CONSTANTINE PORPHYROGENITUS

De Administrando Imperio

A COMMENTARY

F. DVORNIK · R. J. H. JENKINS · B. LEWIS

GY. MORAVCSIK · D. OBOLENSKY · S. RUNCIMAN

edited by

R. J. H. JENKINS

T0337636

DUMBARTON OAKS

RESEARCH LIBRARY AND COLLECTION

WASHINGTON, D.C.

First published by the Athlone Press, University of London
© 1962 F. Dvornik, R. J. H. Jenkins, B. Lewis,
Gy. Moravcsik, D. Obolensky, and S. Runciman

Foreword to the reprint edition © 2012 Dumbarton Oaks
Trustees for Harvard University
Washington, D.C.

Third Printing, 2016

Printed in the United States of America

LIBRARY OF CONGRESS CATALOGING-IN-PUBLICATION DATA
De administrando imperio / Constantine Porphyrogenitus: A Commentary /
by F. Dvornik ... [et al] ; edited by R.J.H. Jenkins.
p. cm.
Originally published: London : Athlone Press, University of London, 1962.
With new introd.
Includes bibliographical references and indexes.
ISBN 978-0-88402-379-1 (pbk. : alk. paper)
1. Constantine VII Porphyrogenitus, Emperor of the East, 905–959.
De administrando imperio.
2. Byzantine Empire—History—Constantine VII Porphyrogenitus, 913-959.
3. Byzantine Empire—History—To 527.
4. Byzantine Empire—History—527-1081.
5. Education of princes—Byzantine Empire.
I. Dvornik, Francis, 1893-1975. II. Jenkins, Romilly James Heald.
DF593.C663D4 2012
949.5′02–dc23
2012008491

www.doaks.org/publications

CONSTANTINE PORPHYROGENITUS

De Administrando Imperio

A COMMENTARY

CONTENTS

FOREWORD TO THE REPRINT EDITION

In 1962 an international team of scholars representing the study of the Byzantine empire and its northern and eastern neighbors published in London at the Athlone Press a commentary on the *De Administrando Imperio* of Constantine Porphyrogenitus. It was intended to complement the critical text of Gyula Moravcsik and the English translation of Romilly Jenkins which had been published in Budapest in 1949. Romilly Jenkins, Professor of Byzantine History and Literature (1960–1969) and later Director of Studies (1967–1969) at Dumbarton Oaks, acted as General Editor; previously he had served as Koraes Professor of Modern Greek and Byzantine History, Language, and Literature at King's College, University of London. Four years later he brought the text and translation under the aegis of Dumbarton Oaks, printing a revised version as the first volume in both the Dumbarton Oaks Texts series and the new international Corpus Fontium Historiae Byzantinae. Although this edition did not brand itself as volume I of the *DAI*, it carefully preserved pagination and alignment so that it could be used with the Athlone commentary, which was explicitly entitled "volume II."

Together the volumes represent an exemplary publication of a foundational text for modern Byzantine Studies. The text and translation have been reprinted seven times, and the commentary was greeted by reviewers with delight at its stellar sextet of contributors and its potential as a lasting reference work. Of Jenkins on his death in 1969 Cyril Mango wrote, "The fruit of his studies was the commented edition and translation of the *DAI*, a monumental collaborative work which he edited and to which he was the principal contributor."

This happy availability of text, translation, and commentary together inspired prolific work in the second half of the twentieth century on encyclopedism, advice literature, administration, historical geography, foreign policy, imperial ideology, ethnography, and above all diplomacy, and through undergraduate special subjects and graduate classes enabled projects for a new generation of scholars. Notable are Arnold Toynbee's monograph *Constantine Porphyrogenitus and His World* of 1973, the 1990 conference on "Byzantine Diplomacy" at Cambridge, at which Constantine Porphyrogenitus himself made an appearance through the mediation of Ihor Ševčenko, and the Budapest conference of 12–14 November 2009 on "Centre and Periphery in the Age of Constantine VII Porphyrogennetos." The perennial appeal of the text is perhaps that it is the (ghost-written) viewpoint of an emperor on his empire and its environs.

The text has continued to be in demand, and a paperback reprint was issued by Dumbarton Oaks in 2008. The commentary however has long been out of print, and it was Joel Kalvesmaki, Byzantine Editor at Dumbarton Oaks, who realized that there was an opportunity to bring both volumes for the first time under the one imprint. We are grateful to the sole surviving author, Bernard Lewis, for his enthusiasm and support for the release, exactly fifty years after its first appearance, of a new paperback reprint, so that text, translation, and commentary can once again provide a basis for teaching and research in Byzantine Studies.

Margaret Mullett
Director of Byzantine Studies, Dumbarton Oaks
Washington, D.C.
February 2012

FOREWORD TO THE FIRST EDITION

THIS Commentary on *De Administrando Imperio* (*DAI*) is arranged for use in conjunction with Gy. Moravcsik's edition of the text (Budapest, 1949; cited as 'Vol. I'): and the words or passages commented on are cited by *chapter* and *line of the chapter* in this edition (*cf.* vol. I, p. 4).

R. J. H. Jenkins has acted as general editor, and the several parts of the work have been distributed amongst the six commentators in the following manner:

General Introduction	R. J. H. Jenkins
Proem	R. J. H. Jenkins
c.1/1–15	R. J. H. Jenkins
c.1/16–28	Gy. Moravcsik
cc.2–8	Gy. Moravcsik
c.9	D. Obolensky
cc.10–13/1–11	Gy. Moravcsik
c.13/12–200	R. J. H. Jenkins
cc.14–22	B. Lewis
cc.23–25/1–55	R. J. H. Jenkins
c.25/56–85	B. Lewis
c.26–29/1–216*	R. J. H. Jenkins
cc.29/217–295, 30–36	F. Dvornik
cc.37–42	Gy. Moravcsik
cc.43–46	S. Runciman
cc.47–53	R. J. H. Jenkins

*The Introductory Note to c.29 is by F. Dvornik.

The number and length of the notes on the several sections have necessarily been left, within broad limits, to the discretion of the individual commentators. Some sections are therefore more fully commented on than others; and this will generally be found to be in accordance with the importance, or controversial nature, of the sections, rather than with their length. The intention of the work is primarily to indicate and document the several problems arising from the text; and only secondarily to offer the solutions favoured by the commentators.

In a book of this kind, written by several authors, it has naturally not been possible to secure unanimity of opinion among them on every problem common to two or more sections. But disagreements are not fundamental. Also, despite the long delay which has intervened between the conception of the book and its appearance, we have made efforts at least to note, if it has not in all cases been possible to exploit, most recent works in the endlessly expanding bibliography of the treatise.

The editor wishes to thank his collaborators for their patience and sympathy; and to include in this category the officers of the Athlone Press, whose help and advice in the arrangement of the material have put us in their debt.

R. J. H. J.

Dumbarton Oaks,
Washington, D.C.
June, 1961.

GENERAL BIBLIOGRAPHY

THE following list contains titles and abbreviated titles of works which are referred to repeatedly in all parts of the *Commentary*. Special bibliographies are prefixed to individual sections.

I. TEXTS

Unless otherwise specified, Byzantine historians are cited by page and line from the Bonn *Corpus Scriptorum Historiae Byzantinae*, the following abbreviations being used:

Theoph. Cont.	Theophanes Continuatus
Sym. Mag.	Symeon Magister
Cont. Geo. Mon.	Georgius Monachus
De Cer.	*De Cerimoniis Aulae Byzantinae*

The following works are cited throughout in editions other than those of the *Corpus*:

Constantine Porphyrogenitus *De Administrando Imperio*, ed. Gy. Moravcsik (Budapest, 1949) [Vol. I]
Costantino Porfirogenito *De Thematibus*, ed. A. Pertusi (Rome, 1952). [*De Them*]
Georgii Monachi *Chronicon*, ed. De Boor (Teubner, 1904). [Geo. Mon.]
Theophanis *Chronographia*, ed. De Boor (Teubner, 1883). [Theophanes]
N.B. also the following:
Cecaumeni Strategikon, edd. Vasilievsky-Jernstedt (St. Petersburg, 1896) [Cecaumenus]
Leonis Imperatoris *Tactica* (*MPG* CVII, cols. 672–1120). [Leo, *Taktika*]

2. MODERN WORKS

L. Bréhier, *Les institutions de l'empire byzantin* (Paris, 1948). [Bréhier, *Institutions*]
L. Bréhier, *La civilisation byzantine* (Paris, 1950). [Bréhier, *Civilisation*]
J. B. Bury, 'The treatise De administrando imperio', *BZ* 15 (1906) 517–77. [Bury]
J. B. Bury, *The Imperial Administrative System in the Ninth Century* (London, 1911). [Bury, *IAS*]
J. B. Bury, *A History of the Eastern Roman Empire from the Fall of Irene to the Accession of Basil I (802–867)*. [Bury, *ERE*]
F. Dölger, *Regesten der Kaiserurkunden des oströmischen Reiches* I (Munich-Berlin, 1924). [Dölger, *Regesten*]
F. Dölger, 'Beiträge zur Geschichte der byzantinischen Finanzverwaltung', *Byz. Archiv* 9 (Leipzig-Berlin, 1927). [Dölger, *Finanzverwaltung*]
F. Dölger, *Byzantinische Diplomatik* (Ettal, 1956). [Dölger, *BD*]
F. Dölger, *Byzanz und die europäische Staatenwelt* (Ettal, 1953). [Dölger, *BES*]
J. Gay, *L'Italie méridionale et l'empire byzantin* (Paris, 1904). [Gay]
E. Gibbon, *The History of the Decline and Fall of the Roman Empire*, ed. J. B. Bury (London, 1896–1900). [Bury's Gibbon]
C. A. Macartney, *The Magyars in the IX Century* (Cambridge 1930). [Macartney]
G. Manojlović, 'Studije o spisu "De administrando imperio" cara Konstantina VII. Porfirogenita' I–IV; *Rad Jugoslavenske Akademije znanosti i umjetnosti* 182 (1910) 1–65, 186 (1911) 35–103, 104–84, 187 (1911) 1–132. [Manojlović I–IV]
J. Marquart, *Osteuropäische und ostasiatische Streifzuge* (Leipzig, 1903). [Marquart]
Gy. Moravcsik, *Byzantinoturcica* I, II (Budapest, 1942, 1943; 2nd ed., Berlin, 1958). [*Byzantinoturcica*]

G. Ostrogorsky, *Geschichte des byzantinischen Staates*, 2nd edition (Munich, 1952).
[Ostrogorsky[2]]
S. Runciman, *The Emperor Romanus Lecapenus and his Reign* (Cambridge, 1927).
[Runciman, *Romanus Lecapenus*]
S. Runciman, *A History of the First Bulgarian Empire* (London, 1930).
[Runciman, *First Bulgarian Empire*]
G. Schlumberger, *Sigillographie de l'empire byzantin* (Paris, 1884).
[Schlumberger, *Sigillographie*]
O. Treitinger, *Die oströmische Kaiser- und Reichsidee* (Jena, 1938; repr. Darmstadt, 1956).
[Treitinger]
A. A. Vasiliev, *Byzance et les Arabes* I: *La dynastie d'Armorium* (820–867), ed. H. Grégoire, M. Canard (Brussels, 1935); *Vizantija i Araby: Politicheskie otnosheniya Vizantii i Arabov za vreme makedonskoy dinastii* (867–959) (St. Petersburg, 1902); *Byzance et les Arabes* II: *La dynastie macédonienne* (867–959), Part 2, Extraits des sources arabes, tr. M. Canard (Brussels, 1950). [Vasiliev I, II, II/2]
A. Vogt, *Le Livre des Cérémonies*, Commentaire I (Paris, 1935), II (Paris, 1940).
[Vogt, *Commentaire*]

The following abbreviations are also commonly used:

AASS	*Acta Sanctorum*
Anal. Boll.	*Analecta Bollandiana*
Byz.-Neugr. Jhrb.	*Byzantinische-Neugriechische Jahrbücher*
BZ	*Byzantinische Zeitschrift*
C.	The Emperor Constantine VII Porphyrogenitus
DAI	*De Administrando Imperio*
Ech. d'Or.	*Echos d'Orient*
EEBΣ	Ἐπετηρὶς τῆς Ἑταιρίας Βυζαντινῶν Σπουδῶν
MGH	*Monumenta Germaniae Historica*
MPG	*Patrologia Graeca*, ed. J.-P. Migne
Rev. Et. Byz.	*Revue des Etudes Byzantines*
S.A.N.	Srpska Akademija Nauka
Sem. Kond.	*Seminarium Kondakovianum*
Viz. Vrem.	*Vizantiiskii Vremennik*

GENERAL INTRODUCTION

Although essays dealing with individual chapters or passages of *DAI* are embarrassingly numerous, those which concern the origins, composition and chronology of the work as a whole are few. The analysis of J. B. Bury[1] remains of permanent value, as may be seen by the frequency with which it is cited in all parts of this Commentary. The long articles of G. Manojlović[2] repay careful study, and contain many useful and acute observations which need to be cited in connexion with individual passages. But, basing himself on Bury's remark that 'the Treatise is disfigured by logical defects of arrangement', he proceeded to re-arrange the material in ten groups according to content, which he then discussed one by one in an arbitrary fashion. This method disguises some of the most important questions which need to be answered. It is only by a study of the material in the order in which it lies before us that we come up against such problems as the illogical position of c. 9, or of the inserted passages at 25/56–26/72. The short sketch of Gy. Moravcsik[3] provides an excellent summary and bibliography. And special mention should be made of the acute suggestions of C. A. Macartney,[4] who often puts us on the right track.

About the purpose of the book as it now stands, and without reference to the origins of its several parts, there can be no dispute. It is a practical manual of statecraft, designed to teach the young prince Romanus II how to govern his empire in the future.[5] As such, it takes its place as an item in the education of a ruler,[6] a conception based ultimately on the Cyprian Hortations of Isocrates.[7] As we know, such practical manuals were frequent and popular in the age of Constantine Porphyrogenitus,[8] which placed great, and perhaps excessive, emphasis on the value of book-learning and inherited precept for the successful conduct of practical affairs.[9] This conclusion as to the purpose of the book is borne out by the style in which it is written, and by the author's comments thereon.[10] The distinction, deriving from classical times, between fine writing worked up for rhetorical display and simple narrative designed for factual instruction, is clearly expressed. This practical purpose of the author must be kept continually and firmly in mind, since it will guard us against some mistaken hypotheses put forward in the past. In the first place, it follows that in all passages where the author instructs his son to do this or that, he has the immediately contemporary political situation in view. Again, it seems to be quite certain that no passages of the book can have been compiled or excerpted as school texts or grammar lessons for a child emperor, as Manojlović contends.[11] Quite apart from the unsuitability of such passages[12] for their intended purpose, the book is addressed to a ruler, and designed to teach him how to rule.

Keeping this principle before us, we may proceed to examine the nature of the material as a whole. It is well to dismiss from it at the outset one or two chapters which consist merely of unedited and largely irrelevant source material, which cannot have been

---

[1] 'The treatise De adm. imp.', *BZ*, 15 (1906), 517–77.
[2] Manojlović I–IV.
[3] *Byzantinoturcica*, I, 209–15; 2nd ed., 361–79.
[4] Macartney 80–151
[5] 1/4–8.
[6] *Byzantinoturcica*, I, 210; 2nd ed., 361.
[7] *Cf. MPG* LXXXVI, cols. 1164 ff.; CII, cols. 665 ff.
[8] *Cf.* A. Rambaud, *L'empire grec au Xme siècle* (Paris, 1870), 78–174; K. Krumbacher, *Geschichte der byzantinischen Litteratur*² (Munich, 1897), 253–64.
[9] *Cf.* Theoph. Cont. 265/16–266/6.
[10] 1/8–15; see note *ad loc.*
[11] I, 8–11, 55, 65.
[12] cc. 23, 24. Manojlović seems to be unaware that these are from Stephanus.

meant to be included in the final arrangement of the book. These chapters are: 23–25/55, three unedited texts from Stephanus of Byzantium and Theophanes about the early history of Spain (these are of course in a different category from the edited and re-arranged texts of Theophanes which form part of the Saracen treatise, cc. 14–22); 48, which is the source of 47; 52, which is the source of 51/199–205; and 53/1–492, which has no relevance to any of the recent or contemporary information about Cherson found in the rest of the book.[1] It is to be noted that none of these chapters is introduced by ἰστέον, ὅτι or ὅτι. They are therefore similar to *De Cer.* Book II, cc. 42, 44, 45, 50, 54, 56 and 57 (*cf. ibid.*, pp. 513–15), which again have no relevance to a Book of Ceremonies, but are documents from which some relevant fact or facts were to be extracted. They have been included by oversight in the final collection, and may be left out of account in any assessment of the material.[2] It may well be that the important c. 9/1–113 of *DAI* should also be placed in this category. It is clear that it has been used as the source for 2/16–23 (*cf.* 9/70–1); and, as Bury (574) has noted, it is itself out of place in the diplomatic section cc. 1–13/11. Bury thought that its proper place was in the third section, on the Nations; but even there it would not be quite homogeneous with the rest of the material. It is simplest to regard it as source material copied erroneously, but very fortunately, into the book.[3]

In the light of the above, it is worth while to consider whether one further section should not be put into this category of simple source material: the much discussed c. 30. 30/2–61 might well be the actual source of 29/3–53 (see on 29/14–53), and the remainder of the chapter (30/61 ff.) have been used for some part of c. 31 (*cf.* 30/71–3 with 31/3–5). Thus, we might see in c. 30 a report, sent perhaps *ad hoc* by a Dalmatian official, from which C. extracted such parts as he thought relevant to the περὶ Χρωβάτων καὶ Σέρβλων συγγραφή of his Περὶ ἐθνῶν. Its position, after c. 29, would agree with this: *cf.* the position of cc. 9, 48, 52, immediately after the cc. in which they are respectively cited. But this interpretation of c. 30 would imply a date *before* 950 for its composition,[4] where-as most scholars are agreed that some of its material must be dated a good deal later than this (see below, pp. 97–9).

The rest of the material of *DAI* is of two kinds: hortatory and didactic on the one hand; informative (that is, historical, topographical or antiquarian) on the other. C.'s own introduction or 'Proem' (P/14–24) divides this material under four heads (P/21–3, = cc. 46/166–48/21, which contains one single item only—see below, pp. 180–1—, is regarded as a sub-section or pendant to the main third section, cc. 14–46). The first two divisions, being essays in practical foreign policy (cc. 1–13 except for c. 9), are of course hortatory and didactic; the second two, being mainly historical or topographical, appear at first sight to fall into the informative category. But it would be a superficial view which regarded these divisions as hard and fast. The long third section (cc. 14–46) with its short pendant, which C. includes under the general heading of 'foreign nations', shows striking differences of treatment and outlook in its various parts. Cc. 43–6 (*cf.* also 53/512–29, and Manojlović I, 21–2) should be included under the first heading rather than the second, since they too instruct and exhort (*cf.* 44/45–9, 115, 125–28; 45/156–75). This contrast in tone between the two halves of C.'s third section, that is, between the Saracen to Magyar chapters (14–42) on the one hand, and the Armenian and Georgian chapters (43–6) on the other, is a point of great significance for study of the origins of the book.

The contrast becomes more striking if we consider the periods of time to which the

---

[1] C. no doubt consulted the documents with reference to the tradition of Chersonite loyalty to the empire (*cf.* 53/110 ff.), having in mind his political note 53/512–35. Even Manojlović can only suppose (I, 20) that the tale was included 'kao zanimljivo štivo'.

[2] *Cf.* Bury in *Eng. Hist. Rev.*, 22 (1907), 214–17, 223–7, 439.

[3] Note especially the *position* of c. 9, between the two final paragraphs of the περὶ Πατζινακιτῶν κεφάλαιον, that is, between 8/34–5 and 9/113: which suggests that the whole chapter was used merely for its references to the Pechenegs (*cf.* 2/16–23; 8/20–2). See however below, p. 20.

[4] *Cf.* W. Ohnsorge, *Abendland und Byzanz* (Darmstadt, 1958), 36: 'bereits vor 950'.

various parts of this section (cc. 14–46) relate. Apart from the bulk of c. 53, which, as we have noted, should not be included at all, the first half of this third section (cc. 14–42) is the least up to date in the book. These chapters, though, as we shall see, they show traces of attempts at modernization, are mainly old, sometimes quite ancient, history.

The Saracen chapters (14–22), excepting for c. 15, are a medley of extracts which bring the history of the caliphate down only as far as the year 813; and even the reference to Crete (22/40–8) takes us no further than 827. The S. Italian and Venetian chapters (27–8) are not concerned with any historical event later than the middle of the 9th cent. The Dalmatian chapters (29–36), excepting for the (?interpolated) chapter 30, are in their original form a historical and topographical account which takes us no further than the reign of Leo VI. And the same is true of the Pecheneg, Turkish and Moravian chapters (37–41),[1] in which the last recorded historical event is the expulsion of the Magyars from Bessarabia in 896, and their subsequent establishment in Moravia some ten years later.

In general, therefore, cc. 14–42, with their emphasis on origins, early history, antiquities, topography and onomatology, bear very clear traces of having been composed as a treatise Περὶ ἐθνῶν, on a plan similar to that of the Περὶ θεμάτων,[2] of which it may well have been intended as a companion volume. The basic structure of the Περὶ ἐθνῶν is clearly discernible under the later accretions. The sections began with an account, often legendary or semi-legendary, of the chief incident or incidents through which the territory in question came to its present state of occupation. The rise of Islam (7th cent.), the capture of Italy by the Lombards (6th cent., here misdated to the 8th), the expulsion to the islands of the Enetikoi (5th cent.), the capture of Dalmatia by the Avars (6th cent.), the settlement of Croats and Serbs (7th cent.), the coming of Turks and Pechenegs (9th cent.): all these are tales concerning origins, often remote origins, of the existing state of affairs. The emphasis is wholly on the past, and the narrative reproduces in most cases what the natives themselves said about their own past. None of this material in any way concerns a De Administrando Imperio. It is followed by topographical lists, with occasional topographical or antiquarian comment.

We are therefore justified in regarding these chapters, in their original form, as the earliest parts of the book, compiled on a different plan and with a different purpose from those adopted later. It is clear that this out of date and antiquarian information could be of no use as a lesson in contemporary government and diplomacy. And when we pass to the second part of C.'s third section, to the Armenian and Georgian chapters (43–6), we note a change both of purpose and material. We are back once more in the East, which we left in c. 22; but we have emerged from the realm of ancient history and entered that of contemporary politics. C. 43, based on Byzantine diplomatic documents, contains no antiquarian or topographical information; instead, we have a detailed account of imperial relations with successive princes of Taron from the beginning of the 10th cent. up to and including the reign of Romanus I (920–44). C. 44 is devoted to establishing the Byzantine claim to the territory of Apahounis (cf. 44/45–9); and ends with an actual piece of instruction (44/115), of the sort given in cc. 1–8, together with a note on the present and practical importance of the territory in question. C. 45 does indeed begin with an antiquarian note on the Iberians (45/2–39); but, after a significant chronological correction (45/39–41), the rest of the chapter is diplomatic history, and, again, it ends with instruction on the policy to be followed with regard to lands near Theodosioupolis (45/156–75). C. 46 is an account of the failure of a diplomatic manœuvre by Romanus I to annex Ardanouj.

A most striking instance of the contrast between the treatment of material in the earlier and later parts of the third section is seen in the respective mentions of Naples on the western, and of Chliat, Arzes and Altzike on the eastern borders of the empire

[1] Cf. on 39/6.
[2] Cf. Manojlović i, 11–16, 56.

(27/58–61; 44/114–15). In the early 950's Naples was in revolt against the empire, and C. sent two expeditions to S. Italy to control the Saracens and recover the city.[1] Yet the entry concerning Naples in *DAI* deals only with its ancient history. Chliat, Arzes and Altzike, on the other hand, are 'the Emperor's property, and he should recover them'.

Thus, the material of C.'s third section (cc. 14–46) may be said to fall into two halves, distinct in nature and purpose: the first, historical; the second, diplomatic and more akin to the final purpose of the book as set out in the Proem. But this clear distinction is to some extent masked by sporadic attempts to bring some of the earlier material in cc. 14–42 up to date by the addition of items of more recent date, chosen for their political importance; and thus to give a superficial air of unity to the whole section on the Nations. These later additions, however, are plainly observable, sometimes by their failure to harmonize with what has gone before, sometimes by the position in which they are inserted. These passages may be listed as follows:

1. 25/56–85: two notices inserted awkwardly at the end of the Saracen συγγραφή.[2] They concern the recent decay of the Saracen autocracy and mention two events which had taken place respectively in 930 and 945. They thus resume Saracen history after a gap of nearly a century and a half (22/75–6); cf. 31/75–82.

2. c. 26: an independent fragment of Italian history from 869–950, based partly on information supplied by Liudprand of Cremona in 949, and certainly written down before 22nd November, 950 (cf. on 26/66). No attempt has been made to insert it in its right place, which would have been at 27/68. But its interest is contemporary and political, since it concerns the descent of C.'s own daughter-in-law Bertha-Eudocia from Charlemagne; and it should be related to the diplomatic passage 13/116–22.

3. 29/54–216: a manifest insertion, or, rather, insertions, as is clear from 29/55–6, which shows that the Croat-Serb συγγραφή (cc. 31–6) was, at least in its original form, already written. Note again the strongly diplomatic flavour of 29/54–88, 213–16.

4. c. 30: this has been generally and rightly recognized as an insertion into, or at least as an interruption of, the περὶ Χρωβάτων καὶ Σέρβλων συγγραφή, from a different hand. It has been suggested above (p. 2) that its position and the fact that it duplicates a large portion of the preceding chapter, might indicate that it is a mere source-document, which properly forms no part of the book. Nor does it at first sight seem probable that a book such as *DAI* would emphasize the virtual abandonment of the coastal cities of Dalmatia to Slav overlordship by the author's grandfather (30/126–42). However, internal chronological evidence appears to confirm that the composition of c. 30 must be later, rather than earlier, than that of cc. 29, 31–6 (see on 30/73–4, 30/75), which would be conclusive for intentional insertion rather than for inclusion by oversight.

5. 31/71–82: that this passage is a later insertion is proved by two details: first, the information in the preceding part of the chapter deals with events probably not later than the 9th cent. (see on 31/42–52), and certainly not later than 927 (cf. 31/61, and contrast 32/126–28). There is no mention in it of King Tomislav. On the other hand 31/71–82, as is generally agreed, contains, first, information of events contemporary with Tomislav, and second, of events which followed the death of King Miroslav (949). Croat history is thus resumed here in two notes after an interval, just as 25/56–85 resumes Saracen history after an even longer gap. Second: the tenses ἐκβάλλει (31/71) and εἶχεν (31/75) prove that the passages were written at different dates.

6. 32/80–145: this passage brings Serbian history up to date, narrating imperial diplomatic relations with Serbian rulers in just the same way that relations with Taronite rulers are narrated in 43/89–133. The rather awkward transition between the earlier

---

[1] Theoph. Cont. 453–4; Cedrenus II, 358–60; Vasiliev II/2, 158–60.
[2] These notices may, as Manojlović (I, 38–9) believed, derive from the same source from which c. 15 also was excerpted. At least, 15/3–4 shows knowledge of Fatimids in Africa, and therefore cannot have been written before 909 at earliest. But the chapter's meaning and reference are so obscure that we cannot say why it was inserted at all.

and later passages is marked by the word ἄρξας (32/78), which means that Peter *began* his reign in the time of Leo VI (for the meaning, *cf.* Cedrenus II, 459/1–2: ἦρξε δὲ κατὰ τὴν ιε' τοῦ Σεπτεμβρίου μηνός). The new passage then starts off properly with Μετὰ δὲ τὸν καιρόν (32/81); and is a simple lesson in diplomacy, which, if it had occurred in cc. 1–13, would have begun with the words ἰστέον, ὅτι ἡ Σερβλία δύναται τοῖς Βουλγάροις πολεμεῖν.

7. 33/16–19: a note on the powerful ruler of the Zachlumi, for whom see on 33/16. It again inserts recent political history into a topographical and antiquarian article.

8. 40/7–22, 51–68: the first of these two passages in C.'s expansion of 38/55–7. That it is out of its place is proved by the ὡς εἴρηται of 40/22, which presupposes 40/37–40. The second passage is generally agreed to be based on information supplied by Magyar envoys in 948 (*cf.* 40/64).

9. 42/24–55: once again, a passage of political and diplomatic importance inserted into a purely topographical account. Its significance lies in the account which it gives of the incorporation of Cherson as an imperial *thema*, and it should be compared with demonstrably late parts of the book such as 43/150 ff. and 50/111–66.

It is to be noted that not all these insertions are in the form of separate paragraphs. 32/81 ff. and 40/7 ff. are introduced simply by Μετὰ δὲ τὸν καιρόν, Μετὰ δὲ ταῦτα, while 42/24–55 has not even this indication. In these cases some care at least has been given to re-editing; whereas 25/56–26/72 are passages of fresh information not worked into their several contexts.

To sum up: C.'s third section (cc. 14–46) falls into two categories: 14–42 containing old or antiquarian information of various kinds, supplemented by later insertions with a strongly political and diplomatic flavour; 43–6 containing up to date and almost wholly diplomatic treatment of Byzantine relations with Armenian and Georgian principalities.

The *date* at which these later additions or insertions were made in cc. 14–42 must be the date at which the author determined to convert his original Περὶ ἐθνῶν into a practical diplomatic hand-book. As we have seen, cc. 43–6 show the new treatment and the new purpose at work. Now, c. 45 is expressly dated to the 10th indiction, A.M. 6460 (45/39–42), which falls between September 951 and August 952. It is thus reasonable to suppose that *the concept of DAI as a political hand-book dates from this year*; and that all the up-to-date, practical, hortatory or diplomatic passages were compiled or inserted not earlier than 951–2. These passages comprise: C.'s first and second sections (cc. 1–8, 10–13); all the later additions to cc. 14–42 detailed above; cc. 43–6; and all the notices dealing with internal affairs (cc. 47–51), which have no relevance to a Περὶ ἐθνῶν, but, as we shall see, much relevance to a treatise *de administrando imperio*. If this is right, we can easily surmise the reason for a sudden change in the purpose of the book at precisely this time. The young emperor Romanus II was born in 938, on a day after 15th March and before 9th November, since he was already 21 when he succeeded in November 959 and still only 24 when he died in March 963. His fourteenth birthday, therefore, the date on which he entered officially into man's estate, fell somewhere in the middle of 952. The new *DAI* was perhaps his father's gift to him on this momentous occasion, a gift which should guide him during the majority which he was then about to enter.

Internal evidence supplies the dates of compilation (though not of collection)[1] for most of the first part of the third section (cc. 14–42). C. 27 on Lombardy (27/3–68) is dated to 948–9 (27/53–4). C. 29, in its original form (29/3–53, 216–95), is dated to the same year (29/234–5). C. 37 (37/13–14) is dated to 950–1. The references to the death of Romanus I (948), specific (13/173) or implied (51/162–86), give no assistance, since they

---

[1] The period during which C. was *collecting* material (as distinct from putting it together) for the Περὶ ἐθνῶν, cannot be established with certainty. A conjectural dating for c. 27 (see Introductory Note to that chapter) might suggest that collection was begun as early as 929, which would imply a collection contemporary with that for the Περὶ θεμάτων.

occur in sections of the book datable to 951–2. But at least it can be said that this method and purpose of a purely historical, topographical and antiquarian Περὶ ἐθνῶν were being followed during the years 948–51, and that its conversion to a diplomatic vade-mecum did not occur until 951–2.

C.'s fourth section, on domestic affairs (c. 48/22–c. 53), must have been added to the book after its new purpose had been resolved upon: that is, in the year 951–2. It appears at first sight to be a jumble of miscellaneous information on historical, territorial, admini-strative, naval, financial and even ecclesiastical matters, set down with little regard to relevance and none at all to order. But, although the order is certainly rather confused, the matter itself can be reduced to certain definite categories which are seen to be very pertinent to contemporary imperial policy. These categories are three: (a) provincial organization; (b) naval administration; (c) civil policy.

(a) It is to be noted that among the 'nations' described in C.'s third section are some whose relations with the empire were ambiguous or transitional. The Serbs and Croats are repeatedly stated to be in subjection to the empire. The same is true by implication of the Armenian and Georgian princes who had accepted imperial titles and who had ceded, or had been expected to cede, territories to the empire (cf. e.g. 43/173–4; 44/45–7; 45/156–7; 46). The contemporary policy of expansion, especially in the east, was to secure, by diplomacy or by war, the incorporation of such territories in the thematic sys-tem of the empire; and this policy had already succeeded in regard to Taron, which was for all practical purposes an imperial province (43/153) before the death of Romanus I, although C. still speaks of it as among the 'nations' outside the pale.

It was therefore obviously important for a ruler to have before him recent precedents for the procedure by which the boundaries of the empire were enlarged and the provinces increased; and for the services and tribute to be exacted from peoples so incorporated at the periphery. The themata which are discussed in this section of DAI (49–50/168)—Peloponnese, Cappadocia, Kephallenia, Lagoubardia,[1] Calabria, Charsianon, Chozanon, Asmosaton, Mesopotamia, Lykandos (cf. 53/507–10)—are all frontier or near-frontier provinces. The provinces of the great central block, reaching from Thessalonike-Nikopolis to Paphlagonia-Bukellarioi-Anatolikoi, are either not mentioned at all, or else mentioned only as ceding territory to other provinces further off towards the frontier. Three of the former group, Peloponnese, Mesopotamia, and Lykandos, are treated at considerable length. Peloponnese, made into a province at the turn of the 8th–9th cents., and pacified successively by Michael III and Romanus I, formed an object lesson in the recovery of imperial territory occupied by barbarians, and in its subsequent financial administration. With the administration and revenue of Peloponnese we must also connect 51/192–204; the relevance of which to contemporary events is no doubt to be seen in the expedition sent to S. Italy under Malakenos in 951.[2] The themata of Mesopo-tamia and Lykandos were foundations of recent date on the eastern frontier, the one acquired by cession, the other by conquest on the part of an allied despot. In each case the method by which an independent thema was built up by the addition of parcels of territory surrounding the nucleus, is carefully described. The thematic part of C.'s fourth section is therefore more closely related to his first and second and to the latter part of his third sections than to the earlier, more antiquarian material of the Περὶ ἐθνῶν. With this thematic part we must also connect the important postscript 53/512–35, which is also a piece of practical instruction concerning a thema.

(b) 50/169–51/191 form three items concerning the naval administration of the empire. The importance of the navy, especially of the imperial navy, to imperial policy at this time is explained on 51/40–5. The Mardaïtes of Attaleia formed a squadron under the immediate control (as is twice emphasized, 50/169–70, 219–21) of the emperor him-self, and independent of the naval governor of the Cibyrrhaiote thema. The plain advice

---

[1] 50/85–7; contrast the antiquarian style of 27/1–68.
[2] Cedrenus II, 358/20; Vasiliev II/2, 158–9: cf. Manojlović II, 63–4.

of C. is that this state of affairs should be maintained; and it is clear that he believes his father to have committed an error in being persuaded to unite the two commands under the governor Eustathios. Even more important to imperial security, and to the security of the imperial palace, was the loyalty of the *corps d'élite* of sailors who manned the private galleys and barges of the imperial family. Not only was the emperor's life in their hands on the many occasions when he put to sea, but they also performed regular guard duties in the Palace itself (51/40–5). The reform of Romanus I (51/173–91), whereby sole authority over both the imperial galleys and barges was vested in a single officer of proved loyalty to the autokrator, was perfectly sensible; and when C. himself recovered power in 945, he does not seem to have restored the old system of dual control (51/188). With the naval notices we must also connect 48/28–32, 53/492–511, which deal with the secret naval weapon of Greek Fire: the first passage records its invention; the second, the oil-wells in the Caucasus and Armenia which supplied its chief ingredient, petroleum.

(*c*) 50/222–56 supply two notices on purely civil and domestic matters, whose relevance it is hard to explain without a more detailed knowledge than we possess of contemporary administrative problems. It is however possible that the list of chamberlains may have been inserted with reference to the promotion of Basil the eunuch from protovestiary to chamberlain, which probably took place shortly before the time of writing: *cf.* on 50/233–4. If this were so, then the passage about Ktenas (50/235–56) may be inserted as a precedent for the appointment of Michael Lecapenus, another cleric, to the lay rank of magister: *cf.* Theoph. Cont. 438/9; Cedrenus II, 327/9–13.[1] It is on the whole probable that this rehabilitation of the surviving Lecapenids took place some years after, rather than before, the death of Romanus I (948).

If it is right to distinguish between the material and purpose of cc. 14–42 (in their original form) and those of cc. 43–51, 53/493–535, then there can be no doubt about the date of cc. 1–8, 10–13. Their tone is didactic and hortatory and they therefore belong to the later part of the book (951–2); and reflect the absolutely contemporary state of affairs. The arguments which have been used to prove that their political background is fifty years or more out of date are refuted in the Introductory Note to the section, pp. 12–13. The chief stumbling-block is certainly 13/3–8, which suggested to Bury (564) that the passage was to be dated to a period before the Magyar conquest of Moravia. But the words are nonsensical as they stand, and it would be dangerous to base any historical conclusions on them. Moravcsik (on 13/5) has given a plausible explanation of them. But there is a simpler explanation still, namely, that at 13/5, between the words ἡ and μεγάλη, a line has fallen out owing to homoioteleuton, and that the original text ran, *e.g.* καὶ πρὸς τὸ μεσημβρινὸν μέρος ἡ Χρωβατία. ἦν δέ ποτε ὁ τόπος ἡ μεγάλη Μοραβία κτλ. The passage, thus restored, falls into line with 40/41–4, on which in fact it is based (Macartney, 151).

On the other hand there is a very strong argument to prove that cc. 1–8, 10–13, were written after the whole of cc. 14–42. C., after deciding to change his Περὶ ἐθνῶν into a *DAI*, was able to give his diplomatic lesson on the Armenian states in its proper place in the third section (cc. 43–6). But the northern ἔθνη, which equally called for a diplomatic lesson, had already been treated in the earlier, historical-antiquarian style in cc. 37–40. It was not possible to convert these chapters into diplomatic lessons without completely rewriting them. Hence a separate περὶ Πατζινακιτῶν κεφάλαιον (cc. 1–8), independent of c. 37, had to be composed with the new purpose in view; and it seems probable, as Macartney (151) has acutely noted, that 13/3–8 represents the embryo of a περὶ Τούρκων κεφάλαιον, independent of cc. 38–40, though using some of their material.

The Proem is obviously the final part of the book, since it contains a list of contents in the right order.

One further question is relevant: how many parts of the book may be regarded as C.'s

---

[1] The suggestion of Manojlović (II, 94) that the Ktenas episode constitutes a lesson in finance does not appear very probable.

own personal composition? On this question the chapter headings may throw some light. As Bury pointed out (520), these headings 'do not correspond to the author's division of the material' in all cases. And he concluded that 'originally there was no division into numbered chapters. The division was based on short summaries or descriptions which were written in the margin, according to a common practice, to facilitate the perusal. But whether these indices were added (as I should consider probable) in the original Ms., or not, they did not represent, and were not intended to determine, adequate subdivisions of the work'; cf. *Byzantinoturcica*, I, 211; 2nd ed., 363. This appears at first sight a satisfactory hypothesis. But, as Obolensky rightly notes, on 9/9, οἱ πακτιῶται αὐτῶν presupposes a mention of the ʽΡῶς, which has previously occurred only in the chapter heading (9/1). C. 40 provides a yet clearer instance: for 40/3–4 would be meaningless without the heading, 40/1–2; cf. also 49/4. Thus it is more likely that the headings, whether in origin capitular or marginal, were already written on the documents from which C. made up his book; and were either put there by the clerks who abstracted his material for him, or else already existed in the documents themselves when they were in their office 'pigeon-holes'. If this is conceded, the lack of a heading to the main part of c. 13 (13/12–194), of which Bury (*ibid.*) complains, is readily explained: c. 13 had no heading because it *did not already exist*, but was an original contribution of C. himself, who wrote it straight into his treatise. This theory is perfectly in accordance with the fact that cc. 1–8, each of which has a separate heading, yet formed in C.'s arrangement a single κεφάλαιον (13/11): he ought to have expunged these existing headings or *marginalia*, but did not do so.

This line of reasoning will certainly suggest C. himself as the author of the main part of c. 13 (cf. Vol. I, p. 11): and indeed the outspoken criticism of Romanus I at 13/147 ff. can hardly have been written by anybody else. But this criticism recurs at 43/89 ff. and 46/135 ff.; moreover, 45/67–175 is a foreign policy directive actually in C.'s name (45/68). Finally, 51/133–91, a passage which combines reminiscences of C.'s own boyhood with the now familiar tone of invective against his father-in-law, must also be his composition. It is noteworthy that all these passages, together with the Proem and the conjunctive sentences in which Romanus II is addressed as 'son', belong to what we now know to be the later, revised portion of the book. While, therefore, we need not doubt that C. took a hand in the compilation of the original Περὶ ἐθνῶν, as of the Περὶ θεμάτων, it is reasonable to believe that the decision to turn the former into a diplomatic guide was C.'s own, and that he took a peculiar and personal interest in the project. This is natural enough: since the work was no longer designed for the ordinary reader, but for his own son, who was to be master of the world. And for him the father personally composed the precepts and advice which give the treatise its importance and charm.

COMMENTARY

Title and Proem

BIBLIOGRAPHY

A. Alföldi, 'Insignien und Tracht der römischen Kaiser', *Römische Mitteilungen*, 50 (1935), 1–171 (Alföldi). W. Ensslin, 'Das Gottesgnadentum des autokratorischen Kaisertums der frühbyzantinischen Zeit', *Atti del V. Congresso internazionale di studi bizantini*, 1 (Rome, 1939), 154–66 (Ensslin, *Gottesgnadentum*). A. Grabar, *L'empereur dans l'art byzantin* (Paris, 1936) (Grabar). G. Ostrogorsky, 'Avtokrator i Samodržac', *Glas Srpsk. kral. Akad.*, 164 (1935), 95–187 (Ostrogorsky, *Avtokrator*).

INTRODUCTORY NOTE

The Proem is divided into four short sections: (1) P/2–12 is a note on the practical value of wisdom for the sovereign (re-emphasized at 1/4–8, 13/12–14, 195–7, 43/3–4, 46/167–9, 48/25–7); (2) P/12–24 is a summary of the contents of the book (partly repeated at 13/197–200, 46/166–7, 48/23–5); (3) P/24–39 is a prophecy of the future glory of Romanus II's reign; and (4) P/39–48 contains a prayer to God to guide and guard him.

The language of the section is Biblical, and derives mainly from passages of the Old Testament which illustrate the wisdom and glory of Solomon. While the ideas of the practical value of wisdom to the ruler derive partly from the classical tradition (see Vol. I, General Introduction, 8), the phraseology in which they are expounded is scriptural and Solomonic (*cf.* Bas. Imp. *Paraen.*, *MPG* cvii, col. lvi B, where the wisdom of Solomon is commended along with that of Isocrates); and the passage is an illustration of the middle Byzantine 'Solomonic' ideal of sovereignty (see Treitinger 135; Grabar 95; *cf.* Vasiliev II/2, 387; G. Schlumberger, *Un empereur byzantin au 10 ème siècle* (Paris, 1890), 185, 263, figs.; *De Cer.*, 455/1, 570/17). It is thus no accident that the 71st Psalm, in which Solomon is depicted in all his glory and omnipotence, is cited or referred to several times in this short Proem; and its ideals of justice towards the poor, subjection of the Arabs (*cf.* verse 10), wealth, fecundity and expanding power are ideals identical with those of the Macedonian rulers of Byzantium. The Proem therefore is a valuable supplementary illustration of 10th-cent. ideas of Byzantine sovereignty, which have been elucidated by Dölger, Treitinger and others: see on Tit/4 (θεοστεφῆ).

The date of composition of the passage is probably 952 (see General Introduction p. 7), since it contains a list of contents in proper order, and must therefore have been written after the final arrangement of the material.

Tit/1–4 Κωνσταντίνου κτλ.
Cf. De Cer., 3, 455. For the double implication, of the emperor as master of the world and slave of Christ, see Dölger, *BES*, 23; Treitinger 146 and note 8.

Tit/2 ἐν Χριστῷ . . . βασιλέως.
See Treitinger 39. βασιλεύς was the official style of the emperors after 629: see Bréhier, *BZ*, 15 (1906), 173; Ostrogorsky, *Avtokrator* 98–9; Dölger, *BD*, 130–1.

Tit/2 Ῥωμαίων.
The word was officially added to the imperial style in the year 812, in order to mark the superiority of the Byzantine emperor to the Frank, whose title of emperor (*sc.* of the Franks) was recognized by Byzantium in that year: see Stein, *Forschungen und Fortschritte*,

6 (1930), 182 ff.; Ostrogorsky-Stein, *Byzantion*, 7 (1932), 195; Treitinger 161, 187, note 117; Dölger, *BES*, 80, note 17; W. Ohnsorge, *Abendland u. Byzanz* (Darmstadt, 1958), 27, 30. For the occasional appearance of this addition before 812, see Dölger, *BES*, 297–300, note 21, who shows that such early uses were not according to protocol (*cf. id., BD*, 135, note 24).

Tit/4 θεοστεφῆ.
Cf. De Cer., 587/6–7. For the emperor as chosen and crowned of God, *cf.* Treitinger 34–8, 61–2, 114; Ensslin, *Gottesgnadentum*, 163–5; Bréhier, *Institutions*, 55. For a brilliant summary of Byzantine conceptions of sovereignty in general, see Dölger, *BES*, 10–13; and *cf.* Ensslin, *Historische Zeitschrift*, 177 (1954), 449–68 (bibliography 468).

Tit/4 πορφυρογέννητον.
That is to say, a child born to a *reigning* sovereign: see Reiske's note, *De Cer.*, II, 253; *cf.* Cedrenus II, 659/12; Zonaras XVIII, 9 (ed. Dindorf IV, 201/24–9). The term πορφύρα, from the exclusive association of the colour with sovereignty (see Alföldi 49–51, 145), early became a synonym of imperial power; *cf.* Ensslin, *Gottesgnadentum*, 156, note 7, and for parallel usages, Ostrogorsky-Stein, *Byzantion*, 7 (1932), 199. This general use of πορφύρα was still alive in the acclamations of the 10th cent.; see *De Cer.*, 39/20, 45/22, 47/14, etc.

For the imperial chamber known as the Πορφύρα and built of porphyry, the traditional birth-place of princes and princesses of the reigning sovereign (τὰ πορφυρογέννητα), see the literature summarized by R. Delbrueck, *Antike Porphyrwerke* (Berlin and Leipzig, 1932), 27, 148. This chamber, though said in the 10th cent. to go back to the time of Constantine the Great (see Liudprand, *Antapodosis*, I, 7, and *cf.* on 13/32), is in fact not heard of until 797 (see Theophanes 472/16); even in the 10th cent. not all πορφυρογέννητα were born in it (*cf.* Cedrenus II, 338/20–339/2), and C. himself gives an alternative explanation of the name (see Theoph. Cont. 147/15–17). *Cf.* also Anna Comnena, ed. Reifferscheid I, 202/30–2, 229/28–30.

The term πορφυρογέννητος itself may derive from either sense of πορφύρα, since it occurs probably not before the time of Leo VI (*cf.* Liudprand, *Antapodosis*, I, 5; and 45/43), and certainly not before that of Theophilus; *cf.* Reiske's note at *De Cer.*, II, 254; Ostrogorsky-Stein, *Byzantion*, 7 (1932), 199 (but *cf.* Dölger, *BZ*, 36 (1936), 151).

P/2-3 σοφὸς . . . φρονίμῳ.
For the combination in this passage of Old Testament and classical ideas of the education of a wise monarch, see Introductory Note to this section; *cf.* Theoph. Cont. 446/1–9.

P/5-6 καθιστᾷ βασιλεῖς . . . τοῦ παντός.
See Treitinger 34–6, 158 ff.; Guilland, *Eos*, 42 (1947), 142–68. For God's gift of universal supremacy, see also Ensslin, *Gottesgnadentum*, 163, note 2.

P/7,12 διδαχὴν . . . διδασκαλίαν.
For the pattern of this instruction, see the prefaces to cc. 1–10 of *Proverbs*. For the education of Romanus by C., *cf. De Cer.*, 455/1–456/6; Theoph. Cont. 458/1–7; Bréhier, *Institutions*, 36–7.

P/11 μεγαλεπήβολος. 'Capable of great achievements': *cf.* Theoph. Cont. 70/3.

P/14-24 πρῶτα μὲν κτλ. See General Introduction, p. 2; and *cf.* Leo, *Taktika*, col. 677 C-D.

P/15 ἔθνος.

Cf. 13/96, etc. The biblical meaning of 'gentiles' (Ps. 2, 1; Matth. 10, 5), that is, nations foreign to the Chosen People of God, was applied by the Byzantines to nations not under the immediate sovereignty, or strange to the religion, of the Byzantine empire, which embraced the Chosen People of the Christian dispensation: *cf.* Dölger, *BES*, 26 and note 62, 142. 'Ethnics' therefore denoted a body of foreigners: either spiritual (*i.e.* heathens, *cf.* De Cer., 58/13–16; Cedrenus II, 382/17–19), or political (as Franks, *De Cer.*, 749/12–13, or Bulgars, Leo Diac. 79/6–7), and very often both. *Cf.* further Treitinger 78–9; Georgakas, *BZ*, 43 (1950), 305–7; K. Lechner, *Hellenen und Barbaren im Weltbild der Byzantiner* (Diss., Munich, 1954), 51. For the political theory of imperial relations with the ἔθνη, see Ostrogorsky, *Sem. Kond.*, 8 (1936), 49–53.

P/15 κατὰ τί μὲν . . . βλάψαι.

The importance of the same knowledge is impressed on the emperor (?) Alexios I by Cecaumenus, in almost the same words (103/30–1): καὶ πῶς διάκειται καὶ εἰς τί βλάπτεται καὶ εἰς τί ὠφελεῖται.

P/33 θρόνος. For the significance of the throne in imperial ritual, see Treitinger 56; Alföldi 125–39.

P/35 ἐξελέξατο. *Cf.* on Tit/4 (θεοστεφῆ).

P/38 δωροφορεῖσθαι.

That is, in token of homage and submission: see *De Cer.*, 40/14–15: τὰ ἔθνη πάντα δουλώσει τοῦ προσφέρειν ὡς οἱ μάγοι τὰ δῶρα τῇ ὑμῶν βασιλείᾳ, and *cf.* Treitinger 76, 184.

P/43 ἕνεκεν ἀληθείας.

This clause τῆς Δαυιτικῆς λύρας (Psalm 44, 5), which doubtless formed a part of the coronation service, is one of which emperors were frequently reminded: see Cyril Mango, *The Homilies of Photius* (Cambridge, Mass., 1958), 137, 189, 315; Sym. Mag. 631/11; Ἐπιστολὴ . . . τῶν ἁγιωτάτων πατριαρχῶν . . . πρὸς Θεόφιλον, ed. Sakkelion (Athens, 1874), 15; Anna Comnena II, 7, 5 (ed. Reifferscheid I, 79/19–21); Codinus 201/13.

P/45 πεσοῦνται . . . λείξουσι.

Future forms with optative sense are very common in contemporary acclamations: *cf.* De Cer., 38/22; 39/13, 20; 40/13, 15; 370/20–1 etc. It is thus fairly certain that the ὁδηγήσαι of P/43 (ὁδιγήση, P) should be written ὁδηγήσει. The future forms in P/28–34 may equally well be optative in meaning, though we have preserved the future sense in the English translation.

P/46–8 Κατασκιασθείη τὸ στέλεχος κτλ.

The image, if not the exact phraseology (*cf.* Theoph. Cont. 212/10–11; 225/20), clearly derives once again from Psalm 71, verse 16. For the imperial tree as *Weltenbaum*, see Treitinger 135, note 20.

P/48 διὰ σοῦ βασιλεύουσι βασιλεῖς. *Cf.* Theophanes 478/16–17; Theoph. Cont. 79/2–3 etc.

1/4–15 Ἄκουσον τοίνυν κτλ.

This passage, consisting still of prefatory matter, belongs more properly to the Proem than to the first chapter on foreign policy.

1/4–8 Ἄκουσον . . . κυβερνᾶν. This merely recapitulates the lesson of P/6–8; *cf. De Cer.*, 455/1–456/6; Bas. Imp. *Paraen.*, *MPG*, cvii, col. xxi A.

1/8–15 Εἰ δὲ σαφεῖ κτλ.
An apology for the simple style in which much of the book is written. For its significance, and its bearing on C.'s part in the work, see Moravcsik, *Atti del V. Congresso internazionale di studi bizantini*, 1 (Rome, 1939), 518–20. For similar apologies, see *De Cer.*, 5/2–4; Leo, *Taktika*, cols. 676 C, 1093 A; Cecaumenus 75/30–76/9; Nicetas Choniata 6/10–17. For κατημαξευμένῳ, *cf.* Callimachus, fr. 1, ed. Pfeiffer 1 (Oxonii, 1949), 5/25; Dionysii Halicarnasei *Opuscula*, ed. Usener-Radermacher 1 (Lipsiae, 1899), 341/12; Psellos, *Stich. Pol.*, ed. Boissonade, *Anecd. gr.*, iii (Paris, 1831), 200, 1. 6, note 2; and *id.*, *Chronographie*, ed. Renauld, 1 (Paris, 1926), xxii; Cedrenus ii, 616/19, 643/12. For the κοινή of the day, *cf. De Them.*, 82/13, 83/21. For ἐπίδειξιν . . . ἀπαγγελίας (1/10, 12), *cf.* Polybius 38, 4: ἐπιδεικτικωτέραν . . . ποιούμενοι . . . τὴν ἀπαγγελίαν, and *id.* 16, 17–18; also General Introduction, p. 1.

Cc. 1/16–28, 2–8, 10–13/11

BIBLIOGRAPHY

See bibliography prefixed to cc. 37–42 (pp. 142–3).

INTRODUCTORY NOTE

Cc. 1/16 to 13/11, except for c. 9, constitute the first section of Constantine's book, as described at P/14–17. Like Section 2 and the latter part of Section 3 (see General Introduction, pp. 2–5), they form a *practical lesson* in the foreign policy to be pursued, in this case towards the 'nations' to the north of Byzantium. The key to this policy at the time of writing is the nation of the Pechenegs (1/16–24); therefore, cc. 1–8 deal with the power and position of the Pechenegs as these affect their ability to serve the emperor (8/18–21), in war or in peace, against or among the peoples to west and east of them. These eight chapters, which in the original arrangement of the book formed a single section περὶ Πατζινακιτῶν (see on 13/10–11), must therefore, *ex hypothesi*, reflect the political situation at the time when the book was compiled, that is, at the middle of the tenth century: otherwise, the lesson which they teach would have been antiquated, unpractical and useless.

Scholars are not agreed upon whether the internal evidence supports this hypothesis. Manojlović (iv, 76–7) maintained that chapters 2–8, 9/114, 12 and 13/9–11 are parts of a monograph on the Pechenegs written in the latter years of the reign of Leo VI. Dvornik (*Les Légendes de Constantin et de Méthode* (Prague, 1933), 243) adopted a similar date. According to Manojlović, these passages represent the ethnographic situation *after* the Pechenegs had expelled the Turks from Atelkuzu northwards towards the upper Dniester, but *before* the Turks had crossed the Carpathians and settled in Hungary (*cf.* Bury 564). He argues (iv, 69–73) that 4/10–11 and 8/21 prove that the Turks were at that time close neighbours of the Pechenegs, whereas after the Hungarian *Landnahme* the Pechenegs could not easily (ῥᾳδίως) have attacked them. This does not seem convincing. We know that in 951 (37/13–14) the Pechenegs were a mere four days journey from Hungary (37/47–8), and thus could easily have been used to overawe it. The further argument that in 950 there would have been no need to incite the Pechenegs against Bulgaria (8/20) is frivolous. Bulgaria had been in need of coercion by the Pechenegs as recently as 924/5 (see on 5/8), and there was no saying when she might not have to be coerced again. She had in fact been ravaged by the Pechenegs as recently as 944 (see *Russian Primary Chronicle*, tr. Cross and Sherbowitz-Wetzor, Cambridge, Mass. (1953), 73), though this time at Russian, not Byzantine instigation. For the notorious crux at 13/5, see note *ad loc.*; but the very same passage states (13/3–5) that the Turks are already on the borders of Francia and south of the Pechenegs.

It thus appears to us that there is nothing in these chapters which points to a period anterior to the Hungarian *Landnahme,* or is inconsistent with the political situation of C.'s own day. On the contrary, the statements that the Pechenegs were already neighbours of Bulgaria and had often attacked her (5/3–14; 8/5–7; 8/22); that the Pechenegs could hinder the Turks from making incursions into Byzantine territory (4/3–13); and that the Turks have already more than once been defeated by the Pechenegs (3/2–5; 4/11–13; 8/21–2; 13/9–11); all point to a time when the Turks were already settled in modern Hungary. *Cf.* Macartney 144, 151; General Introduction, p. 7. On the relationship of this later, diplomatic section to the earlier cc. 37–41, see General Introduction, *ibid.*

1/17 εἰρήνην . . . ἔχειν μετὰ . . . Πατζινακιτῶν. *Cf.* 4/3, 5/5. For the Pechenegs, see *Byzantinoturcica*, I, 46–9 (2nd ed., 87–90); II, 213–14 (2nd ed., 247–9).

1/19 ἀποκρισιάριον. See Treitinger in *Reallex. f. Ant. u. Christ.*, I (1942), 501–4, *s.v.*

1/21 ὄψιδας. Lat. *obsides: cf.* 1/21, 7/5 ff., 8/13 ff., 45/142, and Cedrenus II, 284/2–3.

1/22 τοῦ καθυπουργοῦντος εἰς ταῦτα.
That is, 'the person in charge of these affairs'. The meaning is that the Pecheneg hostages shall be lodged all together in Constantinople in charge of (μετὰ) the competent official. This official was the κουράτωρ τοῦ ἀποκρισιαρείου, for whom see A. Vogt, *Basile Ier* (Paris, 1908), 166; Bury, *IAS*, 93; Bréhier, *Institutions*, 302. For the close supervision of foreign envoys, see *MPG*, CXIII, col. 636 C–D; Liudprand, *Legatio* c. 1; Cecaumenus 13.

1/25 γειτνιάζει τὸ τοιοῦτον ἔθνος. *Cf.* 6/2–3, 37/49.

1/26 τῆς Χερσῶνος.
That is, the city of Cherson, capital of the *thema* of that name: *cf. De Them.*, 98–100, 182–3; and below, 42/39–54 and 53 *passim.*

1/28 τὰ λεγόμενα κλίματα.
That is, the south-east part of the Crimean Peninsula. For references, see Vol. I, p. 323, *s.v.* κλίματα; add A. A. Vasiliev, *The Goths in the Crimea* (Cambridge, Mass., 1936), 117.

2/2 τοῖς 'Ρῶς οἱ Πατζινακῖται γείτονες. *Cf.* 37/42, 47. For the 'Ρῶς, see on 9/1.

2/6 Ἀγοράζουσι γὰρ κτλ. For trade-relations between Pechenegs and Russians see M. V. Levchenko, *Ocherki po istorii russko-vizantiiskikh otnoshenii* (Moscow, 1956), 201.

2/19 εἰς τοὺς φραγμοὺς τοῦ ποταμοῦ. *Cf.* on 9/70–1; and 42/60–2. The former passage (9/70–1) is clearly the source of this one.

3/2 τὸ τῶν Τούρκων γένος.
That is, Hungarians, Magyars; see *Byzantinoturcica*, I, 58–64 (2nd ed., 131–45); II, 270 (2nd ed., 321–2). How the name Τοῦρκοι became attached to the Hungarians is disputed. Some scholars have supposed that the name, as applied to them, was of Byzantine

origin, and of purely geographical and cultural significance: *i.e.*, that the Byzantines called the Hungarians 'Turks' because they had earlier lived between the Don and the Caucasus and had led a nomadic life there (see Darkó, *BZ*, 21, 1912, 475–7); on this supposition Byzantine palace circles simply applied the name 'Turks' to the Hungarians under the influence of literary tradition (*cf.* Czebe, *Kőrösi Csoma-Archivum*, 1 (1921–5), 306–10). Others believe that the name illustrates an historical fact, that is, that the Hungarians got the name as a result of Chazaro-Hungarian relations, and more especially as a result of the fusion of Kavars and Hungarians (see Németh III, 198–202; Manojlović IV, 103; Macartney 124–34; Deér 101, etc.). Our own view is that the Hungarians *called themselves* 'Turks'. This view is based on the facts that Leo VI, who calls the Hungarians Τοῦρκοι (*Taktika*, cols. 957–64), had as early as 894 first-hand information about them through his ambassadors (see Moravcsik, *Acta Historica Academiae Scientiarum Hungaricae*, 1 (1952), 178–80); and that C.'s own information very probably derives from Hungarian sources. If the Hungarians had called themselves anything but 'Turks', the Byzantines must have known of it from themselves.

3/3 διὰ τὸ πολλάκις ἡττηθῆναι. *Cf.* 4/11–13; 8/21–33; 13/9–11; 38/55–7; 40/16–19.

4/3 εἰρηνεύοντος. *Cf.* 1/17; 5/5.

4/10 διὰ γραμμάτων.
Cf. De Cer., 691/4–7. The use of γράμματα in this connexion indicates that the Pechenegs were autonomous, and that the Byzantine government regarded them as quite independent (*cf.* 6/11); see Dölger, *BES*, 37–8; Ostrogorsky, *Sem. Kond.* 8 (1936), 49; Dölger, *BD*, 141.

4/11–13 ἐπέρχεσθαι καὶ ἐξανδραποδίζεσθαι. *Cf.* 3/3; 8/21–2; 13/9–11; 38/55–57; 40/16–19.

5/3 Βουλγάροις. See *Byzantinoturcica*, 1, 50–8 (2nd ed., 108–31); II, 96–101 (2nd ed., 100–6).

5/5 εἰρηνεύειν. *Cf.* 1/17; 4/3.

5/6 πλησιάζουσιν. *Cf.* 8/5; 37/41–8.

5/8 δύνανται κατὰ Βουλγαρίας ἐκστρατεύειν.
So, in 914, the military governor of Cherson, John Bogas, was instructed by the empress Zoë to incite the Pechenegs to invade Bulgaria; see Cont. Geo. Mon. 879/12–19, 882/3–20; Theoph. Cont. 386/23–387/13, 389/20–390/21; *Ep. Nic. Patr.* (*MPG*, CXI) cols. 72–6. Nicholas Mysticus, writing again to the Bulgarian king in 924/5 (*ibid.* cols. 149–53), mentions that the Pechenegs among others are preparing war against Bulgaria.

6/2 ἕτερος λαὸς κτλ. *Cf.* 1/25; 8/5; 9/67; 37/38, 49.

6/3 πραγματεύονται. See 53/530–2.

6/5 Χαζαρίαν καὶ τὴν Ζιχίαν.
For Chazaria see *Byzantinoturcica*, 1, 44–6 (2nd ed., 81–6); II, 280 (2nd ed., 334–6). For the Zichians, who lived on the eastern shore of the Black Sea, *cf.* 42/97–9.

6/8–9 βλαττία . . . Πάρθικα.
For βλαττία, πράνδια, χαρέρια, see *Eparchikon Biblion* IX, 6, ed. I. and P. Zepos in *Jus Graecormanum*, II, 382; Guilland in *Revue des Et. grecques*, 62 (1949), 333–8. For χαρέρια,

lightly woven materials, see Du Cange, *Gloss. Med. et Inf. Graec.*, II (1733), *s.v.* For σήμεντα, see Joh. Lydus, *De Magistratibus*, 2, 4, ed. Wuensch 59/2-5; Alföldi, *Römische Mitteilungen*, 50 (1935), 60. For δέρματα ἀληθινὰ Πάρθικα, see Corippus, *Joh.* IV, 499, *Just.* II, 106 (ed. Bonn. 86, 179); John Lydus, *De Magistratibus*, 2, 13, ed. Wuensch 68/23-4; *Excerpta de Legationibus*, ed. de Boor, I, 132/11; Reiske in *De Cer.*, II, 188, 420. For the mediaeval pepper-trade see A. Schaube, *Handelsgeschichte der romanischen Völker* (Munich and Berlin, 1906), 89, 162-5, and R. E. M. Wheeler, *Rome beyond the Imperial Frontiers* (London: Pelican Books, 1955), 148-9.

6/11 Ἐλεύθεροι γὰρ ὄντες. See on 4/10.

7/1 Περὶ τῶν . . . ἀποστελλομένων.
Cc. 7 and 8 describe the procedure to be followed by Byzantine envoys sent respectively to the eastern and western groups of Pechenegs: see on 6/2, and 37/34-49. The former must be approached from Cherson; the latter might be found perhaps no further off than the mouth of the Danube: see on 8/3. For general instructions to envoys on such missions, see *MPG*, CXIII, col. 637 B-C.

7/2 βασιλικῶν. For these diplomatic and security officials, see on 22/15.

7/5 διασώστας. See Liudprand, *Legatio*, c. 57 (ed. Becker 206/22); and Bréhier, *Institutions*, 310.

7/8-9 ἄπληστοι . . . ἐπιθυμηταί. *Cf.* on 13/15-16.

8/2 χελανδίων. See Introductory Note to c. 51 (p. 195); and Liudprand, *Antapodosis*, V, 9 (ed. Becker 135/3-5).

8/3 τοῦ Δανουβίου.
Though the text does not specifically say so, it is probable that the envoys sent to the western Pechenegs could meet them also at the mouth of the Danube, which at this period formed the frontier between Bulgaria and Patzinacia: see 42/20-1 and Introductory Note to this section; also map in V. N. Zlatarski, *Geschichte der Bulgaren*, I (Leipzig, 1918); D. Rizoff, *Die Bulgaren in ihren. hist., ethnogr. u. pol. Grenzen* (Berlin, 1917), Map IV.

8/5 εἰς τὸ μέρος τῆς Βουλγαρίας. See on 6/2.

8/17 ζάκανα. See Introductory Note to c. 38 (p. 146).

8/18 φίλους.
These are the persons mentioned at 1/20-4. For their status, see Dölger, *BES*, 38, 65-6, note 74. *Cf.* 9/69, if the reading is correct.

8/22 πολλάκις κατ' αὐτῶν ἐλθόντες. *Cf.* 3/3; 4/11-13; 13/9-11; 38/55-7; 40/16-19. For the chronological significance of the phrase, see Introductory Note to this section.

8/23 Τοῦ γὰρ κληρικοῦ Γαβριήλ.
This mission of the cleric Gabriel is not mentioned in any other source, and is even omitted from Dölger, *Regesten*, I, 70. For the date of the mission, see on 8/30.

8/24 ἀπὸ κελεύσεως βασιλικῆς.
The expression indicates that at the time of Gabriel's mission the Turks (Hungarians) were dependent on Byzantium; that is to say, the Byzantine government regarded them as subjects. Leo VI, in his *Taktika* (col. 963 B), writes that the Hungarians are 'anxious

to approve themselves subjects' of Byzantium. The use of the word γράμματα at *De Cer.*, 691/3–4, points to a different sort of relationship: see on 4/10.

8/29 ἄρχοντες. The same word is used in the imperial γράμματα sent to the Turks: see *De Cer.*, 691/4, and preceding note.

8/30 μετὰ τοὺς Πατζινακίτας . . . οὐ βάλλομεν.
The exact meaning of the phrase is uncertain. μετὰ may either be the MGr. μέ, meaning 'with', or else the AGr. μετά with acc., meaning 'after'. K. Amandos ('Ιστορία τοῦ βυζαντινοῦ κράτους,, II, Athens, 1947, 123) gives the following MGr. translation: δὲν τὰ βάζομεν μὲ τοὺς Πατζινακίτας. However, there is in Hungarian an expression which corresponds exactly with the Greek if we suppose μετά to mean 'after': 'we are not putting ourselves after the P.' (*cf.* the colloquial Engl. 'we are not getting after . . .'). It may thus be that the Greek text repeats the actual words of the Hungarian chiefs. The popular tone of the rest of the passage (8/30–3) seems to support this.

As we have stated (on 8/23), no other source mentions the mission of Gabriel. The question arises, what was its date? Manojlović (IV, 66, 72–3) dates it to the time when the Turks were still living near the Dniester. Bury (563, 568) also dates it to the reign of Leo VI (886–912). Fehér (43–5) tries to prove that it took place in 943/4. Runciman (*Romanus Lecapenus*, 108) dates it to 948. As we have noted above (on 5/8), the Byzantines counted on the help of the Pechenegs against Bulgaria, with whom they were at war between 913 and 925. It is not likely that they would have stirred up the Hungarians against the Pechenegs during this period. But after Symeon's death (927) and the conclusion of peace with Bulgaria, the time was ripe to incite foreign nations against the Pechenegs. Our view therefore is that Gabriel's mission took place after 927. Gabriel's words were (8/25–8): 'expel the P. from their seat and settle there yourselves (for you used formerly to be settled there), so that you may be near to my imperial Majesty': that is to say, the Hungarians were to reoccupy the area from which the P. had expelled them; see 38/55–7, 40/15–19. Hungarians living in modern Hungary were far away from Byzantium; but in the district north of the mouth of the Danube they could easily be reached by ship from Byzantium: see on 8/3. The refusal of the Hungarians to adopt Gabriel's plan no doubt refers to their defeat by the Pechenegs in 896; see 38/60–1.

C. 9

BIBLIOGRAPHY

N. P. Barsov, *Ocherki russkoy istoricheskoy geografii. Geografiya Nachal'noy Letopisi* (Warsaw, 1873) (Barsov). P. E. Belyavsky, Article 'Dnepr', *Entsiklopedichesky Slovar'* 20 (St Petersburg, 1893), 791–808 (Belyavsky). S. V. Bernshtein-Kogan, 'Put' iz Varyag v Greki', *Voprosy Geografii* 20 (1950), 239–70 (Bernshtein-Kogan). V. A. Brim, 'Put' iz Varyag v̦ Greki', *Izvestiya Akademii Nauk SSSR*, 7th series, otdel. obshch. nauk, no. 2 (1931), 201–47 (Brim). F. K. Brun, 'Chernomor'e I', *Zapiski Imperatorskogo Novorossiiskogo Universiteta* 28 (Odessa, 1879), 90–108; II, *ibid.*, 30 (1880), 363–79 (Brun, *Chernomor'e*). *A Collection of Voyages and Travels, some now first Printed from Original Manuscripts, others Translated out of Foreign Languages, and now first Published in English*, I (London, 1704) (*Churchill's Voyages*). Cross (see *Povest'*). 'Dneprovskie Porogi', *Zapiski Odesskogo Obshchestva Istorii i Drevnostey* 3 (1853), 581–6 (*Dneprovskie Porogi*). N. Durnovo, 'Vvedenie v istoriyu russkogo yazyka', *Spisy Filosofické Fakulty Masarykovy University v Brně* 20, 1 (Brno, 1927) (Durnovo). R. Ekblom, 'Die Namen der siebenten Dneprstromschnelle', *Språkvetenskapliga Sällskapets Förhandlingar* 1949–51 (Uppsala, 1951), 151–74 (Ekblom, *Die siebente Stromschnelle*). D. I. Evarnitsky, *Vol'nosti zaporozhskikh kozakov* (St Petersburg, 1890) (Evarnitsky). K.-O. Falk, '*Πέραμα τοῦ κραρίου, Traiectus Crarii*', *Slaviska Institutet vid Lunds Universitet, Årsbok* (1948–9) (Lund, 1951), 106–37 (Falk, *Πέραμα τοῦ κραρίου*). K.-O. Falk,

'Dneprforsarnas Namn i Kejsar Konstantin VII Porfyrogennetos' De Administrando Imperio', *Lunds Universitets Årsskrift*, N. F. Avd. 1, Bd. 46, Nr. 4 (Lund, 1951) (Falk). S. Gedeonov, *Varyagi i Rus'*, II (St Petersburg, 1876) (Gedeonov). B. D. Grekov, *Kievskaya Rus'* (4th ed. Moscow-Leningrad, 1944) (Grekov). *Istoriya Kul'tury Drevney Rusi: Domongol'sky period*, ed. N. N. Voronin, M. K. Karger, I (Moscow-Leningrad, 1948); II (*ibid.*, 1951) (*Kul'tura Drevney Rusi*). A. Karlgren, 'Dneprfossernes Nordisk-Slaviske Navne', *Festskrift udgivet af Københavns Universitet i Anledning af Universitetets Aarsfest november 1947* (Copenhagen, 1947) (Karlgren). T. D. Kendrick, *A History of the Vikings* (London, 1930) (Kendrick). B. Kleiber, 'Zu den slavischen Namen der Dnjeprschnellen', *Zeitschrift für slavische Philologie* 28 (1959), 75–98 (Kleiber). *Kniga Bol'shomu Chertezhu*, ed. K. N. Serbina (Moscow-Leningrad, 1950) (*The Book of the Great Map*). G. E. Kochin, *Materialy dlya terminologicheskogo slovarya drevney Rossii* (Moscow-Leningrad, 1937), (Kochin). K. V. Kudryashov, *Russky istorichesky atlas* (Moscow-Leningrad, 1928) (Kudryashov). E. Kunik, *Die Berufung der schwedischen Rodsen durch die Finnen und Slawen*, II (St Petersburg, 1845) (Kunik). 'Izvestiya vizantiiskikh pisateley o Severnom Prichernomor'e', *Izvestiya Gosudarstvennoy Akademii Istorii Material'noy Kul'tury* 91 (1934), containing N. V. Malitsky's revision of V. V. Latyshev's tr. of c. 9 (Latyshev-Malitsky). A. C. Lehrberg, *Untersuchungen zur Erläuterung der älteren Geschichte Russlands* (St Petersburg, 1816) (Lehrberg). M. V. Levchenko, *Ocherki po istorii russko-vizantiiskikh otnosheny* (Moscow, 1956) (Levchenko, *Russko-vizantiiskie otnosheniya*). V. Lyaskoronsky, *Istoriya Pereyaslavl'skoy zemli* (Kiev, 1897) (Lyaskoronsky). V. J. Mansikka, *Die Religion der Ostslaven* I (Helsinki, 1922), *FF Communications* 43 (Mansikka). V. Miller, 'Nazvaniya Dneprovskikh porogov u Konstantina Bagryanorodnogo', *Drevnosti. Trudy Moskovskogo Arkheologicheskogo Obshchestva* V, 1 (1885), Supplement, 19–31 (Miller). A. N. Nasonov, '*Russkaya Zemlya*' *i obrazovanie territorii drevnerusskogo gosudarstva* (Moscow, 1951) (Nasonov). L. Niederle, *Slovanské Starožitnosti* I, 4; III, 2 (Prague, 1924, 1925) (Niederle, *Slovanské Starožitnosti*). L. Niederle, *Manuel de l'Antiquité Slave* I, II (Paris, 1923, 1926) (Niederle, *Manuel*). *Pamyatniki russkogo prava* I, ed. A. A. Zimin (Moscow, 1952) (*Pamyatniki*). H. Paszkiewicz, *The Origin of Russia* (London, 1954) (Paszkiewicz). *Povest' Vremennykh Let*, ed. V. P. Adrianova-Peretts, I, II (Moscow-Leningrad, 1950) (*Povest'*); Eng. tr., S. H. Cross, O. P. Sherbowitz-Wetzor, *The Russian Primary Chronicle*, (Cambridge, Mass., 1953) (Cross). V. I. Ravdonikas, 'Nadpisi i znaki na mechakh iz Dneprostroya', *Izvestiya Gosudarstvennoy Akademii Istorii Material'noy Kul'tury* 100 (1933), 598–616 (Ravdonikas). J. Sahlgren, 'Wikingerfahrten im Osten', *Zeitschrift für slavische Philologie* 8 (1931), 309–323 (Sahlgren). A. Selishchev, *Izvestiya Otdeleniya Russkogo Yazyka i Slovenosti Akademii Nauk SSSR* 32 (1927), 303–30: a review of N. Durnovo's *Ocherk istorii russkogo yazyka* (Selishchev). P. Semenov, *Geografichesko-statistichesky Slovar' Rossiiskoy Imperii* II (St Petersburg, 1863), 77–85, article 'Dnepr' (Semenov). S. M. Seredonin, *Istoricheskaya Geografiya* (Petrograd, 1916) (Seredonin). A. A. Shakhmatov, *Vvedenie v kurs istorii russkogo yazyka* I (Petrograd, 1916) (Shakhmatov, *Vvedenie*). *Id.*, *Drevneishie sud'by russkogo plemeni* (Petrograd, 1919) (Shakhmatov, *Drevneishie sud'by*). G. Y. Shevelov (Yury Šerech), 'On the Slavic names for the falls of the Dnepr in the "De Administrando Imperio" of Constantine Porphyrogenitus', *Slavic Word*, XI, 4 (1955), 503–30 (Shevelov). P. Skok, 'Ortsnamenstudien zu *De administrando imperio* des Kaisers Konstantin Porphyrogennetos', *Zeitschrift für Ortsnamenforschung* 4 (1928) 213–14 (Skok). 'Sochineniya Konstantina Bagryanorodnogo: ,O femakh' (De Thematibus) i ,O narodakh' (De Administrando Imperio)', tr. G. Laskin, *Chteniya v Imperatorskom Obshchestve Istorii i Drevnostey Rossiiskikh pri Moskovskom Universitete* 1899, I (188) (Laskin). A. V. Soloviev, 'Le nom byzantin de la Russie', *Musagetes* 3 (The Hague, 1957) (Soloviev, *Le nom byzantin de la Russie*). I. I. Sreznevsky, *Materialy dlya slovarya drevne-russkogo yazyka* (St Petersburg, 1893–1909) (Sreznevsky). A. Stender-Petersen, *Varangica* (Aarhus, 1953) (Stender-Petersen, *Varangica*). J. C. Stuckenberg, *Hydrographie des russischen Reiches*, III (St Petersburg, 1847) (Stuckenburg). V. Thomsen, *The Relations between Ancient Russia and Scandinavia and the Origin of the Russian State* (Oxford, 1877) (Thomsen, *Relations*). *Id.*, 'Det russiske riges grundlæggelse ved Nordboerne samt bemærkninger til Varægersporgsmålet', *Samlede Afhandlinger* I (Copenhagen, 1919) (Thomsen, *Samlede Afhandlinger*). M. N. Tikhomirov, *Drevnerusskie goroda* (2nd ed., Moscow 1956) (Tikhomirov, (*Drevnerusskie goroda*). V. E. de Timonoff, 'Les Cataractes du Dnièpre' (St Petersburg, 1894), *VIe Congrès International de Navigation Intérieure* (The Hague, 1894) 7e Question (Timonoff). P. N. Tret'yakov, *Vostochno-slavyanskie plemena* (2nd ed., Moscow, 1953) (Tret'yakov). A. A. Vasiliev, *The Russian Attack on Constantinople in 860* (Cambridge, Mass., 1946) (Vasiliev, *Russian Attack*). A. A. Vasiliev, 'Economic Relations between Byzantium and Old Russia', *Journal of Economic and Business History* 4 (1931–2), 314–34 (Vasiliev, *Economic Relations*). M. Vasmer, 'Wikingerspuren in

Russland', *Sitzungsberichte der preussischen Akademie der Wissenschaften*, phil.-hist. Kl. (1931), 649–74 (Vasmer, *Wikingerspuren*). M. Vasmer, *Russisches etymologisches Wörterbuch* (Heidelberg, 1953–8) (Vasmer, *Russisches etymologisches Wörterbuch*). G. Vernadsky, *Ancient Russia* (New Haven, 1943) (Vernadsky, *Ancient Russia*). G. Vernadsky, *Kievan Russia* (New Haven, 1948) (Vernadsky, *Kievan Russia*). N. N. Voronin, *Drevnerusskie goroda* (Moscow-Leningrad, 1945) (Voronin). A. Yuzhny, 'Na Dneprovskikh porogakh', *Vestnik Evropy* (1881), tom. 4, 399–406 (Yuzhny).

INTRODUCTORY NOTE

C. 9 contains a topographical account of the trade route from Kiev to Constantinople, with special reference to the rapids or 'barrages' (φραγμοί) on the lower Dnieper; a list of towns situated on or near the Novgorod-Kiev section of the Baltic–Black Sea waterway; a description of the Russian trading expeditions to Byzantium; a reference to the economic relations between the Russians and their Slav tributaries; and a concluding note on the Uz.

This material is not homogeneous: it falls into at least three sections, each presumably derived from a separate source (*cf.* Manojlović IV, 41–3): (*a*) 9/3–104, a description of the gathering in Kiev of the *monoxyla* from different parts of Russia and of their journey to Constantinople; (*b*) 9/104–13, a fragment on the tribute levied by the Russians on the Slavs during the winter months; and (*c*) 9/114, the note on the Uz. Different origins of (*a*) and (*b*) may be inferred from the transcriptions of the name of the city of Kiev (τὸ Κιοάβα, 9/8, and τὸν Κίοβα, 9/15, in (*a*), and τὸν Κίαβον, 9/106, 111, in (*b*)), and of the Slav tribe of the Krivichi (Κριβηταιηνοί, 9/9–10, in (*a*), and Κριβιτζῶν, 9/108, in (*b*)). As for the note on the Uz, which is related formally to the opening sentence of the next chapter (10/3–4) and in content to the earlier Pecheneg chapters (cc. 1–8), it is clearly out of place where it stands; its incorporation into c. 9 was doubtless due to the absence of a marginal index in the ms. (see Bury 520–1).

It has long been apparent that, with the exception of the note on the Uz, c. 9 as a whole is out of place in the first, didactic, section (cc. 1–13/11) of *DAI*: see Bury 543; Macartney 143; *Byzantinoturcica*, I, 211 (2nd ed. 363). Most scholars believe its proper place to be in the section on the Nations (cc. 14–46). Even there, however, it would not be altogether uniform with the rest of the material: for we find in 9/1–113 neither the historical-antiquarian approach nor the concern with problems of diplomacy which are the distinguishing features of that section (see General Introduction, pp. 2–5). As a detailed itinerary doing duty for a history of the Russians, c. 9 stands apart from the rest of *DAI*[1]; and it may well be, as the General Introduction (p. 2) suggests, that it is source material consulted by C. in the imperial archives in 952 and later copied into his book. Its position in the book, immediately following the περὶ Πατζινακιτῶν κεφάλαιον (cc. 1–8), supports this view; and passages such as 2/16–23 and 8/20–2 suggest that c. 9 was used as a source, consulted when this κεφάλαιον was being written.

The material in this chapter, at least in its main section (9/3–104), was probably compiled about 944. The wording of 9/4–5 suggests that Igor, prince of Kiev, was alive at the time of writing. Igor is believed to have come to the throne in 913 (*Povest'*, I, 31) and died, in all probability, in the autumn of 944 (*ibid.*, II, 295). The passage could not have been written much before 944, since Svyatoslav was still a child when his father died (*ibid.*, I, 40). The reference to his rule in Novgorod—a fact mentioned in no other source —must mean that Svyatoslav resided in that city as Igor's representative during the latter's lifetime: we know that in the 10th cent. the princes of Kiev were in the habit of appointing their sons to the throne of Novgorod (see on 9/4); and from 945 to 972 Svyatoslav was prince of Kiev. The past tense ἐκαθέζετο (9/5) might seem to suggest that the passage was written after Igor's death, when Svyatoslav was already prince of Kiev. In

---

[1] There are, it is true, fragments of itineraries in the section on the Nations, notably in c. 42; but c. 9 is unique in that its account of the Russians and of their waterway betrays no preoccupation with diplomacy or history (with the possible exception of 9/4–5).

that case, however, he and not Igor would have been given the title of ὁ ἄρχων ʿΡωσίας. Attempts have been made to resolve this difficulty by suggesting that the reference to Svyatoslav's reign in Novgorod in 9/4–5 is a later insertion (see Manojlović IV, 42); but this seems a gratuitous complication. It is more likely that the passage was written during Igor's lifetime, and that it consequently referred to Svyatoslav's reign in Novgorod in the present tense: καθέζεται. The alteration to ἐκαθέζετο was probably made in order to bring the text up to date while it lay in the imperial archives, between 944, when Igor died and Svyatoslav removed to Kiev, and 952, when C. consulted it. (For a somewhat similar view, see Gedeonov 531.)

The suggestion that 9/3–104 was compiled about 944[1] receives support from a consideration of who its author could have been. He was obviously a Constantinopolitan: for he compares the width of the 'ford of Krarion' on the Dnieper to that of the Byzantine Hippodrome (9/66–8); and, equally obviously, he moved in court circles: for, in assessing the width of the first rapid, he takes as his measure the imperial polo-ground (9/26–7). It is possible that he obtained at least some of his information on Russia from some Varangian or Slav in Constantinople; however, the vividness and accuracy of his description leave little doubt that it is in the main the account of an eye-witness who had himself travelled up and down the Dnieper. He can scarcely have been a merchant, since, except for two references to the wares (τὰ πράγματα) carried by the Russian ships (9/32, 51), he makes no mention of trade (cf. Manojlović IV, 33, 38–9). It is far more likely that he was a Byzantine envoy who had been sent to Kiev on a diplomatic mission, one of those βασιλικοί whom the imperial government regularly dispatched to negotiate with the empire's northern neighbours: cf. 1/23, 7/3, 8/2, 7, 23–4. In 944 an embassy from Romanus I travelled to Kiev to conclude a treaty with Igor (see Povest', I, 34; Cross 73; and for the date of both embassy and treaty, Povest', II, 289; Cross 237–8). The author of 9/3–104 may well have been a member of this embassy: cf. Bury 543–4. It seems noteworthy in this connexion that the demotic use of the preposition ἀπό followed by accusative is particularly frequent in c. 9 (see Vol. I, p. 334): this suggests that at least part of the chapter was taken down verbally from a diplomatic report.

The complex problem of the sources from which the author of 9/3–104 obtained his information on Russia will be discussed in the commentary below. A study of the Scandinavian and Slavonic proper names which abound in this chapter, notably in the account of the Dnieper rapids, will suggest that our author's informant was in all probability a Northman who, living in the bilingual milieu of Kievan Russia, was familiar with the Slavonic tongue.

If 9/3–104 comes from the pen of a Byzantine author, 9/104–13 seems to have been derived from a different source. It is in this section that traces of Slavonic terminology are most frequent and apparent: the expressions πάντων τῶν ʿΡῶς (9/106) and διατρεφόμενοι (9/110) seem to be literal translations, and πολύδια (9/107) is a direct transcription, of technical terms used at that time by the Eastern Slavs; while the form Κριβιτζῶν (9/108), which is a phonetic transcription of the Slavonic plural Krivichi, corresponds much more closely to the original name of this tribe than the form Κριβηταιηνοί at 9/9–10, which goes back to the singular form of this name. It would seem therefore that 9/104–13 is a Greek translation of a Slav account. There seems no valid reason to suppose that this fragment was written much earlier or much later than 944 (see on 9/104–5). Presumably it lay in the files of the λογοθέτης τοῦ δρόμου in Constantinople, where it was consulted by C., together with 9/3–104, in 952.

There is some evidence that the material embodied in c. 9 was subjected to a certain amount of preliminary editing. It has been suggested above that the form ἐκαθέζετο

---

[1] Some commentators have been struck by the absence in c. 9 of any reference to Igor's great naval attack on the empire in 941. This, however, is no argument for an earlier dating of the chapter, which is essentially a geographical itinerary, containing neither historical excursuses nor diplomatic lessons.

(9/5) betrays an attempt, made between 944 and 952, to bring the text up to date. Furthermore, the words αὐτῶν (9/104) and καθὼς προείρηται (9/112) are clearly editorial comments, whose purpose was to link the fragment 9/104–13 to the preceding section. This evidence of an editorial hand appears to tell against the suggestion made in the General Introduction (p. 2), that the material embodied in c. 9 was later 'copied erroneously into the book'. It seems possible to agree with the view of c. 9 as source material and to believe at the same time that C. may well have intended to include it in *DAI*.

9/1 ἀπὸ 'Ρωσίας.

The word 'Ρωσία, which became the usual Byzantine term for Russia, is first encountered in C.'s writings: *cf. De Cer.*, 594/18, 691/1. The Russians themselves called their country, in the language of the Eastern Slavs, *Rus'* or *ruskaya zemlya* (*Povest'*, *passim*), more rarely *strana ruskaya* (*ibid.*, I, 35, 39); the two latter terms correspond to χώρα τῆς 'Ρωσίας (at 37/43) and γῆ 'Ρωσική (Theodore Prodromus, *MPG*, cxxxiii, col. 1412). Later, the term 'Ρωσία was borrowed by the Russians, in the form *Rosiya*, from the terminology used by the Byzantine Patriarchate. In Russia this form is first attested in the second half of the 15th cent., though it appears in a South Slavonic text as early as 1387: see Soloviev, *Le nom byzantin de la Russie*; see also *Viz. Vrem.* 12 (1957), 134–55. The modern form of the name (with double σ/s) appears in Greek in the 14th cent. (Nicephorus Gregoras III, 199/12, 511/18) and in Russian in the 17th. See also Martel, *Mélanges Paul Boyer* (Paris, 1925), 270–9; Syuzyumov, *Vestnik Drevney Istorii*, 2 (1940), 123; Vasmer, *Russisches etymologisches Wörterbuch, s.v. Rossiya*; Tikhomirov, *Voprosy Istorii* 11 (1953), 93–6.

9/1 Περὶ τῶν . . . 'Ρῶς.

The Greek form of the name is first unequivocally attested in *Annales Bertiniani*, ann. 839, where it is stated by Prudentius of Troyes that a group of Swedes, sent from Constantinople to Lewis the Pious at Ingelheim, 'se, id est gentem suam, Rhos vocari dicebant' (*MGH*, Scr. I, 434; *cf.* Thomsen, *Relations*, 38–45; Vasiliev, *Russian Attack*, 6–13). Attempts to connect the Russian national name with the Syriac *Hros* of the 6th cent. Ps.-Zacharias (Marquart 355 ff.), or with the ῥούσια χελάνδια that formed part of the navy of Constantine V in 773 (Vernadsky, *Ancient Russia*, 279–80), are discountenanced by most scholars today: see Stender-Petersen, *Varangica*, 16; Dvornik, *The Making of Central and Eastern Europe*, 307–9. In Greek sources, οἱ 'Ρῶς are mentioned in the *Life of St George of Amastris*, which some scholars believe to have been written by Ignatius the Deacon in the first half of the 9th cent.: βαρβάρων τῶν 'Ρῶς: see V. G. Vasilievsky, *Trudy*, III, 64. However, the authorship and date of this document are still matters of dispute: for different views, see Vasiliev, *Russian Attack*, 71–89; Lipshits, *Istoricheskie Zapiski*, 26 (1948), 312–31; Levchenko, *Russko-vizantiiskie otnosheniya*, 46–55. The earliest uncontroversial mention of the Russians in Byzantine sources is to be found in the writings of Photius: in the titles of his two Homilies on the Russian attack of 860, where they are called οἱ 'Ρῶς (C. Müller, *Frag. hist. graec.*, v, I, 162–73); and in his encyclical letter of 867, where they are termed τὸ 'Ρῶς (*MPG*, cii, cols. 736–7; Φωτίου ἐπιστολαί, ed. Valetta, London (1864), 178). They are frequently mentioned in 10th cent. sources, both in the form 'Ρῶς (Leo Gramm. 240/19, 240/22–241/1; Sym. Mag. 674/16, 18, 707/3, 746/12; *De Cer.*, 511/6, 579/21, 598/4, 651/18, 654/10–11, 660/18, 664/15–16; Leo Diac. 63/9, 112/1, 135/3, 136/6, 140/16, 141/3, 147/24, 157/20), and in the form 'Ρώς (*MPG*, cv, col. 516; Theoph. Cont. 196/6, 423/15, 20, 826/18); *cf.* Soloviev, *Le nom byzantin de la Russie*, 9–12.

The Greek form 'Ρῶς, 'Ρώς has been derived from the Slavonic *Rus'* (Русь). This derivation has been explained in various ways: (i) by the phonetic proximity and interchangeability of ω and ου in the North Greek language (Ekblom, *Archives d'Etudes Orientales publiées par J.-A. Lundell*, 11 (Stockholm, 1915), 8; *cf.* G. N. Hatzidakis, *Einleitung in die neugr. Grammatik* (Leipzig, 1892), 348 ff.); (ii) by the suggestion that the name *Rus'* may have reached the Byzantines through the language of a Turkic people, such as the Chazars (Thomsen, *Relations*, 99; Stender-Petersen, *Varangica*, 84); and (iii) by the contamination which took place in Byzantium in the 9th and 10th cents. between the name of the Russians and the title of the Biblical King Gog, described in the LXX version of Ezekiel (xxxviii, 2 ,3; xxxix, 1) as ἄρχοντα ʽΡώς. This contamination was made easier by the traditional association of Gog and Magog with the Scythians of the Pontic steppes, and is evidenced in the contemporary belief (Leo Diac. 150/15–19) that the Russian attacks on the empire were in fact fulfilling Ezekiel's prophecy: ἰδοὺ ἐγὼ ἐπάγω ἐπὶ σὲ τὸν Γὼγ καὶ Μαγώγ, ἄρχοντα ʽΡώς (Florovsky, *Sbornik v chest' na Vasil N. Zlatarski*, Sofia, 1925, 505–20; Syuzyumov, *Vestnik Drevney Istorii*, 2 (1940), 121–3; Vasiliev, *Russian Attack*, 166–8). The indeclinable form οἱ ʽΡώς, which may well have been influenced by the Biblical ʽΡώς (also indeclinable), tended however in the course of time to give way to inflected forms of the word: *cf.* τῶν ʽΡώσων (Psellus, *Chronographie*, ed. Renauld, II, 8; Cantacuzenus III, 94/13); οἱ ʽΡῶσοι (Eustathius of Thessalonica: V. V. Latyshev, *Scythica et Caucasica*, I, St Petersburg (1890), 194); οἱ ʽΡωσοί (Glycas 553/4, 595/7) and οἱ ʽΡώσιοι (Balsamon, *MPG*, cxxxvii, col. 485). At the same time, another Greek form, ʽΡούσιοι, appears in the middle of the 10th cent.: see Liudprand, *Antapodosis*, v, 15: gens quaedam . . . quam a qualitate corporis Greci vocant . . . Rúsios, nos vero . . . nominamus Nordmannos; and *cf. ibid.*, I, 11. This false etymology, which connected the name of the Russians with the adjective ῥούσιος, 'red, red-haired', betrays the popular origin of this form (see Syuzyumov, *op. cit.*, 121, 123; Stender-Petersen, *Varangica*, 84; Soloviev, *Le nom byzantin de la Russie*, 12).

The popular form ʽΡούσιοι had no lasting success in Byzantine literature. Yet it was phonetically closer than the more learned form ʽΡῶς to the original name by which the Russians were then widely known in eastern Europe and in the Near East: for the Slavs called them *Rus'* (see *Povest', passim*) and the Arabic writers called them *Rūs* (see Minorsky, *Encyclopaedia of Islam* III (1936), 1181–3). The meaning and origin of this name have been widely, and often fiercely, debated for the past two centuries. The controversy, apart from its many side-issues, was essentially concerned with the elucidation of four problems: (i) the linguistic interpretation of the term *Rus'*; (ii) the ethnic origin of the people who bore that name; (iii) the meaning, or meanings, attached to the name *Rus'* in the sources of the 9th, 10th and 11th cents.; (iv) the rôle played by the Scandinavian Vikings in the creation of the Russian state. For the history of this controversy, see Moshin, *Slavia* 10 (Prague, 1931), 109–36, 343–79, 501–37; *id., Byzantinoslavica*, 3 (1931), 33–58, 285–307; Stender-Petersen, *Varangica*, 5–20; Paszkiewicz 109–32.

The results of modern research may be summarized under four headings, as follows:

(i) *The derivation of the term Rus'.* The most ingenious efforts of the 'anti-Normanist' school (for which, see the works cited above) have not succeeded in undermining the view, argued by Thomsen (*Relations*), who developed some of the views of E. Kunik (*Die Berufung der schwedischen Rodsen durch die Finnen und Slawen*, I, St Petersburg, 1844), that the word *Rus'* is derived from the Old Swedish word *Rōþer*, though the intermediary of the Old Finnish **Rōtsi*. (The modern terms *Ruotsi* and *Rotsi* are the names for Sweden in Finnish and Estonian respectively.) The word *rōþer* itself has been variously explained: as identical with *Roslagen*, the name of the coastal area of the Swedish provinces of Upland and East Götland (*cf.* Thomsen, *Relations*, 95–7; *id., Samlede Afhandlinger*, I, 344); as signifying, in composite forms such as *rōps-karlar*, *rōps-mæn* or *rōps-byggiar*, 'rowers, seafarers' (Thomsen, *Relations*, 95–6); as meaning 'voie ou ligne où on peut ramer, parage ou passe sans grande profondeur' (Ekblom, *Archives d'Etudes Orientales publiées par J. -A. Lundell*, 11 (Stockholm, 1915), 9–10; Stender-Petersen, *Varangica*, 80–1, 244): in this last interpretation, the composite terms such as *rōps-karlar*, *rōps-mæn* and *rōps-byggiar* would mean 'the people who live along, or sail over, the *rōþrar*'. For a different interpretation, see now Vernadsky, *Südost-Forschungen*, 15 (1956), 167–79.

(ii) *The ethnic origin of the Rus'*. Here too, the attempts of the 'anti-Normanist' school to prove that the original *Rus'* were not Scandinavians (the suggested alternatives range over a vast and heterogeneous field which includes Alans, Finns, Chazars, Lithuanians and Slavs) remain wholly unconvincing. Contemporary sources (listed and analysed by Thomsen, *Relations*, 13–15, 37–86) testify with overwhelming weight and virtual unanimity to the fact that the original *Rus'* were Northmen from Scandinavia, mainly Swedes. Not least in importance among these sources is c. 9 of *DAI*, in which the names of the Dnieper barrages are given in the Slavonic and 'Russian' languages, the latter being beyond doubt Old Swedish (see on 9/25). In the course of time, the *Rus'* gave their name to the East Slavonic people over whom they established their rule in the second half of the 9th cent., and by whom they were gradually absorbed. Neither of these processes was, it seems, achieved before the 11th cent.; and may not have been completed before the 12th. Yet the Slavicization of the ruling house of Kiev had certainly begun at the time *DAI* was compiled, to judge at least from the fact that C.'s contemporary Svyatoslav bore so purely Slavonic a name (see Thomsen, *Relations*, 123–5).

(iii) *The different meanings of the term Rus'*. In the Russian sources of the 10th, 11th and 12th cents. the term is used in three distinct, though occasionally overlapping, senses:

(*a*) *Rus'* as an ethnic term for Scandinavians: *e.g. Povest'*, I, 10, 18, 23, 25–8, 36–9. In the last two of these passages, which cite the clauses of the treaties concluded by Oleg and Igor with the Byzantines on behalf of the *Rus'*, it is just possible that the term *Rus'* refers not only to the Varangian ruling class in Kiev, but also, by implication, to their Slav subjects as well. But the primary meaning of *Rus'* is here certainly Scandinavians, and the efforts of 'anti-Normanists' to impugn the veracity of the chronicler's clear and categorical statements on this point (see the recent works of Tikhomirov, *Sovetskaya Etnografiya*, 6–7 (1947), 66–73 and D. S. Likhachev, *Povest'*, II, 243–4) are unconvincing.

(*b*) *Rus'* as a geographical term designating the whole territory inhabited by the Eastern Slavs and governed, directly or indirectly, by the princes of Kiev: *e.g. Povest'*, I, 28, 35, 45, 48, 49, 51. In this sense it was synonymous with *ruskaya zemlya* and with Ῥωσία (see on 9/1, ἀπὸ Ῥωσίας). The extent of this territory varied at different times: in the middle of the 10th cent. it extended approximately from Lake Ladoga in the north to a point on the middle Dnieper some hundred miles south of Kiev, and included a southern enclave which stretched along the southern Bug, the Dniester and the Pruth to the Black Sea; in the west the 'Russian land' reached as far as the Carpathians and the middle courses of the western Dvina and the Niemen; in the north-east it included the upper reaches of the Oka and the Volga: *cf. Atlas Istorii SSSR*, I, ed. K. V. Bazilevich and others (Moscow, 1955), 7–8. The political and economic pivot of this territory was the Baltic–Black Sea waterway along the rivers Volkhov, Lovat' and Dnieper.

(*c*) *Rus'* as a geographical term serving to designate merely the south Russian lands on or by the middle Dnieper, as distinct from, or in contrast to, the remaining East Slavonic territory. In this restricted sense, *Rus'* seems to have comprised the principalities of Kiev, Chernigov and Pereyaslavl'. Evidence in support of this meaning can be found in the Russian chronicles: see Nasonov 28–50; Paszkiewicz 6–10, 333–5. However, in spite of Nasonov's and Levchenko's (pp. 205–6) views to the contrary, there are no grounds for asserting that as early as the 10th cent. the word *Rus'* was restricted to the southern part of the country. Most of the examples of this meaning come from a period no earlier than the 12th cent. Prior to that time *Rus'* as a geographical term undoubtedly referred to all the East Slavonic territories under the sovereignty of the rulers of Kiev: see Likhachev, *Povest'*, II, 238–44.

We may thus still accept, at least in respect to the 9th and 10th cents., Thomsen's statement, made in 1877 (*Relations*, 105): 'The name *Rus'* . . . was at first the appellation of a foreign Scandinavian clan that gained the mastery over the native Slavonic tribes, though the invaders were of course far inferior to them in number. The name of this tribe, *Rus'*, was then naturally transferred, as a politico-geographical appellation, to all land under the rule of the Russ who dwelt at Kiev (= *rus'skaya zemlia*, the Russian land), next to the inhabitants also, Slavs as well as Northmen, and in this latter signification it gradually superseded the old names of the separate Slavonic tribes'.

(iv) *The rôle played by the Scandinavian Rus' in the foundation of the Russian state.* The debate as to whether the 9th cent. Russian state was a Scandinavian creation or the product of earlier Slavonic or Oriental traditions, a debate which has often been befogged by extra-historical considerations, is not over yet. Twenty-five years ago it had seemed that the 'Normanist' and 'anti-Normanist' schools, by renouncing their former extreme positions, were drawing closer to each other on this point (see Moshin, *Slavia*, 10 (1931) 533–7). In recent years, however, Soviet historians have increasingly supported an extreme 'anti-Normanist' position and have vigorously discounted the contribution of the Scandinavians to the political history of Russia. The most objective and temperate of them was B. D. Grekov (*Kievskaya Rus'*). But among scholars in the West a more balanced view has generally prevailed. It is now, indeed, widely recognized that the Kiev state was not born *ex nihilo* with the advent of the Varangians in the 9th cent.; but that its social and economic foundations were laid in the preceding period, during which the Slavs in the Dnieper basin played an active part in the political and commercial life of the West Eurasian and Pontic steppes; and that a pre-existing Slavonic land-owning aristocracy and merchant class remained the mainstay of the country's territorial stability and economic growth under its Viking overlords. It is equally clear, however, that it was the Scandinavian invaders who in the second half of the 9th cent. united the scattered tribes of the Eastern Slavs into a single state based on the Baltic–Black Sea waterway, to which they gave their 'Russian' name. See G. Laehr, *Die Anfänge des russischen Reiches* (Berlin, 1930), 29–43; D. M. Odinets, *Vozniknovenie gosudarstvennogo stroya u vostochnykh slavyan* (Paris, 1935), 151–81; Vernadsky, *Kievan Russia*, 19–28.

9/2 μετὰ τῶν μονοξύλων.

The original meaning of μονόξυλον, used as a neuter noun, was certainly 'a boat hollowed out of a single tree-trunk', *i.e.* a dug-out canoe. Μονόξυλα had long been used by the Slavs for river and sea navigation: they were observed in 448 by Priscus during his journey to Attila's court in Hungary (τοῖς μονοξύλοις πλοίοις: *Excerpta de Legationibus*, ed. De Boor, 131/8); they were used by the Slavs in their attack on Thessalonica in 614–16 (ἐκ μονοδένδρων γλυπτὰς νῆας: *MPG*, cxvi, col. 1325); and they took part in the Avaro-Slav attack on Constantinople in 626 (τοῖς μονοξύλοις ἀκατίοις: Nicephorus, ed. De Boor, 18/10).

The Russians are stated several times to have used μονόξυλα in their wars against the empire: Svyatoslav made use of them during the siege of Silistria in 971 (Cedrenus II, 402/20–3), and in 1043 a fleet of Russian μονόξυλα sailed from Kiev to attack Byzantium: on this occasion we are told explicitly by Scylitzes that this type of boat is indigenous to Russia (πλοίοις ἐγχωρίοις τοῖς λεγομένοις μονοξύλοις: *ibid.*, 551/14–15).

It seems that the Russian μονόξυλα were actually made of hollowed-out tree-trunks. Psellus tells us that, while preparing for their attack of 1043 against the empire, the Russians carved (?hollowed out) boats from the trees they had cut down in the interior of the country (ὑλοτομήσαντες ἄνωθεν καὶ σκάφη μικρά τε καὶ μείζω διαγεγλυφότες: *Chronographie*, ed. Renauld II, 9/16–17). A general picture of the appearance of the Russian dug-outs is given by Constantine Manasses:

καὶ γάρ τοι συμπηξάμενοι θαλαττοπόρα σκάφη
Ταυροσκυθῶν οἱ φύλαρχοι τῶν ἀγριοκαρδίων,
καὶ πλῆθος ἀπειράριθμον τοῖς σκάφεσιν ἐνθέντες,
ἐπῄεσαν καλύπτοντες τὰ νῶτα τῆς θαλάσσης
τοῖς λεμβαδίοις τοῖς πυκνοῖς, τοῖς αὐτοξύλοις πλόοις.
(*Compend. Chron.*, 162)

The μονόξυλα referred to in c. 9 seem to belong to this dug-out type: they were made of trees, felled by the Slavs on their mountains (9/10–11), and their bottoms are termed σκαφίδια (9/17), a word derived from σκάφη, a dug-out. It has been objected, however, that simple dug-outs could not easily have contained a crew sufficient to negotiate the Dnieper barrages and to ward off the Pecheneg attacks (9/50, 70–1, 96), the merchandise (including slaves, 9/32, 52) carried to Byzantium, the merchants who were to sell it, and the sails, masts and rudders necessary for the sea voyage (9/85), while retaining enough sea-worthiness to carry them across the Black Sea: see J. L. Píč, *Zur Rumänisch-Ungarischen Streitfrage. Skizzen zur ältesten Geschichte der Rumänen, Ungarn und Slaven* (Leipzig, 1886), 339 ff. It has hence been suggested (*cf.* Manojlović IV, 33–4, note 4) that C.'s μονόξυλα were something larger than dug-outs. Kendrick (27) thinks that they were Viking ships, contemptuously called dug-outs by the Byzantines (*cf.* the English version, which takes the μονό-ξυλον as referring, not to the single trunk of the keel, but to the single planks or 'strakes' which ran clinkerwise from stem to stern of the Viking vessel). Comparatively large Russian ships are indeed attested in the 10th cent.: according to Mas'ūdī, each of the Russian ships which plundered the coast of the Caspian Sea *c.* 914 was manned by a crew of 100 (Marquart 336); and C. himself mentions seven Russian ships ('Ρῶς καράβια) carrying 415 soldiers, which took part in a Byzantine expedition to Italy in 935 (*De Cer.*, 660/18)—an average of 59 men per ship. However, most of the Russian ships were of comparatively small size and shallow draught, since they were built partly for river navigation: Luidprand states that 'by reason of their small size [they] can move in very shallow water where the Greek *chelandia* because of their greater draught cannot pass' (*Antapodosis*, v, 15; tr. F. A. Wright, 186); and in Leo VI's *Taktika* the Russians are said to sail in light and fast-moving boats (ἀκατίοις) because only in them can they navigate the rivers which flow into the Black Sea (A. Dain, *Naumachica* (Paris, 1943), 1, 78; *cf.* 6, 70).

It may be doubted whether all the Russian ships which sailed from Kiev to Constantinople in the 9th and 10th cents. were μονόξυλα in the true sense of the word. The Russian fleet which attacked Constantinople in 860 is believed by Vasiliev (*Russian Attack*, 190–2) to have consisted of Viking ships; and the same may be true of the ships launched by Oleg of Kiev against Byzantium in 907, which were provided with sails and anchors, and each of which was manned by 40 oarsmen (*Povest'*, 1, 24–5, 11, 266–7; Cross 64–5). It is noteworthy that the Russian vessel depicted as attacking Constantinople on a miniature in the 15th cent. Königsberg ms. of the *Primary Chronicle* bears a close resemblance to a Viking ship (reproduced in *Povest'*, 1, 24–5).

On the other hand, the Russian sources provide some additional evidence suggesting that actual μονόξυλα, or at least a modified form thereof, were used by the Russians at that time. The *Primary Chronicle*, in describing the Russian vessels, uses mainly two terms: *lod'i* and *korabli* (the latter deriving from Greek καράβιον: see Vasmer, *Russisches etymologisches Wörterbuch*, 621–2): *cf. Povest'*, 11, index, 537 *s.v. korabl'*; I. Smorgonsky, *Korablestroitel'nye i nekotorye morskie terminy ne russkogo proiskhozhdeniya* (Moscow-Leningrad, 1936), 78–82. In the Chronicle these terms seem to be used in a generic sense and sometimes are clearly synonymous (*e.g. Povest'*, 1, 34–6, 103–4). But the *Pravda Russkaya*, the Code of Laws, in its expanded version compiled in the 12th cent., contains a clause listing four categories of boats in order of their price: *mor'skaya* (or *zamor'skaya*) *lod'ya* = a seafaring boat; *naboinaya lod'ya* = a boat provided with lateral planks; *strug*; and *cheln*: *Pravda Russkaya*, ed. B. D. Grekov, 1 (Moscow-Leningrad, 1940), 113, 131, 158, 174, 196, 225, 256, 288, 310, 336, 357, 384, 436–8; 11 (1947), 577–8: article 79; *Pamyatniki*, 173–4; *cf. Medieval Russian Laws*, tr. G. Vernadsky (New York, 1947), 49 (Vernadsky, contrary to most authorities, translates *naboinaya lod'ya* as a 'decked boat'). A number of scholars believe that the Russian μονόξυλα were in fact a variety of the *naboinaya lod'ya*: the hollowed-out tree-trunk served merely as a foundation for such a boat; the sides of this framework were raised by external planks, nailed or sewn on in clinker-built fashion, in order to increase the size, displacement, stability and safety of the craft. Such ships were light and solid enough to negotiate the Dnieper barrages, and sufficiently stable and safe to sail along the Black Sea coast to Constantinople. They were capable of carrying between 40 and 60 men, and are thought to have resembled—though on a smaller scale— the later sea-going Cossack *chaiki*, deckless boats which were generally about 60 ft. long, 10 to 12 ft. wide, and about 12 ft. deep; *cf.* on 9/16–19. For the relationship between the μονόξυλον, the *naboinaya lod'ya* and the *chaika*, see Lyaskoronsky 240–5; P. I. Belavenets, *Materialy po istorii russkogo flota* (Moscow-Leningrad, 1940), 15–16; Voronin in *Kul'tura Drevney Rusi*, I, 282–8; Vernadsky, *Kievan Russia*, 29–30; Levchenko, *Russko-vizantiiskie otnosheniya*, 64–5, 143–7. For a detailed discussion of the various types of Russian boats, including the μονόξυλον, see Niederle, *Slovanské Starožitnosti*, III, 2, 446–62, and the summary of it in his *Manuel*, II, 256–60.

We do not know what the Slavs called their μονόξυλα in the Middle Ages. The more recent Russian equivalent of μονόξυλον—*odnodrevka, odnoderevka*—is first attested, in adjectival form, in the 16th cent. (*struzhok odnodrevy*: Sreznevsky II, 619). It seems likely, however, that C.'s μονόξυλα approximated most closely to the boats known in Kievan Russia as *naboinye lod'i*, which some historians have identified with the *nasady*. For the *nasady*, see Bogorodsky, *Uchenye Zapiski Leningradskogo Gosudarstvennogo Pedagogicheskogo Instituta*, 104 (1955), 227–58.

We may find some support for the view that the μονόξυλα were dug-out canoes with their sides raised by rows of planks in c. 9 itself. For C. tells us that on two occasions during the voyage from Russia to Constantinople various 'tackle' was added to the original dug-outs (9/16–19, 84–6). It seems likely enough that, among the λοιπὰς χρείας with which the μονόξυλα were equipped, together with oars and rowlocks in Kiev, and sails, masts and rudders on the island of St Aitherios at the mouth of the Dnieper, were included these lateral planks, which would have offered greater safety and comfort for the journey over the Black Sea.

9/3 ἀπὸ τῆς ἔξω ʻΡωσίας.
Many attempts have been made to explain this *hapax legomenon*. The majority of scholars have accepted one of the two following views:

(i) 'Outer Russia' was, in the eyes of C. or of his informant, the whole of that part of Russia which was outside Kiev and the districts immediately adjoining that city. It thus included all the Russian cities mentioned by C. (9/4–7, 20) with the exception of Kiev, and comprised those 'Slavonic regions' which paid tribute to the Kievan Russians (9/9–10, 20–1, 107–9): see Thomsen, *Relations*, 52; Shakhmatov, *Vvedenie*, 90; Grekov 176; Vernadsky, *Kievan Russia*, 31. This interpretation has the advantage of conforming strictly to the syntax of the text, the correlative clauses beginning with εἰσὶ μὲν (9/4) and εἰσὶ δὲ (9/5) both being taken to refer to the subject of the sentence τὰ ἀπὸ τῆς ἔξω ʻΡωσίας μονόξυλα. This reading however raises logical difficulties: for the antithetically implied ἔσω ʻΡωσία, if restricted to Kiev and its immediate neighbourhood, would be disproportionately small by comparison with an 'outer Russia' extending from Novgorod to the middle Dnieper; it is hard to believe, moreover, that a town such as Vyshgorod (9/7), which was virtually a suburb of Kiev (see on 9/6–7), could have been placed on the periphery of a large realm of which Kiev was the centre. Nor do these logical difficulties vanish if we assume that 'inner Russia' comprised the southern districts of Chernigov and Pereyaslavl' as well as Kiev (as is stated by V. Mavrodin, *Drevnyaya Rus'* (Leningrad, 1946), 132), particularly as C. himself places Chernigov (9/6) on a par with the other Russian cities outside the capital.

(ii) 'Outer Russia' consisted only of the city of Novgorod and its surrounding districts: see Manojlović IV, 42; Moshin, *Byzantinoslavica*, 3 (1931), 305. Nasonov, who shares this view (20–1, 31, 39, 70, 162), believes that in 9/3–9 'outer Russia', with its centre in Novgorod, is contrasted with *Rus'* proper, situated on the middle Dnieper, and ruled by Igor, prince of Kiev; in his opinion, the passage need not be taken to mean that any other of the cities enumerated therein was included in 'outer Russia' (31). This interpretation has the drawback of deviating somewhat from the literal sense of the passage, for the correlative clauses εἰσὶ μέν . . . εἰσὶ δὲ . . . certainly imply that all the cities enumerated here, from Novgorod to Vyshgorod, are part of 'outer Russia'. It has, however, the advantage of restoring a more literal and accurate meaning to the adverb ἔξω, which is well suited to the peripheral position occupied by Novgorod and its district on the map of 10th cent. Russia, from the viewpoint of both Kiev and Constantinople.

In addition to these two widely held opinions, the following views have also been expressed regarding the meaning of 'outer Russia'. It has been identified with a Scandinavian settlement on the middle Volga (Smirnov, *Zbirnik Istorichno-Filologichnogo Viddilu*, Ukrains'ka Akademiya Nauk, LXXV (1928), 180-1); with the district of Roslagen in Sweden (A. Pogodin, *Belićev Zbornik* (Belgrade, 1937), 77-85); with the Swedish colonies in north Russia in the area between Beloozero, Ladoga, Novgorod, Izborsk, Polotsk and Rostov (Stender-Petersen, *Varangica*, 82-3); with the entire Russian territory colonised by the Vikings (Paszkiewicz 122-3, 323, note 6: he believes that the implied 'inner Russia' was Scandinavia); and, tentatively, with all the Russian lands and cities mentioned in c. 9, *i.e.* the whole of Russia from Novgorod to Vitichev, except the extreme south of the country which bordered on the Black Sea (Soloviev, *Byzantion*, 13 (1938), 227-32). Cf. also the suggestion of M. A. Shangin and A. F. Vishnyakova (*Viz. Vrem.* 14, 1958, 97-8) that the word 'Ρωσία is a later insertion, and that the passage originally read τὰ ἀπὸ τῆς ἔξω μονόξυλα.

It seems to us that those interpretations which would include Kiev in 'outer Russia' twist the straightforward meaning of the text, and are hence unacceptable. It is quite clear that the passage in 9/3-9 intends to suggest that Kiev forms the nucleus of an implied 'inner Russia' (ἔσω 'Ρωσία). It seems most natural and satisfactory to identify ἡ ἔξω 'Ρωσία with northern Russia. It is hard to say whether this term should be restricted to Novgorod and its neighbourhood; it is probably wrong to seek for too precise a delimitation of a geographical term which is doubtless used here in a general and rather vague sense. It seems perhaps most likely that for C. or his informant the southern boundary of 'outer Russia' was somewhere between Novgorod and Smolensk.

Although the term ἡ ἔξω 'Ρωσία is a *hapax legomenon*, similar or analogous expressions have been noted both in Greek and Slavonic. H. Stürenburg has pointed out that the correlative expressions ἐντός (ἔσω) and ἐκτός (ἔξω) were often used by the Greeks to designate places situated more or less close to the Mediterranean: thus we find 'Ιβηρία ἡ ἐντός (the Hispania citerior of the Romans) and ἡ ἔξω 'Ιβηρία (Hispania exterior), as well as ἡ ἔξω θάλασσα, the Atlantic Ocean: *Relative Ortsbezeichnung; zum geographischen Sprachgebrauch der Griechen und Römer* (Leipzig-Berlin, 1932), 14-18 (cited by Soloviev, *Byzantion*, 13 (1938), 230-1). A curious example is provided by Balsamon, who observed that the ῥουσάλια (a pagan feast widely celebrated in Slavonic lands, and notably in Russia) were still kept in his day 'in the outer regions' (ἐν ταῖς ἔξω χώραις): see *MPG*, CXXXVII, cols. 728-9, and, for the ῥουσάλια, Niederle, *Manuel*, II, 55, 132, 166-7. A possible Slavonic parallel to the term ἡ ἔξω 'Ρωσία is offered by the expression *Verkhnyaya zemlya* ('the upper country'), used in the 12th cent. in Russia to designate the territories of Novgorod and Smolensk: *Ipat'evskaya Letopis'*, ann. 1148: *Polnoe Sobranie Russkikh Letopisey*, II², 369; *cf. Povest'*, II, 350-1; Gedeonov 436.

9/4 ἀπὸ τοῦ Νεμογαρδάς.

The emendation to Νεβογαρδάς, proposed by Bury (543, note 1), is accepted today: see Latyshev-Malitsky 52, note 14; Grégoire, *La Nouvelle Clio*, 4 (1952), 279-80. The name presumably occurs here in the genitive form (Durnovo 205). The ending -γαρδάς leaves little doubt that we have here the Greek transcription of a Scandinavian name for Novgorod, similar in form to *Hólmgarðr*, the Old Norse name by which that city is known in the Icelandic sagas; this strongly suggests that this passage at least is based on evidence supplied by a Scandinavian informant: see Tikhomirov, *Drevnerusskie goroda*, 14; Levchenko, *Russko-vizantiiskie otnosheniya*, 210. It is notable, in this connexion, that Novgorod retained close commercial ties with Scandinavia until the 12th cent., and that the Norse sagas invariably regard Novgorod, and not Kiev, as the principal city of Russia: see Brim 227; Braun, *Festschrift für Eugen Mogk* (Halle, 1924), 170–1; Stender-Petersen, *Varangica*, 256–7.

The city of Novgorod, situated on the upper reaches of the Volkhov river, was in the 10th cent. the largest Russian town after Kiev. Its importance was mainly due to its position on the Baltic–Black Sea waterway (it dominated the northern sector of this waterway, which linked the gulf of Finland, by the Neva, Lake Ladoga, the Volkhov, Lake Il'men' and the Lovat', with the portages that led over the western Dvina to the upper Dnieper), and to its proximity to the upper reaches of the Volga: see Tikhomirov, *Drevnerusskie goroda*, 375–6. It was the principal city of the *Slovene*, the most northerly of the East Slavonic tribes, who occupied a large part of the basins of Lake Il'men', of the Volkhov, the Lovat' and the Msta, the upper course of the Mologa, and the northern section of the Valdai hills: for the *Slovene*, see Vernadsky, *Ancient Russia*, 324–7; Tret'yakov 228–33. The origins of the city are shrouded in mist: the *Primary Chronicle* records its foundation among the earliest traditions of the Slavonic people (*Povest'*, 1, 11; Cross 53). The 'old' town which Novgorod (lit. 'new town') superseded as capital of the *Slovene* has been tentatively identified as Staraya Ladoga (the Aldegjuborg of the Norse sagas). A Slavonic settlement on the site of present-day Novgorod may have existed as early as the 7th or 8th cent. of our era: see N. G. Porfiridov, *Drevny Novgorod* (Moscow-Leningrad, 1947), 11–24; Voronin 35. In the second half of the 9th cent., according to written sources, Novgorod was the centre of an important Scandinavian colony in north Russia (*Povest'*, 1, 18, 11, 244–6; Cross 59–60). Archæology, however, has to date revealed virtually nothing on this site prior to the 10th cent.: see A. V. Artsikhovsky, *Osnovy Arkheologii*[2] (Moscow, 1955), 237. The political allegiance of the city to the Varangian dynasty of Kiev probably dates from the early 10th cent.: see Nasonov 69.

Doubts have sometimes been expressed as to whether the Slavs of the Novgorod region really supplied μονόξυλα for the journey to Constantinople. Thus, Bernshtein-Kogan (250) thinks it unreasonable to believe that the dug-outs would have been dragged over the two portages that separated the Lovat' from the Dnieper, when, on C.'s own showing, they could all have been obtained from cities on or near the Dnieper. V. A. Parkhomenko, on the other hand, suggests that the Novgorod mentioned at 9/4 is not the northern city, but another town of that name situated further south (*U istokov russkoy gosudarstvennosti*, Leningrad, 1924, 34, note 8). Such scepticism seems quite unwarranted. Novgorod was an important enough centre on the Baltic–Black Sea waterway to take an essential part in the Russian trade with Byzantium. There is no reason to doubt that the *Slovene* of the Novgorod area, along with the other 'Slavonic regions' (9/10), contributed their quota of μονόξυλα to the rulers of Kiev.

9/4 *Σφενδοσθλάβος*.

The name of Svyatoslav, prince of Kiev during the regency of his mother Olga (945–69) and sovereign of Russia from 969 to 972, is Slavonic; and in accordance with the contemporary Byzantine transcription, his name (*cf.* Leo Diac. *passim*) is rendered in a nasalized form, *Σφεν-*, corresponding to the Old Church Slavonic Svę-. This is remarkable, because it is generally considered that the nasal vowels were no longer pronounced in Russia by the middle of the 10th cent. (See Shakhmatov, *Entsiklopediya slavyanskoy filologii*, 11, 1, Petrograd, 1915, 112–13). They were, however, still in use among the Bulgarians; and it has been assumed that the name *Σφενδοσθλάβος* passed into Greek through a South Slav intermediary: *cf.* Durnovo 207. It is a fact that the influence of the Old Bulgarian language has been detected in the transcription of several other Slavonic proper names in c. 9: see Shakhmatov, *Vvedenie*, 81, and on 9/25.

Svyatoslav's name probably became known in Byzantium in 944, for among the Russian ambassadors sent to Constantinople in that year to conclude a treaty with the empire there figured a personal envoy of Svyatoslav: *Povest'*, I, 34; Cross 73. Svyatoslav was doubtless then still prince of Novgorod; 9/4-5 is the only source which refers to Svyatoslav's residence in Novgorod, presumably as representative or deputy of his father Igor, who was then prince of Kiev (see Introductory Note, p. 18). It was a common practice for the rulers of Kiev in the 10th cent. to appoint one of their sons to the subordinate throne of Novgorod (see *Povest'*, I, 49–50, 83; Cross 87, 119; *cf.* Nasonov 31–2); and the existence of princes who ruled in different cities of Russia as vassals of the sovereign of Kiev is attested in the Russo-Byzantine treaties of the 10th cent. (*Povest'*, I, 25–6, 34–5; Cross 66, 73; *cf.* Grekov 177–8).

This passage, and the reference to Igor which follows it, permit a tentative determination of the date at which the main section of c. 9 was compiled. Paszkiewicz (161–2) claims that this passage was written after Igor's death, *i.e.* not earlier than 945, when Svyatoslav, as he believes, ruled over Russia from Novgorod. But this conclusion seems to be incompatible both with the evidence of the Russian sources and with the wording of 9/4-5. The prince of Novgorod never wielded authority over the whole of Russia; and, *pace* Paszkiewicz, 9/5 suggests that at the time of writing Igor was ruler of Russia, *i.e.* prince of Kiev. On this point, and for the view that this passage is not a later insertion but was written during Igor's lifetime, probably about 944, see Introductory Note, pp. 18–19.

9/5 ὁ υἱὸς Ἴγγωρ, τοῦ ἄρχοντος Ῥωσίας.

The *Hypatian Chronicle* states that Svyatoslav was born in 942 (*Polnoe Sobranie Russkikh Letopisey*, II², 34). This dating is justifiably suspect: for although the *Primary Chronicle* tells us that in 945/6 Svyatoslav was still a child (*Povest'*, I, 40, 42; Cross 78, 80), he was at least old enough to wield a spear in battle (*ibid.*). His parents, Igor and Olga, are said to have married in 903 (*Povest'*, I, 23; Cross 64); this date is even more dubious (see *Povest'*, II, 262; Tikhomirov, *Sovetskaya Etnografiya*, 6–7, 1947, 71).

The chronology of the early part of Igor's life is exceedingly uncertain (*cf. Povest'*, II, 249–50). According to the *Primary Chronicle* (*Povest'*, I, 31; Cross 71), his reign in Kiev began in 913, and he died in all probability in the autumn of 944 (*Povest'*, II, 295). While his reign was noteworthy for three unsuccessful campaigns waged by the Russians in Transcaucasia (see Vernadsky, *Kievan Russia*, 32–5), it was for his dealings with Byzantium that he was chiefly remembered in his own country. The *Primary Chronicle* usefully supplements the evidence of Byzantine sources on the Russian campaign in Anatolia in 941, which ended in the destruction of Igor's fleet; adds the information that in 944 Igor's army, which was marching against Byzantium, was halted on the Danube by the diplomacy of Romanus I; and gives the Russian text of the treaty concluded between the Russians and the empire in that same year (see *Povest'*, I, 33–9; Cross 71–7). For the Russo-Byzantine war of 941, see Bártová, *Byzantinoslavica*, 8 (1939–46), 87–108; Runciman, *Romanus Lecapenus*, 111–13; Levchenko, *Russko-vizantiiskie otnosheniya*, 128–71. At the time c. 9 was compiled, Igor was thus well known in Byzantium; and it seems quite likely that the author of 9/3–104 was one of Romanus I's envoys who travelled to Kiev in 944 to conclude the treaty with him (see Introductory Note, p. 19).

The name Ἴγγωρ has retained the Scandinavian nasal consonant, which is absent in the Slavonic Igor'. The same form is adopted by Leo Diac. (106/5, 144/6: he cites the genitive case Ἴγγορος, which may derive from a nominative Ἴγγωρ or Ἴγγορ), and a similar transcription, *Inger*, is given by Liudprand, *Antapodosis* v, 15. Ἴγγωρ is an intermediate form between *Ingvarr*, the Old Norse form of the name (Thomsen, *Relations*, 135) and the Slavonic Igor'; it may be regarded either as a blend of both forms or as reflecting a form presumably used in Kiev before the complete Russification of this name. (In this connexion, it is worth noting that C.'s own great-grandfather was called Ἴγγερ,

Theoph. Cont. 235/8, a form which is close to Liudprand's version of Igor; and *cf. MPG*, cxvi, col. 69 B; *AASS*, Nov. ii/1, 360 B, 406 C).

The title ἄρχων 'Ρωσίας was in the middle of the 10th cent. the official designation of the imperial chancellery for the prince of Kiev: see *De Cer.*, 690/21–691/1; *cf.* Ostrogorsky, *Sem. Kond.*, 8 (1936), 49. In the Old Russian text of the Russo-Byzantine treaty of 944, presumably translated from the Greek at the time of its conclusion, Igor is given the title of *veliky knyaz' rusky* (*velikyi kŭnyazĭ rusĭskyi*), 'the Great Prince of Rus'': *Povest'*, 1, 35; Cross 73–4. The same title was applied to Oleg in the treaty of 911: *Povest'*, 1, 25; Cross 66. Its Greek equivalent, μέγας ἄρχων 'Ρωσίας, is cited in an inscription on a recently discovered seal attributed to Mstislav II of Kiev (1167–9): see Blifel'd, *Arkheologiya*, 3 (Kiev, 1950), 102–10; Rybakov, *ibid.*, 111–18; A. Soloviev, *Festschrift für H. F. Schmid; Wiener Archiv für Geschichte des Slawentums und Osteuropas*, ii (1956), 144–9.

9/5 ἐκαθέζετο.

It is suggested in the Introductory Note (p. 18) that the compiler of this section of c. 9, who wrote while Svyatoslav was still prince of Novgorod, used the present tense καθέζεται, and that the verb was later altered to a past tense in the Byzantine archives, in order to bring it up to date.

It may be that we have in ἐκαθέζετο a direct and literal translation of the Slavonic *sěde*: since the Old Russian verb *sěděti*, whose original meaning is 'to sit', was often used at that time in the special sense of 'to occupy a throne, to reign' (see Sreznevsky, *s.v.*). The translation into Greek of a technical term used by the Russian rulers, or at least by their Slav subjects, would suggest that the writer of c. 9 was supplied with part of his information by someone familiar with the Slavonic language. C. 9 contains other instances of Slavonic idioms probably translated, and in one case directly transcribed, into Greek: see on 9/107, 110; and *cf.* on 8/30.

9/5–6 ἀπὸ τὸ κάστρον τὴν Μιλινίσκαν.

The term κάστρον is used in this chapter (9/6, 8, 21) in the sense of a stronghold or fortified town. It corresponds exactly to the East Slavonic *gorod* (Old Church Slavonic *grad*). A *gorod* or *grad* was, for the Eastern Slavs in the early Middle Ages, an inhabited place often situated on the high bank of a river or at the confluence of two rivers, enclosed by an earthwork or a wooden palisade and serving as a centre of craftsmanship and trade. Archaeology has shown that the earliest East Slavonic *goroda* arose in the 8th and 9th cents. in the valleys of the middle Dnieper, Dniester and Bug. Written sources reveal a remarkable growth of these fortified towns on Russian territory in the 9th and 10th cents. The chronicles mention more than twenty in this period alone: see Tikhomirov, *Drevnerusskie goroda*, 3–17. The rapid development of town life and urban economy in the early Kievan period has often been discussed by historians: *e.g.* A. Eck, *Le Moyen Age Russe* (Paris, 1933), 3 ff.

The Northmen, by establishing their power and promoting trade along the rivers of Russia, certainly contributed to the further growth of these Slavonic towns. However, contrary to the statement of H. Pirenne (*Economic and Social History of Medieval Europe*, London, 1949, 22–3), there is no reason to believe that any of the large Russian κάστρα was actually built by the Northmen. In fact the name *Garðaríki*, the land of the *goroda* or towns, which the Scandinavians gave to Russia, suggests that they were struck by the number and size of the cities in their newly acquired Slavonic lands: see Stender-Petersen, *Varangica*, 17–18, 84. The Old Norse word *garðr* (a yard, a stronghold) is akin to the Slavonic *grad*, *gorod*. It forms the ending of the Old Norse names *Hólmgarðr* and *Kœnugarðr*, by which the Northmen designated Novgorod and Kiev respectively, and is clearly identifiable in Νεμ[β]ογαρδάς (see on 9/4, ἀπὸ τοῦ Νεμογαρδάς). It has been suggested that the use of the term *garðr* in these names is an imitation of the Slavonic *grad*, *gorod*: see Thomsen, *Relations*, 80, note 1.

τὴν Μιλινίσκαν is the town of Smolensk on the upper Dnieper. The first ι was undoubtedly caused by assimilation to the two following iotas. The omission of the initial Σ has been variously explained. Durnovo (238) suggests that the name stood originally in the genitive case—ἀπὸ τῆς Σμιλινίσκας (or *Σμολινίσκας)—and that one of the consecutive sigmas dropped out; however, the preposition ἀπό with accusative is common enough, especially in this chapter (9/5, 6, 96, 106). The omission could also be explained by supposing that the Greek form ἀπὸ τὴν *Μολινίσκαν goes back to the Slavonic group i- Smolĭnĭska, which the author obtained from a Slav-speaking informant and which he could easily have interpreted as iz Molĭnĭska; by further interpreting the genitive in this latter group as the name of the city (cf. on 9/6-7), he would naturally have taken the nominative form to be Μολινίσκα, from which he then formed the accusative Μολινίσκαν, required by the demotic use of ἀπό (this explanation was suggested to me by Professor R. Jakobson).

The position of Smolensk, near the watershed between the Dnieper, the western Dvina, the Lovat' and the Volga, gave it considerable commercial, and later political, importance. Archaeologists are still undecided as to the exact location of 9th and 10th cent. Smolensk: see Avdusin, *Vestnik Moskovskogo Universiteta*, 7 (1953), 123-37. The view that it was situated 10 km. to the west of the present-day city, on the right bank of the Dnieper, on the site of the celebrated Gnezdovo burial ground, has been strongly impugned by Tikhomirov (*Drevnerusskie goroda*, 28-32), who believes that the medieval and modern sites of Smolensk are identical. It was one of the oldest towns in Russia, and is mentioned in the opening section of the *Primary Chronicle* as the principal city of the Slavonic Krivichians: *Povest'*, I, 13; Cross 55 (for the Krivichians, see on 9/9-10). Its political importance was enhanced when it became part of the Kievan realm, an event which the Chronicle dates to the late 9th cent.: *Povest'*, I, 20; Cross 61. By the middle of the 10th cent. Smolensk was a fortified stronghold, beside which a new burg (a faubourg), inhabited by merchants and artisans, was growing up. For the importance of Smolensk at this period, see Brim 233-4; Voronin 28-9; Nasonov 159-65; Tikhomirov, *Drevnerusskie goroda*, 352-4.

9/6-7   ἀπὸ Τελιούτζαν καὶ Τζερνιγῶγαν καὶ ἀπὸ τοῦ Βουσεγραδέ.

Τελιούτζαν: practically all commentators agree in identifying this town with Lyubech, situated on the middle Dnieper, north of Kiev and not far to the north-west of Chernigov. Different explanations have been offered of this much corrupted Greek form: suggested readings vary between τε Λιού‹β›τζαν (Rački), τε Λιούτζαν (Manojlović iv, 34, note 2) and τὰ Λιούβτζα (Shakhmatov, *Vvedenie*, 89; Latyshev-Malitsky 52, note 15). A sceptical view is expressed by Durnovo (205), who points out that the Slavonic vowel ю was rendered by C. by the Greek υ, and never by ιου: cf. πολύδια, 9/107, and note *ad loc.* There certainly seems to be a linguistic difficulty in the traditional interpretation Lyubech⟩ Τελιούτζα, but on geographical and historical grounds the identification is well-nigh irresistible.

Lyubech is mentioned in the *Primary Chronicle* as early as 882; in 907 it is listed among the Russian cities subject to the prince of Kiev and receiving tribute from Byzantium: *Povest'*, I, 20, 24; Cross 61, 64. The close commercial relations Lyubech had with Kiev in the 10th cent. explain the part it played at that time in the trade with the empire: see Tikhomirov, *Drevnerusskie goroda*, 345.

Τζερνιγῶγαν: this comparatively uncorrupted form of the name Chernigov is given, as are the other place names in 9/6, in the accusative case. The Greek nominative must have been Τζερνιγῶγα. Durnovo (207) believes that the form may go back to the Slavonic genitive *Chernigova*, and may have preserved in its terminal the case-ending used by the author's Slav-speaking informant: *iz Chernigova*, i.e. 'from Chernigov'. The second γ in Τζερνιγῶγαν, instead of the expected β, is probably due to a graphic assimilation to the first γ.

Chernigov was situated near the bank of the lower Desna, north-east of Kiev. Its economic importance was assured by its proximity to the Dnieper waterway; and its political significance is apparent in 10th cent. sources: it is first mentioned along with Lyubech, as subject to Kiev and receiving tribute from Byzantium, in 907; and then, in 944, it was clearly considered to be the most important city in South Russia after Kiev, a position it retained during the following centuries: *Povest'*, 1, 24–5, 36; Cross 74; *cf.* Tikhomirov, *Drevnerusskie goroda*, 338–40.

τοῦ Βουσεγραδέ: this is undoubtedly the town of Vyshgorod, situated on the right bank of the Dnieper, 20 km. upstream from Kiev, near the confluence of the Desna and the Dnieper. Its Slavonic name means 'the upper (or higher) city', the acropolis. It is first mentioned in the *Primary Chronicle*, ann. 946, where it is described as a possession of Princess Olga: *Povest'*, 1, 43; Cross, 81, 243, note 83. For Vyshgorod, see Nasonov 53–5; Tikhomirov, *Drevnerusskie goroda*, 294–8.

The form Βουσεγραδέ is derived, not from the Russian (East Slavonic) *Vyshgorod*, but from the South Slavonic *Vyshegrad*. It is generally attributed to the influence of Old Bulgarian (see Durnovo 207–8), though one scholar suggests the possibility of a Serbo-Croat source of the form -ρα- in this name (Selishchev 311–12). The terminal ε comes perhaps from the Slavonic locative case *Vyshegrade* (see Durnovo 207; Skok 237): this may provide further evidence for the belief that the author of this passage used a Slavonic written or oral source: *cf.* on 9/5–6. The Slavonic ы is, at least after labials, commonly rendered by the Greek diphthong ου in *DAI*: see Skok 221, 243.

9/7–8　διὰ τοῦ ποταμοῦ κατέρχονται Δανάπρεως.

The Dnieper was the principal artery in that intricate network of rivers, lakes, portages and seas which led from Scandinavia to Byzantium, and which was one of the most important trade routes of early medieval Europe. The international importance of this route dates from the second half of the 9th cent., when, along most of its length, the Northmen founded their trading colonies and carved out their military kingdoms. In this way the Dnieper, which about that time superseded the Volga as the true Swedish *austrvegr*, the great highway for the Eastern adventure, became the spinal cord of the new Kievan state. There are two detailed accounts of this trade route in medieval sources: the Russian *Primary Chronicle*, which gives it its classic name, 'the route from the Varangians to the Greeks' (*put' iz Varyag v Greki*), mainly describes its northern half: the waterway from the Baltic, up the Neva, the Volkhov, Lake Il'men', the Lovat' into the Dnieper (*Povest'*, 1, 11–12; Cross 53). The other account, *DAI*, c. 9, is particularly detailed on the southern section of this waterway, the section from Kiev to Constantinople, known in medieval Russia as 'the Greek route' (*grechesky put'*). C. 9 does, however, sketch the principal landmarks along its northern sector as well: the towns of Novgorod, Smolensk, Lyubech, Vyshgorod and Chernigov, whence the μονόξυλα 'come down' the river Dnieper. The last of these, standing by the lower Desna, lies in the Dnieper basin; the other towns, except Novgorod, were on the banks of that river. It is only from Novgorod to the Dnieper that the exact itinerary followed by the Slavs and their μονόξυλα remains uncertain: for between the upper Lovat' and the Dnieper there lies an expanse of land, about 140 km. across, which the *Primary Chronicle* vaguely terms 'a portage' (*volok*), ignoring both the fact that this territory is bisected by the western Dvina and the existence of several portages and a large number of alternative routes within it. The problem is best formulated by Seredonin (227–8): 'The Varangians, and the Russians after them, pulled and dragged their boats over comparatively small distances, making use of every little river, every lake, to sail their boats, or at least to drag them over water rather than over dry land. The chronicler was evidently but poorly acquainted with the conditions of navigation along the great waterway. The modern investigator must show how the boats passed firstly from the Lovat' into the western Dvina, and secondly from the Dvina into the Dnieper.' Seredonin himself attempted to trace the different itineraries, using geographical and historical evidence (227–40); and his conclusions have been followed and amplified by Brim (230–2) and Bernshtein-Kogan (252–60). (i) The shorter of the two sections, that between the Lovat' and the western Dvina, is a maze of rivulets and small lakes; Brim mentions four possible itineraries, and Bernshtein-Kogan nine. The most convenient route, it seems, led through the town of Toropets, which was reached either by sailing up the Kun'ya (an affluent of the Lovat') and thence up the Serëzha, over a portage to the Toropa river; or by moving up the Pola river over several portages into the Toropa, and thence down the Toropa into the western Dvina: see map in Bernshtein-Kogan 253. (ii) Between the western Dvina and the Dnieper there were two main routes: either up the Kasplya river, over Lake Kasplya, up the Vydra, over Lake Kuprino, up the Krapivka (or Lelekva), up to a small portage to the Katynka, and down that river into the Dnieper a little below Smolensk; or else up the Mezha river and its affluent the El'sha, over a portage to the Votrya, down that river and the Vop' to the Dnieper above Smolensk: see map in Nasonov 160.

9/8 τὸ κάστρον τὸ Κιοάβα.

The name Kiev (Киевъ, Кыевъ) is transcribed in c. 9 in three different ways: τὸ Κιοάβα (9/8), τὸν Κίοβα (9/15), and τὸν Κίαβον (9/106, 111). The last form is nearest to, and Κιοάβα furthest removed from, the Slavonic pronunciation.

Kiev was probably the oldest city in Russia. Excavations carried out on its site between 1938 and 1947 by a group of Soviet archaeologists under M. K. Karger revealed distinct traces of at least three Slavonic settlements dating back to the 8th or 9th cent., and evidence of still earlier habitation: see Kul'tura drevney Rusi, I, 197–8 (including a plan of early medieval Kiev); M. K. Karger, Arkheologicheskie issledovaniya drevnego Kieva. Otchety i materialy (Kiev, 1951). The Primary Chronicle recounts the story, whose details are clearly legendary, of the foundation of Kiev by the eponymous Kii and his two brothers Shchek and Khoriv: Povest', I, 12–13; Cross 54. A variant of this story, however, occurs in a 7th cent. Armenian source: see Marr, Izvestiya Rossiiskoy Akademii Istorii Material'noy Kul'tury, III (1924), 257–87; cf. Rybakov, Izvestiya Akademii Nauk SSSR, ser. ist. i filos., VII (1950), 239; and Karger claims to have found some factual corroboration of this story in the topography of 8th and 9th cent. Kiev (op. cit., 6).

The historical records of Kiev begin with an entry in the Primary Chronicle ann. 862, which relates how two Varangians, Askold and Dir, captured the city from the Chazars: Povest', I, 18–19; Cross 60. It was then the capital city of the Slavonic Polyanians, for whom see on 9/108–9. Its rôle as the political centre of the whole Russian realm, which it was to retain until the second half of the 12th cent., is dated by the Chronicle from its capture by Oleg in 882, when this Varangian ruler allegedly declared Kiev to be 'the mother of the Russian cities' (Povest', I, 20; Cross 61).

In the middle of the 10th cent. Kiev was already a city of some importance, with a palace partly constructed of stone (see Povest', I, 40; Cross 78), a pagan sanctuary and a Christian church (see Povest', I, 39; Cross 77). It was situated on a hill overlooking the right bank of the Dnieper; the later mercantile and artisan faubourg of Kiev, the Podol, was still uninhabited at that time: see Povest', I, 40; Cross 78; cf. Tikhomirov, Drevnerusskie goroda, 17–22, 286–8.

9/8–9 τὸ ἐπονομαζόμενον Σαμβατάς.

The name, despite many attempts, has not yet been explained to the satisfaction of most philologists. In his critical survey of his predecessors' views on the subject up to 1928, Il'insky (Yuvileinii Zbirnik na poshanu M. S. Hrushevs'kogo, II, Kiev (1928), 166–77) lists twenty-two different theories (not counting his own) of the etymology and meaning of Σαμβατάς. Lyashchenko (Doklady Akademii Nauk SSSR (1930), B, no. 4, 66–72) and Latyshev-Malitsky (52–3) have further lengthened the list, while adding their own different interpretations. The identification of Σαμβατάς with Zānbat, a city which several

Arab sources, Ibn Rosta, Gardīzī and possibly Ḥudūd al-'Ālam, place on the borders of the Slav lands, was suggested by Marquart (509), but has not found universal acceptance: see V. Minorsky, Ḥudūd al-'Ālam (London, 1937), 431. The more noteworthy attempts to explain Σαμβατάς have been made with reference to the following languages: Old Norse (Thomsen, Relations, 145–6; cf. Pipping, Studier i nordisk filologi, II (Helsingfors, 1911), 25–6); Slavonic (Il'insky, loc. cit., 176–7; cf. Latyshev-Malitsky 53); Armenian (N. Ya. Marr, Izbrannye raboty, II (Leningrad, 1936), 284); Hebrew (Heinzel, Sitzungsber. der phil.-hist. Cl. der Akad. der Wiss. 114, (Vienna, 1887), 479–80); Hungarian (Gedeonov, Otryvki iz issledovany o varyazhskom voprose (St Petersburg, 1862), 107); and Turkic. The view that Σαμβατάς may be derived from the Turkic language of the Chazars has recently found acceptance, wholehearted or qualified, in the works of a number of scholars. It was put forward by Yu. D. Brutskus in 1924 (Pis'mo khazarskogo evreya ot X. veka, Berlin, 19–20), and is argued by him in considerable detail in The Slavonic and East European Review, 22 (May, 1944), 108–24. In his view, the word is formed by the juxtaposition of two Turkic roots: sam, which means 'high' or 'top', and was used as a designation of a large number of towns in the Chazar empire; and -bat, meaning 'strong'. *Sambat would thus mean 'high fortress', an epithet appropriate to the geographical position of Kiev. Brutskus' interpretation was wholeheartedly endorsed by Moshin (Byzantinoslavica, 3 (1931), 53–4, note 74); cf. also Manojlović IV, 45; L. P. Yakubinsky, Istoriya drevnerusskogo yazyka (Moscow, 1953), 346–7. Lyashchenko (op. cit., 69–72), without adducing any linguistic arguments, also believed in the Chazar origin of the name, and took 9/8–9 to mean 'the fortress of Kiev, which is also called Sambatas'. He suggested that Σαμβατάς is a name for the Kievan fortress on the hill, as distinct from the lower settlement on the Dnieper. From the historical viewpoint, these explanations have their weaknesses: the foothill below the fortress of Kiev was still, it seems, uninhabited in the middle of the 10th cent. (see on 9/8); Vyshgorod, the Slavonic equivalent of 'high fortress', was a separate town, albeit very near Kiev, and not, as Brutskus believes, identical with that city. Yet this theory has the advantage of taking into account the Chazar cultural and political influences to which the area round Kiev was subjected for more than a hundred years before the late 9th cent.

9/9   οἱ πακτιῶται αὐτῶν.
There has been some controversy as to the meaning of πακτιῶται, which comes from the noun τὸ πάκτον, itself derived from Latin pactum. In Byzantine Greek πάκτον meant both 'pact' and 'tribute': see Du Cange 1, 1080–1. Eck argued that the relationship between the Russians and the Slavs is shown in this passage to be based on a mutual contract or treaty, on a 'symbiose volontaire et profitable pour les deux parties' (Annuaire de l'Institut de Philologie et d'Histoire Orientales, 2 (1934), 343–9). This view has been controverted by Dujčev (Sem. Kond., 10 (1938), 145–54), who refers to a passage in Theophanes (359/12–17) stating that in the late 7th cent. the Slavonic tribes in Moesia were ὑπὸ πάκτον vis-à-vis the Bulgarian invaders. This, he convincingly shows, means that the Slavs were the tributaries, not the allies, of their conquerors; and he concludes that in DAI as well (9/9, 109) the Slavs are described as the tributaries of the Russians. Contractual relations between the two parties, as he further points out, are excluded by the wording of 9/105–10, where the Russians are said to be 'maintained' during the winter months by their Slavonic πακτιῶται.

If further proof were needed of the accuracy of Dujčev's conclusions, it could be found at 37/43–5, where the lands of the Slavonic tribes are said to be 'tributary' (ὑποφόροις) territories of the country of Russia; and one at least of these tribes, the Λενζενίνοι/ Λενζανῆνοι, is also listed among the πακτιῶται of the Russians at 9/10. The term ὑπόφορος quite unambiguously suggests a relationship of subjection or dependence; and it is clear from a comparison of the two passages that ὑπόφοροι and πακτιῶται are used synonymously.

The pronoun αὐτῶν refers logically to οἱ ῾Ρῶς who, however, are not mentioned in the preceding passage, except in the chapter-heading (9/1). If the appositional clause οἱ πακτιῶται αὐτῶν was not mechanically inserted during the editing that preceded the incorporation of c. 9 into *DAI*, from the passage οἵτινές εἰσιν πακτιῶται τῶν ῾Ρῶς in 9/109, the conclusion seems inescapable that the heading (9/1–2), either capitular or marginal, formed part of the original ms. of c. 9: see General Introduction, p. 8.

9/9–10   οἱ Κριβηταιηνοὶ λεγόμενοι.

The first of the five Slavonic tribes referred to in c. 9 as Σκλαβηνίαι (9/9–10, 107–9) are the Krivichians (*Krivichi*). All of them, except the Λενζανῆνοι (9/10), occur in the list of thirteen East Slavonic tribes mentioned in the opening section of the *Primary Chronicle* (*Povest'*, I, 11–14; Cross 53–6). The long-standing controversy among Russian scholars as to whether these 9th and 10th cent. 'tribes' were separate ethnic groups or merely more or less transitory territorial units, is summarized by Tret'yakov (217–28). Tret'yakov, relying on recent archaeological evidence, concludes that most (though not all) of them were compact and stable groups which had lived for five or six hundred years on the territory they occupied in the 10th cent., each of them united by common social and cultural traditions and by a common language. He appears to regard most of them not so much as tribes, but rather as ethnic groups, which were gradually absorbed into the Kievan state.

The Krivichians were among the oldest and most stable of these groups. The *Primary Chronicle* tells us that they lived on the upper reaches of the Volga, the Dvina and the Dnieper (*Povest'*, I, 13; Cross 55); and that their principal city was Smolensk. This has been strikingly confirmed by the excavation of the Krivichian burial mounds in that area, dating from 4th to 10th cents. The considerable commercial importance of this territory, which lies at the very centre of the great East European watershed, explains its colonization by the Northmen as early perhaps as the end of the 8th cent., and the importance acquired by Smolensk at the time c. 9 was written (*cf.* on 9/5–6). For the Krivichians, see Vernadsky, *Ancient Russia*, 324–7; Tret'yakov 228–36; Paszkiewicz 436–41; V. V. Sedov, *Sovetskaya Arkheologiya* 1960, 1, 47–62.

The name of the Krivichians is transcribed in c. 9 in two different ways: Κριβηταιηνοί (9/9–10) and Κριβιτζῶν (9/108). The form Κριβιτζοί reproduces, as faithfully as the laws of Greek phonetics would allow, the Slavonic (Old Russian) plural *Krivichi*. As for Κριβηταιηνοί, which Marquart (107) wrongly derived from an impossible singular *Kriwičin, B. Unbegaun has shown that it is a Greek plural formed from an Old Russian singular *Krivitin. This conclusion is all the more important since medieval Slavonic sources have preserved no examples of the names of the old Russian tribes in the singular form, the chronicles invariably treating them as collective plurals: *La langue russe au XVIe siècle* (Paris, 1935), 288–9.

9/10   οἱ Λενζανῆνοι.

This name, which recurs at 37/44 in the form Λενζενίνοις, remained for long a puzzle. It was most commonly identified with that of the *Luchane*, the inhabitants of the city of Lutsk in Volynia (*cf. Povest'*, I, 136; Cross 168): so Barsov note 114; Seredonin 128; and, with reservations, Niederle, *Manuel*, I, 215. Shakhmatov, who in 1916 half-heartedly accepted this identification (*Vvedenie*, 89), repudiated it in 1919 (*Drevneishie sud'by*, 30, note 3). *Cf.* Latyshev-Malitsky 54, note 17. Though several scholars still support this interpretation (*e.g.*, uncertainly, Likhachev, *Povest'*, II, 215; see other works cited by Paszkiewicz 366, note 5), it has now become a minority view. Tret'yakov, writing in 1953, still regards the Λενζανῆνοι/Λενζενίνοι as 'mysterious', and the question of their identity 'an open one' (218, 224).

However, as early as 1925 G. Il'insky proposed a much more convincing solution (*Slavia*, IV/2 (1925), 314–19). He derived Λενζανῆνος/Λενζενίνος from the Common Slav root *lęd-, meaning 'uncultivated, virgin soil', and the Common Slav suffix -janin- ('inhabitant of'). The Common Slav *lędjaninŭ ('an inhabitant of the virgin soil') must have produced the Old Russian forms *lędžaninŭ, *lęžaninŭ, either of which, in Il'insky's view, may provide the model for Λενζανῆνοι. Moreover, the term *lędjaninŭ is known to have given rise to the word Lęchŭ, which became a common name for a Pole (cf. Niederle, Slovanské Starožitnosti, III, 226–9; Manuel, I, 164–6). The Poles were indeed called Lyakhy in medieval Russia, Lengyel by the Hungarians, Lenkai by the Lithuanians, and Lechitae in medieval Latin sources: cf. Paszkiewicz 365–6. The inescapable conclusion is that the Λενζανῆνοι are Poles: cf. Durnovo 206; Skok 240; Paszkiewicz 366. The preservation of the nasal in this name raises the same problems as does the form Σφενδοσθλάβος: see on 9/4.

The geographical location of the Λενζανῆνοι raises some awkward questions. Il'insky believes that 9/9–10 must mean that they were neighbours of the Krivichians and that they lived near enough to the Dnieper to bring their monoxyla to this river without too much difficulty; he suggests that this position precisely fits that of the Slavonic Radimichians who lived in the basin of the Sozh, an affluent of the Dnieper, and points to the remarkable fact that the Radimichi are said by the Primary Chronicle to be descended from the Lyakhy, or Poles. Paszkiewicz (365–80), who accepts this view, believes that the Λενζανῆνοι included the Slavonic Vyatichians on the upper Oka as well as the Radimichians, the Polish origin of both tribes being vouched for by the chronicler. For the Radimichians and the Vyatichians, see Povest', I, 14; Cross 56; Vernadsky, Ancient Russia, 316–20; Tret'yakov 238–41, 244–5; Solov'eva, Sovetskaya Arkheologiya, 25 (1956), 138–70. However, the identity of the Λενζανῆνοι with the Radimichians and Vyatichians is questionable; and Soviet scholars (Likhachev, Povest', II, 225–6; Tret'yakov 244–5), as well as Vernadsky, deny, on archaeological grounds, the Polish origin of these two tribes. Furthermore, the position of the Radimichians and Vyatichians is inconsistent with that ascribed to the Λενζενίνοι at 37/42–4: these are placed in South Russia, west of the Dnieper, in the neighbourhood of the Pechenegs. As C. in his account of Patzinacia and its neighbours at 37/34–45 seems to be surveying these territories in a general direction from east to west and then to north-west, the Λενζενίνοι could best be located to the west of the Derevlyanians, on the upper Pripet and the upper Bug, in the borderland between Russia and Poland: see Il'insky 317; Paszkiewicz 366. See also on 33/18–19.

9/10 αἱ λοιπαὶ Σκλαβηνίαι.

The term ἡ Σκλαβηνία (Σκλαυηνία)/αἱ Σκλαβηνίαι (Σκλαβινίαι, Σκλαυινίαι) was frequently used in the 7th, 8th and 9th cents. to mean the Balkan lands colonized by Slavs: more particularly, (i) the left bank of the Danube (Simocatta 293/2; Acta S. Demetrii, I, MPG, cxvi, col. 1285); (ii) Thrace (Scriptor Incertus de Leone Armenio, Byzantion, 11, 1936, 423); (iii) Macedonia (Theophanes 347/6–7, 364/11, 430/21–2, 486/12). See Vizantiski Izvori za istoriju naroda Jugoslavije, ed. G. Ostrogorsky, I (Belgrade, 1955), 125, 177, note 7, 251–2, 222, 226, 230, 235–6. By extension the term came to mean any region occupied by the Slavs (ibid., 177, note 7). Cf. on 49/15.

9/10–11 εἰς τὰ ὄρη αὐτῶν κόπτουσι τὰ μονόξυλα.

The reference to the 'mountains' on which the Slavs cut the monoxyla is somewhat puzzling. The nearest mountain range, the Carpathians, was far distant from any of the Slavonic regions mentioned in c. 9. The few hills that exist in the neighbourhood of Kiev and Chernigov are scarcely important enough to fit the picture here sketched. It may be that the author has in mind the Valdai Hills (from 900 to 1000 ft. high) near the great water-divide that separates the upper courses of the Volga, the Dnieper and the western Dvina, which the Primary Chronicle calls Okov'sky les, the upland Oka forest (Povest', I, 11–12, II, 217; Cross 53). However, since the ὄρη in c. 9 refer to all the Slavonic regions, it seems possible that this word is a translation of the Slavonic term gory, plural of gora, which in Old Russian meant not only 'mountain' but also 'dry land', as opposed to water; it is also noteworthy that in the Russian language of the time the notions of 'mountain' and 'forest' were closely connected: see Sreznevsky, *s.v. gora*; *cf.* V. Dal', *Tolkovy slovar'*, 1 (St Petersburg-Moscow, 4th ed., 1912), cols. 926-7; Barsov 15. It is significant that the Kievan Polyanians are described in the *Primary Chronicle* as living 'in the forest on the hills (*v lese na gorakh*) over the river Dnieper': *Povest'* 1, 16; Cross 58; *cf.* Seredonin 143. It may thus be surmised that the author of this passage, who learnt from his Slav-speaking informant that the Slavs cut their *monoxyla* in the forests (*na gorakh*) misinterpreted this statement to mean that this activity took place on the mountains (εἰς τὰ ὄρη). In the primeval forests which then covered so much of central and northern Russia, there must have been many trees large enough to serve as *monoxyla*. *Cf.* Vernadsky, *Kievan Russia*, 30. In the 15th cent. Giosafat Barbaro saw on the islands of the Volga trees from which were hollowed out boats of one piece, capable of carrying 8 to 10 horses and the same number of men: see J. Barbaro and A. Contarini, *Travels to Tana and Persia*, tr. W. Thomas, ed. Lord Stanley of Alderley (London, Hakluyt Society, 1873), 31.

9/11-12 καὶ καταρτίσαντες αὐτά.
This first stage in the preparing or fitting of the *monoxyla*, performed *in situ*, must have been the actual hollowing-out process. Voronin (*Kul'turá Drevney Rusi*, 1, 282) thus reconstructs the method of manufacture: 'the trunk of a thick tree was first hollowed out with an axe and then trimmed with an adze. Then the log was steamed, and the sides distended to the required breadth; the bow and the stern were firmly tied to avoid any cracks; the process of stretching was consolidated by the insertion of thwarts made of stiff branches. . . . Perhaps the tree was sometimes fitted out before being felled: in this case wedges were gradually driven ever deeper into the trunk; after two to five years the tree would fall, and the manufacture of the dug-out would be completed in the ordinary way; this method ensured greater solidity for the boat, but was too slow. A dug-out made in this way might have a bow and stern either blunt or sharp. The size of these dug-outs varied considerably, from small canoes to enormous boats.' This preparation of the *monoxyla* in the interior of Russia is alluded to by Psellus, in the passage cited on 9/2.

9/13-14 ἐκεῖναι εἰσβάλλουσιν εἰς τὸν . . . Δάναπριν.
Taken literally, this is of course incorrect, for the Dnieper does not flow out of any lake. The λίμναι in question may be those which were studded over a large part of the great Russian waterway and which were particularly numerous in the sector between the Baltic and the upper Dnieper; but see on 9/59.

9/16-19 Οἱ δὲ 'Ρῶς . . . ἐξοπλίζουσιν αὐτά.
This is the second stage of the κατάρτισις (9/11-12) or ἐξάρτισις (9/16) of the *monoxyla*: for the first stage, see on 9/11-12. The operation is now taken over by the Russians (*i.e.* the Varangian ruling class), who equip the σκαφίδια ('dug-outs', see on 9/2) with oars and rowlocks for the journey down the Dnieper. It seems probable that the 'other tackle' (9/19) with which the *monoxyla* were rigged out in Kiev included external planks which served to raise their sides (see on 9/2). The French engineer Guillaume Levasseur de Beauplan, who visited the Dnieper region towards the middle of the 17th cent., describes the Cossack boats of that period, which, as has been pointed out (on 9/2), bore a close resemblance to the early Slavonic *monoxyla*: the Cossacks, he wrote, 'build Boats about 60 foot long, 10 or 12 foot wide, and 12 foot deep; these Boats have no Keel, but are built upon Bottoms made of the Wood of the Willow about 45 foot in length, and rais'd with Planks 10 or 12 foot long, and about a foot broad, which they pin or nail one over another . . . till they come to 12 foot in height, and 60 in length, stretching out in length and breadth the higher they go. . . . They have great Bundles of large Reeds put together as thick as a Barrel end to end, and reaching the whole length of the Vessel, well bound

with Bands made of Lime or Cherry-tree; they build them as our Carpenters do with ribs and cross-pieces, and then pitch them.' *Churchill's Voyages*, 1, 591–2; original text, *Description d'Ukranie* (Rouen, 1660), 55–6. The *monoxyla* could scarcely have been loaded in Kiev with all the merchandise, traders and crew they carried down the Dnieper (see on 9/2) unless their sides were raised with such planks: cf. *Kul'tura Drevney Rusi*, 1, 283–4.

9/17–18   τὰ παλαιὰ αὐτῶν μονόξυλα καταλύοντες.
The dismantled *monoxyla* are presumably those which, in the autumn of the previous year, had returned from the journey to Constantinople. C. 9 seems to imply that these Russian trading expeditions thither took place every year: see Manojlović IV, 41; Levchenko, *Russko-vizantiiskie otnosheniya*, 200. Yet this could hardly have been so, for C. himself tells us that they were possible only when there was peace between the Russians and the Pechenegs: see 2/16–23 and cf. 9/70–1.

9/19   'Ιουνίου μηνός.
The *monoxyla* gathered in Kiev during April (9/110); the month of May was doubtless spent in rigging them out. The time of departure, which was conditioned by the seasonal melting of the ice on the Russian rivers in early April (9/110–11), was also governed by the sailing conditions in the Black Sea, which is at its calmest in June and July. On the other hand, an early departure was desirable, since the Russian merchants were required by the Byzantine authorities to leave Constantinople by the autumn (*Povest'*, 1, 36–7; Cross 75–6); and the expedition had to be back in Kiev for the *polyudie*, which started in November (9/105–7). The duration of the journey can be calculated only approximately: the section from Kiev to the rapids, including the stop for two or three days at Vitichev (9/20–2), probably took almost ten days; the rapids were possibly passed in a day; another day would perhaps be spent on the Island of St Gregory (9/72–8); from St Gregory to the Island of St Aitherios at the mouth of the Dnieper was four days sailing (9/80), and here the travellers stopped for two or three days (9/83–4). About eighteen or nineteen days out from Kiev, they began the voyage across the Black Sea: here their speed must have varied considerably with weather conditions. Kendrick states (149) that Constantinople lay at a distance of about ten days sail from the Dnieper mouth along the western coast of the Black Sea; this may be true of the Russian naval campaigns against the empire, but would scarcely apply to a convoy of merchant ships, obliged to put in to shore at frequent intervals (9/88–104). About twenty days for the sea voyage would seem to be a conservative estimate. Probably, therefore, the whole journey from Kiev to Constantinople, under the most favourable conditions, took about six weeks; in stormy weather, or when the Pechenegs were troublesome (9/50, 70–1, 78–9, 93–4), considerably more. The Russians must consequently have arrived in Constantinople by the middle of July at earliest, more often probably during the second half of that month.

We know that on several occasions Russian armed flotillas appeared in the neighbourhood of Constantinople as early as June: on the 18th June in 860 (Vasiliev, *Russian Attack*, 102, 149); in 941 the Russian fleet was seen approaching the Bosphorus on 11th June (Runciman, *Romanus Lecapenus*, 111–2); and in June 1043 the Russian navy was sighted in the same place (Vernadsky, *Südost-Forschungen*, 12 (1953), 52). But these were military expeditions, and even the faster moving Russian combat ships could scarcely have taken less than three weeks to sail from Kiev to the Bosphorus.

9/20   τὸ Βιτετζέβη.
This is the town of Vitichev on the Dnieper, about 60 km. downstream from Kiev. As the assembly-point of all the *monoxyla* and one of the last Russian fortresses on the fringe of the Pecheneg steppe, it must then have been a place of some importance. No early mention of it, however, is made in Russian sources: a deserted 'hill of Vitichev' is referred to in the *Primary Chronicle*, ann. 1095 (*Povest'*, 1, 149; Cross 181). Some historians

identify Vitichev with Uvetichi, mentioned in the Chronicle, ann. 1100 (*Povest'*, 1, 181; Cross 198): see Grekov 295; Likhachev, *Povest'*, 11, 460. The identification is, however, not proved; and is not accepted by Tikhomirov (*Drevnerusskie goroda*, 14, 55, 286); *cf.* O. P. Sherbowitz-Wetzor in Cross, 281, note 350.

9/21 πακτιωτικὸν κάστρον τῶν ῾Ρῶς. For πακτιωτικόν, πακτιῶται, see on 9/9. For κάστρον, see on 9/5–6.

9/22–3 ἡνίκα ἂν ἅπαντα ἀποσυναχθῶσι τὰ μονόξυλα.
The choice of Vitichev as the assembly-point of the *monoxyla* may seem at first sight surprising. Why was this relatively minor city, and not Kiev, the place where the boats were 'all collected'? And why this extra two or three days' wait at Vitichev? The text clearly suggests that the flotilla was joined in this town by a further contingent of *monoxyla*; and it seems natural to assume that these late arrivals came from Pereyaslavl'. This city stood on the lower course of the Trubezh, not far from its confluence with the Dnieper, some 50 km. downstream from Vitichev. Its contemporary importance may be gauged from the fact that among the Russian towns mentioned or alluded to in Russo-Byzantine treaties of the 10th cent., Pereyaslavl' is listed third in order of priority, immediately following Kiev and Chernigov: see *Povest'*, 1, 24–5, 36; Cross 64–5, 74. The same treaties provide solid evidence that Pereyaslavl', along with other Russian cities, traded with Byzantium in the 10th cent. (*ibid.*); *cf.* Lyaskoronsky 262. For Pereyaslavl', see also Tikhomirov, *Drevnerusskie goroda*, 308–13. Though Pereyaslavl' is nowhere mentioned in *DAI* (its omission from c. 9 may be due to its position which precluded its dugouts from joining the others at Kiev), there can be little doubt that *monoxyla* which had been cut and prepared in the forests surrounding that city took part in the common voyage to Constantinople; we may thus suppose that the *monoxyla* from Pereyaslavl' were taken down the Trubezh and then up the Dnieper to Vitichev, where, before their inclusion in the assembled flotilla, they were in their turn furnished with oars, rowlocks and side-planks.

9/24 εἰς τὸν πρῶτον φραγμόν.
The φραγμοί (literally, 'barrages'), or, as the Russians called them in Slavonic, *porogi* (literally, 'thresholds', 'ridges': *cf.* Old Church Slavonic *pragŭ*), of which the celebrated description begins here, were a series of rapids formed by the Dnieper for a distance of 67·7 km. between the modern towns of Dnepropetrovsk (formerly Ekaterinoslav) and Zaporozh'e (formerly Aleksandrovsk). They are caused by granite formations which extend across south-west Russia in a south-easterly direction from the Carpathians to the Sea of Azov; the Dnieper, which, until its confluence with its left bank tributary the Samara, flows parallel to these crystalline rocks, at this point abruptly changes its course and is forced to cut through them in a north–south direction. As a result, the river-bed intersects a large number of granite ridges, which often protruded above the surface of the water, forming sharp or dome-shaped ledges from 200 to 850 m. in length, nine of which extend right across from one bank to the other, and some thirty more over part of the river-bed: the former are the *porogi* proper; the latter are called in Russian *zabory*. The water, finding its way blocked by these natural barrages, sought to rise over or pass between them; and the ensuing turbulence rendered the rapids highly dangerous, and in some cases impossible, for river craft. The hazards of navigation in this area were further increased by the strong and variable winds which blow during spring, by the large number of isolated rocks, scattered over the sandy bed of the river in the intervals between the rapids, some of which jutted out above the surface, and by the sixty-odd islands with which this sector of the Dnieper was studded. The speed of the current, which over the rest of the river's course averages between 40 and 50 m. a minute, rose in the rapids to

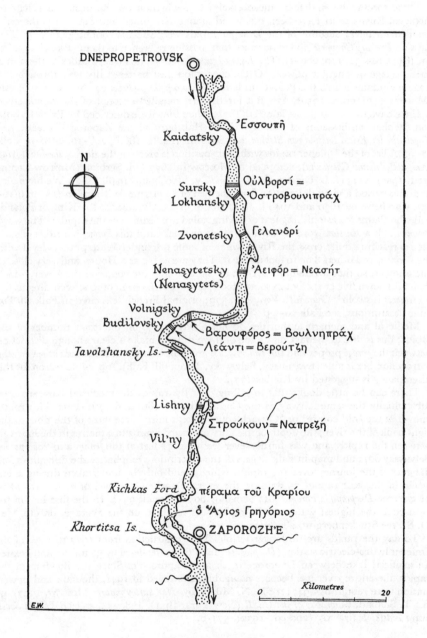

The Dnieper rapids

between 200 and 320 m. a minute. See map, p. 39; *Dneprovskie Porogi*, 581-6; Semenov 79-81; Evarnitsky 33-40; Belyavsky 799-802; Timonoff 14-59.

These spectacular and fearsome obstacles to navigation on the principal artery of medieval Russia must have been renowned among Northmen and Slavs. Yet the only detailed medieval account of the Dnieper rapids we possess is contained in c. 9. The Russian *Primary Chronicle* makes no more than passing reference to them (*Povest'*, I, 52-3, 80, 184; Cross 90, 116, 200-1). The *Lay of Igor's Campaign*, it is true, alludes to them in a poetic image of singular power: 'O Dnieper, thou hast battered thy way through the stone mountains across the Polovtsian land' (*Slovo o polku Igoreve*, ed. Adrianova-Peretts (Moscow-Leningrad, 1950), 27). But for the first detailed account of the rapids since *DAI* we have to wait until the late 16th cent., when they were described by Erich Lassota von Steblau, ambassador of Rudolph II of Habsburg to the Zaporog Cossacks: see *Tagebuch des Erich Lassota von Steblau*, ed. Schottin (Halle, 1866), 208-10, cited in Falk 17-19. A list of the Dnieper rapids with their position is given in the *Book of the Great Map* (*Kniga Bol'shomu Chertezhu*), compiled in Moscow in 1627 (ed. Serbina (Moscow-Leningrad, 1950), 111; cf. L. Bagrow, *Imago Mundi*, V, Stockholm, 1948, 81-2). We have also from this period a vivid description from the pen of Levasseur de Beauplan (see on 9/16-19), who between 1630 and 1648 built fortresses in the Ukraine for the King of Poland, and who claims the astonishing feat of having sailed upstream over the rapids: 'The word *Porouy* . . . is a *Russian* word signifying a Stone or Rock; and this *Porouy* is a ridge of such Stones reaching quite cross the River, whereof some are under Water, others level with the surface, and others 8 or 10 foot above it. They are as big as a House, and very close to one another, so that it resembles a Dam or Bank to stop the course of the River, which then falls down five or six foot in some places, and six or seven in others, according as the *Boristhenes* is swoln': *Churchill's Voyages*, I, 579; original French text cited in Falk 20. For later descriptions, see Falk 20-33.

Medieval and modern authorities do not always agree on the exact number of the rapids; this is due to the fact that some of them did not make a clear enough distinction between the *porogi* proper and the *zabory*. C. 9 gives the number of the rapids as seven: the correct number is nine (Evarnitsky, Belyavsky, Timonoff, Falk). A possible reason for this discrepancy is suggested by Kleiber (77).

There can be little doubt that in sailing over the rapids the medieval Russians used substantially the same fairway as the Cossacks in the 16th and 17th cents. This route, known as the 'old course' or 'Cossack course', kept fairly close most of the time to the right bank of the river; the depth of this fairway varied from 2 to 4 metres in the intervals between the rapids, and was hardly ever less than $3\frac{1}{2}$ feet at the *porogi* and *zabory*: see Belyavsky 801; and map in Falk *ad fin*. All the descriptions emphasize the difficulties and dangers of the journey over the rapids, which could only be undertaken during a few weeks in the year (about 75 days on the average), when the level of water was at its height: see *Dneprovskie Porogi*, 581; Semenov 80; Timonoff 93-4. In the first half of the 19th cent. the highest water on the rapids was reached, on the average, on 9th May O. S.: see Stuckenberg III, 282, note 1.

To-day the rapids are no longer visible. The construction from 1927 to 1932 of the Dnieper hydro-electric station (*Dneproges*) raised the water-level by 37 metres and created an artificial lake between Dnepropetrovsk and Zaporozh'e. Since the flooding of the rapids, the entire river has become navigable. Destroyed in 1941, the dam and power-station were rebuilt by 1947: see N. N. Mikhailov, *Nad kartoy rodiny* (Moscow, 1947), 98 ff.; T. Shabad, *Geography of the USSR* (New York, 1951), 438, 444, 454; *Bol'shaya Sovetskaya Entsiklopediya*, XIV (2nd ed., 1952), 577-8.

9/25 'Ρωσιστὶ καὶ Σκλαβηνιστί.
The celebrated names of the Dnieper rapids, here given in two languages, 'Russian' and 'Slavonic', raise a large number of problems which philologists and historians have

discussed for more than two centuries. A detailed review of the principal explanations of these names offered up to 1951, and a comprehensive bibliography of the subject, can be found in Falk 59–272 (German summary *ibid.*, 244–56).

The researches of T. S. Bayer (1736), J. Thunmann (1774), and above all the arguments of V. Thomsen (1877) established beyond doubt that the 'Russian' names of the rapids are Scandinavian—Old Norse or Old Swedish. Even the more extreme adherents of various 'anti-Normanist' theories (see on 9/1) have been unable to refute this conclusion; they have hence either glossed over the 'Russian' names, or, in Thomsen's words (*Relations*, 67), 'contented themselves with vague allusions or loose postulates of the most unscientific kind'. To some extent at least this charge can be directed against those contemporary Soviet scholars who, in defiance of the clear evidence of c. 9, are most reluctant to admit that in the middle of the 10th cent. the 'Russian' language (*i.e.* the language of the *Rus'*) was Scandinavian: see Tikhomirov, *Sovetskaya Etnografiya*, VI–VII (1947), 75–7; S. V. Yushkov, *Obshchestvenno-politichesky stroy i pravo Kievskogo gosudarstva* (Moscow, 1949), 51–3; Levchenko, *Russko-vizantiiskie otnosheniya*, 208–10.

As for the 'Slavonic' names, no scholar has ever doubted that they are derived from the language of the Eastern Slavs, who themselves later adopted the national name of 'Russians' from their erstwhile Scandinavian conquerors. Some philologists, however, have detected in the Greek transcriptions of these East Slavonic names traces of a phonetic and morphological influence of the Old Bulgarian language: see Shakhmatov, *Vvedenie*, 81; Shevelov 509, 526; and on 9/4. On the other hand, Falk, basing his arguments on the palaeographic study of the oldest ms. of *DAI* and on his interpretation of the linguistic methods used by the Byzantines in transcribing foreign proper names, has recently concluded that the Slavonic names of the rapids are Ukrainian (226–30 and *passim*). This conclusion has been strongly challenged by a number of leading philologists, who have pointed out that it accords neither with the evidence of the oldest South Russian documents nor with the results of a comparative study of the East Slavonic dialects. See the highly critical comments on Falk's methods and conclusions by Shevelov (*passim*), the review of Falk's book by the same author (writing under the name Yu. Šerech) in *Ukraïna*, 5 (1951), 324–30, and Falk's reply *ibid.*, 8 (1952), 627–32; 9 (1953), 722–5. *Cf.* also the discussion between Falk and J. Sahlgren, cited by Shevelov (503).

One of the difficult problems which face the scholar who seeks to interpret the names of the rapids is, as Shevelov (505) succinctly puts it, that of discovering the correct relationship between the three basic parts of the material: the Slavonic and the Scandinavian names, and their etymology or translation into Greek; 'the relationship between the three parts varies from one case to the other, and the scholar must decide whether he is going to approach each instance completely individually or whether he is going to look for some general system'.

A controversial and still unsolved question is that of the relative priority of the 'Russian' and of the Slav names. If, in accordance with the text, we assume that the Greek interpretations of the names apply to both categories (for a different view, however, see Karlgren 14–25), it would follow that one of these two groups represents a translation from the other. The view of Yushkov, *loc. cit.*, and of other Soviet scholars (*cf.* Levchenko, *Russko-vizantiiskie otnosheniya*, 209), that the 'Russian' names belong to a separate 'international nomenclature' consisting of names taken from various languages, is neither clear nor convincing. It has been suggested that the Northmen who discovered and explored the Dnieper during the 9th cent. gave to the rapids names in their own language, and that these names were borrowed and translated by the Eastern Slavs into their own tongue. Falk accordingly (39–40, 67–8) believes most of the Slavonic names to be direct translations of the Scandinavian ones; and he points out, in support of this view (34–5), that place-names similar to the ones brought by the Northmen to Russia are found in regions of Viking colonization in Scotland, England and Normandy; *cf.* however Shevelov (526) for a different interpretation of this fact.

On the other hand, though the boundary between the area settled by the Eastern Slavs and the Pecheneg steppe in the mid-10th cent. crossed the Dnieper about half-way between Kiev and the rapids, there is every reason to believe that the Slavs had sailed down the lower Dnieper, and were thus familiar with the rapids, long before the advent of the Northmen. Miller (29) therefore believed that the Scandinavian names are translations of the Slav ones. Ekblom (*Die siebente Stromschnelle*, 163–4) suggests that there existed a set of Slav names for the rapids by which the Scandinavians, when giving their own names to them, were 'influenced'. Shevelov, who considers the question of the relative priority of the two groups of names to be an open one, likewise inclines (526) to the view that the Northmen translated the names of the rapids 'directly from the local language'.

Equally controversial is the problem of the source from which these names were derived. Was the author's informant a Northman or a Slav? Or was each category of names obtained from a different source? Levchenko (*Russko-vizantiiskie otnosheniya*, 210) seems to postulate two separate sources, the one a Bulgarian merchant who had travelled in Russia, the other a Varangian in Constantinople: this view is, to say the least, unproven. As Falk (231–4) has pointed out, the semantic correspondence between the 'Russian' and the Slavonic names of the rapids, and the fact that both lists are incomplete and omit the same rapids, strongly suggest that the names were given to the author by one person. Bury, who drew attention to the fact that the Slav names are on the whole less seriously corrupted than the Scandinavian, believed (541) that the source must have been a Slavonic one. See also Shevelov 526; Miller 30. However, on the assumption that the author of c. 9 was a Byzantine envoy who travelled to Kiev in 944 (see Introductory Note, p. 19), it is equally possible to believe that he obtained both sets of names from a Varangian who, living in the bilingual world of Kievan Russia, knew the Slavonic language, which, as Bury justly observed (542), was at that time 'a sort of *lingua franca*' in Eastern Europe. This view is argued by Falk (*ibid.*).

The twelve names of the Dnieper rapids preserved in c. 9 are of great importance to philologists. The Scandinavian names are the only direct specimens we have of the language spoken by the Swedish *Rus'*. They reveal features typical of the Swedish language of the Viking age and, alongside the Russian place-names of Scandinavian origin, provide valuable evidence of Scandinavian toponymy in Eastern Europe. They offer one of the most striking proofs we possess of the Scandinavian origin of the *Rus'*: see Thomsen, *Relations*, 67; Falk 223–6. The Slavonic names are among the earliest recorded examples of the language spoken by the Eastern Slavs, which in respect of the following centuries is termed Old Russian. Despite the scepticism of scholars like Selishchev (309) and Shevelov (529–30), who discount their value as linguistic material, they can still, if used with necessary caution, provide important evidence on the history of Old Russian phonetics and morphology: *cf.* Durnovo 205–9.

9/**25–6**   τὸν ἐπονομαζόμενον Ἐσσουπῆ, ὃ ἑρμηνεύεται . . . 'μὴ κοιμᾶσαι'.

It is fairly commonly agreed that this is the Slavonic name of the first rapid: the exact equivalent of 'do not sleep' (μὴ κοιμᾶσαι) is *ne sŭpi* in Old Church Slavonic, *ne spi* in Old and modern Russian. The first form can be obtained if it be supposed that Ἐσσουπῆ was miswritten for *Νεσσουπῆ or *Νεσουπῆ, a mistake all the more natural as the preceding word ἐπονομαζόμενον ends with a ν. This explanation was already proposed by Banduri in 1711 (as Νεσσουπί; *MPG*, cxiii, col. 173), and has been accepted by the majority of commentators; see Falk 72–83. Falk, however, proposes a completely different explanation of this name. He suggests that the original and correct form was *Οὐστουπῆ, a transcription of *ustupi, nom. pl. of *ustupŭ, 'a ledge, a projection'. In his opinion, the initial οὐ- (ȣ-) was misread as ε, and στ as σσ, when the origina lms. of c. 9 was compiled from the documents in C.'s archives; and the false etymology *ne sŭpi* was invented at the the same time (83–92, 249–50; *cf.* the photographic reproduction of Paris and Vatican

mss. of c. 9, *ibid.*, 275–94; *Ukraïna*, 8, 1952, 629–31; Shevelov 507–8). Falk's interpretation tallies well with the description of the first rapid at 9/27–30; and it is noteworthy that
the modern Russian word *ustup* is cited as a synonym for *porog* in dictionaries of both
medieval and modern Russian: see Sreznevsky and Dal' *s. v. porog.* Falk's reading of
Εσσουπῆ as *Ούστουπῆ is accepted as a possibility by Shevelov (507–8, 527); and, more
wholeheartedly, by Ekblom (*Die siebente Stromschnelle*, 167–9), who supports it by different
and rather simpler palaeographic arguments and confirms Falk's suggestion that the
Slavonic *ustupi* corresponds to the Old Norse *stup* (or *stupi*), 'a fall, a precipice'; the formal
and semantic resemblance between the two words suggests, in Ekblom's opinion, that the
original form *ούστουπῆ 'reproduced the East Slavonic *ustupi* and besides reminded the
writer of the Old Norse *stup(i)*'.

Attempts have been made, however, to derive ʼΕσσουπῆ from a Scandinavian word.
Thus Thomsen, who endorsed the traditional derivation *Νεσσουπῆ in 1877 (*Relations*,
54–5), abandoned it in 1919 (*Samlede Afhandlinger*, I, 299 ff.) in favour of the Swedish *Ves
uppi*, 'be awake'; but this latter has not been generally accepted: see Sahlgren 320. And
Sahlgren himself has recently suggested derivation from the Scandinavian *äsupi*, 'always
(*ä*-) sucking in (*-supi*)' (*Bygd och Namn*, 38 (1950), 145; 39 (1951), 153 f.; cited by
Shevelov 508). *Cf.* Kleiber 87–8.

The wording of 9/24–6 certainly suggests that the 'Russian' and the Slavonic names of
the first rapid were the same. In view of the fact that all the other rapids except the third
have double names, it has been supposed that one of the names, probably the Scandinavian, was omitted here, either by the author (Falk 91) or by a copyist; and Kunik
(428), who held the latter view, believed that the order of the words was shifted from
τὸν ἐπονομαζόμενον ʽΡωσιστὶ μὲν . . . Σκλαβινιστὶ δὲ Νεσσουπῆ, ὃ ἑρμηνεύεται κτλ.
(*cf.* Thomsen, *Relations*, 54–5). However, it is equally possible that the author was given
both a Scandinavian and a Slavonic name for the first rapid, but that these names were
phonetically so close to each other that he took them to be the same word: see Karlgren
26–30; Shevelov 505–6, 527.

This first rapid is generally identified with that known as *Kodak* (or *Kadak*) in the 17th
cent. *Book of the Great Map* (*Kniga Bol'shomu Chertezhu*, 111; see on 9/24), and as *Kaidatsky*
or *Staro-Kaidatsky* in the 19th cent.: see Evarnitsky 35; Falk 90–1; Timonoff 60–2;
Kleiber 88; and the map in Kudryashov III, 12. It lay 18 km. downstream from Dnepropetrovsk (Belyavsky 799) and consisted of four ridges; its dimensions are given by
Evarnitsky as follows: width, 331 m.; length, 512 m. by the right bank, 544 m. by the left
bank; fall, 1.94 m. (it should be noted that the measurements given by Evarnitsky for the
rapids, cited here and below, differ slightly from those given by Timonoff). After the
Nenasytets (9/45–55), this was considered one of the most dangerous of the rapids; see Falk
24–5.

9/26–7 ὅσον τὸ πλάτος τοῦ τζυκανιστηρίου.

The τζυκανιστήριον was the imperial manège in Constantinople; it served more
particularly as the Polo-ground of the emperor and the court. The word comes from the
Persian *čougān*, 'polo'. Hence τζυκάνιον, 'the game of polo, polo-stick'; τζυκανίζειν,
τζουκανίζειν, 'to play polo'. The game, imported from Persia in the first half of the 5th
cent., was popular at the Byzantine court till the fall of the empire. From Constantinople
the French Crusaders brought it to France, where it was known as *chicane*. The first τζυκανιστήριον in Constantinople was built by Theodosius II to the east of the Palace, near the
Sea of Marmora. Basil I demolished it to make room for the Nea Ekklesia, and built a
new and larger ground further east, by the sea: see Theoph. Cont. 144/13–15; and, for
Basil's exploits at the game, Genesius 127/8–15. *Cf.* plan in Vogt, Commentaire I, *ad fin.*;
D. F. Belyaev, *Byzantina*, I (*Zapiski Russkogo Arkheologicheskogo Obshchestva*, V/I (1891)), 76;
J. Ebersolt, *Le grand palais de Constantinople* (Paris, 1910), 75, 140–1, 147, 151, 160, 173–4,
215; Koukoulès, *EEBΣ*, 13 (1937), 114–17; C. Diem, *Asiatische Reiterspiele* (Berlin,

1942), 111, 120–8, 260–2; R. Janin, *Constantinople byzantine* (Paris, 1950), 40, 119, 188–9; L. Bréhier, *La Civilisation Byzantine* (Paris, 1950), 66–7.

The exact dimensions of the τζυκανιστήριον are not known. On Vogt's plan its width is about 70 metres. This reference, as well as the allusion to the width of the Hippodrome (9/68), shows that the author of this section of c. 9 was a Constantinopolitan and a courtier: see Introductory Note, p. 19; Manojlović IV, 37; *cf.* on 29/14–53.

9/30–5 Καὶ διὰ τοῦτο κτλ.

For this use of punting-poles in rocky, shallow water, *cf. Vita S. Hilarionis, Analecta Hierosol. Stachyologias*, 5 (1898), 131–2: ὑφάλου (*cf.* on 9/68–70) καὶ στενῆς τῆς τοῦ πλοίου διαβάσεως οὔσης, μὴ δυνάμενοι κώπαις χρήσασθαι, ἠναγκάζοντο κοντοῖς τὸ πλοῖον διωθούμενοι μετὰ πολλοῦ δέους τὸν τόπον διανήχεσθαι.

9/31 πλησίον σκαλώσαντες. On the assumption that the Russians used the same fairway as the Cossacks in later times (see on 9/24), this would be the right bank.

9/32 τὰ . . . λοιπὰ πράγματα.

This, together with a later passage referring to τὰ πράγματα and slaves (9/51–2), is the only explicit mention of trade in c. 9; but *cf.* 2/16–18. There can be no doubt that the annual expeditions described in c. 9 were primarily undertaken for trading purposes, although, as Manojlović (IV, 43) has pointed out, Russian merchants travelling to Constantinople were sometimes employed on diplomatic missions.

The nature of these Russian goods which were shipped to Constantinople is revealed by contemporary Russian sources. The *Primary Chronicle*, ann. 969, attributes to Svyatoslav of Kiev the statement that furs, wax, honey and slaves are exported from Russia to Little Preslav on the lower Danube: *Povest'*, 1, 48; Cross 86. These were in the 10th cent. the staple articles of Russian export to the South. The great importance of the Russian slave-trade at that time is attested in many sources. 'The slaves in their chains' were an essential part of the shipload of the Kievan *monoxyla* (9/52). The Russo-Byzantine treaties reveal that some of these slaves shipped from Russia to Constantinople were natives of the empire: the treaty of 911 provides for the return home of Greek and Russian prisoners of war who had been sold into slavery, against a specified ransom (*Povest'*, 1, 28; Cross 67–8); while the treaty of 944 contains two clauses relating to the return of fugitive slaves: a Russian slave who escapes to Byzantium, or who finds his way to the St Mamas quarter (the suburb of Constantinople where the Russian merchants were forced to reside), is to be returned; likewise a Byzantine slave who escapes to Russia must be brought back, and, if the property he has stolen is found to be intact, the Russians will be paid two *nomismata* (*Povest'*, 1, 36; Cross 75).

Furs from the forests of central and northern Russia were highly prized in the markets of Europe and Asia. In the tribute gathered by the Russians from their Slav subjects during the winter (9/105–9) furs were the standard contribution (*Povest'*, 1, 42; Cross 81). Igor, on concluding his treaty with the empire in 944, presented the Byzantine envoys to Kiev with furs, slaves and wax (*Povest'*, 1, 39; Cross 77). The same commodities, according to the chronicler, were promised to the emperor by Olga of Kiev (*Povest'*, 1, 45; Cross 83). Contemporary evidence shows that the furs exported by the Russians at that time included beaver, sable, ermine, black fox and squirrel.

Wax, as is evidenced in the passage cited above, was a commodity highly rated on the Byzantine market (*cf.* 53/531): it was used to make candles for the Church. Together with honey, it was gathered in the Russian forests.

The Russian merchants referred to in c. 9 are clearly armed to the teeth. Since a considerable part of their itinerary passed through territory infested by hostile Pechenegs, this is scarcely surprising. In a more general sense, however, the boundary between trader and warrior was a slender one in 10th cent. Russia. The merchants of the principal

Russian cities still belonged to the military aristocracy, to the prince's retinue; and the monopoly of the trade with Byzantium was in their hands: Manojlović IV, 38. For the trade between Russia and the empire, which was then done mostly by barter, see the Russo-Byzantine treaties (*Povest'*, I, 24–9, 34–9; Cross 64–8, 73–7); Pargoire, *Echos d'Orient*, II (1908), 203–10; Istrin, *Izvestiya Otdel. Russk. Yazyka i Slovesnosti Ross. Akad. Nauk*, 29 (1924), 383–93; Vasiliev, *Economic Relations*; Levchenko, *Viz. Vrem.*, 5 (1952), 105–26; *id.*, *Russko-vizantiiskie otnosheniya*, 91–127, 152–71. For the Russian export trade in the 10th cent. see *Kul'tura Drevney Rusi*, I, 319–26, 335–41, 365–6.

9/39–40   τὸν ἕτερον φραγμόν, τὸν ἐπιλεγόμενον 'Ρωσιστὶ . . . Οὐλβορσί.
The 'Russian' name of the second rapid raises no great difficulties. It is derived from the Scandinavian (*H*)*ulmforsi*, a dative-locative singular of *Holmfors* or *Hulmfors*, a compound of the common Scandinavian word *holm* (Old Norse *hólmr*), 'an islet', and *fors*, a waterfall, a rapid. See Falk 93–109, 250; *cf.* Thomsen, *Relations*, 55–6; Sahlgren 316–7 Vasmer, *Wikingerspuren*, 669. As Falk has shown, a large number of Swedish place-names are formed with the element *holm-*, and the Old Norse word *holmr*, or *holmi*, also occurs in Scandinavian place-names in England, Scotland and Normandy.

9/40   Σκλαβηνιστὶ . . . 'Οστροβουνιπράχ.
The meaning of the Slavonic name of the second rapid is perfectly clear. It is a combination of an adjective formed from *ostrov*, an island, and *prag* (*porog*), a rapid. Philologists are, however, not all in agreement on the original form of the adjective: in recent times the majority have favoured the form *ostrovĭnyi* (островьныи): see Thomsen, *Relations*, 55; Shakhmatov, *Vvedenie*, 89; Durnovo 205. Falk, however (109–13, 250–1; *cf. Ukraïna*, IX, 1953, 722), believes that the form was originally written *ὀστρουνουνι, that the copyist rendered the compound *ονου as οβου, and that the latter form reflects the South Russian, Ukrainian, diphthong *uụ*. His interpretation has been criticized by Ekblom (*Die siebente Stromschnelle*, 169–70). The form πράχ exhibits two striking peculiarities: it is derived not from the East Slavonic form *porog*, but from the South Slavonic, Old Bulgarian *prag* (but see a different view in Selishchev 312); and the final χ (instead of γ) strongly suggests that the *g* in *prag* was pronounced by the author's informant as a fricative consonant, in accordance with South Russian phonetics. These facts prompted Shakhmatov (*Vvedenie*, 81) to write: 'Constantine Porphyrogenitus . . . obtained his information [about the Dnieper rapids] from an inhabitant of South Russia, but this educated man used in conversing with the emperor, whenever it was necessary, words and names not in their Russian [*i.e.* East Slavonic] but in their Old Bulgarian form, while revealing at the same time his South Russian pronunciation.' Shakhmatov's views on the genesis of c. 9 may not be wholly acceptable on historical grounds; but his linguistic explanation of the form πράχ has been endorsed by a number of scholars.

9/40–1   ὅπερ ἑρμηνεύεται 'τὸ νησίον τοῦ φραγμοῦ'.
Both the Scandinavian and the Slavonic names of the rapid are formed of words meaning 'island' and 'rapid'. It has been observed, however, that the Greek translation of the names is not quite correct: the words should be reversed: the exact equivalent of *Holmfors* and *Ostrovĭnyi prag* would be ὁ φραγμὸς τοῦ νησίου. See Thomsen, *Relations*, 55; Latyshev-Malitsky 55, note 21. Sahlgren (317) attributes the inversion to the absent-mindedness of the author or copyist. See however Kleiber 84–5.
This rapid has been identified with either of the two which lie downstream from the first one: with the second rapid, called *Sursky* in modern times, or with the longer and more dangerous third rapid, the *Lokhansky*. Both have islands adjoining them. As these two rapids are only about half a kilometre distant from one another, it may be that the name *Holmfors-Ostrovĭnyi prag* comprised both of them: see Thomsen, *Relations*, 56; Falk 93–103. The *Sursky* rapid was 7½ km. downstream from the first; it consisted of two ridges;

its length was 102 m. by the right bank and 72½ m. by the left bank; its fall was 50 cm. The *Lokhansky* had three ridges and the following dimensions: width, 128 m.; length, 271 m. by the right bank, 166 m. by the left; fall, 1·6 m. See Evarnitsky 35; Falk 25; and the sketch-map of these two rapids in Timonoff 63.

9/43-5 τὸν τρίτον φραγμόν . . . ' ἦχος φραγμοῦ '.

The name of the third rapid has been assigned to the wrong language and the Slavonic name is lacking. Γελανδρί is a transcription of the Old Swedish present participle *Gællandi* (Old Norse *Gellandi, Gjallandi*), which means 'loudly sounding, ringing'. For the problem raised by the insertion of the Greek *rho*, see Vasmer, *Zeitschrift für slavische Philologie* 28 (1959), 99–100. As at 9/40-1, the author makes a slight error in translation: the meaning is not 'the sound of the rapid', but 'the sounding (ringing) rapid', perhaps ὁ φραγμὸς τοῦ ἤχου. It is quite possible, as Kunik (429 f.) suggested, that the Slavonic name was inadvertently omitted by the copyist and that the original text read τὸν λεγόμενον 'Ρωσιστὶ μὲν Γελανδρί, Σκλαβηνιστὶ δὲ . . . ὃ ἑρμηνεύεται 'ἦχος φραγμοῦ'. It may be that this missing Slavonic name bore some resemblance to the modern Russian name of this rapid—*Zvonets* or *Zvonetsky*—which is derived from *zvon*, 'a ringing sound', and is thus exactly synonymous with *Gællandi*. See Thomsen, *Relations* 56-7; Sahlgren 317; Latyshev-Malitsky 55, note 22; Falk 117–28, 251; but *cf.* also Shevelov 510. Kleiber (89–90) believes that *Zvonets* may already have been the Slavonic name of the rapid in C.'s time: if so, the name—probably Zvonici—might have been transcribed as *Σβονίτσι: see Vasmer, *loc. cit.* The peculiar sound made by the water passing over the Dnieper rapids has struck several observers: *cf.* 9/29–30; Falk 127–8. The *Zvonets* was situated 5 km. downstream from the *Lokhansky* rapid; it consisted of four ridges; its length by the right bank was 186 m., and by the left 218 m.; its fall was 1½ m. (Evarnitsky 36; Timonoff 64; Falk 25).

9/45-6 τὸν τέταρτον φραγμόν . . . 'Αειφόρ.

The 'Russian' name of the fourth rapid still raises some difficulties. Its correct interpretation became possible only in 1876, when Cobet (*Mnemosyne*, 4, 1876, 378–82) published c. 9 according to a fresh collation of the Paris ms. of *DAI*: it then became apparent that the correct form of the name is not 'Αειφάρ, as previous editors had given it, but 'Αειφόρ. See Thomsen, *Relations*, 143-4; Falk 135.

At the present time there are two principal explanations of 'Αειφόρ. The first was proposed by Thomsen (*loc. cit.*): in his opinion, the word is a compound of the Old Norse particle *ei, ey, æ* (Old Swedish *ai*), 'ever', and the Old Norse adjective *forr*, 'forward, precipitate, violent'. *Eiforr* (in Old Swedish *Aiforr*) thus means 'the ever violent, the ever rapid, *perpetuo praeceps*'. The name *Aiforr* was transcribed as 'Αειφόρ. Thomsen's interpretation is accepted by Falk (142–50, 252), who considers that it is supported by the punctuation of the Paris ms. of *DAI*. A different explanation was put forward by Sahlgren (320–3): criticizing Thomsen for ignoring Swedish toponymy, he points out that the great majority of Swedish waterfalls have names ending in *-fors*, and cites the Swedish word *ed*, pronounced *aið* in the 10th cent., which designated a place where boats were dragged or carried, *i.e.* a portage. He accordingly takes 'Αειφόρ to be a transcription of *Aiðfors, which he renders 'the portage-rapid', 'die Stromschnelle mit dem danebenlaufenden Transportpfad'. In support of his view he refers to the description given in c. 9 of the fourth barrage, the only one impassable for *monoxyla* and round which they had to be dragged and ported (9/47–57). The omission of the σ in *'Αειφόρς he explains by supposing that the ms. was written from dictation and that this letter was consequently not distinguished from the initial σ of the following word σκλαβηνιστί. Sahlgren's reconstruction of *Aiðfors is supported by Vasmer (*Wikingerspuren*, 669) and Karlgren (108–9).

The explanations of both Thomsen and Sahlgren have recently been reconsidered by Ekblom (*Die siebente Stromschnelle*, 171–3). He, like Falk (143–6), rejects the reconstructed

*Aiðfors on palaeographical grounds, and further observes that a term with this meaning would provide no suitable parallel with Νεασήτ, the Slavonic name of this rapid (see on 9/46–7). But he also regards with some scepticism Thomsen's and Falk's Aiforr, and concludes that the name 'Αειφόρ still awaits a satisfactory explanation.

About 1870 at Pilgård on the island of Gotland a Runic inscription was discovered on a stone. As deciphered by H. Pipping (Nordiska Studier tillegnade A. Noreen, Uppsala, 1904, 175–82), the inscription referred to a certain Hegbiarn who, together with his brothers, erected stones in memory of Rafn at Rufstain in the south and penetrated as far as Aifur. The inscription has been dated about 1000 A.D., and most scholars have identified Aifur with 'Αειφόρ. The search for Rufstain has yielded no conclusive results, though it has been tentatively identified with the Rvany Kamen', 'the cloven stone', which the Russian traveller A. Afanas'ev-Chuzhbinsky described as situated on the upper reaches of the rapid: Poezdka v yuzhnuyu Rossiyu, 1, 2nd ed. (St Petersburg, 1863), 101. For the Pilgård inscription, see F. Braun, in Sbornik arkheologicheskikh statey, podnesenny A. A. Bobrinskomu (St Petersburg, 1911), 270–6; T. J. Arne, La Suède et l'Orient (Uppsala, 1914), 11; Latyshev-Malitsky 55, note 23; Falk 136–9. For a sceptical view of its decipherment, see Sahlgren 321, note 1.

9/46–7 Νεασήτ, διότι . . . εἰς τὰ λιθάρια τοῦ φραγμοῦ.
The Slavonic name of the fourth rapid has been satisfactorily explained. Contrary to our author's assertion, its connexion with pelicans seems dubious. It is true that the Old Church Slavonic word for pelican is nejęsytĭ, which became neyasyt' in the East Slavonic language of Russia. It has been argued, however, notably by Thomsen (Relations, 58–61; cf. Latyshev-Malitsky 55, note 23), that the connexion between the name of this rapid and that of the pelican is impossible on grounds of logic and ornithology. If any such connexion had really existed, the rapid would have been called by a compound name meaning something like 'Pelican rapid', and not simply 'the Pelican'; pelicans, moreover, do not live in the Dnieper valley, nor do they nest in rocks. The 'pelican theory' is thus regarded by most scholars today as an invention either of the author or of his etymologically minded informant. The attempts of some more recent commentators to substitute for pelicans other less improbable birds, such as storks, vultures, swans or owls, were even more misguided: for these embroideries, see Falk 129–42; Latyshev-Malitsky 55, note 23. See, however, Kleiber 80–1.

The name Νεασήτ is indeed derived from nejęsytĭ, neyasyt'. But the primary meaning of this word, which is a negative adjective from syt, is both in Old Church Slavonic and in Old Russian (East Slavonic) 'insatiable'. This is not only an eminently suitable name for the largest and most fearsome of the rapids, the only one which, even in the spring, is never wholly covered by the water, and whose violence is thus never diminished (see below); but also the derivation of its name from the Slavonic adjective meaning 'insatiable' is confirmed by the fact that from the 17th cent. onwards the rapid was invariably called Nenasytets or Nenasytetsky, which can only mean 'insatiable': see Kniga Bol'shomu Chertezhu, 111; Thomsen, Relations, 60–1; Falk 129–54.

There is still some difference of opinion over the origin of the modern name Nenasytets. Thomsen (Relations, 60, note 3) suggests the possibility that the form Νεασήτ is a mistake for Νεναϭήτ. Selishchev (311) also believes that as early as the 10th cent. the Slavonic name of the rapid may have been Nenasytĭcĭ or Nenasytĭnyi, but suggests Nejęsytĭ as an alternative. Falk, however (151), regards Nenasytets as a later form, related by popular etymology to the verb nasytiti, 'to satiate'. He suggests that the suffix -ets was added to the name by analogy with Zvonets, the Slavonic name of the third rapid (see on 9/43–5), as a kind of rhyme. The suffix, moreover, serves to personify this rapid, which was also popularly known as Did, 'Grandfather', and Razboinik, 'the Robber' (Falk 151–2, 252–3).

The epithet ὁ μέγας was well suited to Νεασήτ. It was indeed a giant among the rapids. Situated about 6½ km. below the third rapid, it consisted of twelve ridges, covering an overall distance of 2·454 km. by the right bank and 1·65 km. by the left. Its fall was 5·9 m. For a distance of about 2 km. upstream from the rapid, the Dnieper was about 2½ km. wide; after passing the two large islands of Kozlov and Tkachev, the current accelerated and, on entering the rapids, began to zig-zag violently from one bank to the other between the numerous rocky islets by the left bank and the promontories and ridges that jutted out from the right bank, sometimes to the middle of the river. The strength and turmoil of the current were further increased by the many underwater stones and by a transversal barrier of steep rocks, whose summits, jagged or rounded, rose up to seven feet above the surface of the water. 'For all these reasons the river, which above the *Nenasytetsky* rapid flows freely and smoothly on its course, on reaching the rapid and encountering there impassable obstacles in the form of ledges, rocks, ridges and promontories, hurtles with inconceivable violence in different directions and rushes from one rock to another; the current, as a result, becomes terribly agitated . . . billions of particles of spray fly up in all directions . . . bottomless whirlpools are formed between the rocks: all this produces a terrible noise, resembling a groan, which can be heard far away from the rapid and which drowns all other sounds—the cry of the birds and the voice of man . . . *Nenasytets* looks particularly majestic and enchanting viewed from the top of the right bank when the river is in spate and its surface is covered with silvery, pearl-like foam . . . when it roars, and groans, and throws up its waters high in the air, and suddenly breaks off and falls into so deep a silence that one may hear the water gently splashing its way from stone to stone, from one ridge to another, thus enabling the local inhabitants to foretell changes in the weather.' Evarnitsky 37–8 (Falk 27).

The *Nenasytets* doubtless enjoyed the same terrifying reputation in the 10th cent. as it did in modern times. It was the only rapid over which the Russians did not risk their *monoxyla* (9/47–57). In later times the Zaporog Cossacks were more intrepid: their pilots took boats and rafts through a narrow passage free of rocks in the middle of the river: see map in Falk *ad fin.* It must have been a terrifying experience. See also Yuzhny 405–6; D. I. Evarnitsky, *Zaporozh'e*, 1 (St Petersburg, 1888), 121 ff.; Timonoff 64–8; Falk 153–4.

9/50 τοὺς Πατζινακίτας. See on 9/66–7, 70–1.

9/52 τὰ ψυχάρια. See on 9/32.

9/53 μίλια ἕξ.

The length of *Nenasytets* was 2·454 km. by the right bank (see on 9/46–7), along which, presumably, the portage round the rapid was made. But six Byzantine miles were equivalent to 8·887 km. This would imply that the Russians put in to land (9/48) and re-embarked (9/57) respectively several miles up- and down-stream from the rapid.

9/57–8 τὸν πέμπτον φραγμόν . . . Βαρουφόρος.

The name has most commonly been derived from the Old Norse *Báru-fors*, a compound of *bára* (genitive *báru*), 'a wave', and *fors*, 'a waterfall, a rapid'. It would thus mean 'the wave-rapid'. The ending *-fors* was hellenized to make *-φόρος*. See Thomsen, *Relations*, 64; Sahlgren 317–18; Ekblom, *Die siebente Stromschnelle*, 171; and earlier works cited in Falk 155–63. Falk himself (163–6, 253), on the other hand, claims that the name should read *Varuforos* and relates it to the Swedish *varu-, var-*, meaning 'an elevation, an island, bank or rock rising above the surface of the water'.

9/58–9 Σκλαβηνιστὶ . . . Βουλνηπράχ.

The great majority of commentators are of the opinion that the Slavonic name of the fifth rapid has exactly the same meaning as the Scandinavian: Βουλνηπράχ is a compound of *vlŭna* (влъна), 'a wave', and *pragŭ*, 'a rapid' (*cf.* on 9/40). See Thomsen, *Relations*, 64; Shakhmatov, *Vvedenie*, 89; Durnovo 205. Here again, however, Falk (166–71, 253) rejects what he calls the 'wave theory', and connects βουλνη- with the adjective *volĭnyi*, 'free'; he attempts to corroborate this view by identifying Βουλνηπράχ with *Vil'ny*, the name given in modern times to the ninth and last rapid, which does mean 'the free' (see on 9/65). Βουληπράχ, he thus concludes, means 'the rapid which is free (of water)'. The transcription of *volĭnyi* as βουλνη- is interpreted by Falk as evidence that the weak ĭ (ь) in non-final positions had disappeared in East Slavonic by the middle of the 10th cent. (in Greek it would have been rendered as ε or as ου), and that an early stage in the phonetic development *o* > *u* > *i*, characteristic of the Ukrainian language, had already been reached by that time (as instanced in the transcription of *o* as ου).

Falk's interpretation of this name has been criticized by Ekblom (*Die siebente Strom-schnelle*, 169–71), who points out with justice that Falk's arbitrary change in the sequence of the names of the rapids has no basis in fact: *cf.* Shevelov 511. It is hard to believe that the name *Vil'nyi* (*Vol'noy, Vol'ny*), which since the 17th cent. has invariably designated the last, *i.e.* the most southerly, of the rapids, should ever have been applied to the fifth rapid, which lay 26 km. upstream. Ekblom reverts to the 'wave theory' and suggests that Βουλνηπράχ may well have been derived from 'a South East-Slavonic' form **Vŭlni(hŭ)-prah(ŭ)*. (For the possibility that the Slavonic form of this name in the 10th cent. contained a labio-velar ł, see also Selishchev 311.) In this case, Falk's linguistic conclusions would have no relevance: the Slavonic ŭ (ъ) was transcribed in Greek as ου, and the name never contained any ĭ (ь). The name Βουλνηπράχ, like Βαρουφόρος, means 'die Wogenstromschnelle'.

Pace Falk, there can be no doubt that the rapid Βαρουφόρος/Βουλνηπράχ is the one known in more recent times as *Volnigsky, Volneg* (Ukrainian *Vovnih*): *cf.* Miller 26. For the various forms of this name see Falk 19, 28, 32. It lay about 14 km. downstream from *Nenasytets*, and was one of the largest of the rapids; it consisted of four ridges and covered a distance of 576 m. by the right bank and 501 m. by the left: its fall was 2·4 m.: see Evarnitsky 39 (Falk 28); *cf. Dneprovskie Porogi* 583; Belyavsky 800; Timonoff 68, 80.

9/59 διότι μεγάλην λίμνην ἀποτελεῖ.

It is not clear why the name 'the wave-rapid' should be given to a rapid 'because it forms a large lake'. Lehrberg (366–7) therefore proposed the emendation from λίμνην to δίνην, 'a whirlpool'. This was accepted, as approximating more closely to the rapid's name, by Thomsen (*Relations*, 64), Niederle (*Slovanské Starožitnosti*, I, 4, 109) and by Shakhmatov and Krims'ky in their Ukrainian translation of c. 9 (*Zbirnik Istor.-Filolog. Viddilu Ukraïn. Akad. Nauk*, XII, 1924, 138, note 1). However, Malitsky, in his notes to Latyshev's Russian translation of c. 9, points out that there were no special grounds for singling out the whirlpool of this particular rapid, whose fall was considerably less than that of *Nenasytets*. He proposes to retain λίμνην, translates this (following Laskin 71, 73) as *zavod'*, 'creek' or 'backwater', and mentions the existence of a small harbour by the exit from the rapid: Latyshev-Malitsky 56, note 24; *cf.* Likhachev, *Povest'*, II, 216. But the problem cannot be said to have been solved. *Cf.* Kleiber 85–6.

9/61–2 τὸν ἔκτον φραγμόν . . . Λεάντι.

The name Λεάντι is quite clear. It is a Scandinavian present participle, formed like Γελανδρί (see on 9/43–5). It corresponds to the Old Swedish participle *le(i)andi*, from *lea*, 'to laugh' (*cf.* Old Norse *hlæjandi*), which, as Falk has pointed out, was an onomatopoeia. The 'Russian' name of the rapid thus means 'the Laughing'. See Thomsen, *Relations*, 65; Miller 27; Sahlgren 318; *cf.* Falk 183–8, 253–4. Thomsen plausibly suggests that this rapid 'may have been so called both from its rippling or babbling sound and from the glittering or sparkling of the foam'. *Cf.* G. B. Ravndal (*Stories of the East-Vikings*, Minneapolis (1938), 92): 'Number 6 vaunts the name of Leanti or "Laughing", corresponding to the Minnehaha of America's Indians. Seemingly, they were a dauntless, rollicking crowd, those early river-men . . . who first baptized the rapids of the Dnieper.'

9/62 Βερούτζη, ὅ ἐστιν 'βράσμα νεροῦ'.

The Slavonic name of the sixth rapid is semantically linked to its 'Russian' name. Βερούτζη is generally acknowledged to be a transcription of the East Slavonic participle *vĭrūčii* (вьручии) from vĭrěti, 'to boil, to bubble'. The name thus means 'the boiling, or bubbling, rapid', and approximates closely to βράσμα νεροῦ: here, as in the case of other rapids (*cf.* on 9/40–1, 43–5), the Greek expression is a free rather than a literal translation of the original name. See Thomsen, *Relations*, 64–5; Miller 27; Shakhmatov, *Vvedenie*, 89–90; Durnovo 206 and note 2; Latyshev-Malitsky 56, note 25; Falk 188–91, 253. *Cf.* Vasmer (*Zeitschr. f. slav. Phil.* 28 (1959), 98), who criticizes Kleiber's attempt (*ibid.* 90–1 and *Scando-Slavica* 5 (1959) 143–7) to relate Βερούτζη to the Slavonic *ruchey*, 'a stream'. The Slavonic *ch* (*č*) is quite regularly transcribed in *DAI* as τζ: see on 9/6–7; *cf.* Durnovo 206; Skok 227, note 1. As for ε, it seems to do duty for ĭ (ь) that had not yet disappeared from the Slavonic name: see Ekblom, *Die siebente Stromschnelle*, 169. *Cf.*, however, Shevelov 512–4.

Commentators have not always agreed in identifying Λεάντι/Βερούτζη. Thomsen tentatively identified it with the *Tavolzhansky*, mentioned in the 16th and 17th cents., and situated between the *Budilovsky* and the *Lishny* rapids, near the island that bore its name: *cf.* Falk 18–20; map p. 39. But the *Tavolzhansky* was not a proper rapid, and it is not even marked on recent maps. Falk (191, 235) leans uncertainly towards the view that the sixth rapid is the *Volnigsky* (or *Vovnih*): but this cannot be accepted, as the latter rapid must be Βαρουφόρος/Βουλνηπράχ (see on 9/58–9). It seems most satisfactory to identify Λεάντι/Βερούτζη with the *Budilo* or *Budilovsky* rapid: see Evarnitsky 39–40 (Falk 28); and map p. 39. It lay about 5½ km. downstream from the *Volnigsky*, consisted of two ridges, and was 399 m. long by the right bank and 218 m. by the left; its fall was 1 m. It was one of the dangerous rapids. See Evarnitsky, *ibid.*; Belyavsky 800; Yuzhny 406.

9/64 τὸν ἕβδομον φραγμόν . . . Στρούκουν.

Cobet's edition of c. 9 (1876: see on 9/45–6) restored the correct reading Στρούκουν, which is found in the Paris ms. (Falk 281), in place of the faulty Στρούβουν of the Vatican ms. (Falk 291), given by all previous editions. See Thomsen, *Relations*, 144; Falk 207. For the common confusion between β and κ in Greek minuscule, see *Byzantinoturcica*, II, 56 (2nd ed. 47).

Στρούκουν is fairly generally derived from the Old Swedish (or Old Norse) *Strukum*, the dative plural of *struk(a)* or *struke*, meaning 'a rapid current in a river, especially where it is narrow' (Thomsen), 'Verengung im Flusslauf, kleine Stromschnelle' (Falk), 'Stromstrich' (Ekblom.) The dative case was a locative one, and the Old Swedish original may have read *at* (*ā*) *Strukum*. Such locatives occur in large numbers in Viking place-names, not only in Scandinavia but also in England and Scotland. Another instance of a locative dative is provided by Οὐλβορσί (see on 9/39–40). The substitution of the Greek ending ουν for *um* can be explained by the natural aversion of Greek classicizing writers from a word ending in μ (*cf. Byzantinoturcica*, II, 47; 2nd ed. 39): in accordance with the practice of hellenizing foreign proper names by adapting them to the Greek system of declension, a practice commonly resorted to in *DAI*, *Strukum* was transcribed as Στρούκουν, a form which would have suggested a neuter singular. See Thomsen, *Relations*, 144–5; Falk 207–17, 254; Ekblom, *Die siebente Stromschnelle*, 153–6, 161, 165–6.

A somewhat different explanation of Στρούκουν is given by Sahlgren (318–20), who derives it from the Old Swedish word *strukn, 'a stream, a small waterfall'. He suggests that a second *u* was added to the name in the Greek transcription for phonetic reasons, and draws attention to the concordance of meaning between 'a small waterfall' and the Greek μικρὸς φραγμός: *cf.* Vasmer, *Wikingerspuren*, 669. Ekblom, however (*Die siebente Stromschnelle*, 166, note 1), points out that the word *strukn is nowhere attested. For other explanations, see Latyshev-Malitsky 56, note 26; Falk 192–206.

The precise meaning of *Strukum*/Στρούκουν is a matter of dispute between Falk and

Ekblom. The former (207–17, 254), largely, it seems, in order to bring the sense of this word into full accord with his explanation of the Slavonic name of this rapid, Ναπρεζή, *Ναστρεζή (see on 9/65), extends the meaning of *Strukum* to include not only 'the small rapids' or 'the narrow places where the current is rapid', but also 'the area surrounding the rapids or narrow places'. The difference may appear comparatively slight; but Ekblom (*Die siebente Stromschnelle*, 153–4, 166), while accepting Falk's etymology of Στρούκουν, will not agree to any such extension of meaning: *Strukum*, he insists, could in this context mean only 'Stromstrich' (or more precisely 'den Stromstrichen'), but not 'Stromstrich mit anliegendem Gebiet'.

9/65 Ναπρεζή.

The name Ναπρεζή has caused commentators much trouble. In this form it has proved to be an insoluble conundrum, and those who have tried to solve it have been driven to emend the text: see Falk 192–206. It was not until 1951 that Falk's *Dneprforsarnas Namn* fully explored the promising line on this problem proposed by him in 1944. He suggested the reading Ναστρεζή, and showed on palaeographical grounds how στ could have been mistaken for π. The root of this word, in his opinion, is the Old Church Slavonic feminine noun *streži* (стрежь), meaning 'the rapid current of a river, that part of the river where the current is most rapid and impetuous': cf. Sreznevsky, *s.v.* стрьжьнъ'; Vasmer, *Russisches etymologisches Wörterbuch s.v. strezh*.

Falk's interpretation (217–22, 254–5), apart from its simplicity, has the great merit of establishing a close semantic relation between the Slavonic and 'Russian' names of the seventh rapid, since *streži* and *struk(a)* are synonyms (see on 9/64). The next step, however, proved somewhat harder, as the exact relationship between *streži* and Ναστρεζή was difficult to establish. Falk suggested that Ναστρεζή corresponds to *Nastrežje (from an earlier *Nastrežije), which he rendered as 'the area surrounding the rapid and narrow current (*streži*)'. This view was searchingly criticized by Ekblom (*Die siebente Stromschnelle*, 151–4, 156–67, 174), who pointed out that, contrary to Falk's belief, the name *Strukum*, which is identical with *streži* but not synonymous with the area surrounding it, is by no means a synonym of *Nastrežije*. In attempting to explain Ναστρεζή, he argues, one should start not from the hypothetical derivative *Nastrežije, but from the well attested, basic form *streži*. He shows that in Germanic languages place-names with nominative meanings commonly occurred in medieval times in the form of locative datives preceded by prepositions governing the locative case; and he suggests that the form Ναστρεζή (*Nastrezi*) may similarly be a compound of the Slavonic preposition *na* ('on', 'at') and *streži*, a locative of *streži*. It is thus possible, he claims, that a Slav-speaking Northman, when questioned by the author as to the name of the rapid, may have replied in his own language '*Heitir at (ā) Strukum*' ('it is called *Strukum*'), and have added in Slavonic, when giving the other name, '*Imenujetй sę na Streži*' ('it is called *Streži*'). In this manner, Ekblom believes, the Slavonic name *Streži* (стрежь) was accidentally recorded by the author of c. 9 as *na Streži* and transcribed as Ναστρεζή.

Though the exact relationship between Ναστρεζή and *streži* may remain controversial, it is Falk's great merit to have restored the first of these terms to the correct Greek transcription of the Slavonic name of the seventh rapid, and to have notably advanced our understanding of its meaning by revealing the Slavonic root that for so long remained hidden within it.

It has not been possible to identify Στρούκουν/Ναστρεζή with certainty. It has generally been identified either with the penultimate (eighth) or with the last (ninth) rapid, known in modern times as *Lishny* and *Vil'ny* (*Vol'noy*) respectively. *Lishny* is favoured by Lehrberg (373), Thomsen (*Relations*, 66), and Evarnitsky (40; Falk 29); *Vil'ny* by Ravdonikas(614), and Kudryashov (see his map of the rapids, III, 12). Falk takes Στρούκουν/Ναστρεζή to be the narrow fairway below the *Vil'ny* rapid and above *Kichkas* 'the ford of Krarion': see on 9/66): Falk 213–4, 235. Cf. Karlgren 81; Kleiber 94–5.

Lishny was situated 15 km. downstream from *Budilo*; its length was 469 m. by the right bank, and 186 m. by the left; its fall was only 40 cm.: this, coupled with the fact that its fairway was relatively unimpeded by stones, could well justify the epithet 'μικρὸς' φραγμός. See Evarnitsky 40 (Falk 29); Belyavsky 800; Timonoff 68–9. *Vil'ny* or *Vol'noy* lay 6 km. downstream from *Lishny*, and consisted of six ridges; its length was 990 m. by the right bank and 811 m. by the left; its fall was 2·90 m. The shallow water and an abundance of stones and rocky islands in this sector of the river made the *Vil'ny* a dangerous rapid: in a particularly difficult spot was a narrow passage known as *Vovche horlo* ('the wolf's gullet'), later used by the rafts of the Cossacks to sail between two small islands close to the right bank. See Evarnitsky 40 (Falk 29); Lehrberg 374–7; *Dneprovskie Porogi*, 583; Belyavsky 800; Timonoff 69, 96; and map in Falk *ad fin.*

9/66 εἰς τὸ λεγόμενον πέραμα τοῦ Κραρίου.

This is by common consent identified with the ford of *Kichkas*, mentioned from the late 16th cent. onwards, and situated about 15 km. downstream from *Vil'ny*, the last rapid. For references to Kichkas and for different forms of the name, see Falk, Πέραμα τοῦ κραρίου 107–10.

A few kilometres downstream from the last rapid, the Dnieper, which, save for a westerly bend between *Nenasytets* and *Budilo*, had been flowing through the area of the rapids in a north-south direction, abruptly altered course and made a sharp bend towards the south-west. At the same time the river-bed, which at the last rapid was about 1 km. wide, suddenly narrowed between the bend and Kichkas to a mere 183 m. The curve in the river-bed, the enormous rocks that protruded from the water by the right bank, and the current flowing with considerable force towards the left bank, made this passage particularly hazardous. The river banks, high in the whole area of the rapids, here rose precipitously to form a narrow gorge flanked on both sides by steep cliffs reaching to a height of 75 m. See Lehrberg 332; *Dneprovskie Porogi* 583; Semenov 80; Belyavsky 801.

Attempts were made to explain the expression πέραμα τοῦ Κραρίου by deriving the latter of these terms from either the Turko-Tatar or the Armenian languages; but, as Falk (Πέραμα τοῦ κραρίου 110–12) has pointed out, they are unconvincing. His own explanation is simple; it can be supported by sound palaeographic and linguistic arguments, and agrees well with the topography of this section of the river. He proposes to read πέραμα τοῦ *βραρίου. The letters β and κ were often confused in Greek minuscule writing: see on 9/64. According to Falk, πέραμα τοῦ *βραρίου goes back to an Old Swedish *Vrár færia: the form vrár, genitive of vrá, 'an angle, a corner', was, in accordance with the Byzantine custom of hellenizing foreign loan-words, given the Greek ending -ιον; while færia, 'ferry', was naturally translated as πέραμα. Both these Old Swedish words, he shows, are frequently found in Scandinavian place-names, and notably, in the forms *wray* and *ferry*, in England. And finally he points out that *Vrá* names are mainly found by river-bends and confluences: a significant fact when related to the position of πέραμα τοῦ *βραρίου, 'the ford of the bend', just by the sudden and spectacular curve of the Dnieper: see map p. 39. But see Vasmer, *Zeitschr. f. slav. Phil.* 29 (1961), 379–81.

9/66–7 ἐν ᾧ διαπερῶσιν ... ἐπὶ Χερσῶνα.

The Kichkas ford, it appears from this passage, was a kind of main junction on the road from Kiev to the South. Here the land-route from Cherson forked off in a southward direction from 'the Greek route', which led by water down the lower Dnieper to the Black Sea: see on 9/7–8. Here both the Chersonites returning home from Russia and the Pechenegs on their way to the Crimea crossed over from the right to the left bank of the river. This route from Kiev to Cherson must be one of the two roads, mentioned at 42/84–6, along which the Pechenegs are said to 'pass through' on their journey to the

Crimea; and it seems likely that the Russians too, when travelling to Black Bulgaria and Chazaria (*cf.* 42/76–7), crossed the Dnieper at the ford of Kichkas. In all probability, therefore, this ford was also an important landmark on the trade-route that linked Kiev with the Don, with the lower Volga and with Tmutarakan' (Ταμάταρχα).

This land-route over the Kichkas ford was an alternative to the longer, though commercially more convenient, waterway from Kiev to Cherson which led down the Dnieper to its estuary, and thence eastward over the Black Sea. For this route, see Spitsyn, in *Sbornik statey, posvyashchennykh S. F. Platonovu* (St Petersburg, 1911), 243–5. Its latter section, between the mouth of the Dnieper and Cherson, is mentioned at 42/69–71. The land-route over the Kichkas ford retained its importance for several centuries. The Russians used it until the early 13th cent. for trading through Cherson with Constantinople: see Vasiliev, *Economic Relations*, 326–7. In the 16th and 17th cents. Kichkas was known as 'the Tatar ford': see Falk, Πέραμα τοῦ κραρίου 108.

Direct economic and diplomatic relations between Kiev and Cherson are attested in the 10th cent.: see Vasiliev, *Economic Relations*, 326–8; Likhachev, *Povest'*, II, 219. As for the Pechenegs, who at this time controlled the entire lower course of the Dnieper, they had many occasions to use the Kichkas ford: when crossing over to the left bank of the river at the beginning of every summer (8/34–5); while accompanying Byzantine diplomatic agents from Cherson to Western Patzinacia (7/1–8); when 'performing services' for Chersonites and for the emperor in Russia (6/4–5); or when acting as middlemen in the trade between Russia and Cherson: for it may be presumed that the wax which the Chersonites obtained from the Pechenegs and sold in Byzantium (53/530–2) came from Russia: see on 9/32.

9/67–8 ἔχον τὸ αὐτὸ πέραμα . . . ὅσον τοῦ ἱπποδρομίου.
Recent excavations have revealed that the width of the Hippodrome was 117·50 m., the tiers included: see *Preliminary Report upon the excavations carried out in the Hippodrome of Constantinople in 1927 on behalf of the British Academy* (by S. Casson and others; London, 1928), 3–8; E. Mamboury, Th. Wiegand, *Die Kaiserpaläste von Konstantinopel* (Berlin and Leipzig, 1934), 40; E. Mamboury, *The Tourists' Istanbul* (Istanbul, 1953), 355. The width of the actual course has been calculated, with slight variations, to have been between 72·50 and about 75 m. See Vogt, *Byzantion*, 10 (1935), 472–3; Vogt, Commentaire II, 114 ff. and plan *ad fin.*; Latyshev-Malitsky 57, note 28. Levasseur de Beauplan (see on 9/16–19), describing the Kichkas ford, said that, 'there the Channel cannot be above 150 paces over' (*Churchill's Voyages*, I, 579). According to Belyavsky (801), the width of the Dnieper by Kichkas was 86 *sazheni* (that is, 183·52 m.). These figures, the first of which is obviously approximate, do not differ much from that established for the Hippodrome by modern archaeologists.

9/68–70 τὸ δὲ ὕψος . . . ἐκεῖσε.
The text as it stands is a hopeless conundrum and clearly requires to be emended. The offending words are παρακύπτουσιν οἱ φίλοι. A popular emendation proved to be that proposed by Banduri in his edition of 1711: ὀφθαλμοί instead of φίλοι. He translated: 'altitudinem vero ab inferiori parte quantum oculi perspicere possunt' (*MPG*, CXIII, col. 175). But this reading is neither logically nor syntactically satisfactory, and was aptly criticized by Malitsky (Latyshev-Malitsky 57, note 29). But Malitsky's own retention of the unsatisfactory φίλοι renders his own version of the passage, to say the least, obscure: see also Likhachev, *Povest'*, II, 216).

The only emendation so far suggested that (*pace* Dujčev, *BZ*, 46, 1953, 121) makes sense of the passage is that of Jenkins (see Vol. I, p. 61, apparatus): he proposes to read προκύπτουσιν ὕφαλοι, 'underwater (rocks) project', and suggests the following translation for 9/67–70: 'this ford is as wide as the Hippodrome and, measured upstream from the bottom as far as the rocks break surface, a bow-shot in length'. We would thus have here the latitudinal and longitudinal measurements of the πέραμα. Such ὕφαλοι (sc. λίθοι), whose jagged or rounded summits projected above the surface of the water, were found in large numbers all over the area of the rapids (see on 9/24); and it is noteworthy that a particularly large rock called Shkola is marked on the map of the rapids at what appears to be a distance of 100 m. from the ford: see Falk 214 and map ad fin. By what is surely a curious coincidence, Levasseur de Beauplan in his notes on the Kichkas ford (Churchill's Voyages, I, 579) wrote: 'I have seen Polanders with a Bow shoot across the River, and the Arrow has fallen above 100 paces beyond the Bank.'

9/70-1   "Οθεν καὶ . . . πολεμοῦσι τοὺς 'Ρῶς.

It seems clear that this passage was used as a source for 2/16-23: see General Introduction p. 2; Introductory Note pp. 18, 20; cf. Macartney 145. It should be noted, however, that 2/16-23 shows the Pechenegs attacking while the Russians are porting their ships round a rapid, and must hence have been based also on 9/47-55.

The Russian sources clearly show that in the 10th cent. relations between the Russians and Pechenegs were close, in peace as well as in war. The *Primary Chronicle* refers to hostilities between the two in the years 920, 968, 971-2, 988, 992 and 997 (*Povest'*, I, 32, 47, 52-3, 83, 84-5, 87-8; Cross 71, 85, 90, 119-20, 122-3); and to peaceful relations in 915, 944, 968 (*Povest'*, I, 31, 33-4, 48; Cross 71, 72-3, 86). The same dual relationship is suggested in *DAI*, notably in c. 9. The deadly peril to the Kievan state presented by the Pechenegs, who so often threatened to cut the trade-route to Byzantium, Russia's economic life-line, is only too apparent from such passages as 9/50, 70-1, 93-4, 95-6, 103-4. Yet trade relations between the two are hinted at at 9/66-7 (see note *ad loc*); and if we consider the statement at 2/16-18 that the Russians are only able to travel to Constantinople when they are at peace with the Pechenegs, and relate it to the picture of regular traffic between Kiev and Byzantium painted in c. 9, we shall be forced to conclude that, at least in the middle of the 10th cent., peaceful relations between the Russians and their Turkic neighbours in the steppe were maintained for long periods at a time. As Parkhomenko (*Slavia*, VIII, 1 (1929), 138-44) has rightly pointed out, the Pechenegs, by controlling the Dnieper rapids, played a vital part in the fortunes of the Russian export trade.

In 1928, during the construction of the Dnieper dam, five swords were extracted from underneath the river-bed just opposite Kichkas, on the site of the πέραμα τοῦ Κραρίου. The workmanship of these swords and the Latin inscriptions on their blades suggested that they were made in the 10th cent., probably in Western Europe, and that they had belonged to a group of Vikings. V. I. Ravdonikas, who was the first to decipher the inscriptions, suggested that the swords had belonged to the Varangian retinue of Prince Svyatoslav of Kiev, who, on his return from Bulgaria in the spring of 972, was ambushed by the Pechenegs at the Dnieper rapids and slain in battle (*Povest'*, I, 52-3; Cross 90). Evidence supplied by the find that these swords had been simultaneously immersed in the Dnieper, suggesting a sudden catastrophe, together with the striking concordance between the Chronicle story and the passage at 9/70-1, certainly give support to this hypothesis: see Ravdonikas 598-616; cf. Kul'tura drevney Rusi, I, 328-9.

9/72   τὴν νῆσον, τὴν ἐπιλεγομένην ὁ Ἅγιος Γρηγόριος.

A few km. downstream from Kichkas, opposite the site of the modern Zaporozh'e, lay the island of St Gregory, known to the Russians as *Khortitsa*. For this island, see Brun, *Chernomor'e*, II, 363-79; Vasmer, *Wikingerspuren*, 669. It was about 11 km. in length; its greatest width was slightly over 2 km. Flanked on the north, east and south by high cliffs rising at times to 20 m., it lay in the middle of the river 'like a gigantic ship cleaving the waters of the Dnieper' (Brun 364). The river itself, which had gradually widened and deepened after Kichkas, and whose banks were now much lower, assumed at this point the appearance it had had above the rapids (see Belyavsky 801). The island of *Khortitsa* was used in the following centuries by the Russians as a base for their campaigns against the Polovtsy and the Mongols: see *Povest'*, I, 183–4; Cross 200–1 (ann. 1103); *Polnoe Sobranie Russkikh Letopisey*, VII, 130 (ann. 1223: in this source, the *Voskresenskaya Letopis'*, Khortitsa is called 'the Varangian island'). In Brun's opinion, the island was given the name of St Gregory by the Byzantines after St Gregory the Illuminator, the apostle of Armenia.

9/73–8 ἐν ᾗ νήσῳ . . . ἐάσειν αὐτούς.

In performing their pagan rites on the island, the Russians presumably expressed both their thankfulness and relief at having completed the most dangerous part of the journey and their hopes of a safe passage from Khortitsa to Constantinople. The nature of these rites is a matter of some dispute: the fact that some of them are attested among the Scandinavians may suggest that we have here an account of Viking sacrifices (Mansikka 323–4). On the other hand, the description also tallies well with our knowledge of Slavonic pagan ritual (Gedeonov 547–51).

(i). Oak-trees seem to have played an important part in Slavonic paganism, notably in Russia. The trees under which the pagans were said to pray in the 'Statute of Vladimir I' (*Pamyatniki*, 245, 251), and which, in a later source, they were alleged to worship (N. M. Karamzin, *Istoriya Gosudarstva Rossiiskogo*, I (St Petersburg, 1892, note 216), were probably oaks (*cf.* Mansikka 244–5). In the 12th cent. Helmold described some sacred oaks consecrated to a divinity of the Baltic Slavs (*Chronica Slavorum*, tr. F. J. Tschan, New York, 1935, 218). An oak-tree which 'had lived for thousands of years' and was 'of colossal width' was described on this same island by a Russian traveller in 1876. It had died a few years previously, and was thought to have been the traditional meeting-place of the Zaporog Cossacks: see Laskin 73, note 297.

(ii). The slaughtering of cocks and/or hens for sacrificial purposes is ascribed to pagan Russians in several sources: see *Pamyatniki drevne-russkoy tserkovno-uchitel'noy literatury*, III (St Petersburg, 1897), 224, 227; *cf.* *Kul'tura Drevney Rusi*, II, 72. Ibn Fadlan, in his celebrated account of a Russian ship-burial on the Volga in the 10th cent., describes the ritual killing of a cock and a hen which were thrown into the funeral ship: *Puteshestvie Ibn-Fadlana na Volgu*, tr. I. Yu. Krachkovsky (Moscow-Leningrad, 1939), 82. Leo Diaconus (149/22–4) tells us that during the siege of Silistria in 971 the Russians in Svyatoslav's army sacrificed cocks by throwing them into the Danube. Finally, Thietmar of Merseburg (*MGH*, Scr., n. s. IX, 24/5) refers to the practice of sacrificing cocks which existed in Lederun (Lejre) in Denmark.

(iii). Arrows, and weapons in general, were used by the Russians as sacred objects in their pagan ritual: see Likhachev, *Povest'*, II, 290. In 907, when concluding their treaty with the empire, the Russians took the oath on their weapons 'in accordance with the Russian religion': *Povest'*, I, 25; Cross 65. In 944 they ratified the treaty with Byzantium by ritually laying down their weapons before the statue of Perun, the pagan god of the Slavs, in Kiev: *Povest'*, I, 38–9; Cross 77; *cf.* Mansikka 29–38. The arrows, pegged in the ground in a circle (9/74–5), were probably used for divination: similar use was made of spears by the Baltic Slavs: see Thietmar of Merseburg, *ed. cit.*, 302/25 ff.

(iv). Both the Slavs and the Northmen offered food to their pagan divinities. The 'Sermon of a certain Lover of Christ', written in Kievan Russia against the remnants of paganism, refers to the custom of setting meals in front of idols, which meals included loaves of bread: see *Pamyatniki drevne-russkoy tserkovno-uchitel'noy literatury*, III, 227; Mansikka 147–60. Ibn Fadlan relates that the Russians in the first half of the 10th cent. placed meals of bread, meat, onion, milk and intoxicating drink before wooden effigies of their gods: *Puteshestvie na Volgu*, tr. Krachkovsky, 79. Finally, the 'History of St Olaf' in the *Heimskringla*, describing the idol of Thor, states: 'four loaves of bread are brought to him,

5—D.A.I.

and meat withal': *Heimskringla*, tr. E. Monsen and A. H. Smith (Cambridge, 1932), 331.

It seems that boatmen and sailors of all times were accustomed, after passing through the Dnieper rapids, to express at this stage of their journey their thankfulness and relief in their several and characteristic ways. A Russian traveller who in 1880 was taken down the rapids on a raft relates that after passing Budilo, the last dangerous rapid (see on 9/62), the pilots stood in a circle and sang a prayer (Yuzhny 406). In recent times too the Dnieper pilots would come ashore at Kichkas and shout in chorus 'davay horilku!', that is, 'bring the vodka!': see Falk 13, note 6.

It is quite possible that in the middle of the 10th cent. the island of St Gregory, during these brief halts of the Russian flotillas, may also have echoed the sound of Christian prayers: we know that by 944 there were already many Christians in Kiev, notably among the Varangians (*Povest'*, I, 38-9; Cross 77); and C. himself (*De Cer.*, 579/21) refers to οἱ βαπτισμένοι 'Ρῶς.

9/78-9 'Ἀπὸ δὲ τοῦ νησίου τούτου . . . τὸν Σελινάν.

For the Selinas, see on 9/92-3. The words οὐ φοβοῦνται are puzzling, in view of the later statement that the Pechenegs keep pace with the Russians until they are past the Selinas, in the hope that one of their *monoxyla* will be wrecked on the shore (9/93-6). Meursius, accordingly, in his edition of 1611 (see Vol. I, pp. 23-4), omitted the negative particle οὐ. But this is inadmissible on logical grounds, since the Russians had begun to fear the Pechenegs long before they reached the Island of St Gregory. The passage probably means that the danger of Pecheneg attacks, which had been particularly acute by *Nenasytets* (9/50) and the πέραμα (9/70-1), subsided between the Island of St Gregory and the mouth of the Danube: the Dnieper below St Gregory was too wide and its banks too low to allow the Pechenegs effectively to attack or to shoot at the Russians; the Island of St Aitherios was probably under some form of Byzantine protectorate (see on 9/82); and for most of the time between the mouth of the Dnieper and the Selinas the Russians were out at sea. However, as 9/94-6 shows, the Pechenegs could still be a real danger during the voyage to the mouth of the Danube, in the event of the Russian flotilla's being driven ashore by bad weather.

9/82 ἡ νῆσος τοῦ 'Ἁγίου Αἰθερίου.

The Island of St Aitherios is the small island of Berezan', 856 m. long and a mere 350 m. wide, lying in the large estuary common to the Dnieper and the southern Bug, 5 km. from the mainland. Its importance in the 10th cent. was due to the fisheries of the Chersonites in the mouth of the Dnieper, to the strategic value offered by this estuary to the Byzantines, and to its rôle as a station and emporium on the trade-route to Byzantium. Two special clauses of the Russo-Byzantine treaty of 944 inhibit the Russians from interfering with the Chersonite fisheries at the mouth of the Dnieper and from spending the winter on the Island of St Aitherios on the return journey from Constantinople: *Povest'*, I, 37; Cross 76.

In 1905 a Swedish Runic inscription was discovered on the island, which reads: 'Grani erected this mound in memory of Karl, his comrade'. There is little doubt that these two names belonged to Northmen who had stopped at Berezan' on their way to or from Constantinople, and the second of whom was buried there by his comrade. The inscription has been tentatively dated to the 11th cent. See Brun, *Chernomor'e*, I, 90–108; Braun, *Izvestiya Imperatorskoy Arkheologicheskoy Kommissii*, 23 (1907), 66–75; Cleve, *Eurasia Septentrionalis Antiqua*, 4 (1929), 250–62; Boltenko, *Arkheologiya*, I (Kiev, 1947), 39–51; Levchenko, *Russko-Vizantiiskie Otnosheniya*, 163, 303–4.

The distance by river from Kiev to the mouth of the Dnieper was 953 km. (see Soloviev, *Byzantion*, 13 (1938), 232); and from the Island of St Gregory (Khortitsa) to the Dnieper estuary, 347 km. (Timonoff 115).

9/84-6 Καὶ πάλιν . . . ἐπιφέρονται.

This is the third, and final, stage in the fitting of the *monoxyla*: cf. on 9/11–12, 9/16–19. In preparation for the long sea voyage, they are now equipped with sails, masts and rudders which the Russians have brought with them from Kiev.

9/89 τὸν Δάναστριν ποταμόν. Cf. 42/66–7.

9/91 τὸν ποταμὸν τὸν ἐπιλεγόμενον Ἄσπρον.

According to Niederle (*Slovanské Starožitnosti*, I, 4, 121), Ἄσπρος was a river in the basin of the Dniester. Its name was doubtless connected with the Ἄσπρον κάστρον mentioned at 37/60–1, known as *Belgorod* in Russian (*Akkerman* in Turkish, and *Cetatea Albă* in Rumanian), which stood on the southern shore of the estuary of the Dniester and was in the middle of the 10th cent. controlled by the Pechenegs. See Skok 242, note 1; Honigmann, *Byzantion*, 17 (1944–5), 160; Nasonov 138, 142.

9/92–3 τὸν Σελινάν . . . παρακλάδιον.

Generally identified as Sulina, the present name of the central of the three mouths that form the Danube delta, between the Kilia mouth in the north and the St George mouth in the south. See Seredonin 159; Skok 242; Bromberg, *Byzantion*, 13 (1938), 12–13. The word παρακλάδιον, a *hapax legomenon*, was translated by Meursius as 'divergium' and interpreted by Du Cange as 'ubi Danubius in ramos finditur'. Though it has been derived from a West Slavonic *překlad*, 'a ferry' (Gedeonov 534), it is surely more satisfactory to connect it with the Greek κλάδιον, κλάδος, 'a small branch': see Manojlović IV, 36. Indeed, it is found in MGr.

9/97–8 τὴν τῆς Βουλγαρίας γῆν . . . ἔρχονται.

The lower Danube formed at that time the northern frontier of Bulgaria: see S. Runciman, *A History of the First Bulgarian Empire* (London, 1930), 150, note 2, 160. On the other hand, we are told at 37/48 that Patzinacia was distant half a day's journey from Bulgaria. If taken literally, this statement would mean that in the middle of the 10th cent. the two countries were separated by a kind of no-man's-land several miles in depth.

Within Bulgarian territorial waters danger from the Pechenegs no longer existed. The Bulgarians could raise no objection to the voyage of Russian traders along their coast, for at this time they were close allies of the empire. The efficacy of this alliance was demonstrated in 941, when the Bulgarians warned the Byzantine authorities that a hostile Russian fleet was sailing past their coast to attack Constantinople: *Povest'*, I, 33; Cross 71–2.

9/99 εἰς τὸν Κωνοπάν.

There is a striking resemblance between this mysterious name and that of an island in the Danube delta which Pliny (*Nat. Hist.*, ed. Teubner, I, 336/15–16) called 'insula Conopon Diabasis'. Bromberg (*Byzantion*, 13, 1938, 11–12), pointing out this similarity, suggests that Κωνοπάς, or Κωνοπά, as he prefers to read, may be either the St George Island, between the Sulina and the St George mouths of the Danube, or Dranov Island, between the latter mouth and Lake Razelm.

9/99–100 εἰς Κωνστάντιαν . . . Βάρνας.

Κωνστάντια, later known as Constanza and Kustenje (Constanţa in Rumanian), is a town on the sea-coast of the Dobrudja. Varna was already then an important Bulgarian city. The river mentioned here, at whose mouth Varna lay, is known today as the Provadiya.

9/100–1 εἰς τὸν ποταμὸν τὴν Διτζίναν.

This river has been identified with the Βιτζίνα mentioned by Anna Comnena (VII, 3; ed. Reifferscheid, I, 233/17). The latter, known in antiquity as Πάνυσος (see Pauly-Wissowa, *RE, s. v.* Panysos) and in modern times as the Kamčiya or Kamčyk, flows into the Black Sea between Varna and Mesebr (Mesembria). Its medieval Slavonic name must have been either Dichina or Vichina. See Seredonin 159; Kulakovsky, *Viz. Vrem.*, 4 (1897), 319–22; G. I. Brătianu, *Recherches sur Vicina et Cetatea Albă* (Bucharest, 1935), 1–96; Bromberg, *Byzantion*, 13 (1937), 173–80; Bănescu, *Byzantion*, 12 (1938), 83–8; P. Ş. Năsturel, *Studii şi cercetări de Istorie Veche*, 8 (1957), 1–4, 295–305.

9/101 ἅπερ πάντα εἰσὶ γῆ τῆς Βουλγαρίας.

It is clear from 9/101–4 that the frontier between Bulgaria and the empire ran at this time along a line that reached the Black Sea between the Ditzina and Mesembria. This passage allows us to conclude that the coastal cities of Mesembria, Anchialus, Sozopolis and Agathopolis, which had belonged to Symeon's empire, were recovered by the Byzantines by the treaty of 927: see Runciman, *First Bulgarian Empire*, 180.

9/102–4 εἰς τὰ τῆς Μεσημβρίας μέρη . . . πλοῦς.

The Russians are here said to end their voyage at Mesembria. This probably means simply that they are now within Byzantine waters and are thus safe. The safety of Russian merchant ships in these waters was expressly guaranteed by the treaty of 911: *Povest'*, I, 27; Cross 67.

9/104–5 Ἡ δὲ χειμέριος . . . αὕτη.

It was suggested in the Introductory Note to this chapter (p. 19) that 9/104–13 is probably a separate account, derived from a Slavonic source, which was joined to the preceding, longer section of c. 9 at the time when the material for this chapter was collected and sorted in the office of the λογοθέτης τοῦ δρόμου in Constantinople. This fragment, which describes how the Russians levied tribute from the Slavs during the winter months, is linked chronologically to the early part of c. 9 which tells of the labour performed by the Slavs in cutting and preparing the *monoxyla* in the winter (9/11). Its position as an appendix, or at the most a kind of explanatory footnote, is only saved from being redundant and illogical by its implication that at least part of the tribute collected by the Russians from their Slav subjects during the winter was shipped to Byzantium in the *monoxyla* in the spring. It is clear that an attempt was made by some editorial hand to relate the second passage to the first: see Introductory Note p. 20.

An attempt to define the differences between 9/3–104 and 9/104–13 was made by Manojlović (IV, 41–4). Some of his remarks are discerning and helpful; but his main contentions, that 9/3–104 describes the northern Russians whose centre was Novgorod, while 9/104–13 is centred on Kiev as the capital of Russia, and that 9/3–104 refers to an earlier period, perhaps even to the late 9th cent., cannot be accepted (*cf.* Levchenko, *Russko-vizantiiskie otnosheniya*, 204–5, who in some measure accepts his theses). There is no evidence to show that 9/104–13 was composed later than the first section, which was probably written about 944 (Introductory Note p. 18). The position occupied by Kiev in the two sections is rather the reverse of what Manojlović considered it to be: in 9/3–104 Kiev is the true centre of Russia, and upon this city, from the most distant parts of Russia, the *monoxyla* converge; it seems more likely, therefore, that the whole of this section is based on the verbal account of a Russian Varangian from Kiev, who witnessed and perhaps took part in the fitting out of the *monoxyla* in the city harbour, and who possessed first-hand and detailed knowledge on the itinerary to Constantinople. By contrast, 9/104–13 appears centrifugal: here the Russians are shown leaving Kiev and going on their 'rounds' over the dependent Slav territories. If we further observe that traces of Slavonic technical terminology are more numerous and striking in 9/104–13 than in any other part of c. 9 (Introductory Note p. 19), we may well be justified in concluding that this section originates in the account of a Slavonic observer who had personal experience of the tax-collecting methods of his Russian overlords.

9/106 ἄρχοντες μετὰ πάντων τῶν Ῥῶς.

The expression πάντες οἱ Ῥῶς, which here designates the aristocratic retinue, or *druzhina* (see Vernadsky, *Kievan Russia*, 137–40), of the princes (ἄρχοντες) of Kiev, is to all appearance a literal translation of the Slavonic idiom *vsya Rus'* (*cf. Povest'*, 1, 18, 52). This passage may be compared with the *Primary Chronicle*'s account of Igor setting out from Kiev in 944, accompanied by his *druzhina*, to collect tribute from the Derevlyanians: *Povest'*, 1, 39–40; Cross 78.

9/107 τὰ πολύδια, ὃ λέγεται γύρα.

πολύδια was taken by the earlier editors and commentators to be a diminutive of πόλις (*cf.* the alternative reading πολύδρια proposed by Meursius). Du Cange, accordingly, has the following entry *s.v.* πολύδιον: 'municipium, oppidum . . . Nisi legendum sit πολύδρια'. Banduri also translated πολύδια as 'oppida', giving πολύδρια as a possible variant (*MPG*, CXIII, col. 177). This explanation was accepted by Niederle (*Slavia*, VII, 4 (1929), 979–80).

As early as 1851, however, a different and much more satisfactory explanation of πολύδια was proposed by S. M. Soloviev (*Istoriya Rossii s drevneishikh vremen*, 1 (St Petersburg, 1894), 215–16): he recognized that this Greek *hapax legomenon* is simply the phonetic transcription of the Slavonic (Old Russian) word *polyudie* or *polyud'e*. *Polyudie* was a technical term, occuring fairly frequently in medieval Russian sources, which meant (i) the tribute collected by the princes from their subjects, and (ii) the journey, or circuit, undertaken by the prince round his lands in order to levy tribute, administer his realm and dispense justice: see Sreznevsky, Kochin, Vasmer (*Russisches etymologisches Wörterbuch*), *s.v. polyudie, polyud'e*. It is now generally accepted that πολύδια corresponds to the second meaning of *polyudie*, and that 9/105–7 refers to these 'circuits' undertaken by the Russian rulers and their retainers over the lands of their Slav subjects. See Vvedensky, *Izvestiya Obshchestva Arkheologii, Istorii i Etnografii pri Kazanskom Universitete*, XXII, 2 (1906), 149–63; Popov, *Byzantinoslavica*, 3 (1931), 92–6; and the valuable bibliographical survey of the question in Latyshev-Malitsky 57–8, note 34.

The evidence of Russian sources confirms and supplements the brief description of the *polyudie* given at 9/105–10. It generally took place in the autumn or winter (*Povest'*, 1, 39; Cross 78, ann. 945). The dues of the local population included both the maintenance of the prince and his retinue (*cf.* on 9/110) and contributions in kind, generally furs, honey and wax; some of these were subsequently exported to Byzantium. The tribute was collected from each homestead or from each tilling unit. The right of *polyudie* was occasionally granted by the princes to their more important retainers and companions in arms. Whenever the dues were collected by a subsidiary ruler, he was expected to retain one-third of the tribute for his personal use and to send the remaining two-thirds to Kiev (*Povest'*, 1, 43, 88–9; Cross 81, 124). See Vernadsky, *Kievan Russia*, 189–92; *Kul'tura Drevney Rusi*, 1, 305–6, 11, 13–14.

The practice of *polyudie*, which at its best was an onerous burden to the Slavonic population, and at its worst little different from organized robbery, cannot have been popular among the Slavs. It was on one of these foraging expeditions that Igor was killed by the furious Derevlyanians in 944 (*Povest'*, 1, 39–40; Cross 78). It is noteworthy that the system of *polyudie* seems to have been thoroughly overhauled in 946 or 947, that is, in all probability, a few years after c. 9 was written. The *Primary Chronicle* alludes to new regulations relating to taxes and tribute introduced by Princess Olga: *Povest'*, 1, 43; Cross 81–2. It has been plausibly suggested that the aim of Olga's financial and administrative reforms was to replace the periodic and arbitrary visitations by a more equitable system, whereby the taxes were to be locally collected at specially determined posts throughout the land and the amount of the contributions fixed in advance. See Grekov 180–2; Vernadsky, *Kievan Russia*, 39–40, 190; Kul'tura Drevney Rusi, II, 13–15; Levchenko, *Russko-vizantiiskie Otnosheniya*, 213–16. But there is no reason to think that Olga 'abolished the custom of poliudie' (Vernadsky, *Kievan Russia*, 39), still less that the information given about it in c. 9 is 'somewhat out of date' (Levchenko, *Russko-vizantiiskie otnosheniya*, 213).

The word γύρα, translated by Du Cange as 'circulationes, circuitiones', is clearly the Greek synonym of *polyudie*. It is obviously related to the adjective γυρός, 'round, circular', to the noun γῦρος, 'a circle', and to the adverb γυρόθεν, *cf.* 9/75. Commentators have varied in their grammatical analysis of the form γύρα: Popov (*Byzantinoslavica*, 3, 1931, 93–4) regards it as a neuter plural of the adjective γυρός, and, contrary to the readings of Paris and Vatican mss., places the accent on the second syllable; the passage would thus mean 'the πολύδια, which are called circular'. Stender-Petersen (*Varangica*, 162–3), on the other hand, takes γύρα, with better reason, to be a feminine singular noun, meaning 'a circuit'. This view has not only the advantage of retaining the parallelism of the two synonyms πολύδια and γύρα; it is also supported by a passage from the *Epanagoge*, whose relevance to 9/107 was already perceived by Nevolin (*Finnsky Vestnik*, 20 (1847), no. 8,1–10 = *Sobranie Sochineny* (St Petersburg (1859), 527), who, however, following Leunclavius (*Jus graeco-romanum*, II (1596), 92), wrongly ascribed it to the *Ecloga*. It reads: κελεύομεν μηδενὶ τῶν ἀρχόντων ἐξεῖναι χωρὶς ἀναγκαίας χρείας ἀποδημίας ποιεῖσθαι ἢ τὰς λεγομένας γύρας (*Epanag.*, VII, 8, ed. Zepos, *Jus graeco-romanum*, II (Athens, 1931), 250). It is clear that ἀποδημίας/τὰς λεγομένας γύρας are a pair of synonyms exactly corresponding to τὰ πολύδια, ὃ λέγεται γύρα, and that the meaning of γύρα is hence 'a circuit'. The singular form may be influenced by the fact that *polyudie* is a collective singular noun.

Stender-Petersen (*Varangica*, 151–64) has recently drawn attention to a passage from the *Heimskringla* which describes the activities of Harald Hadrada in Byzantium and Russia: the saga tells us that Harald had, while in Constantinople, gathered much wealth by going three times on *pólútasvarf* (ed. F. Jónsson (Copenhagen, 1911), 457). Stender-Petersen suggests that the difficult word *pólútasvarf*, which has been interpreted in various ways, is a compound formed from the Old Norse *svarf*, one of whose meanings is 'a circuit, a round', and from a transcription of *polyudie*. Thus, *pólútasvarf* is a tautology, similar to the synonymous tautologies ἀποδημία/γύρα and πολύδια/γύρα. He believes accordingly that the Scandinavian source which is at the origin of this passage of the Saga of Harald Hadrada in the *Heimskringla* stated that Harald had gone off three times on administrative and tax-gathering circuits (*polyudie*).

9/107–8   τῶν . . . Βερβιάνων.

The majority of commentators have proposed the reading Δερβιάνων, and have identified this Slav tribe as Derevlyanians (the *Derevlyane* of the *Primary Chronicle*), mentioned at 37/44 in the form Δερβλενίνοις: see Marquart 107; Manojlović IV, 40; Shakhmatov, *Vvedenie*, 90; Durnovo 206; Latyshev-Malitsky 58, note 35. The latter form is clearly derived from the Slavonic singular *Dervlyanín*, the former from the plural *Dervlyáne*.

This tribe lived to the west of the middle Dnieper, between the Pripet in the north and the Teterev in the south. In the first half of the 10th cent. they carried on a fierce struggle against the rulers of Kiev, which ended in their defeat by Olga (*c.* 945): *Povest'*, I, 39–43; Cross 78–81. For the Derevlyanians, see also Vernadsky, *Ancient Russia*, 323–4; Tret'yakov 245–51; I. P. Rusanova, *Sovetskaya Arkheologiya*, 1960, 1, 63–9.

9/108   τῶν Δρουγουβιτῶν.

These are the Dregovichians (the *Dregovichi* of the *Primary Chronicle*). They lived immediately north of the Derevlyanians, north of the Pripet river: see Vernadsky, *Ancient Russia*, 323–4; Tret'yakov 246–7. The name in this form corresponds to the Slavonic singular *Dregovitin*: *cf.* on 9/9–10, 9/107–8.

9/108 Κριβιτζῶν. See on 9/9–10.

9/108 τῶν Σεβερίων.
These are the Severians (the *Severyane* or *Sever* of the *Primary Chronicle*). Their homes lay to the east of the Dnieper, in the basins of the middle Desna, of the Seim and of the upper Sula: see Vernadsky, *Ancient Russia*, 316–19; Rybakov, *Sovetskaya Etnografiya*, 6–7 (1947), 81–95; Tret'yakov 242–4; Solov'eva, *Sovetskaya Arkheologiya*, 25 (1956), 138–70.

9/108–9 καὶ λοιπῶν Σκλάβων.
It has been observed that among the Slav tribes enumerated at 9/9–10, 9/107–9 and 37/44–5, no mention is made of the Polyanians (*Polyane*), a leading East Slavonic tribe which lived on the middle Dnieper and of whose territory Kiev was the principal city (see Vernadsky, *Ancient Russia*, 313–15; Rybakov, *Sovetskaya Etnografiya*, 6–7 (1947), 95–105). This fact has been interpreted by several historians to mean that in *DAI* the Polyanians are identified with οἱ ῾Ρῶς: see V. A. Parkhomenko, *U istokov russkoy gosudarstvennosti* (Leningrad, 1924), 54; Tikhomirov, *Sovetskaya Etnografiya*, 6–7 (1947), 77; Levchenko, *Russko-vizantiiskie otnosheniya*, 205–8. If this view is taken to mean that the ῾Ρῶς were Slavonic Polyanians, it is wholly unacceptable: see Nasonov 16, and on 9/1; for the Russians in *DAI* are very clearly distinguished from their Slav tributaries. On the other hand, the Polyanians appear to have been among the first of the East Slavonic tribes to lose their tribal name and to adopt the 'Russian' national appellation of their former Scandinavian overlords: they are mentioned for the last time in the Chronicle in 944 (*Povest'*, i, 33, ii, 240; Cross 72), and this source has an earlier, and significant, reference to 'the Polyanians, who are now called Rus'' (*Povest'*, i, 21; Cross 62). It seems quite possible that by the time c. 9 was written the tribal name of the Polyanians was no longer in current use and was hence passed over in silence by our author.

9/110 διατρεφόμενοι.
This word has every appearance of being a literal translation of an East Slavonic (Old Russian) verb, whose infinitive mood was *kormitisya*, meaning (i) 'to feed' or 'to be fed'; (ii) 'to be maintained'; hence the Old Russian technical terms *kormlenie*, 'the maintenance of officials at the expense of the population', 'the collection of tribute', and *korm*, 'the duty of the population to maintain officials': see Kochin, *s. vv. kormitisya, kormlenie, korm*. The term occurs in the form *pokorm*, in the *Primary Chronicle*, ann. 1018: *Povest'*, i, 97; Cross 132.

9/110–11 ἀπὸ μηνὸς Ἀπριλίου . . . ποταμοῦ.
For the dates when the ice melts at various points on the Dnieper, see Stuckenberg 268–82. At Smolensk the average date of melting is 1st April: Bernshtein-Kogan 270, note 56.

9/113 ῾Ρωμανίαν. *Cf.* Dölger, *BES*, 77 ff.

9/114 οἱ Οὖζοι.
The Uz (or Ghuz) were a Turkic nomadic people who in the 10th cent. lived northeast of the Caspian Sea, between the Volga and the Aral Sea; see Marquart 337–41; R. Grousset, *L'empire des steppes* (Paris, 1941), 240–1; *Byzantinoturcica*, i, 46–9 (2nd ed., 90–4), ii, 197 (2nd ed., 228). The illogical position of this note in c. 9 has often been pointed out: see Bury 520–1; Manojlović iv, 43; and Introductory Note p. 18. Macartney (146–7) convincingly suggests that this reference to the Uz was brought in from 37/5–8, where the Uz are said to have defeated the Pechenegs: 'therefore, C. argues, they can defeat them again'. *Cf.* Latyshev-Malitsky 58–9, note 36.

Cc. 10–13/1–11

BIBLIOGRAPHY

See bibliography to Cc. 37–42, below, pp. 142–3.

INTRODUCTORY NOTE

See above, p. 12.

10/3 Χαζάρους. See on 37/4.

10/4 ὁ ἐξουσιοκράτωρ 'Αλανίας.
For the title, see *De Cer.*, 688/2; Ostrogorsky, *Sem. Kond.*, 8 (1936), 52; Soloviev. *Byzantinoslavica*, 9 (1947), 34 and note 10. For the Alans, see J. Kulakovsky, *Alany po svedeiniyam klassicheskikh i vizantiiskikh pisateley* (Kiev, 1899).

10/5 τὰ ἐννέα κλίματα. We do not know exactly where this district lay.

11/8 Σάρκελ. See on 42/54–5

11/8 κλίματα . . . Χερσῶνα. See on 1/26, 28.

12/1 ἡ μαύρη λεγομένη Βουλγαρία.
Black Bulgaria is mentioned again at 42/77. Black Bulgars are referred to also in the *Russian Primary Chronicle* (ed. Cross and Sherbowitz-Wetzor, Cambridge, Mass., 1953), 76. The locality of Black Bulgaria is debatable. Some have thought that it was in the region of the Kuban (see G. Laskin, *Sochineniya Konstantina Bagryanorodnogo* (Moscow, 1899), 76; V. N. Zlatarsky, *Istoriya na Blgarskata Drzhava prez Srdnite Vekove*, I (Sofia, 1918), 114); others that it lay between the Dnieper and the Don (see Westberg, *Zapiski Imp. Akad. Nauk*, v, 2 (St Petersburg, 1901), 103, 107; Marquart 503; A. A. Vasiliev, *The Goths in the Crimea* (Cambridge, Mass., 1936), 101). It is however not probable that these Bulgars were identical with the so-called Volga Bulgars, well known to us from Arabic sources. See F. Brun, *Chernomor'e: Sbornik izsledovanii po istoricheskoy geografii Yuzhnoy Rossii*, I (Odessa, 1879), 31–2, 100, 107; Macartney, *Byz.-Neugr. Jhrb.*, 8 (1930–1), 150–8; A. P. Smirnov, *Volzhskie Bulgary* (Moscow, 1951).

13/3–8 τὰ τοιαῦτα ἔθνη. *Cf.* 40/41–4.

13/4 δυτικώτερον . . . βορειότερον.
The orientation is inaccurate. The Pechenegs lived to the north-east of the Turks. However, Manojlović (IV, 116) suggested that in C.'s work the expressions δυτικώτερον and βορειότερον mean respectively 'south-west' and 'north-east'.

13/5 πρὸς τὸ μεσημβρινὸν . . . Μοραβία.
This statement is quite at variance with the facts. Scholars have given different explanations. Bury (564) believed that the information derives from an older source, of the time of Leo VI, when the Magyars had not yet conquered Pannonia. Fehér (48–51) believed that C.'s statement is based on southern Slav tradition, according to which Svatopluk was ruler of a great southern Slav empire. Manojlović (IV, 106–13) was probably nearer the mark in seeing here the traces of a conception of a southern Moravia. His thesis is supported by an additional text, published by Lambros in *Néos Ἑλληνομνήμων*

9 (1912), 133: οἱ παρὰ τὸν Δούναβιν οἰκοῦντες Βούλγαροι, Μόραβοι, (Σέρβοι καὶ
Βλάχοι) καὶ Σλαῦοι τῆς Ἰλλυρίας ἦταν πεφωτισμένοι διὰ τοῦ ἀγίου βαπτίσματος περὶ
τὰ μέσα τοῦ θ' αἰῶνος ἐπὶ Μιχαὴλ αὐτοκράτορος καὶ τοῦ διασήμου πατριάρχου
Φωτίου. Here, then, we are dealing, not just with a series of names connected with the
river Morava, but with actual Μόραβοι, who are said to be living there. We believe therefore that C.'s source has simply confused the northern Moravia with the district of the
southern Moravians. (For an alternative solution of the puzzle, see General Introduction
p. 7.)

13/7–8 Οἱ δὲ Χρωβάτοι . . . παράκεινται.
These Croats are not, as some have supposed, the southern, but the northern Croats
(cf. vol. I, p. 313, s. vv. Χρωβατία, Χρωβάτοι), who were the northern neighbours of the
Turks. See Fehér 38–45; F. Dvornik, *Les Légendes de Constantin et de Méthode* (Prague,
1933), 246.

13/9–11 δύνανται . . . ἐπιτίθεσθαι. Cf. 3/3; 4/11–13; 8/21–2; 38/55–7; 40/16–19.

13/10–11 ἐν τῷ περὶ Πατζινακιτῶν κεφαλαίῳ.
C. here refers to cc. 1–8, on the Pechenegs. The present division into chapters does not
correspond to the author's arrangement of his book, in which cc. 1–8 formed a single
section: see General Introduction p. 8. Note the suggestion of Macartney (151) that
13/3–11 represents the embryo of a chapter περὶ Τούρκων, parallel to that περὶ Πατζινακιτῶν.

C. 13/12–200

BIBLIOGRAPHY

A Alföldi, 'Insignien und Tracht der römischen Kaiser', *Römische Mitteilungen*, 50 (1935), 1–171
(Alföldi).   J. Deér, 'Der Ursprung der Kaiserkrone', *Schweitzer Beiträge zur allgemeinen Geschichte*,
8 (1950), 51–87 (Deér).   A. Grabar, *L'empereur dans l'art byzantin* (Paris, 1936) (Grabar).   C.
Neumann, *Die Weltstellung des byzantinischen Reiches vor den Kreuzzügen* (Leipzig, 1894) (Neumann).
G. Ostrogorsky, 'Avtokrator i Samodržac', *Glas Srpsk. kral. Akad.*, 164 (1935), 95–187 (Ostro-
gorsky, *Avtokrator*).

INTRODUCTORY NOTE

This diplomatic section, written in all probability by C. himself in 952 (cf. 13/147–94,
and General Introduction pp. 7–8), lays down the lines along which requests from the
northern barbarians (Chazars, Turks, Russians, Pechenegs, Slavs, cf. 13/24–5) for
imperial vesture, for Greek Fire or for marriage alliances with the imperial house are to
be answered and refused. The Saracen east would, for obvious reasons, not prefer
requests of the first and third kinds; and the Frankish west, while also unlikely to make
requests for vesture, acceptance of which would imply submission to Byzantium (cf.
Treitinger 194, 195), is specially exempted from the ban on foreign marriages (13/116–
22). It is moreover clear from 1/16 ff. that at this time the northern tribes were the
government's chief preoccupation in foreign affairs.
  The chief of the πιθαναὶ ἀπολογίαι (13/20–1) and εὐπρεπεῖς λόγοι (13/105) are in
each case the same: a plea that the inviolable principles which forbid these concessions
derive from Constantine the Great and came to him directly from God. This *legitimis-
tische Fiktion* (see Neumann 3; cf. on 13/32) is certainly conscious fiction, since C., as
emperor, very well knew what was and what was not inscribed on the Holy Table
(13/48–9, 84–5, 112–13), and was aware that the invention of Greek fire was no earlier

than the reign of Constantine IV (48/28–30). Moreover, many other statements in the section on vesture are deliberate falsifications, all designed to emphasize the religious significance of this vesture. The religious significance was, in itself, real enough (*cf.* Bréhier, *Institutions*, 75–6); but it was the outcome of an imperial *Weltanschauung* and an historical tradition of such complexity and antiquity that no illiterate barbarian could be expected to grasp them. Instead, much concrete, if erroneous, corroboration had to be drawn from the visible manifestations of the state religion: hence the emphasis laid on the connexion of the imperial vesture with Santa Sophia and with its high priest, the patriarch, though in fact the vesture had an origin far more antique than the Christian church, and much of the church's ceremonial had been modelled on that of the Sacred Palace (*cf.* Treitinger 57–8, 62–3).

The religious association claimed for Greek fire is of course wholly fictitious. The objection to marriages with ἐθνικοί, which again rose from the Byzantine imperial *mystique*, had again to be explained in terms of a hard and fast religious sanction, and this could not properly and consistently be done. There was indeed a canon of the Trullan Synod which forbade marriages with heretics (see on 13/144); and this might justify the condemnation of Constantine V's marriage with the Chazar Irene, though she became a Christian before marriage (Theophanes 410/1). But C. is on very weak ground in condemning the marriage of Maria Lecapena with a Bulgarian (13/161); and it is to be feared that C.'s motive here was not so much love of the 'Christian order' or jealousy for the imperial dignity as hatred of his father-in-law; see on 13/147–94.

13/13   ἐκ πατρικῶν θησαυρῶν προφέρειν. *Cf.* Isocrates, *Ad Demonicum*, 11 E, and Introductory Note to Title and Proem p. 9.

13/15–16   ἐν χρήμασι λίχνον. *Cf.* 7/8–9; Leo Diac. 77/7–9.

13/24   Χάζαροι. The imperial garment known as τζιτζάκιον was Chazar in origin: see *Byzantinoturcica*, ii, 264; (2nd ed., 313); Moravcsik, *Sem. Kond.*, 4 (1931), 69–76.

13/26   ἐσθήτων.
The imperial vesture, like all the emperor's material surroundings (see Treitinger 50–1), was itself endued with sanctity, a sanctity which communicated itself to the legitimate wearer for the period during which he wore it, and which endangered any who wore it illegitimately: see Nicephorus Gregoras I, 518/22–519/3, and Reiske's notes at *De Cer.*, ii, 138–9, 282–3. For a striking parallel from elsewhere, see J. G. Frazer, *Taboo and the Perils of the Soul* (London, 1911), 3–4. Formal deprivation of such vesture denoted deposition: *cf.* Cedrenus ii, 413/4–7, 9–12. See further on 13/42–5; Dölger, *BES*, 144; Grabar, *Sem. Kond.*, 7 (1935), 112; and the remarks on 'hierarchy through clothing' of Lopez, *Speculum*, 20 (1945), 10, 21–2, 29, 41–2.

13/26   στεμμάτων. See Alföldi 145 ff.; Treitinger 26, note 77; Deér *passim*.

13/28–9   παρ' ὑμῶν καμελαύκια.
The *kamelaukion* (for the Latin derivation of which, see Reiske's note at *De Cer.*, ii, 654–5) denoted either a dome-shaped baldequin (*cf.* Treitinger 57, note 42) or, as here, a *closed*, hemispherical head-dress or crown. Deér (69–81) has shown that the imperial crown of the 10th cent. derived from the imperial triumphal helmet girt with a diadem, which since the 6th cent. had adopted the cross and globe as a crest; and that this helmet form is the *kamelaukion* here in question. The term was also used for crowns worn by the Caesar (*De Cer.*, 628/6) or by a subordinate ruler (Theophanes 228/22), which proves that it was not a technical term for one specific type of crown, but a general term, current in the day-to-day language of the Court, and indicating a certain shape, *i.e.* a closed

hemisphere as opposed to an open circlet. Deér (79, note 131) rejects the distinction made by Ebersolt and others between technical meanings of στέμμα and στέφανος. Crowns of an order inferior to the imperial *stemma* were occasionally sent by an emperor to a client prince in token of the latter's dependence on Byzantium (see Treitinger 203-4; Grabar 7, note 3; *id.*, *Sem. Kond.*, 7, 1935, 114-15; W. Ohnsorge, *Abendland u. Byzanz*, Darmstadt, 1958, 45, note 167), but the northern Scyths were not powerful enough to warrant the dispatch of these. The reading παρ' ὑμῶν (*cf.* ὑμεῖς, 13/34) puts the term *kamelaukion* into the mouths of the barbarians: this is explained by Moravcsik (*Acta Antiqua Acad. Sci. Hung.*, 1/1-2, 1951, 231, 233) on the hypothesis that C. is here using 'un terme byzantin susceptible de réléver le sens précis des dénominations étrangères correspondantes'; the barbarians are thus asking for '*stemmata* which you call (by a name which we Byzantines should translate) *kamelaukia*'.

13/32　Κωνσταντῖνον ἐκεῖνον.

See Neumann 3; Alföldi 149; Treitinger 129-35; Ostrogorsky[2] 25, note 1. For Constantine as ἰσαπόστολος, see Downey, *Dumbarton Oaks Papers*, 6 (1951), 59, note 25. For the crown's celestial origin, and for the relation of the ἄγγελος to the pagan Νίκη, see Grabar 115, 116.

13/35　θεῖναι . . . ἐκκλησίᾳ.

The imperial vesture had indeed a sacred character: see Introductory Note to this section, and on 13/26. But, with a very few exceptions (see on 13/38-42; Treitinger 62, 63, note 78), it was kept, not in the church, but in the οἰκειακὸν βασιλικὸν βεστιάριον: see *De Cer.*, 466/10, 13, 519/9-10; Nicetas Choniata 66/3-4; Dölger, *Finanzverwaltung*, 33, 34; Ebersolt, *Mélanges Ch. Diehl*, 1 (Paris, 1930), 81-3. This was a treasury adjacent to the κοιτών of the emperor, in the palace of the Chrysotriklinos: see Vogt, Commentaire 1, plan 2 nos: 46, 47. Here the robes were kept in chests (ταβλία) and the *stemmata* in cylindrical cases (κορνίκλια): see *De Cer.*, 7/2-4. The emperor as a rule took off the *stemma* before entering the cathedral (see Treitinger 150 and note 31).

13/37-8　ἀλλ' ὅτε . . . ἑορτή.

The wearing of imperial vesture was in fact not confined to purely religious festivals: it was also worn at festivals associated with the emperor-cult, as when the emperor appeared as Universal Victor at the races (see *De Cer.*, 190/18-20; Treitinger 170-2), or sat on the throne of Solomon as Master of the World (*De Cer.*, 522/5-9, 567/11-19, 583/17-18; Treitinger 199-202). For δεσποτικαὶ ἑορταί, see *MPG*, cxi, cols. 397 D ff.

13/38-42　Διὸ δὴ . . . ἐφαπλούμενα.

It is true that a *stemma* might from time to time be dedicated to the church, and hung from the ciborium εἰς κόσμον αὐτῆς: see Theophanes 281/15-18, 453/27-8; Paulus Silentiarius 101-2; Treitinger 63, note 78; Christophilopoulou, *Hellenika*, 15 (1957), 279 ff. Yet even such dedicated objects could be borrowed occasionally: see Reiske's note at *De Cer.*, II, 647-9. That ἱμάτια and σαγία served for altar-cloths, as here stated, is certainly false: for the ὕφασμα, κατασάρκιον, ἐνδυτή (*cf.* Theoph. Cont. 430/5), and the ἀέρες or εἰλητά covering the communion plate, see Reiske's notes at *De Cer.*, II, 108 and Vogt, *Commentaire*, 1, 60, 61. For the σαγίον, *ibid.* 30.

13/42-5　Ἡνίκα δὲ κτλ.

The festivals and processions (προελεύσεις) in question are those described in the first thirty-five chapters of *De Cer.*, Book 1 (*cf.* Treitinger 152); and the various garments appropriate to these and other occasions are detailed *ibid.*, c. 37. But the patriarch had nothing to do with their selection, which was a matter of rule, carried out by οἱ τῶν ἀλλαξίμων τοῦ κουβουκλείου (*De Cer.*, 7/1-3). The patriarch blessed the *stemma* and crowned the emperor with it only at the coronation of an αὐτοκράτωρ (*ibid.*, 193/1-3). That the emperor in his *stemma* and *chlamys* was invested with a strongly religious character is true: see on 13/26, and *cf.* Cantacuzene I, 200/6-7 (= Codinus 93/20-1). But it is not true that he wore them only on religious occasions, or that they were generally laid up in the church: see preceding notes.

13/48 κατάρα.
Cf. 13/84-5, 111-13. There were of course no such inscriptions. It is to be noted that C., both here and at 13/39-42, adduces evidence that could not possibly be checked by any foreigner, even though he visited Santa Sophia itself; (*cf.* however Cont. Geo. Mon. 868/14-16). In point of fact, the Holy Table in question was made by Justinian I; see Paulus Silentiarius 35, lines 72 ff., with Du Cange's notes *ibid.*, 115-22, and Cedrenus I, 677/7-19. For the true inscription, see Cedrenus I, 677/14-19.

13/55 ὅμοια καμεῖν.
There were no heirloom regalia at Byzantium; see Sickel, *BZ*, 7 (1898), 554, note 96. The sanctity lay, not in the objects themselves, but in their substance and form. Hence imperial vesture and insignia could be increased or renovated without difficulty, as by Theophilus (Sym. Mag. 627/14-16) and C. himself (*De Cer.*, 582/1-2; Theoph. Cont. 447/1-2; *cf. ibid.*, 452/13-19). But C. again exceeds the truth in postulating the approval of bishops and senate (13/56-7).

13/61-6 Εἷς γάρ τις . . . ἐπεσπάσατο.
See Theophanes 453/25-30; Geo. Mon. 765/8-14. Leo IV (750-80) was not husband, but son of a Chazar princess: see Theophanes 426/14-16, and *cf.* on 27/14-37. For criticism of the story, see Reiske's note at *De Cer.*, II, 649; but certainly the *stemma* was endued with a magical power that made its misuse dangerous, see on 13/26 (ἐσθήτων). For κακιγκάκως see Kurtz, *BZ*, 3 (1894), 152-5; Nestle, *BZ*, 8 (1899), 157-8.

13/68 ὀμνύειν.
For the coronation oath, originally a confession of faith, see Evagrius III, 32; *De Cer.*, 422/19-21, with Reiske's notes at II, 438, 746; and *cf.* Treitinger 30; J. B. Bury, *Constitution of the Later Roman Empire* (ed. Temperley, Cambridge, 1930), 114; *id.*, *ERE*, 39-40; Svoronos, *Rev. Et. Byz.*, 9 (1951), 121, note 3. For the later formula, see Codinus 86-7. Michael I (811) is the first emperor after Leo IV (ἔκτοτε, 13/67) of whose coronation oath we have a summary (Theophanes 493/10-14), though it of course contains no provision such as that here described.

13/70-1 ὑπὸ τοῦ πατριάρχου στέφεσθαι.
For the importance in middle-Byzantine thought of the religious coronation by the patriarch, see Ostrogorsky, *BZ*, 41 (1941), 212-18; Charanis, *Byzantion*, 15 (1940-1), 60 ff. But it does not appear that a church coronation was ever a *constitutional* necessity: *cf.* Ensslin, *Historische Zeitschrift*, 177 (1954), 462; Dölger, *BES*, 293, note 13.

13/73 ὑγροῦ πυρός.
See 48/28-32, with references in Apparatus I (add Genesios 34/9-13, although his testimony is erroneous). For contemporary references, see Theophanes 499/13-14; Anon., *De Obsidione Toleranda*, ed. Van den Berg (Leiden, 1947), 107, 108; Vasiliev II/2, 150; and for modern bibliography, see P. Charanis in Ch. Diehl, *Byzantium, Greatness and Decline* (Rutgers University Press, 1957), 340; add J. R. Partington, *A History of Greek Fire and Gunpowder* (Cambridge, 1960), 10-41. For a prohibition of such exports to enemies, see the 63rd Novel of Leo VI (ed. Noailles-Dain (Paris, 1944), 231-3). The Russians may well have made this request during the negotiations of 945: see *Russian Primary Chronicle*, ed. Cross and Sherbowitz-Wetzor (Cambridge, Mass., 1953), 73-8.

13/76 ἔχεις ἀποκρούεσθαι.   For the construction, see Vol. I, p. 335, and Reiske's note at *De Cer.*, II, 279.

13/76-8 Καὶ αὐτὸ . . . τῷ . . . Κωνσταντίνῳ.   A manifest absurdity, since Greek Fire was not in use until 674-8: see 48/28-32, and Ostrogorsky[2] 101.

13/94-103 Συνέβη δέ ποτε κτλ.   The incident is not recorded elsewhere, and may be a fiction.

13/107 συμπενθεριάσαι.

On this famous passage, see generally Bury's Gibbon VI, 86-8; Neumann 22-3; Ostrogorsky[2] 243-4 (*cf. id.*, *Sem. Kond.*, 8, 1936, 53-4); Guilland, *Byzantinoslavica*, 9 (1948), 311-12; Bréhier, *Institutions*, 31-3, 38-40. There was, undoubtedly, a strong feeling against such marriages: see Liudprand, *Legatio*, c. 15; Anna Comnena I, 10, 2 (ed. Reifferscheid, I, 35/7-9), where even unions with the Frankish west are condemned. But C. himself was in no position to condemn Frankish alliances (*cf.* Dölger, *BES*, 286, note 5): his half-sister Anna, who, though born out of wedlock and not properly speaking a *porphyrogenita*, had acted as Augusta after her mother's death, married Lewis the Blind (see on 26/17; and Ohnsorge, *BZ*, 45, 1952, 321-3, and 51, 1958, 78-81, as against Kolias, *EEBΣ*, 23, 1953, 342-6, who believes that Anna was a *prophyrogenita*, but that the marriage did not take place); while his son Romanus married the bastard of Hugh of Arles (see on 13/121-2, 26/66-72), and was then betrothed to the German Hedwig (Ohnsorge, *BZ*, 45, 1952, 325-6). The fact is that such unions, however distasteful in theory, were matters of political expediency (*cf.* W. Ohnsorge, *Abendland u. Byzanz*, Darmstadt (1958), 155-6); and the proudest emperors made very little trouble about doing what C. here reprobates. It is instructive to contrast the words of Nicephorus II's council to Liudprand (*Legatio*, c. 15) with Nicephorus's own plan to marry Basil II and Constantine VIII to Bulgarian princesses (Leo Diac. 79/18-20). The fate of their sister Anna is well known: *cf.* Ostrogorsky[2] 243.

13/121-2 Διὰ τὴν . . . περιφάνειαν καὶ εὐγένειαν.

For this 'exception' in favour of the Franks, see Dölger, *BES*, 286 and note 5. W. Ohnsorge, *Das Zweikaiserproblem im früheren Mittelalter* (Hildesheim, 1947), 44-5, relates it to the spiritual *Brotherhood* in the imperial hierarchy accorded to Charlemagne in 812 and not removed from his successors: *cf. De Cer.*, 689/12, and on 26/5-8. The value of a Frankish marriage is stressed in a passage of the Μονῳδία 'Ρωμανοῦ Β', a funeral lament for Bertha-Eudocia (†949) put into the mouth of the young widower Romanus II: see *Bulletin de Correspondance Hellénique*, 2 (1878), 269: ταύτην δὲ οὔτε ἀπὸ τῶν ἐθάδων καὶ ἡμεδαπῶν λαβεῖν εὐαγὲς ὑπείληφα οὔτε ἀπὸ τῶν ἐν τέλει καὶ πλούτῳ κομώντων καὶ παντοίαις αὔραις εὐτυχίας περιρρεομένων — ἦν γὰρ ⟨ἂν⟩ οὕτω τὰ τῆς δόξης ἐμοὶ ἐν παραβύστῳ καὶ ἐν γωνίᾳ καὶ ὥσπερ ὑφ' ἓν περικλειόμενά τε καὶ συμπνιγόμενα — ἀλλὰ ἐξ ἐθνῶν τῶν ἐξ Εὐρώπης, καὶ τούτων ἐπισήμων καὶ διαβοήτων ἐπί τε γένους λαμπρότητι καὶ ἐξουσίας μεγαλειότητι καὶ τῶν ἰταλικῶν χωρῶν νεμομένων τὸ εὐτραφὲς καὶ πιότατον. Τί δή ποτε; Ἵνα εἴη μοι τὸ κλέος ἐπ' ἐσχάτης γῆς θαυμαζόμενον καὶ τοῖς πατρικοῖς τελοῖεν ὑπόφοροι θεσμοῖς οἱ ἐξ οὗ περ αὕτη προύκέκριτο.

While the first part of this passage is purely rhetorical, the last betrays the political motives which brought such unions about.

13/126-38 Λέων ἐκεῖνος ὁ βασιλεὺς κτλ.

See on 13/61-6. It was his father who married a Chazar, as Justinian II had done before him (Theophanes 373/1). If the clause ἅπαξ . . . ἑαυτὸν (13/132-3) refers to the episode of the *stemma*, the accusation is in any case nonsensical, since the misuse of the *stemma* was, *ex hypothesi*, Leo's last act on earth. For Leo's position in the ikonoklast movement (13/138), see Ostrogorsky[2] 142. ἐκεῖνος (13/138) is emphatic: *he* was a mere heretic, from whom little better could be expected; but Romanus I, against whom the venom of the passage is directed, had not even this excuse.

13/144 κανόνος τοῦτο κωλύοντος.
The 72nd canon of the Trullan Synod (Rhallis-Potlis II, 471; *cf. ibid.*, VI, 534, *s.v.* γάμος αἱρετικῶν πρὸς ὀρθοδόξους), which C. here has in mind (*cf.* on 13/175–86), did in fact forbid marriages between orthodox and heretics, a canon which Theophilus seems to have contravened (Theoph. Cont. 112/15–17; *cf.* Bury, *ERE*, 124). But there could be no suggestion that the Bulgarians were heretics, and C. finds no answer to the defence suggested at 13/161.

13/145 Χριστιανικῆς καταστάσεως. *Cf.* Theoph. Cont. 868/16; *Vita Euthymii*, ed. De Boor (Berlin, 1888), 16/14.

13/147–94 Πῶς ὁ κύρις Ῥωμανὸς κτλ.
For this attack on Romanus, *cf.* on 51/141–92, and *De Cer.*, 606/9–19. It by no means follows from 13/143–5, which deals with the church's prohibition of marriage with ἄπιστοι, whereas the Bulgarians were not only Christians but Orthodox Christians (13/161). C. plays on the two meanings of ἔθνος (see on P/15), that is, 'foreigners' and 'infidels'; *cf.* Rhallis-Potlis III, 364: ἐθνικοὺς ἐνταῦθα τοὺς ἀπίστους νοεῖν δεῖ. Εἰ γὰρ ἐθνικός τις πιστὸς ᾖ, οὐ κωλυθήσεται κτλ. There was no question of Romanus's putting himself outside the canon and ecclesiastical tradition, as C. says at 13/167–8: indeed, the marriages of C.'s own relatives to Franks came nearer to an infringement of the canon: *cf.* on 13/107.

13/147–9 μετὰ Βουλγάρων συνεπενθερίασεν κτλ.
On 8th October, 927; see Theoph. Cont. 412/16–415/9; Sym. Mag. 740/19–741/15; Cont. Geo. Mon. 904/15–906/13; *cf.* Runciman, *Romanus Lecapenus*, 97; Ostrogorsky[2] 215; Dölger, *BES*, 154–5. That the marriage could be, and was, adduced as an instance, not of unorthodoxy, but of derogation from dignity, is clear from Liudprand, *Legatio*, c. 16 (ed. Becker, 184/13–17).

13/150 ἰδιώτης καὶ ἀγράμματος.
Cf. Acts 4, 13; C. uses ἰδιώτης in the same context at Δελτίον Ἱστ. καὶ Ἐθνολογ. Ἐταιρίας 2 (1885), 264/15. On the usage here, see Guilland, *Byzantinoslavica*, 9 (1948), 307.

13/161–2 οὐδὲ αὐτοκράτορος καὶ ἐνθέσμου βασιλέως.
For αὐτοκράτωρ, see Dölger, *BD*, 107–17 (a fundamental passage, fully documented), 139. The translation presents difficulties. Ostrogorsky, *Avtokrator*, 110–11, who notes (*cf.* Stein, *Mélanges Bidez*, II, Brussels, 1934, 906; Dölger, *BD*, 117) that C.'s second αὐτοκρατορία started officially only with the deposition of Romanus (944), regards the αὐτοκράτωρ here (927) as Romanus and the ἔνθεσμος βασιλεύς as C. himself: he puts it (120): 'Christophor Lakapin nije bio avtokrator niti legitimni vasilevs'. Stein (907) has: 'Christophore Lécapène n'était pas "un αὐτοκράτωρ et un βασιλεύς légitime"', which is a little closer to the Greek. The text certainly suggests that the αὐτοκράτωρ and the ἔνθεσμος βασιλεύς are regarded as one person; since, therefore, C. had been αὐτοκράτωρ between 913 and 922 (see 51/136; *Vita Euthymii*, ed. De Boor, 71/32), and since he manifestly regarded the whole reign of Romanus (920–44) as an usurpation, it is simplest to conclude that he here regards himself as both αὐτοκράτωρ and ἔνθεσμος βασιλεύς.

13/162 τρίτου.
This would be accurate if Christopher's promotion to second rank in the imperial hierarchy came at or immediately after his daughter's wedding, as Theoph. Cont. (414/15–18) says it did ; but Ostrogorsky[2] 218, note 1 shows that this promotion must be dated between April 922 and December 924. C. is therefore wrong here, unless, as in the previous note, he is understood to be regarding himself as *de jure* αὐτοκράτωρ throughout.

13/164–6 οὐδὲν διέφερεν κτλ.
C. again exaggerates: it is obvious that a 'porphyrogeniti porphyrogenita' was in fact in quite a different category from her more distant relatives: *cf.* Liudprand, *Legatio*, c. 15. The marriage recorded at 43/153–5 passes without censure; and *cf.* on 13/107.

13/175–86 Ἕκαστον γὰρ ἔθνος κτλ.
For the edification of his son, C. here adds a scholion to the words of the 72nd Quini-Sext canon (see on 13/144): οὐ γὰρ χρὴ τὰ ἄμικτα μιγνύναι, οὐδὲ τῷ προβάτῳ λύκον συμπλέκεσθαι.

13/177 ἀνάκρασιν. The emendation ἀνάκρασιν is certain: Plutarch, an author beloved by C. (see Jenkins, *Acad. roy. de Belgique, Bull. Cl. Lettres*, 5e série, 34 (1948), 72), uses the word in this sense (*Vita Alexandri*, c. 47); *cf.* C.'s use of συνανεκιρνᾶτο (Theoph. Cont. 216/11), and of ἀνεκράθην (*BZ*, 17 (1908), 81/29–30); also *MPG*, cxi, col. 64 B.

13/187–90 μιμεῖσθαι . . . μιμήσεως. *Cf.* Theoph. Cont. 48/19–21; Isocrates, *Ad Demonicum*, 4 B.

13/196–7 θαυμαστότερον.
Cf. Isocrates, *Ad Demonicum*, 10 B: τὸν ἐν μοναρχίᾳ κατοικοῦντα τὸν βασιλέα προσήκει θαυμάζειν. The conjunctive passage leads on from C.'s second section (P/17–18) to his third (P/18–23).

Cc. 14–25

BIBLIOGRAPHY

1. TEXTS (translated)
'*Abd al-Malik ibn Hisham, Das Leben Mohammed's nach Mohammed Ibn Ishak*, etc. Aus dem Arabischen übersetzt von G. Weil. 2 Bd. (Stuttgart, 1864). (Eng. tr. from the Arabic, A. Guillaume, *The Life of Muhammad*, Oxford, 1955) (Ibn Hishām). P. K. Hitti, *The Origins of the Islamic State*, being a translation . . . of the . . . Futûh al-Buldân of . . . al-Balâdhuri; 1 (New York, 1916) (Hitti, *Origins*). *Chronique de Michel le Syrien*, ed. et tr. J. -B. Chabot, 3 vols. (Paris, 1899–1904) (Mich. Syr.).

2. MODERN WORKS
A. d'Ancona, *Giornale Storico della Letteratura Italiana*, 13 (1889), 199–281 (d'Ancona). L. Caetani, *Annali dell'Islam*, 10 vols. (Milan, 1905–26) (Caetani, *Annali*). Id., *Chronographia Islamica* (Paris, 1912–18 and Rome, 1923) (Caetani, *Chronographia*). Id., *Studi di Storia orientale*, i iii (Milan, 1911, 1914) (Caetani, *Studi*). *Encyclopaedia of Islam*, first edition (Leiden 1913–38), second edition (Leiden 1954–) (*EI¹* and *EI²*). G. Glotz, *Histoire Générale, Histoire du Moyen Age;* tome iii, *Le Monde oriental de 395 à 1081;* par C. Diehl et G. Marçais (Paris, 1936) (Diehl-Marçais). C. Güterbock, *Der Islam im Lichte der byzantinischen Polemik* (Berlin, 1912) (Güterbock). H. Lammens, *Etudes sur le siècle des Omayyades* (Beyrouth, 1930) (Lammens, *Etudes*). J. Wellhausen, *Skizzen u.Vorarbeiten*, 6 Parts (Berlin, 1884–99) (Wellhausen, *Skizzen*). Id., *The Arab Kingdom and its Fall* (Calcutta, 1927) (Wellhausen, *Arab Kingdom*).

INTRODUCTORY NOTE

With c. 14 we begin the material originally compiled for the historical and antiquarian Περὶ ἐθνῶν, material which, apart from some insertions probably added in 952, continues until the end of c. 42: see General Introduction pp. 2–4. Cc. 14–22 contain C.'s account of Muḥammad and the rise of Islam until the beginning of the 9th cent. (22/40–8, mentioning the capture of Crete in 827, is the only entry outside the range of Theophanes). The account is based in the main on Theophanes, with some omissions and some additions from other sources: see on 14/10; Bury 525–33. For the eastern Christian sources, and for Byzantine accounts of Islam generally, see Brooks, *BZ*, 15 (1906), 578–87; Güterbock; and Eichner, *Der Islam*, 23 (1936), 133–62, 197–244. For the western medieval legend of Muḥammad, based, in the pre-crusading period, almost exclusively on these passages from Theophanes, see d'Ancona; H. G. Prutz, *Kulturgeschichte der Kreuzzüge* (Berlin, 1883); A. Malvezzi, *L'Islamismo e la Cultura Europea* (Florence, 1956); and N. Daniel, *Islam and The West* (Edinburgh, 1961).

14/1 Περὶ τῆς γενεαλογίας.
For the traditional Arab genealogy of the 'Ishmaelite' tribes, see H. F. Wüstenfeld, *Genealogische Tabellen der arabischen Stämme u. Familien* (2 vols., Göttingen, 1852, 1853). For alternative Greek versions, see Apparatus 1 on 14/2–28, and also Phrantzes 294/19–303/23; *MPG* cv, col. 842, note 13.

14/4 Ζιναρὸς. Nizār, ancestor of the northern tribes.

14/5–6 Μούνδαρον καὶ 'Ραβίαν. Muḍar and Rabīʿa.

14/6–7 Κούσαρον καὶ Κάϊσον καὶ Θεμίμην. Quraish, Qais, Tamīm and Asad were among the most important northern tribes.

14/9 ἐνδότεροι. Cf. Theoph. Cont. 55/5–6.

14/9 τοῦ 'Ιεκτάν.
Qaḥṭān, in Muslim tradition, is the eponymous ancestor of all the S. Arabian or Yemenite (= 'Αμανῖται) tribes and nations, including the Himyarites (= 'Ομηρῖται). The name is an Arabized version of the Hebrew Joktan (LXX, 'Ιεκτάν), who appears in a similar rôle in *Gen.* 10, 25 and 1 *Chron.*, 1, 19. See Fischer, *EI¹*, *s. v.* Ḳaḥṭān.

14/10 'Αναδείκνυται δὲ οὕτως.
For authoritative accounts of the life of Muḥammad, see F. Buhl, *Muhammeds Liv* (Copenhagen, 1903; German tr. by H. H. Schaeder, *Das Leben Muhammeds*, Leipzig, 1930); Caetani, *Studi*, iii; Tor Andrae, *Muhammad, his Life and his Faith* (London, 1936); R. Blachère, *Le problème de Mahomet* (Paris, 1952); W. Montgomery Watt, *Muhammad at Mecca* (Oxford, 1953); id., *Muhammad at Medina* (Oxford, 1956). For the latter part of the Prophet's career, and for the Caliphate until 660, see Caetani, *Annali*. The chief traditional text is that of Ibn Hishām. C.'s account here and in c. 17 goes back to Theophanes, although in c. 14 he is verbally dependent on Geo. Mon., whereas in c. 17 he borrows from Theophanes directly (see Bury 526–7, 532). Theophanes' own account seems to be based on eastern Christian sources, which, though lost, are still traceable in the works of later Syriac chroniclers (see Buk, *BZ*, 14, 1905, 532–4; Brooks, *BZ*, 15, 1906, 578–87): these in turn were based on Muslim history and tradition, which remain the sole original sources for the genesis of Islam. Most of the items in Theophanes' account are recognizable parts of the Muslim tradition, distorted to give then an anti-Islamic tone, together with some extraneous matter of dubious origin.

14/15 λαμβάνει αὐτὴν εἰς γυναῖκα. Thus far the account tallies, except in tone, with the Muslim tradition.

14/15–16 ἐπιχωριάζων ἐν Παλαιστίνῃ.
Modern criticism has cast doubt on Muḥammad's alleged visits to Palestine, and on his previous studies. The Muslim tradition of course regards Muḥammad as illiterate: see C. A. Nallino, *Raccolta di Scritti*, II (Rome, 1940), 60–6. *Cf.* however, Grégoire, *Mélanges Diehl*, I (Paris, 1930), 107–19.

14/17–18 τὸ πάθος τῆς ἐπιληψίας. Theophanes (334/5, 7) would appear to give us the first surviving occurrence of the oft repeated story of Muḥammad's epilepsy.

14/22 Ἀρειανοῦ τινος μοναχοῦ.
Theophanes (334/10–11) speaks only of 'a certain monk exiled for heresy and living there', without giving his sect; but John of Damascus, *de Haeresibus*, 101 (*MPG*, XCIV, cols. 764–5), speaks of an *Arian* monk who helped Muḥammad to study the Old and New Testaments and to prepare his own 'sect'. Theophanes appears here to have conflated two separate Muslim traditions. One of them tells of a certain Waraqa ibn Nawfal, an aged cousin of Khadīja, who was an ascetic and a seeker after truth. He is said to have known Hebrew, read the Bible, and eventually adopted Christianity. It was he who assured Khadīja of the authenticity of her husband's visions; (see d'Ancona 213–15; Ibn Hishām, tr. Weil, I, 114, tr. Guillaume 83, 107). The other tradition tells of a Syrian monk called Baḥīrā or Buḥairā, who, when Muḥammad visited Syria as a lad in a trading caravan, recognized him as a future prophet; see Ibn Hishām, tr. Weil, I, 86, tr. Guillaume 79–81). Another version places the episode some years later and gives the monk's name as Nestor. Masʿūdī, *Prairies*, I, 146, identifies Baḥīrā with Sergius, as does also a Syriac apocalypse published by Gottheil, *Zeitschr. für Assyriologie*, XIII (1898), 118–210; XIV (1899–1900), 203–68; XV (1901), 56–102; XVII (1903), 125–66 (see especially XIV, 213). *Cf.* d'Ancona 204–13; Abel, *EI²*, *s.v.* Baḥīrā; Abel, *Annuaire de l'Inst. de phil. et de l'hist. orientales*, III (1935), 1–12; Bignami-Odier, Levi Della Vida, *Mélanges d'arch. et d'hist. publiés par l'Ecole fr. de Rome* (1950), 125–48.

14/25 Βουβάχαρ. *Cf.* 17/3–4, Ἀβουβάχαρος, Βουπάκτωρ. The name is Abū Bakr.

14/26 καταλείψασα.
George Monachus, whom C. copies here, has misunderstood his source (*cf.* Phrantzes 296, 11–13): it was not Khadīja who left Muḥammad behind to succeed her, but Muḥammad who left Abū Bakr behind to succeed him; see 17/3, 13–14 and Bury 527.

14/28 τῆς Αἰθρίβου. A rather elliptical reference to the Hijra to Medina, previously known as Yathrib (Lathrippa in Ptolemy VI, 7, 31; Iathrippa in Stephanus Byzantinus, ed. Meineke 321/13).

14/30 φονεύων . . . παράδεισον.
The Muslim delight in war and the Muslim carnal paradise were favourite subjects of attack by Byzantine polemists. For the former, *cf.* Leo, *Taktika*, col. 972 C, and the outcry caused by the proposal of Nicephorus II to canonize Christian warriors (Zonaras, ed. Dindorf, IV, 82/25–83/4; *cf.* S. Runciman, *History of the Crusades*, I (Cambridge, 1950), 83–4). For the latter, see 17/16–22; John of Damascus, *de Haeresibus* (*MPG*, XCIV), col. 769 B-D (*cf.* Niket. Byz. *Refut. Mohamedis*, *MPG*, CV. cols. 744 C-D, 780–1); and Abel, *Byzantion*, 24 (1954), 368–9. Theophanes appears to refer to Sūra 56; *cf.* Eichner, *Der Islam*, 23 (1936), 213 ff. For Muslim conceptions of paradise, see Gardet, *EI²*, *s.v.* Djanna.

14/31-6 Προσεύχονται κτλ.

There is, of course, no foundation in Islam for these strange statements. The association of God and Venus may go back to the Orotalt and Alilat (Arabic, Al-Lāt) of Herodotus III, 8. The well-known Muslim cry of Allahu akbar ('God is very great'; cf. Geo. Mon. 706/7-12, ὁ Θεός, ὁ Θεὸς μείζων κτλ.) may be misconstrued to fit this association. 'Kubar' may possibly be a remote echo of the Ka'ba of Mecca, to which John of Damascus refers when he speaks of the 'stone of the Khataba' which the Muslims worship and which, he says, 'is none other than the idol of a goddess whom you adore': see Güterbock 11; and cf. Nicet. Byz. Refut. Mohamedis (MPG, cv) cols. 720 D, 793 B. The Arabic sources mention an idol called Hubal (see EI², s.v.) who was worshipped in the Ka'ba in pre-Islamic times; it is however described as being in the form of a man. The association of the Arabs with Venus, whether archaeological or astronomical, conveniently confirmed the Byzantine conviction that the Arabs were devoted to lechery: see 17/16-22; Cedrenus I, 744/9-24; Anna Comnena x, 5 (ed. Reifferscheid II, 75/7-15); Bullialdi Notae ad Ducae Hist., 625, 'Stephanus qui...Mahometis sectatores venereis rebus deditos fore praevidet'; Bury's Gibbon v, 378, note 171.

15/1 τῶν Φατεμιτῶν.

The source of this chapter has not been discovered. Manojlović (I, 35-9) has noted parallels between it and 25/51-62: hence it may well be that both c. 15 and 25/51-62 are later insertions into the Saracen συγγραφή. At least c. 15 shows a knowledge of the African Fatimids (15/4), which provides a terminus post of 909: see General Introduction p. 4, note 2. The contents of the chapter are puzzling: it is not easy to see to whom they refer, or how Muḥammad could have made war with the help of his daughter's descendants (to avoid this difficulty, one might render: 'Fatem was a daughter... Fatemites. But these, that is, the people I am now to speak of, are not from Fatemi etc.', and are thus not to be confused with the African Fatemites, cf. 25/58-61). That C. has some specific sect or tribe of Muslim warriors in mind is clear from Leo, Taktika, cols. 972 D, 973 B, which describe Saracens in general both as riding horses and wearing corselets (λωρίκια); contrast 15/10-11. From C.'s indications that these 'Fatemites' come from the north (15/4) and form the core of the Saracen army (15/8-10) it is just possible to suppose that he is drawing on some account of Turkish (?Farganese: cf. Marquart 216, 227) mercenaries in Saracen service: see Bury, ERE, 237-8, and for the Saracen regiment of 1,000 men, ibid. The description of camel-riders without armour would, however, only really be appropriate to Bedouin Arabs, and it is most likely that some such are meant. One possibility is the Carmathians, who were Arabs, camel-riders and Shi'ites (usually, though not always, supporters of the claims of the line of Fāṭima); other possibilities are the Ismā'īlī and Zaidī claimants and their supporters, active in the Yemen and elsewhere: see M. J. de Goeje, Mémoire sur les Carmathes...² (Leiden, 1886); B. Lewis, The Origins of Ismā'īlism (Cambridge, 1940).

15/11 θώρακας. The word here = λωρίκια, though at Leo, Taktika, col. 724 A θώρακες = κλιβάνια: for both, see on 51/82-4.

15/12 περιβόλαια. Cf. Theoph. Cont. 478/3.

16/1-2 Στέφανος ὁ μαθηματικός.

For Stephen, see H. Usener, De Stephano Alexandrino (Bonn, 1879); cf. K. Krumbacher, Gesch. d. byz. Litt.² (Munich, 1897), 621. For this famous horoscope, which in its original form appears to be a forgery of the latter part of the 8th cent. (Usener 9-14), see also Bury 526, 532, 533-7. C.'s familiarity with the prophecies of Stephen is further witnessed by Theoph. Cont. 338/10; we should not therefore reject the chapter with Meursius (see 16/8, Apparatus 2), especially since it has an important place in C.'s scheme (see Bury 532). That such a prophecy was made at the time stated is witnessed by Fredegarius, MGH, scr. rer. Mer. II, 153/6-9.

16/1 κανόνος . . . ἐθεμάτισεν.

The 'Canon' is the chronological chart cast in the horoscope ('thema'); cf. Cedrenus
I, 717/9, κανονίσαντος κρατῆσαι, 'measured the term of their empire'. For θέμα,
θεμάτιον, θεματίζω, see Du Cange, s.vv. (cols. 488, 489).

16/11-12 ἔτη ἐννέα. From the Hijra in 622, when Muḥammad became ruler of the
community in Medina, until his death in 632; see Bury 532.

17/1 Χρονικοῦ . . . Θεοφάνους.

Here begins C.'s second series of extracts relating to the Arabs, that series which is
borrowed directly from Theophanes; see Bury 531-2. C. 17 derives wholly from Theophanes, ann. 6122, except for the annus mundi at 17/2 and for the lines 17/10-12, which
are transitional between two excerpts.

17/4 Οἱ δὲ πεπλανημένοι ῾Εβραῖοι.

Theophanes' story of the Jewish inspiration of Islam is found also, with some variations, in a Jewish version, in two Geniza texts, one in Hebrew and the other in Arabic,
published by Mann, *Jewish Quarterly Review*, XII, n. s. (1921), 123 ff., and Leveen, *Jewish
Quarterly Review*, XVI, n. s. (1925–6), 399 ff. Both Jewish and Christian versions appear to
be based on a common source, probably on the Muslim tradition of the nine Rabbis who
pretended to accept Islam in order to mock the prophet; see Ibn Hishām tr. Weil, I,
266, tr. Guillaume 246, and Theophanes, 333/8, ἦσαν δὲ τῷ ἀριθμῷ δέκα οἱ τοῦτο
πεποιηκότες κτλ.: cf. A. J. Wensinck, *Mohammed en de Joden te Medina* (Leiden, 1908), 65
ff. The divergences in the versions can easily be explained by the respective prejudices of
the Jewish and Christian writers. There is nothing in the Muslim or Jewish versions about
Jews inciting Muḥammad against the Christians. This is probably an addition by
Theophanes, whose story (333/11–12) is a little fuller than C.'s version of it, or else by his
eastern Christian source; cf. other cases where Theophanes puts the blame for Muslim
crimes on a Jew, e.g. the removal of crosses in Jerusalem (342/24), and the destruction of
ikons (401/29-402/4, with parallel accounts in Syriac sources). Nor do the Jewish sources
mention a revulsion of the Jews after seeing Muḥammad eat camel's flesh (17/8; cf. also
Theodos. Diac., *De Expugn. Cret.*, ap. Leon. Diac., 266/68); but in the Muslim tradition
(see Ibn Hishām, tr. Weil, I, 277, tr. Guillaume 255) the Jews, seeking to test Muḥammad's claim to prophethood, question him about the dietary laws, and are told that
camel's milk and camel's meat were favourite delicacies forsworn by the Jews in gratitude
to God. In Muḥammad's day the eating of camel's meat was a sign of a Jew's conversion
to Islam: see R. Leszynski, *Die Juden in Arabien zur Zeit Muhammads* (Berlin, 1910), 27.
On the whole question, see Schwabe, *Tarbiz*, 2 (1930), 74–90; S. D. Goitein, *G. E. Weil
Jubilee Volume* (Jerusalem, 1952), 10–23 (in Hebrew); id., *Journ. of Jewish Stud.* 9 (1958),
149–62; id., *Jews and Arabs; Their Contacts through the Ages* (New York, 1955), 46 ff., where
the broader question of Muḥammad's relations with the Jews is discussed.

17/10-12 Οὗτοί εἰσιν . . . Σαρακηνοί. See on 17/1. The circumcision is mentioned,
but not in these words, by Geo. Mon. 700/6.

17/14 κατέλιπεν. See on 14/26.

17/14-16 ᾿Εκράτησεν δὲ κτλ.

Theophanes says (334/18–20): 'his heresy prevailed in the district of Ethribos through
war at the last; at first in secret ten years, and through war another ten years, and openly
nine'. The chronology is not very clear. The ten years of war may refer to the period
between the Hijra and Muḥammad's death.

17/16–23   Ἐδίδαξεν δὲ κτλ.   See on 14/30; and *cf.* Qur'ān xxxvii, 39 ff., xlvii, 16 ff., lv, 46 ff., lvi, 14 ff., lxxvi, 11 ff.

18/1   ἀρχηγὸς τῶν 'Αράβων.
Cc. 18–20 cover the caliphates of Abū Bakr (632–4), 'Umar (634–44) and 'Uthmān (644–56) (*cf.* Diehl-Marçais 185–97), and consist of brief notes of which Theophanes is the source.

18/3   πόλιν Γάζαν.
Gaza, betrayed to the Muslims by disappointed Arab mercenaries, was captured in 633; see Theophanes 336/1–3, and *cf.* Nicephorus, ed. de Boor, 23/17–22. The victory of Ajnādain (30th July, 634) followed, and gave the Arabs control of most of Palestine. For the chronology, see Bury's Gibbon v, 540–2; Wellhausen, *Skizzen*, vi, 51 ff.; M. J. de Goeje, *Mémoire sur la conquête de la Syrie* (Leiden, 1900).

19/3   ἐπολιόρκησεν τὴν 'Ιερουσαλήμ.
For the date of the capture of Jerusalem, variously given as 636, 637 and 638, see Bury's Gibbon v, 542; Ostrogorsky[2] 89. Arabic sources vary also; Balādhurī (Hitti, *Origins*, 213–14) gives A. H. 17 (= 638); *cf.* Abel, *Conférences de S.-Etienne* (Paris, 1911), 105–44; De Goeje, *op. cit.*, 152 ff.

19/4   δόλῳ.
The correct reading is λόγῳ, a 'pact' (see 19/5 and Theophanes 339/16; *cf.* 50/119 and Phrantzes 303/9, μετὰ συμβάσεως). The pact of 'Umar with Sophronius is also related by eastern Christian sources; see Mich. Syr. ii, 425–6; Bar-Hebraeus, *Chronographia*, 37a; Agapius of Manbij, *Kitāb al-'unwān*, ed. Cheikho (Beirut, 1912), 343. Some traces of it are found in Muslim annals; see Ṭabarī i, 2405; *cf.* Hitti, *Origins*, 214. On the vexed question of its authenticity, see De Goeje, *Mémoire sur la conquête de la Syrie* (Leiden, 1900), 136 ff; Caetani, *Annali*, iii, 920 ff.; A. S. Tritton, *The Caliphs and their Non-Muslim Subjects* (London, 1930), ch. 1.; Cahen, *E.I.*[2], *s.v.* Dhimma. For subsequent violations see G. Vismara, *Bizanzio e l'Islam* (Milan, 1950), 23, note 59.

19/11   προσκυνητήριον.
For 'Umar's mosque in Jerusalem, see Theophanes 342/22–3; Caetani, *Annali*, iii, 941–3 and 950–1. It should not be confused with the Umayyad mosque now called the 'Mosque of Omar'; see Diehl-Marçais 209.

20/2   λαμβάνει τὴν 'Αφρικήν.
For the westward expansion of the Arabs in Africa during the reign of 'Uthmān, see Caetani, *Chronographia*, 290, 296, 302, 354, 361; and Bury's Gibbon v, 459–63, and notes 158 and 168. The invasion was begun in 647.

20/4   τὸν κολοσσὸν Ρόδου.   See on 21/56–65.

20/4   Κύπρον τὴν νῆσον.
For Arab raids on Cyprus during the reign of 'Uthmān (A.H. 28, 33 = 648–9, 653–4), see Caetani, *Chronographia*, 308, 339, 353; Wellhausen, *Nachr. d. kgl. Ges. d. Wiss. Göttingen* (1901), 418 ff.; M. A. Cheira, *La lutte entre Arabes et Byzantins* (Alexandria, 1947), 99 ff.; G. Hill, *A History of Cyprus*, i (Cambridge, 1940), 283–5.

20/5   νῆσον τὴν 'Άραδον.
Cf. Mich. Syr. ii, 442; Dionysius of Tell Mahré, ed. et tr. Chabot (Paris, 1895), 7; Caetani, *Chronographia*, 315; Wellhausen, *Nachr. d. kgl. Ges. d. Wiss, Göttingen* (1901),

419; Cheira, *op. cit.*, 101. The date was A.H. 29 = 650. Arabic sources often confuse Aradus (Arwād) with Rhodes (Rūdus), and also with the island or peninsula near the Bosphorus held by the Arabs during the siege of Constantinople: see Canard, *Journal Asiatique*, CCVIII (1926), 78–9.

20/7–10 Οὗτος τὴν νῆσον . . . χαλκόν. See on 21/56–65.

20/10–12 Οὗτος ὁ Μανίας . . . Ἰωνίας.

For Muʿāwiya's expedition into Asia Minor during the caliphate of ʿUthmān, see Caetani, *Chronographia*, 330, 338, 360; Ostrogorsky[2] 94; Brooks, *Journal of Hellenic Studies*, 18 (1898), 182–206. For the expedition to Constantinople, see on 21/52–3.

21/3 πρὸς τῇ τελευτῇ . . . ἀρχηγοῦ.

These words are not in Theophanes, though the remaining part of the paragraph (21/4–16) derives from him. Muʿāwiya died in 680, and the peace here referred to was concluded in 678, more as a result of the catastrophic defeat of the Arabs at Constantinople (674–8) than of the Mardaïte depredations: see Diehl-Marçais 241–2; Ostrogorsky[2] 101–2.

21/4 οἱ Μαρδαῖται.

For the Mardaïtes, for whom Theophanes is one of our chief sources, see also on 50/169–70; Lammens, *EI*[1] *s.v.*; *id.*, *Etudes*, 14–21, where the identity of the Mardaïtes with the Jarājima of the Arabic sources is suggested; (*cf.* Hitti, *Origins*, 246 ff.). The word appears to come from a Semitic root meaning 'rebel'. The Maronite tradition, elaborated by Lammens, identifies the Mardaïtes with the early Maronites; but this is far from certain.

21/10–11 Κωνσταντίνου . . . Πωγωνάτου.

Cf. 21/46–7. Brooks, *BZ*, 17 (1908), 460–2, shows that Pogonatus was not Constantine IV, but his father, Constans II. These passages confirm his thesis. *Cf.* also 21/28–30, where Muʿāwiya's alleged grandson is contemporary with the grandson of Pogonatus. See also Ostrogorsky, *Zgodovinski Časopis*, 6–7 (1952–3), 116–23.

21/13 ἔγγραφον . . . εἰρήνης. See Dölger, *Regesten*, 239; *cf.* Caetani, *Chronographia*, 628, and Lammens, *Etudes*, 21–2.

21/16–17 διῃρέθη ἡ τῶν Ἀράβων ἀρχή.

Cf. 21/71–106. Both passages describe the first Civil War in Islam (656–61), at one stage of which ʿAlī held Medina (Yathrib) and the east, Muʿāwiya Syria, Palestine and Egypt. For the Civil War generally, see Caetani, *Annali*, IX and X; Wellhausen, *Skizzen*, VI, 113–46; *id.*, *Arab Kingdom*, 75–112. For the rôle of ʿAlī, see especially F. Buhl, 'Alī som Prætendent og Kalif (Copenhagen, 1921); L. Veccia Vaglieri, *Annali dell'Istituto Universitario Orientale di Napoli*, n.s. IV (1952), 1–94 (based on new, Kharijite material); and *id.*, *EI*[2], *s.v.* ʿAlī ibn Abī Ṭālib.

21/23–34 Καὶ μετ' αὐτὸν κτλ.

For the significance of this passage, which does not derive from Theophanes, see Bury 527–9. Despite a nearly accurate estimate of the chronology of the Umayyad caliphate (21/23: 85 years instead of 89 or 94), C. goes on to antedate the death of Marwān II ('Marouam') and the rise of the ʿAbbasids (750) by about forty years, in order to bring them into relation with the conquest of Spain in 711. However, the 'grandson of Mauias', that is, ʿAbd ar-Raḥmān, who went to Spain and founded the emirate of Cordova (21/28–30), did not do so until 756. The earlier conqueror, contemporary with Justinian II, was Ṭāriḳ.

21/24 ἐξῆλθον οἱ λεγόμενοι Μαυροφόροι.

A reference to the rise of the 'Abbasids in Khurāsān and their eviction of the Umayyads (750); see Diehl-Marçais 346–7. The black robes and banners were adopted by the 'Abbasid revolutionaries in order to comply with messianic and apocalyptic prophecies current at the time, and retained by them as distinctive emblems of the dynasty and as the uniform of their Khurāsānī troops after their accession to power; see G. Van Vloten, *Recherches sur la domination arabe* (Amsterdam, 1894); and, more especially, *id.*, *De Opkomst der Abbasiden in Chorasan* (Leiden, 1890); Moscati, *Rendiconti dell'Accad. Naz. dei Lincei*, cl. di sci. mor. &c., ser. VIII, 4 (1949), 323–35, 474–95 and 5 (1950), 1–17; Lewis, *EI²*, 15 ff., *s.v.* 'Abbāsids.

21/29 διεπέρασεν εἰς τὴν Ἱσπανίαν.

See 22/36–40, and on 21/23–34. For 'Abd ar-Raḥmān's crossing into Spain (755) and capture of Cordova (756), see Diehl-Marçais 396–8. He was, in fact, grandson of Hishām (724–43); *cf.* 22/54).

21/31-4 τοῖς ἡμετέροις ἱστορικοῖς οὐ γέγραπται. For the significance of this remark, unjust as it is, see Bury 528 and below, note on cc. 23–5.

21/34-5 ἔχει δὲ τοῦ . . . οὕτως.

We now return to extracts from Theophanes, dealing with the successors of Mu'āwiya: Yazīd I (680–3); Marwān I (684–5); and 'Abd al-Malik (685–705). For the omission of Mu'āwiya II (683–4) from the list of Umayyad caliphs, see Wellhausen, *Arab Kingdom*, 169.

21/38-9 ἐταράχθησαν . . . Ζουβέρ.

'Abdallah ibn Zubair was leader of the Medinese party ('the Arabs of Aithribos') in the second civil war in Islam (680–92); see Wellhausen, *Arab Kingdom*, 146–52.

21/41 Οὐσάν.

Ḥassān ibn Mālik ibn Bahdal, an Arab of Kalb and maternal uncle to Yazīd I. For his rôle in the second civil war and his decisive part in the victory of Marj Rāhiṭ (684), which assured the succession of Marwān I, see Wellhausen, *Arab Kingdom*, 170–83, and Sir Wm. Muir, *The Caliphate* (new ed., Edinburgh, 1924), 317 ff.

21/44-5 χειροῦται τοὺς τυράννους.

For 'Abd al-Malik's defeat of 'Abdallah ibn Zubair (692) and other challengers to his authority, see Wellhausen, *Arab Kingdom*, cc. III and IV, and Muir, *loc. cit.*

21/49-126 Ἰστέον, ὅτι ὁ τῶν Ἀράβων ἀρχηγὸς κτλ.

After recording the death of Constantine IV and the succession of Justinian II in 685 (21/46–8), C. now inserts a passage, the sources of which are unknown (see Manojlović I, 47), dealing with Mu'āwiya I: first, his exploits as general of 'Uthmān (654–5); next, his campaign against 'Alī during the first civil war in Islam (657); and lastly, his blood-connexion with Maslama, who commanded the Arab expedition against Constantinople in 717–18. The passage thus gives a fuller account of two matters which have already been dealt with more summarily above, at 20/3–13 and 21/16–23; but its position is awkward, as it interrupts the narration at 21/48 which should proceed immediately with 22/5. See Bury 529–30.

21/50 οὐκ ἐκ τοῦ γένους.

Mu'āwiya was of the family of Umayya, one of the chief families of pre-Islamic Mecca. Muḥammad was of the Meccan family of Hāshim. Both families were part of the tribe of Quraish.

21/52–3 ἀπεστάλη κατὰ τῆς 'Ρωμαίων πολιτείας.

Probably a reference to the naval campaign of 655, which however can hardly be called an expedition against Constantinople: see Caetani, *Chronographia*, 526, 535; Wellhausen, *Nachr. d. kgl. Ges. d. Wiss. Göttingen* (1901), 414–47; Canard, *Journal Asiatique*, ccviii (1926), 63–7; M. A. Cheira, *La lutte entre Arabes et Byzantins* (Alexandria, 1947), 102. For Mu'āwiya's preparatory raids on Ionia, see 20/11–12, and Ostrogorsky[2] 94. For the real assault of 674–8, see on 21/116–26.

21/56–65 'Ελθὼν δὲ ἐν τῇ 'Ρόδῳ κτλ.

Cf. 20/4, 7–10. An Arab force under Abu'l-A'war landed in Rhodes in 654: see Caetani, *Chronographia*, 339; Wellhausen, *op. cit.*, 419; Ostrogorsky[2] 94; Cheira, *op. cit.*, 101. For the colossus, see J. A. Overbeck, *Die Antiken Schriftquellen* (Leipzig, 1868), 291–4 (nos. 1939–54); Robert, Pauly-Wissowa, *R.E.*, iii, cols. 2130, 2131, *s.v.* Chares; Haynes, *Journal of Hellenic Studies*, 77 (1957), 311–12. Begun shortly after 304 B.C., and completed in twelve years, it fell in an earthquake in 227 B.C., and was apparently not re-erected (see, however, in addition to our text, Mich. Syr. ii, 442–3, who gives a circumstantial account of its being *pulled down* by the Arabs). The inscription, despite the impossible τὸν ἐν 'Ρόδῳ κολοσσὸν, has the imperfect ἐποίει to commend it; for emendations, see the Apparatus. It is obvious that 980 camels is a mistake for 90; see C. Torr, *Rhodes in Ancient Times* (Cambridge, 1885), 96–7. The story is not known to the Arabic sources, but is again found in Mich. Syr. ii, 443.

21/69 'Ο δὲ 'Αλὴμ.   Alim, the Ali of 21/18–22, is the caliph 'Alī ibn Abī Ṭālib (†661).

21/73 πάσης Συρίας.   That is, the Islamic empire; *cf.* 25/56–7.

21/73 παρὰ τὸν Εὐφράτην ποταμόν.

The forces of 'Alī and Mu'āwiya met at Ṣiffīn, a ruined Roman town near the Euphrates, in 657. For a discussion of the Oriental sources, see Caetani, *Annali*, ix, 429 ff.; *cf.* F. Buhl, '*Alī Som Prætendent og Kalif* (Copenhagen, 1921), 62 ff.; Wellhausen, *Arab Kingdom*, 77 ff. To the Oriental sources discussed in these works we may add the *Waq'at Ṣiffīn* of Naṣr ibn Muzāḥim (†827), the oldest Shi'ite historian (Cairo, 1946). See the article of L. Veccia Vaglieri cited on 21/16–17: and *id.*, *EI*[2], *s.v.* 'Alī i. Abī Ṭālib.

21/74–106 Τοῦ δὲ πολέμου κρατοῦντος κτλ.

The arbitration of Adhruḥ, which followed the battle of Ṣiffīn, is described by the Arabic sources in numerous different versions, presenting a tangled and contradictory story from which only one fact emerges clearly, the promulgation of a verdict unsatisfactory to 'Alī. C.'s account tallies broadly with the pro-'Alid accounts in the Muslim sources, the general burden of which is that somehow Mu'āwiya's arbitrator outwitted 'Alī's. On this passage Caetani, *Annali*, x, 59, observes: 'the episode of the ring is not related in its entirety by any of the Arabic sources that have reached us (instead, Mas'ūdī has the turban, and the '*Iqd* the sword), but the narratives of Ya'qūbī and Bar-Hebraeus presuppose it. The translator has not understood the double meaning of *Khala'tu* ("to deprive someone" and "to take off a garment, a ring") which his Arabic original presented, and has paraphrased it so as to disfigure the sense completely and thus constrain himself to introduce the story of the handing over of the rings to the two arbitrators, along with the observation that the ring was the symbol of power among the Arabs. The story of the departure of 'Alī for Medina and his death there may be a false induction by the Byzantine author.' From all this, it would seem fairly certain that C.'s account is based, at one or more removes, on a Shi'ite or pro-Shi'ite Arabic account, with some adaptations where the original version was imperfectly understood. For the use of the ring as an emblem of authority among the Arabs, see Allan, *EI*[1], *s.v.* Khātam; and *cf.* Achmetis,

Oneirocriticon (ed. Drexl, Teubner, 1925), 212/20. For the arbitration generally, see Caetani, *Annali*, x, 12–76; Buhl, *op. cit.*, 72–8; Wellhausen, *Arab Kingdom*, 89 ff.; Lammens, *Etudes*, 125 ff.; *EI²*, *s.v.* Adhruḥ; L. Veccia Vaglieri, *op. cit.*, 85 ff. *Cf.* also Naṣr ibn Muzāḥim, 627–8, where the arbitrators 'depose' (*Khalaʿ*) their principals without reference to any material object.

21/76   Τίνι τρόπῳ.   = not 'how?' but 'why?'; *cf.* 51/1; *De Cer.*, 637/14; *Vita Euthymii* (ed. De Boor, Berlin, 1888), 45/11–12.

21/96, 100   ἐκβάλω . . . εἰσαγάγω.   For aor. subj. as fut. see N. Bănescu, *Entwicklung des gr. Futurums* (Bucharest, 1915), 72–4; and *cf.* Theoph. Cont. 27/21.

21/109   Μανίας ἀπέκτεινεν ἅπαντας.
The massacre of 'Alī's family, including Ḥusain, took place at Karbala on the 10th October 680; the caliph was not Muʿāwiya, but Yazīd I: see Diehl-Marçais 202–3.

21/111   ἔκγονος . . . Σοφιάμ.   Muʿāwiya was son of Abū Sufyān.

21/112   Ἔκγονος . . . ὁ Μάσαλμας.   Maslama ibn 'Abd al-Malik was grandson of Marwān I, not of Muʿāwiya.

21/114   μαγίσδιον.
For the mosque of Constantinople, see Du Cange, *Constantinopolis Christiana* (Paris, 1680), II, 164, and Reiske's note at *De Cer.*, II, 727; *cf.* *MPG*, cxi, col. 312 D and Vasiliev II/2, 286–90; also, Vasiliev, *Mélanges Ch. Diehl*, I (Paris, 1930), 294; Nomikos, *ΕΕΒΣ* I (1924), 199–209. For the Saracen gaol in the Pretorium, see *Vita Euthymii*, ed. De Boor (Berlin, 1888), 8/11; Theoph. Cont. 372/23-373/1; *De Cer.*, 743/1–2, 767/16; and, generally, R. Janin, *Constantinople byzantine* (Paris, 1950), 163 ff.

21/116–26   Ἦλθεν δὲ Σουλεϊμὰν κτλ.
For this attack on Constantinople, *cf.* 22/49–52 and see Caetani, *Chronographia*, 1193, 1208, 1223; Wellhausen, *Nachr. d. kgl. Ges. d. Wiss. Göttingen* (1901), 442; Canard, *Journal Asiatique*, ccviii (1926), 80 ff.; Cheira, *op. cit.*, 180 ff.; R. Guilland, *Etudes byzantines* (Paris, 1959), 109–33. The date is August 717–August 718: see Ostrogorsky² 126, note 1. The great siege of 674–8 (*cf.* on 21/3) is mentioned only incidentally, at 48/28–32. For Maslama, see Gabrieli, *Rendiconti dell' Accad. Naz. dei Lincei*, cl. di sci. mor. &c., ser. VIII, 5 (1950), 22–39.

21/115, 116   Σουλεϊμὰν . . . Σουλεϊμὰν.
C.'s account confuses the caliph Suleiman (715–7) with Maslama's lieutenant of the same name. The caliph took no part in the siege, and in fact died shortly after it had begun.

21/125   ἁγίαν εἰκόνα.
For this famous talisman, the Hodegetria, see, *e.g.* Genesios 102/15–16; Theoph. Cont. 204/12–14; Psellos, *Chronographie*, ed. Renauld I, 39/23–6; Bullialdi *Notae ad Ducae Hist.*, 615–6. *Cf.* J. Ebersolt, *Sanctuaires de Byzance* (Paris, 1921), 69–70; A. Van Millingen, *Walls of Byzantine Constantinople* (London, 1899), 257; *id.*, *Churches of Constantinople* (London, 1912), 227; Wolff, *Traditio*, 6 (1948), 319–28. For miraculous deliverances of Constantinople by the Virgin, see A. A. Vasiliev, *The Russian Attack on Constantinople in 860* (Cambridge, Mass., 1946), 97–100; N. H. Baynes, *Byzantine Studies and Other Essays* (London, 1955), 258. This use of an icon by Leo III, shortly before his edict against images (730), is interesting, if historical.

22/1 *Ἐκ τοῦ Χρονογράφου κτλ.*
C. now resumes his account of the caliphate, which was broken off at 21/46 in the middle of the reign of 'Abd al-Malik. The chapter is based on Theophanes, except for the passage 22/36–48; see Bury 529–31.

22/6–9 *Αὕτη ἐστὶν . . . ἀποκτείνας.*
A conjunctive passage, explaining the circumstances of Justinian II's reign. He reigned from 685–95, Leontius from 695–8, Tiberius Apsimarus from 698–705, and Justinian again from 705–11 (see Ostrogorsky² 105).

22/9–14 *βεβαιῶσαι τὴν εἰρήνην κτλ.*
For this renewal, in 688, of the peace of 678 (*cf.* on 21/3), see Dölger, *Regesten,* 257; Ostrogorsky² 106. For the Mardaïte invasions, see on 21/4. For the agreement over Cyprus, see Canard, *Bull. d' Et. orient. de l'Inst. fr. de Damas,* 13 (1949–51), 62–9; Jenkins, *Studies presented to D. M. Robinson,* II (1953), 1006–14; and Introductory Note to cc. 46/166–9; 47–8 (p. 180).

22/15 *μαγιστριανόν.*
The *μαγιστριανοί* or *Agentes in Rebus* of the Magister Officiorum were concerned (*a*) with diplomacy (*cf. De Cer.,* 400/16–17) and (*b*) with internal security. With the decline of the Magistracy in the 8th cent., the name *μαγιστριανός* also tends to disappear; see A. E. R. Boak and J. E. Dunlap, *Two Studies in Later Roman and Byzantine Administration* (New York, 1924), 74. But the same corps with the same duties continued under the name of *βασιλικοί,* or *βασιλικοὶ ἄνθρωποι.* The change of title may perhaps be attributed to Justinian II, since just at this time (698) we find Tiberius Apsimarus sending a *βασιλικός* to the caliph (see 47/18). But the old title occasionally recurs even as late as the 10th cent.; *cf. Vit. Basilii Jun. (MPG,* CIX), col. 656 A.

22/19–22 *Πᾶσαι γὰρ . . . μέχρι τοῦ νῦν.*
That is to say, the eastern frontier of the empire from Tarsus in the south to Theodosioupolis in the north. For Armenia Quarta see E. Stein, *Histoire du Bas-Empire,* II (Paris, 1949), 471 and note 3; Hitti, *Origins,* 305; *MPG,* CVII, cols. 348–9. For the use which the Arabs made of these frontier fortresses, see Hitti, *Origins,* 263–5; Bar-Hebraeus, tr. Wallis-Budge (Oxford, 1932), I, 105.

22/24 *χάλκεον τεῖχος διαλύσας.* For the significance of Justinian's transfer of populations, see Ostrogorsky² 107.

22/24–6 *Παρέλυσε . . . τύπους.*
For Justinian's Bulgarian campaign (688–9), see Ostrogorsky² 106. For Constantine IV's peace with the Bulgarians (681), see Theophanes 359/19–25; Dölger, *Regesten* 243; Ostrogorsky² 103–4. For his peaceable policy, see Theophanes 359/27.

22/27–9 *ἐπεστράτευσαν . . . τῇ Ἀφρικῇ.*
The subjugation of North Africa, begun by the great 'Uqba (†683), was continued in 697 by Ḥassān ibn an-Nu'man, who finally captured Carthage in the following year; see Diehl-Marçais 207; Ostrogorsky² 113–14.

22/33 *Οὐαλὶδ.* Walīd (705–15).

22/35–6 *τῆς Ἀφρικῆς . . . ὁλοσχερῶς.*
For the final subjugation of Africa by Mūsā ibn Nuṣair, ending with the capture of Ceuta (711), see Diehl-Marçais 337; Bury's Gibbon v, 469–71.

22/36-40 Τότε ὁ τοῦ Μανίου ἔγγονος κτλ.
Cf. 21/28-30. The same confusion between Ṭāriḳ (711) and 'Abd ar-Raḥmān (756) is apparent here; see on 21/23-34. 'Mauiates' is an obvious error for 'Umayyads', in Arabic, Umawī.

22/40-8 οἱ τὴν Κρήτην οἰκοῦντες κτλ.
For the Spanish Arab occupation of Crete (827), see Gaspar, *Homenaje a D. Francisco Codera* (Saragossa, 1904), 217-33; Brooks, *English Historical Review*, 28 (1913), 431-43; Vasiliev I, 49-61 (date, 56, note 1). The rebellion of Thomas lasted from 821-23; see Ostrogorsky[2] 166-7. The invaders of Crete did not come by way of Sicily, as here stated, but by way of Egypt; C. confuses the event with the first systematic assault on Sicily by African Saracens, which took place in the same year (827); see Vasiliev I, 61 ff. For the 'richness' of Crete, cf. Theoph. Cont. 74/20-2. With 22/41-5, cf. also Theoph. Cont. 474/1-7.

22/49-52 διαδέχεται Σουλεϊμάν. Sulaimān (715-17). For his expedition against Constantinople see on 21/116-26.

22/52-60 διαδέχεται Οὔμαρ κτλ.
The caliphs here listed are: 'Umar (II) ibn 'Abd al-'Azīz (717-20); Yazīd II (720-4); Hishām (724-43); (the brief reigns of Walīd II, Yazīd III and Ibrāhīm (743) are omitted); Marwān II (744-50); Ṣaffāḥ (750-4) and Manṣūr (754-75) (the first two 'Abbasid caliphs are confounded under the one name (22/56), since both were called 'Abdallah); Mahdī (775-85); Hārūn ar-Rashīd (786-809).

22/61-2 Ἐν τούτῳ τῷ χρόνῳ κτλ. For this incomplete and, as it stands, meaningless reference to the year 796, see Bury 530.

22/62-76 Τῷ δ' αὐτῷ ἔτει κτλ.
For the civil war (809-13) between Muḥammad al-Amīn (809-13) and 'Abdallah al-Ma'mūn (813-33), the sons of Hārūn, see Gabrieli, *Rivista degli Studi Orientali*, XI (1928), 341 ff.; Diehl-Marçais 355-8.

22/71-5 αἱ . . . ἐκκλησίαι.
For the destruction of Christian monasteries during this revolt, see also Theophanes 499/17-25; Mich. Syr. III, 23-4. For the monasteries here in question, see E. Schwartz, *Kyrillos von Skythopholis* (Leipzig, 1939), 290, 292, 294; and for the terms λαύρα and κοινόβιον, ibid., 289.

22/77-8 Ἀγροῦ, μητρόθειος.
For the Monastery of Agros at Sigriane (cf. 25/2), see Theophanes II, 557, s.v., and Bury, *ERE*, 74 and note 1. The precise degree of relationship implied by μητρόθειος is hard to determine: since Theophanes died in 818, and since Photeinos, great-grandfather of the Augusta Zöe, was active in the following decade (see Theoph. Cont. 76/8-10), we must postulate at least four generations between historian and emperor. Cf. Theoph. Cont. 5/3-4.

22/80 σοφωτάτου.. Cf. Dölger, *BES*, 201, note 13; Mango, *Zbornik Radova S.A.N.*, Viz. Inst. 6 (1960), 68, 90-2.

23, 24, 25/1-55
These passages consist of source material to be used in the Περὶ ἐθνῶν for the composition of a geographical and historical section on Saracen Spain, the history of which, C. complains (21/31-4), has hitherto been neglected by Byzantine historians. The

material is not edited or rearranged in any way (of c. 25 only lines 29–32 are relevant), as is the material borrowed from Theophanes for use in cc. 17 ff.; it is merely transcribed en bloc, from Stephanus of Byzantium and from Theophanes A.M. 5931: see General Introduction pp. 1–2. We must suppose that the section on the caliphate of Cordova was either never written or has been lost. This is the more regrettable since C.'s knowledge of 8th–9th cent. Spain must have been at least as exact as his knowledge of 8th–9th cent. Italy, and we should have been justified in expecting a section on Cordova at least as informative as is c. 27 on Italy. During the years 946–52 embassies, both political and cultural, were exchanged between Constantinople and Cordova: see De Cer., 571/15–16; Liudprand, Antapodosis, VI, 4–6; Vasiliev II/2, 185–7, 218–19, 276–81; cf. Vasiliev II, 272–8; and 25/61–2. Pilgrims were another source of information; see Synaxar. Cp. (AASS, November, Propylaeum), 320. C.'s knowledge of Saracen Spanish history was doubtless faulty in detail (see on 21/23–34, 22/36–40), but it was correct in essentials.

Since these chapters are unedited transcripts from other and much older books, and are besides irrelevant in subject and time to the period of which C. is writing, it is superfluous to comment on them in detail. For cc. 23, 24 the relevant bibliographical material will be found in Apparatus 1 of Vol. 1, pp. 98, 100, 102. For c. 25/1–55, which is Theophanes's account of the Vandal invasion of Africa (429–32), the reader may, in addition to the sources cited in Vol. 1, p. 102, consult J. B. Bury, History of the Later Roman Empire, 1 (London, 1923), 244–9; E. Stein, Geschichte des spätrömischen Reiches, 1 (Vienna, 1928), 472–8; and especially J. L. M. de Lepper, De Rebus Gestis Bonifatii Comitis Africae et Magistri Militum (Breda, 1941), x, xi (bibliography), and 75–106.

25/56–85 Ἰστέον, ὅτι τρεῖς ἀμερουμνεῖς κτλ.
After his notes on Spain, C. now returns to the Saracens, with a final, short passage summarizing present-day intelligence on the political state of the Saracen empire and its rulers: see Bury 531. That this passage is a later addition to the Saracen συγγραφή is shown in General Introduction p. 4.

25/56–62 τρεῖς ἀμερουμνεῖς κτλ.
At the beginning of the 10th century there were three caliphs in Islam: the 'Abbasid in Bagdad, who claimed descent from an uncle of Muḥammad; the Fatimid in Tunisia, claiming descent from Muḥammad through his daughter Fāṭima and his son-in-law 'Alī; and the Umayyad in Cordova. At the time of writing the three were, respectively, Muṭi' (946–74), Manṣūr (946–53) and 'Abd ar-Raḥmān III (912–61).

25/63–4 κατ' ἀρχὰς . . . Βαγδάδ.
Baghdad was not, of course, the first capital of the caliphs. The patriarchal caliphs had their seat in Medina; the Umayyads in Damascus and other places in Syria. Manṣūr founded Baghdad in 762–3 as his new capital.

25/67 Περσίαν, ἤγουν τὸ Χωρασάν. Khurāsān was the largest and most important of the provinces into which Persia was divided.

25/69–71 ἀμηραδίαν τὴν Φιλιστίημ κτλ.
See Hitti, Origins, 202. Syria was divided by the Arab conquerors into the four Junds (military districts) of Filasṭīn (Palestine), Jordan, Damascus and Ḥimṣ, corresponding to former Byzantine administrative districts; cf. Diehl-Marçais 200 and note 87. The administrative centre of the Jund of Palestine was Ramla (25/69). Mu'āwiya added the Jund of Qinnasrīn in the north, which included Aleppo, sometimes its chief town. About 786, under Hārūn ar-Rashid, the Jund of Qinnasrīn was subdivided, the frontier marches being organized into the separate Jund al-'Awāṣim (Jund of the Border-Fortresses). Antioch (25/71) is variously reported as being in the Jund of Qinnasrīn and the Jund of the marches, sometimes as the centre of the latter; see G. Le Strange, Palestine under the

Moslems (London, 1890), 24 ff. From 877, when Aḥmad ibn Ṭūlūn incorporated Syria into his virtually autonomous governorship of Egypt (Diehl-Marçais 391–2), most of Syria was under the jurisdiction of the ruler of Egypt. In 944 the Hamdanid Saif ad-Daula captured Aleppo from the Egyptian garrison and made it the centre of an autonomous principality (Diehl-Marçais 393).

25/72–4 ἀμηραδίαν τὸ Χαρὰν κτλ.
Harran, Āmid (later Diyārbekir), Naṣībīn and Takrīt were all towns in the province of Jazīra or Mesopotamia. Takrīt was transferred some time in the 10th cent. to the province of Iraq; see G. Le Strange, *Lands of the Eastern Caliphate* (repr. Cambridge, 1930), 37, 86 ff.; Rice, *Anatolian Studies*, 2 (1952), 36–84.

25/74 ’Αφρικῆς ἀποσπασθείσης. A reference to the rise of the Fatimids in Tunisia (909); see Diehl-Marçais 424–7.

25/77–9 ’Αρτίως δὲ πάλιν κτλ.
This is no doubt an allusion to the rise of the Buwaihid dynasty in Persia, and to the seizure of Baghdad by Aḥmad Mu'izz ad-Daula in 946 (*cf.* ἀρτίως). Though the Buwaihids usurped the effective power of the caliph, they left him the title, adopting for themselves the title of Amīr al-Umarā', literally, Prince of Princes, or Commander of Commanders, which a Byzantine observer, seeing the usurpation of the real authority of the caliph, might easily confuse with Amīr al-Mu'minīn (ἀμερουμνῆς), Commander or Prince of the Faithful; see Manojlović I, 37–8. The Buwaihids were Shi'ites but did not themselves claim 'Alid descent. They came from western Persia, not from Khurāsān. For the dynasty generally, see V. Minorsky, *Domination des Dailamites* (Paris, 1932) *passim*; Diehl-Marçais 389; Cahen, *EI²*, *s.v.* Buwayhids.

25/80–1 τὸ κουρὰν . . . δίκην μανιακίου.
Cf. the ἐγκόλπια of Byzantine emperors, and see Du Cange *s. vv.* ἐγκόλπιον, φυλακτόν. For the Saracens' talismanic use of the Koran, see Reiske's note at *De Cer.*, II, 132–3; and for their cult of relics generally, see Goldziher, *Muhammedanische Studien*, 2 (1890), 356–68.

25/83–4 τῆς εὐδαίμονος ’Αραβίας.
The general trend towards provincial autonomy in the Islamic empire affected the Yemen at the beginning of the 9th cent., and from about 924–5 no further governors were appointed from Baghdad. Various local dynasties flourished, several of them professing different forms of Shi'ism. The Zaidī Imāms, claiming descent from 'Alī, established themselves towards the end of the 9th cent., and an Ismā'īlī mission serving the Fatimid Imām was also able to win some successes: see A. Van Arendonk, *De Opkomst van het Zaidietische Imamaat in Yemen* (Leiden, 1919; French tr. *Les débuts de l'imamat zaidite au Yemen*, Leiden, 1960). Manojlović (I, 37–8) connects this notice with the Carmathian revolt of the early 10th cent.: (Abū Ṭāhir took Mecca in January 930), but it seems more likely that the Zaidi Imām is meant.

C. 26

BIBLIOGRAPHY

Cambridge Medieval History III (Cambridge, 1922) (*CMH*).   E. Dümmler, *Geschichte des ostfränkischen Reiches* II, III (Leipzig, 1887, 1888) (Dümmler).   L. M. Hartmann, *Geschichte Italiens im Mittelalter* III/I, 2 (Gotha, 1908, 1911) (Hartmann).   A. Hofmeister, 'Markgrafen und Markgrafschaften im italischen Königreich', *Mitteilungen des Instituts für österreichischen Geschichtsforschung*, Ergänzungsband 7, Heft 2 (Vienna, 1907) 386–404 (Hofmeister).   W. Ohnsorge, *Abendland und Byzanz* (Darmstadt, 1958) (Ohnsorge).

INTRODUCTORY NOTE

This chapter is a later (political) insertion to the Italian section of the original Περὶ ἐθνῶν (c. 27), as may be seen by its contents and also by the facts that it is out of place and immediately follows a similar insertion (25/56–85): see General Introduction p. 4. The passage must have been written down and placed in the records before, or very shortly after, 22nd November, 950, the date of young Lothair's death (26/66). Its addition to *DAI* may be dated to 952.

The chapter gives a short, often inaccurate, summary of the history of the Regnum Italicum between the years 869 and 944, that is, from the death of Lothair II, king of Lorraine, down to the marriage of his great-granddaughter Bertha with C.'s son Romanus (26/67). The object of the passage is to glorify Hugh of Arles, C.'s συμπένθερος, by illustrating his descent from Charles the Great (*cf.* 13/116–22); and Hugh's virtual deposition (945) and death (947) are not mentioned, although his son Lothair is described as 'now king of Italy' (26/66).

C.'s sources of information for this chapter were certainly the numerous embassies, Byzantine and Frank, which passed between Constantinople and the west during the reigns of Leo VI, Romanus I and himself: see Liudprand, *Antapodosis* III, 22; V, 20; VI, 2–3; Gay 225; Ohnsorge 227 ff. Liudprand's own conversations with C. in 949 were doubtless a chief source (Bury 553–6); but we should not regard them as the only one. The inaccuracies in the account are probably due to its being based on oral, not on written historical information. Ohnsorge has rightly pointed out (see on 26/11) that what interested the Byzantine government was the succession of wearers of the imperial crown in the west, and on them it kept a careful watch. About the development of western politics as such, it was less well informed, because less interested. Even so, it is hard to explain why C. should make three errors regarding the parentage of his own daughter-in-law's father (see on 26/15).

Other possible sources of information are C.'s half-sister Anna (see on 13/107; but her marriage to Lewis III was very brief); and, of course, Bertha-Eudocia herself. For the relationship of the persons mentioned in c. 26, see the accompanying genealogical table. For Byzantine policy towards King Hugh until 945, see Ohnsorge 35, 234, 522.

26/2 ὁ μέγας Λωθάριος.
Lothair II (825–69), second son of the emperor Lothair I and great-grandson of Charlemagne. He was not, as is here stated, king of Italy; but see Ohnsorge 246, note 89. His elder brother, the emperor Lewis II (see 29/104–69), ruled over Italy: see *CMH*, 34, 44. μέγας here, as μεγάλου in the next line and μεγάλην, μεγάλης at 26/15, 70, means 'elder': see Dölger, *BES*, 286, note 7; *cf. De Cer.*, 644/7, 11, and on 30/73–4.

26/4 ἐγκώμιά τε καὶ διηγήματα. See Einhard, *Vit. Karol. Magn.*, c. 29; *cf.* G. Paris, *Histoire poétique de Charlemagne* (Paris, 1905), 37–52.

26/5–8 Οὗτος οὖν ὁ Κάρουλος . . . ὑπόσπονδοι αὐτοῦ.
A passage of great importance for Byzantine political theory in the 9th cent.: see Ohnsorge 242–4; *id., Das Zweikaiserproblem im früheren Mittelalter* (Hildesheim, 1947), 28–47; Dölger, *BES*, 288 ff. The title of emperor (*sc.* of the Franks: *cf.* Theophanes 494/21) was conceded by Byzantium to Charles in his capacity of *Gesamtherrscher* over the united West (μονοκράτωρ . . . μεγάλην Φραγγίαν), a status which his successors could not claim and were hence, after 871 officially, degraded to the rank of ῥῆγες (*cf.* 29/105), though allowed to retain spiritual *Brotherhood* in the imperial family hierarchy (*De Cer.*, 689/12): see Ohnsorge, *Zweikaiserproblem*, 40, 42, 45. The terms μονοκράτωρ and ἐβασίλευσε are carefully distinguished from the official titles of the eastern emperor, αὐτοκράτωρ and βασιλεὺς τῶν Ῥωμαίων: see Dölger, *BES*, 287, note 7, 304, 307. For μονοκράτωρ, see also Dölger, *BD*, 110; and Soloviev, *Byzantinoslavica*, 9 (1947), 36.

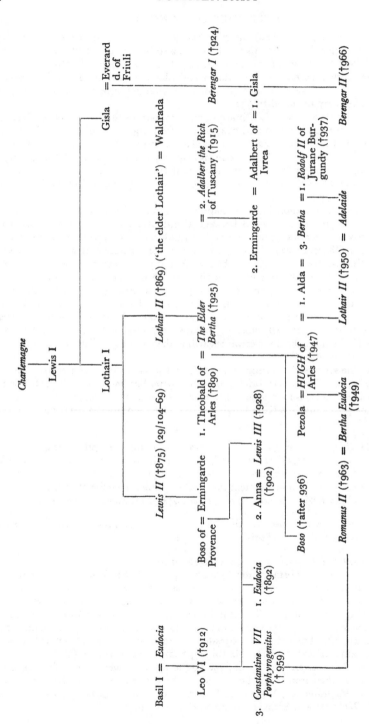

Genealogical Tree of *persons mentioned* in chapter 26.

26/7–8 οὐδεὶς τῶν ὑπολοίπων ῥηγῶν . . . καλέσαι.

Cf. Einhard, *Vit. Karol. Magn.*, c. 16. The 'kings' in question were Charles's three sons: see on 28/18–19; Ohnsorge 243. For the status of ῥήξ in the Byzantine diplomatic hierarchy, see Dölger, *BZ*, 31 (1931), 439–40, who cites *De Cer.*, 679/8 (*cf.* Reiske's note *ibid.*, II, 811–13) and Kinnamos 219/1–3; Stein, *Mélanges Bidez*, II (Brussels, 1934), 903 and note 1; Ohnsorge 248–51.

26/9 ἐν Παλαιστίνῃ . . . μοναστήρια.

For Charles's relations with the caliphate and the Holy Land, see Einhard, *Vit. Karol. Magn.*, cc. 16, 27; F. W. Buckler, *Harun'l Rashid and Charles the Great* (Cambridge, Mass., 1931), 29–31, 35–6 and bibliography 57–64; *cf.* Runciman, *English Historical Review*, 50 (1935), 606 ff. For the monasteries, that is, hostels founded by Charles, see S. Runciman, *A History of the Crusades*, I (Cambridge, 1951), 43 and note 3.

26/11–12 κατὰ ῾Ρώμης . . . τοῦ τότε πάπα.

This is inaccurate. As Dr Ohnsorge has kindly suggested to me, C. is probably confusing Lothair II with his father, the *emperor* Lothair I; *cf.* Dümmler II, 242, note 4. For Lothair's mission to pope Hadrian at (Cassino and) Rome, and his death of the plague at Piacenza (8th August, 869), see *Annales Bertiniani* (*MGH*, Scr. 1), 481–2; Reginonis *Chronicon* (*MPL*, CXXXII), cols. 97–9; Dümmler II, 240–4; *CMH*, 44.

26/11 ἐστέφθη.

Though the western emperors ceased to be recognized as such by Byzantium in 871, Byzantium carefully noted who was, or was not, crowned at Rome: see 26/19, 23; Ohnsorge 240, 245–6, 254.

26/15 ἔτεκεν δὲ υἱόν.

C. commits three errors regarding the parentage of Hugh: Adalbert the Rich, Marquis of Tuscany (†915), was not son, but son-in-law of Lothair; Bertha was not daughter-in-law, but daughter of Lothair, by his mistress Waldrada; and finally Hugh's father was not Adalbert, but Bertha's first husband, Theobald of Arles (†890); see Hofmeister 391–2. Gay (225) believes that the first two errors were made deliberately, in order to trace Hugh's descent from Charles through the male line; *cf.* Liudprand, *Antapodosis*, V, 14. But the third at least must be due to ignorance. It is noteworthy that these errors might have arisen from a reading of *Antapodosis*, I, 39; II, 36, but less understandably from conversation with Liudprand. For a similar error regarding notorious parentage, *cf.* Psellus, *Chronographie*, ed. Renauld, I, 3/9–10; and on 13/61–6.

26/15–16 τὴν μεγάλην Βέρταν.

That is, the 'elder' Bertha: see on 26/2. *Cf.* 26/69–70, and Hofmeister 393. At *MPG*, CXI, col. 197 D, Lewis III is referred to as ἀνεψιὸς Βέρτας.

26/17 Λοδόϊκος ὁ ἴδιος τοῦ Λοδοΐκου.

Lewis III, the Blind, of Provence, grandson of the emperor Lewis II (but Ohnsorge 241, note 69, thinks Λοδοΐκου corrupt, and would read Λωθαρίου). For his two invasions of Italy, in 900 and 905, see Liudprand, *Antapodosis*, II, 35, 36–41, with ed. Becker (*Die Werke Liudprands von Cremona*[3], 1915), 53, notes 1, 2; *Gesta Berengarii Imperatoris*, ed. Dümmler (Halle, 1871), IV, 1–65; Kolias, *EEBΣ*, 23 (1953), 331. For the date of his blinding, 21st July, 905, see *CMH*, 138, note 1. For his marriage to C.'s half-sister Anna, see on 13/107. For ἴδιος = 'kinsman', *cf.* Cont. Geo. Mon. 851/5; *De Cer.*, 597/11 598/1. Dujčev, *BZ*, 46 (1953), 121, would supply ἔγγονος after ἴδιος.

26/18 ἀπὸ τῆς μεγάλης Φραγγίας. See on 28/4–5; Ohnsorge 241–2.

26/19 ἄστεπτος.

In fact, Lewis received the crown of Italy at Pavia on 12th October, 900, and the imperial crown at Rome in the following February: see Hartmann III/2, 180 and 203, note 4.

26/21-2 ἐκράτησεν Βεριγγάριος.

Cf. Liudprand, *Antapodosis*, II, 41; Berengarius regno potitur. Berengar I, great-grandson of Charlemagne, was king of Italy 888-924 and emperor after 915; see Liudprand, *Antapodosis*, I, 15, 43. It was against him that Bertha and Adalbert persuaded Lewis III to rise; see *Gesta Berengarii Imperatoris*, IV, 1 ff. He was grandfather of Berengar II: see Liudprand, *Antapodosis*, II, 33.

26/23 ἐστέφθη. Berengar received the imperial crown in December 915; see Hofmeister 401; Hartmann III, 2, 188 and 205, note 7.

26/23 τῷ ʿΡοδούλφῳ.

Rodolf II of Jurane Burgundy. For his expedition to Pavia (922) and defeat of Berengar at Fiorenzuola (17th July, 923), see Liudprand, *Antapodosis*, II, 60 and 64-7; Hartmann III, 2, 191-2 and 206, note 9. Of a victory of Berengar over Rodolf before the battle of Fiorenzuola there is no mention elsewhere; C. is perhaps thinking of the victory over Adalbert of Ivrea near Brescia (see Liudprand, *Antapodosis*, II, 61-2), after which Adalbert saved his purse by a trick similar to that by which Berengar is here said to have saved his life.

26/26 ὁ μὲν ἥμισυς λαός. *Cf.* Liudprand, *Antapodosis*, II, 65: media pars populi etc.

26/31, 33 δόρκας . . . μεναύλου.

For δόρκα (? *cf.* Italian *targa*), see on 51/82-4; *De Cer.*, 579/2, 670/7, with Reiske's note *ibid.*, II, 682. For μέναυλον, see Leo, *Taktika*, col. 732 A; Theophanes 221/3.

26/38 συνεβιβάσθησαν. See Hartmann III/2, 192 and 206, note 9.

26/41-53 Καὶ μετὰ τοῦτο ἦλθον κτλ.

For this unsuccessful expedition of Hugh and of his full brother Boso (Liudprand, *Antapodosis*, III, 47; Hofmeister 392, note 4), see Liudprand, *Antapodosis*, III, 12 with ed. Becker 79, note 3; Hartmann III/2, 207, note 11. *Gesta Berengarii Imperatoris*, ed. Dümmler, 46, note 1 and *CMH*, 139 date the expedition to 923; but Previté-Orton, *English Historical Review*, 32 (1917), 340 places it before the coming of Rodolf. For Hugh Tagliaferro, see Previté-Orton, *ibid.*, 341. For the Gospels carried in supplicatory processions, see Reiske's note at *De Cer.*, II, 100.

26/54-5 ἀπέκτεινεν αὐτὸν Φαλέμβερτος.

For the murder of Berengar, see Liudprand, *Antapodosis*, II, 68-73; Hartmann III/2, 193 and 206, note 9. For the date, 7th April, 924, see Liudprand, *Antapodosis*, ed. Becker 69, note 3. With ἐκράτησεν ὅλον τὸ ῥηγᾶτον ὁ ʿΡοδούλφος, *cf.* Liudprand, *Antapodosis*, III, 8: regnum potenter obtinuit.

26/56-8 Καὶ μετὰ τοῦτο κτλ.

For the second coming of Hugh, see Liudprand, *Antapodosis*, III, 12, 16; Hartmann III/2, 196-7 and 207, note 12. Rodolf's tenure of ὅλον τὸ ῥηγᾶτον lasted from 924 to 926. Hugh was crowned at Pavia in July 926.

26/62 τελευτήσαντος.

For Rodolf's death (July 937) and the subsequent marriages of his widow and daughter, see Liudprand, *Antapodosis*, IV, 13; Hartmann III/2, 201, 236; Bury 555.

26/66 τῷ νυνὶ ὄντι . . . ῥηγί. Lothair reigned from 947 until his death on 22nd November, 950; see Hartmann III/2, 237.

26/66–72 Ἡ δὲ ἀνελθοῦσα κτλ.

See Liudprand, *Antapodosis*, V, 14, 20; Theoph. Cont. 431/11–19; Cont. Geo. Mon. 917/11–18; and the text cited on 13/121–2. The marriage took place in September 944, and the girl died five years afterwards, in 949: cf. Runciman, *Romanus Lecapenus*, 196. If we are right in emending the ἤτοι of 26/68 to an imperfect ἦτο, the implication would be that she was already dead at the time of writing. But if ἤτοι is right, ἡ ἀνελθοῦσα must be the subject of ἐβασίλευσε, and we must place a lacuna after ἀνδρὸς αὐτῆς and supply πέντε after ἔτη (944–9): see on 26/71. Bertha-Eudocia and her husband are represented on a frequently published ivory plaque in the Bibliothèque Nationale: *e.g.* R. Byron, *The Byzantine Achievement* (London, 1929), pl. 4.

26/68 φιλοχρίστου δεσπότου.

For φιλόχριστος, an epithet not applied to iconoclast emperors, see Reiske's note at *De Cer.*, II, 493–4. For δεσπότης, a term originally applied to a junior emperor but at this period a simple alternative to βασιλεύς or αὐτοκράτωρ, see Bréhier, *BZ*, 15 (1906), 176; Ostrogorsky, *Glas Srpsk. Kral. Akad.*, 164 (1935), 105, note 1; Dölger, *BD*, 131.

26/71 ἐβασίλευσεν ἔτη ⟨δέκα⟩.

If the elder, and not the younger, Bertha is the subject of ἐβασίλευσεν, then we must supply δέκα after ἔτη, that is, the ten years from her second husband's death in 915 to her own in 925. For her rule, cf. Liudprand, *Antapodosis*, II, 55; Hofmeister 402; Hartmann III/2, 195. But the reading is not certain: see on 26/66–72. For the ambiguous meaning of the verb, see on 26/5–8.

26/71–2 μάμμης καὶ ἀδελφῆς.

The two Eudocias in question were Eudocia Ingerina and Eudocia daughter of Leo VI by his first wife St Theophano; see *De Cer.*, 643/11–12; *Vita Euthymii*, ed. De Boor (Berlin, 1888), 19/20, 20/13–14, 126.

Cc. 27–28, 29/54–216

BIBLIOGRAPHY

I. TEXTS

Annales Bertiniani Auctore Hincmaro; MGH scr. 1 (Hincmar). *Chronicle of Ahimaaz*, tr. Salzman (Columbia Univ. Pr., 1924) (*Chron. Ahimaaz*). *Chronicon Casinense, MGH* scr. III (*Chron. Cas.*). *Chronicon Saleritanum, MGH* scr., III (*Chron. Sal.*); new ed. U. Westerbergh, Lund, 1956 (W.) *Chronicon Venetum, MGH* scr., XIV (*Chron. Ven.*). *Chronicon Venetum Andreae Danduli, scr. rer. ital.*, XII (Dandolo). *Chronicae quae dicuntur Fredegarii scholastici, MGH* scr. rer. Merov., II (Fredegarius). *Cronaca veneziana del diacono Giovanni*, ed. Monticolo, *Cronache veneziane antichissime* (Rome, 1890) (John the Deacon). *Cronica de singulis patriarchis Novae Aquileie* and *Chronicon Gradense*, ed. Monticolo, *Cronache veneziane antichissime* (Rome, 1890) (*Cron. Ven. Ant.*). *Erchemperti Historia Langobardorum, MGH* scr., III (Erchempert). *Pauli Historia Langobardorum. MGH* scr. rer. Lang. et Ital. saec. VI–IX (Paul the Deacon).

2. MODERN WORKS

S. Abel–B. Simson, *Jahrbücher des fränkischen Reiches unter Karl dem Grossen*, ii (Leipzig, 1883) (Abel–Simson). M. Amari, *Storia dei Musulmani di Sicilia* i² (Catania, 1933) (Amari). F. Dvornik, *Les Slaves, Byzance et Rome au IXe siècle* (Paris, 1926) (Dvornik, *Les Slaves*). L. M. Hartmann, *Geschichte Italiens im Mittelalter* ii/2, iii/1 (Gotha, 1903, 1908) (Hartmann). F. Hirsch, *Das Herzogthum Benevent bis zur Untergang des langobardischen Reiches* (Leipzig, 1871) (Hirsch). F. Hirsch, *Byzantinische Studien* (Leipzig, 1876) (Hirsch, *Byzantinische Studien*). H. Kretschmayr, 'Die Beschreibung der venezianischen Inseln bei Konst. Porph.', *BZ*, 13 (1904), 482–9 (Kretschmayr, *Beschreibung*). H. Kretschmayr, *Geschichte von Venedig*, i (Gotha, 1905) (Kretschmayr). E. Lentz, *Das Verhältnis Venedigs zu Byzanz nach dem Fall des Exarchats bis zum Ausgang des neunten Jahrhunderts*, i (Berlin, 1891) (Lentz). W. Ohnsorge, *Abendland und Byzanz* (Darmstadt, 1958) (Ohnsorge).

INTRODUCTORY NOTE TO c. 27/1–70

(For Introductory Note to 29/54–216 see below, p. 101).

Cc. 27, 28 belong to the original scheme of the Περὶ ἐθνῶν, and should follow immediately on c. 22: see General Introduction pp. 3–4. The first passage (27/1–70) contains an incomplete and often inaccurate summary of the history of the Byzantine province of Lombardy (Lagoubardia) during the two preceding centuries (the coming of the Lombards is misdated to the 8th cent.). Lombardy was incorporated as an independent *thema* during the reign of Leo VI: see on 50/85 and Gay 173. Its territory covered in theory all of Southern Italy except Calabria, as far north as the Papal State: see Gay, pl. 2. The date of its incorporation probably coincided with the Byzantine occupation of Benevento (891). We may, however, note with Gay (170) that C. occasionally regards Lombardy as covering all of Italy reconquered by Belisarius and Narses in the 6th cent.: cf. *De Them.*, 97/16–18.

The emphasis laid on the supremacy of Capua (27/50, 61) led Gay (170, note 1) and Bury (544) to conclude that C.'s sources of information were Lombard and Capuan. The story of Narses and Irene (27/14–37) can hardly be of Byzantine origin, nor have been subjected to Byzantine historical criticism. But the date at which the information reached Constantinople is uncertain. Gay (170 and note 1) thought that it came with the Capuan embassy of Landolf in 909. Banduri (*MPG*, cxiii, col. 239, note 42), relying on the statement at 27/66 that Capua Nova was founded 73 years before, argued that C. wrote down this item in 929, since the date of the foundation was c. 856. Bury (545) disputed this, and maintained that the passage was, as we should have expected, written in 949, since at 27/55 it is stated that the division of Lombardy (*i.e.* between Radelchis and Sikenolf in 849) took place '200 years ago', and 200 he thought to be an obvious mistake for 100. However, if we are to emend σ′ (200) at all, it is just as easy, if not easier, to amend to π′ (80) as to ρ′ (100), and to assume that the words ἥτις . . . ͵ϲυνζ′ are an insertion of 949, which would make it possible to retain Banduri's date for both notices: and if this were right, we should have a rare indication that material for the earlier Περὶ ἐθνῶν was being amassed *pari passu* with that of the Περὶ θεμάτων: see General Introduction p. 5, note 1. The information contained in the passage is in any case so inaccurate that arguments based on its chronological data must be precarious: cf. Hirsch 3, note 2.

27/2 πριγκιπάτων καὶ ἀρχοντιῶν.

The πριγκιπᾶτα are the Lombard principalities of Benevento (since 774; Capua-Benevento since 899) and Salerno (since 849): see *De Cer.*, 690/4–5. The ἀρχοντίαι are the governments of the nominally Byzantine but practically independent states of Amalfi and Gaeta: see *De Cer.*, 690/6.

27/6 τὸ βασίλειον. Cf. *De Them.*, 84/tit., 94/4.

27/7 διεμερίσθησαν . . . εἰς ἀρχὰς δύο.

See Gay 173, 174. This twofold division may, however, vaguely recall the two divisions of Byzantine authority in Italy before the fall of Ravenna to the Lombards (751), to which the following version of the Narses story clearly refers (see next note): that is to say, in the north the exarchate, though this had no authority over the Lombard cities of Benevento, Papia and Capua, and in the south the province of Sicily, whose military governor did in fact exercise authority over Calabria, Naples and Amalfi: see 27/58-61; Gay 7, 8, 17; Hartmann III/1, 163; *Cambridge Medieval History*, II (1913), 232-3.

27/14-37 Ἐν δὲ τοῖς καιροῖς Εἰρήνης κτλ.

That the Lombard invasion of Italy (566) was in response to the invitation of Narses is stated by *Liber Pontificalis*, lxiii (Iohannes III), and by Isidore of Seville (*MPL*, LXXXIII, col. 1055 A); see Bury's Gibbon V, 9-10, note 20. The incident of the distaff is told first by Fredegarius III, c. 65, and repeated by Paul the Deacon II, c. 5 and by John the Deacon, 61. For the various sources, see Bury's Gibbon V, 509-11; Hartmann II/1, 33, note 16. C.'s narrative is close to that of Fredegarius: eo quod agusta ei adparatum ex auro facto muliebri, eo quod eonucus erat, cum quo filaret, direxit; et pensiliariis regerit, non populo. At ille respondens: 'Filo filabo, de quem Justinus imperator nec agusta ad caput venire non possit'. With μέχρις ἂν ζῶσιν (27/29) *cf.* also John the Deacon, *loc. cit.*: qualem ipsa dum viveret deponere non posset. C.'s version transfers the story from the 6th to the 8th cent., and makes Narses contemporary with pope Zacharias (741-52); this suggests, as Bury (545-7) has noted, that the Lombard source has transferred the incident from the invasion of Alboin to the fall of Ravenna (751). But if this is so, it is more reasonable to assume that the empress Irene here mentioned is not the wife of Leo IV but the wife of Constantine V (see Theophanes 410/1). The story of Byzantine losses in Italy would be more justly connected in Lombard memory with the neglect and heresy of Copronymus (see Ostrogorsky[2] 137; A. Lombard, *Constantin V*, Paris, 1902, 79-81) than with the conciliatory policy of the younger Irene (see Gay 36-8).

27/16 ὁ πάπας . . . ἐκράτει τὴν Ῥώμην.   *Cf. De Them.*, 94/3-4; in fact, however, the Papal State dates from 767: see Hartmann II/2, 218-9.

27/31 εἰς Παννονίαν.   *Cf.* Procopius, *B. G.*, III, 33, 10; Paul the Deacon I, c. 22.

27/32 ὀπώρας παντοίας.   *Cf.* Paul the Deacon II, c. 5: multimoda pomorum genera.

27/37 ἦλθον εἰς Βενεβενδόν.

Beneventum fell to the Lombards in 571, but the story here told of its capture is apocryphal: see Hirsch 3, note 2. In any case the walls had been destroyed by Totila and not yet rebuilt: see Procopius, *B. G.*, III, 6, 1. The origin of the tale may be the same as of that told of the capture of Bari by the Saracens in *Chron. Cas.*, 225: obsitis siquidem vestimentis et calciamentis, saltem nec tara bene succinctis, sed solis harundinibus manu gestantes.

27/40 οἰκοδομήσαντες . . . κάστρον μικρόν.   For such Lombard forts, *e.g.* Cividale or Castel Seprio, see G. P. Bognetti, *S. Maria di Castelseprio* (Milan, [1948]), 55-6.

27/45-6 ἐπὶ τὸ αὐτό.

The phrase is normally used of persons or things collected together on the same spot (*cf.* 46/153); but this meaning is unsatisfactory here, since there would be no point in stating that the Lombards directed their assault towards the same objective. However, ἐπὶ τὸ αὐτό is sometimes used almost with the sense of ὁμοῦ (cf. Theoph. Cont. 475/22; AASS, Sept. vol. III, 857 A), and may be used so here: 'they wheeled about in the church, and attacked all together'.

27/47 θέματος. This is of course an anachronism: cf. on 32/16–20 fin., and on 50/85.

27/48–9 ἄνευ τῆς Ὑδρεντοῦ . . . Ῥουσιάνου. See Gay 6, 14, 169.

27/49–50 Νεαπόλεως . . . Ἀμάλφης. See 27/67-8; Gay 21-2, 169. For Amalfi see also Hofmeister, Byz.-Neugr. Jahrb., 1 (1920), 94 ff.

27/50 Πρῶτον δὲ κάστρον. See on 27/61.

27/52 ᾠκίσθη.
This statement refers to the forcible translation of the Amalfitans to Salerno by Sicard in or about 837; see Chron. Sal., cc. 72-4; Gay 41; Hartmann III/1, 209; Hofmeister, Byz.-Neugr. Jahrb., 1 (1920), 96.

27/52-3 διεμέρισαν . . . τὰ πριγκιπᾶτα.
See Radelgisi et Siginulfi Divisio Ducatus Beneventani (MGH, Leg. IV), 221 ff.; Gay 62-4; Hartmann III/1, 219-20. For the date (849) see Gay 62; Hartmann III/1, 229, note 15.

27/55 ἔτη σ'. See Introductory Note to this Section; and on 27/66.

27/55 ἀδελφοὶ δύο.
Sico (817-31) was father, not brother, of Sicard (831-9), who succeeded him as prince of Beneventum; see Gay 39-43. The division was between Radelchis, the thesaurarius, who succeeded Sicard on the throne of Beneventum (see Erchempert c. 14), and Sikenolf, brother of Sicard, who became prince of Salerno after the division of the principality: see Gay 50-1.

27/58 Νεάπολις . . . πραιτώριον. See on 27/7. For the πραιτώριον, cf. De Them., 82/3.

27/60 δούξ.
See Dölger, BZ, 31 (1931), 440: ein byzantinischer Titel für einen Fürsten, der zum mindesten nominell zu jener Zeit noch unter oströmischer Oberhoheit steht.

27/61 Κάπυα . . . ὑπερμεγέθης.
See 27/50 and Introductory Note to this Section. Capua had in fact since 899 been the capital of the duchy of Capua-Benevento: cf. De Cer., 690/4; Gay 151. The old city was destroyed by Gaiseric in 456, but, as Hirsch, 2, note 2, observes, it is an exaggeration to say that it was an ἐρημόκαστρον when the Lombards occupied it in 571.

27/63 πάλιν τῶν Ἀφρικῶν.
These are the Saracens of Bari under Kalfon (29/90) who at the hest of Radelchis devastated the territories of Sikenolf during the 840's; see Chron. Cas., 225: cum his (sc. Saracenis) quoque Radelchis totam devastavit Siconolfi regionem, Capuamque primariam universam redegit in cinerem. Cf. Vasiliev I, 209.

27/64 ᾠκοδόμησεν . . . κάστρον.
For the foundation of New Capua (856), see Erchempert cc. 24, 25 (supra pontem qui vulgo Casilinium dicitur); Chron. S. Ben. (MGH, scr. III), 205; Gay 68; Hartmann III/1, 247; Amari I, 502.

27/66 ἔτη ογ'.

See Introductory Note to this Section. The figure 73 (+856 = 929) does not harmonize with 27/54 (949); and the figure 200 at 27/55 gives a third discrepancy. It is suggested above that ἥτις . . . ‚συνζ' (27/53–4) are an insertion of 949 and that π' should be read for σ' at 27/55: this would give the year 929 in both cases for the *original* composition of the passage. But other solutions are possible.

27/69–70 Ἰστέον, ὅτι μαστρομίλης κτλ.

That is to say, '*Magister militum* corresponds to the Greek katepano of the army'. The reference is to the Duke of Naples, who bore this title: see *De Cer.*, 690/23. For the significance of the term at this period, see Reiske's note at *De Cer.*, II, 817–8; Kretschmayr 39, 416. For κατεπάνω, see on 45/147, 50/169–70; it is clear from the equation with δούξ that κατεπάνω still retains its limited, local significance. For knowledge of Latin at Byzantium, *cf.* Dölger, *BES*, 18 and note 28.

INTRODUCTORY NOTE TO c. 27/71—c. 28

This passage on the early history of Venice also belongs to the original Περὶ ἐθνῶν (see General Introduction pp. 3–4), and falls into four sections: 1. Topography (27/71–96); 2. Foundation of Venice (28/1–16); 3. Pippin's attack in 809–10 (28/17–43); and 4. Origin of the independent Duchy (28/43–51). The sources of C.'s narratives are purely Venetian: see Kretschmayr 19, and *id.*, *Beschreibung*, 486; Bury 552–3. They represent 'Venetian living tradition'; and while most of the incidents recur in the earliest Venetian chronicles, there is no single extant Venetian source from which C. could have borrowed wholesale. On the other hand, the selection of material is made from the Byzantine point of view: see Kretschmayr 58. Thus, emphasis is laid on the conquest by Pippin, which brought about a memorable revolution in Byzantine diplomacy in relation to Charlemagne (*cf.* on 26/5–8).

27/72 ἐκαλοῦντο Ἐνετικοί.

For the traditions, see Paul the Deacon II, c. 14; *Chron. Ven.*, 33; John the Deacon 63: proximas insulas petierunt, sicque Venetie nomen, de qua exierant, eisdem insulis indiderunt, qui et actenus illic degentes Venetici nuncupantur. Heneti vero, licet apud Latinos una littera addatur, grece laudabiles (*sc.* αἰνετοί) dicuntur. For the significance of the terms 'Venice', 'Venetians' in these chapters, see Kretschmayr, *Beschreibung*, 484, note 3.

27/73–4 Κόγκορδα . . . Νούνου.

For Concordia, see Kretschmayr 12 and *Enciclopedia Italiana*, XI (1931), 82–3, *s.v.* Concordia Sagittaria. Justiniana and Nonum are not easily identifiable. The former is perhaps Aegida, refounded by Justin II with the name Justinopolis, the modern Capodistria: see *MPG* CXIII, col. 240, note 45; Philippi Cluveri, *Italia Antiqua* (Leyden, 1624), I, 210. If so, C.'s designation is both inaccurate and anachronistic. Nonum may be the Ad Nonum mentioned in the Itinerarium Hierosolymitanum (*Itinerarium Antonini Augusti et Hierosolymitanum*, ed. Parthey and Pinder, Berlin, 1848, 265; *cf. Itineraria Romana*, ed. Cuntz, Teubner, 1929, 88, no. 559/5) as lying between Padua and Altinum; *cf.* Cluverius, *tom. cit.*, 162: AD NONUM autem LAPIDEM opidum *Mestre* VII millaria à Venetiis dissitum. Neither can compare in importance with Padua, Aquileia or Oderzo.

27/75–96 Ἰστέον, ὅτι περασάντων κτλ.

This section has been so thoroughly explored by Kretschmayr (*Beschreibung*) that we need do little but refer to his article. C. begins with a brief mention of the capital, Rialto (27/76–8); then follows an enumeration of the Lidi (νῆσοι κατ' ἀνατολὰς τοῦ αὐτοῦ κάστρου) from north to south, that is, from Grado (Κογράδον) to Loreo (Λαυριτῶν) (27/78–88); lastly come islands lying behind the Lidi, Torcello (Τορτζελῶν), Murano (Μουράν) and Rialto ('Ρίβαλτον), and cities of the mainland (27/89–95). As Kretschmayr, *Beschreibung*, 488, has noted, it is by a *lapsus calami* that C. places all the third group ἐν τῇ στερεᾷ (27/90), since at 27/77 and 28/50 he is aware that Rialto is an island. C.'s account lies between the earlier *Chron. Ven.*, 7–9, 15, 16, 39, and the later John the Deacon 63–6. The close similarity of C.'s description from Grado to Litus mercedis (Λιτου-μαγκέρσης) to that of *Chron. Ven.* justifies Kretschmayr in postulating a common origin.

27/76 ἐν πρώτοις.

This dubious statement is clarified at 28/47–51: see Kretschmayr, *Beschreibung*, 484–5. The original seat of the doge was Heracliana (Νεόκαστρον, 27/92; Τζιβιτάνουβα, 28/47): see on 28/47.

28/4–5 Φράγγοι . . . Φραγγίας.

This is not strictly accurate, since the earliest intervention of the Franks in Venetia was a brief occupation of Βενετιῶν τὰ πολλά in the middle of the 6th cent.; see Kretschmayr 17; E. Stein, *Histoire du Bas-Empire*, II (Paris, 1949), 526 and note 2, 610. But clearly C. uses the terms in the general sense of 10th cent. Byzantium: *cf.* Liudprand, *Legatio*, c. 33 (ex Francis, quo nomine tam Latinos quam Teutones comprehendit); Gay 225–6; Ohnsorge 241–2, who distinguishes Φραγγία = regnum italicum, Papia, from μεγάλη Φραγγία (26/18; *cf.* 30/73–4) = Transalpine Francia.

28/6–7 Ἀττίλα, τοῦ βασιλέως τῶν Ἀβάρων.

For the connexion of Attila with the foundation of Venice, see *Chron. Ven.*, 33; *Cron. Ven. Ant.*, 7, 48, 49, 70; Dandolo cols. 75–6; *cf.* Kretschmayr 411. Kretschmayr 16 shows that as a matter of fact the land-cities of Venetia recovered after the Hunnish invasion; *cf.* Hartmann II/2, 102. But folk-memory seized on the sack of Aquileia (452) as the fixed point of what was a gradual process. The Avars did not appear till the 6th cent. (Stein, *op. cit.*, 541), but it was common to confuse them with the Huns: see John the Deacon 75; Dandolo col. 94; Einhard, *Vit. Karol. Magn.*, c. 13; *Byzantinoturcica* II, 202 (2nd ed. 234).

28/10 ποιεῖν ἐκεῖσε καλύβια. For the Venetian versions, see *Cron. Ven. Ant.*, 19 and note 2.

28/17–39 παρεγένετο πάλιν Πιπῖνος κτλ.

For the Frankish version, see Einhard, *Annales* (*MPL*, CIV), col. 473 B, ann. 810. For Venetian versions, see *Chron. Ven.*, 52–6; Dandolo col. 158; John the Deacon 104. *Cf.* Kretschmayr 56–7, 422, note 3; Abel-Simson 415–22; Lentz 37–9; Hartmann III/1, 62, 89, note 10; Dölger, *BES*, 325–6. For the date, autumn 809–spring 810, see Kretschmayr 57.

28/18–19 τῆς τε Παπίας . . . Σκλαβηνιῶν.

Pippin's brothers were Charles and Lewis and the bastard Pippin: see Einhard, *Vit. Karol. Magn.*, cc. 18, 20 and *cf.* on 26/7–8. For the antithesis Παπίας/πασῶν τῶν Φραγγιῶν, see Ohnsorge 241–2. For Charles's 'Reichstheilungsgesetz' (806), see Abel-Simson 344–53; and for the Slavs, *ibid.*, 347 and note 3. *Cf.* Hartmann III/1, 77–9, 90, note 21. For Σκλαβηνιῶν, *cf.* on 9/10, 49/15.

28/22 Ἀειβόλας.

C.'s account of these operations is condensed. Pippin occupied the coast; then, attacking from the south, transferred his troops by ship to Chioggia, Brondolo and the Lido of Palestrina. Up the last of these he advanced as far as Alviola/Ἀειβόλα, where, in his attempt to cross over to Malamocco, he was temporarily brought to a stand: see John the Deacon 104 and note 1; Kretschmayr 57 and plan 1; Hartmann III/1, 62. It is clear that C. regards the assault on Malamocco as launched from the mainland: see 28/25.

28/33-9 Ἀπορήσας οὖν . . . πλεῖστα πάκτα.

The source of these details is unknown: see Bury 552; Dölger, *BES* 326, note 82. Venice was at that time in no position to make a peace-treaty on her own account: Pippin took her from Byzantium in 810, and his father handed her back in 812: see Dölger, *Regesten*, 385, and *cf*. Lentz 31 ff.; Hartmann III/1, 64. That the annual tribute mentioned here was exacted by Pippin is accepted by Kretschmayr (58), but doubted by Hartmann III/1, 89, note 12. A tribute of 25 lbs. in silver pence was exacted by Berengar I (888), and by his successors Rodolf (924) and Hugh (927): see *MGH*, Legum Sectio, II, Capitularia Reg. Franc. II, 146: et promisistis nobis cum cuncto ducatu Veneticorum annualiter inferre de denariis Papiensibus libras viginti quinque; *ibid.*, 149, 151; *cf*. Kretschmayr 431-2.

28/35 ἀπὸ τῆς ἐμῆς χώρας. Pavia had in fact once been the capital of Venetia: see Kretschmayr 12.

28/42 διβάρια.

In view of the passages from the *Kaiserpakta* cited on 28/33-9, it is natural to assume that C. wrote δινάρια, and that the text should read δινάρια ἀσήμιν λίτρας κέ, where ἀσήμιν would have its later connotation of 'silver' (*cf*. 50/248), and not the original meaning of 'uncoined silver'. It is, however, just possible that διβάρια may be a literal rendering of 'dupondia' in the pejorative sense of 'two-pennyworths', or 'pepper-corns'; *cf*. MGr. δίλεφτο. 25, or even 36, lbs. of silver would certainly have been a nominal fee. Bury, *ERE*, 326 and note 1, wrongly supposes the fee to have been paid in gold.

28/45 ἀνηγόρευσαν ἑαυτοὺς δοῦκα.

For the origins of the Doge, see *Chron. Ven.*, 33; John the Deacon 91, 94; Dandolo col. 127. *Cf*. Kretschmayr 42, 43; Hartmann II/2, 120, note 29, III/1, 55-6; Lentz 3. The first *named* doge is certainly Paulutius, and the date of his election certainly after 680. Kretschmayr inclines to accept Dandolo's date, 697.

28/45 εὐγενείᾳ . . . διαφέροντα. *Cf*. Dandolo col. 127: nobilitate perspicuum.

28/47 Τζιβιτάνουβα.

That is, Civitas Nova or Heracliana: see on 27/76; Kretschmayr 415, note 2; Kretschmayr, *Beschreibung*, 488, note 1. The transfer of the doge's seat to Rialto was made by the doge Agnello in 811, after Pippin's attack; see Bury, *ERE*, 327.

Cc. 29/1-53, 217-295; 30-36

BIBLIOGRAPHY

I. TEXTS

A. Dandolo, *Chronicon Venetum*, in L. A. Muratori, *Scr. rer. italicarum*, XII (1728) (Dandolo). *Letopis popa Dukljanina*, ed. F. Šišić; *Posebna izdanja Srpsk. kral. Akad.*, kn. LXVII, filos. i filol. spisi kn. 18, Beograd, 1928 (Priest of Dioclea). F. Rački, *Documenta historiae chroaticae periodum antiquam illustrantia*; Monumenta spectantia historiam Slavorum meridionalium, VII (Zagreb, 1877) (Rački, *Documenta*). T. Smičiklas, *Codex diplomaticus regni Croatiae, Dalmatiae et Slavoniae*, i–ix (Zagreb, 1904–11) (Smičiklas, *Cod. dipl.*). Thomas Archidiaconus, *Historia Salonitana;* ed. F. Rački, *Monumenta spectantia historiam Slavorum meridionalium*, xxvi (Zagreb, 1894) (Thomas the Archdeacon).

2. MODERN WORKS

H. Cons, *La province romaine de Dalmatie* (Paris, 1882) (Cons, *Province romaine*). E. Dümmler, 'Ueber die älteste Geschichte der Slaven in Dalmatien', *Sitzungsberichte der k. Akad. Wien*, phil.-hist. kl., xx, 1856, 357–68 (Dümmler, *Älteste Geschichte*). F. Dvornik, *Les Slaves, Byzance et Rome, au IXe s.* (Paris, 1926) (Dvornik, *Les Slaves*). F. Dvornik, *Les Légendes de Constantin et de Méthode vues de Byzance* (Prague, 1933) (Dvornik, *Légendes*). F. Dvornik, *The Making of Central and Eastern Europe* (London, 1949) (Dvornik, *The Making*). F. Dvornik, *The Slavs, their Early History and Civilization* (Amer. Acad., Boston, 1956) (Dvornik, *The Slavs*). D. Farlati and J. Coleti, *Illyricum Sacrum* (Venice, 1751–1819) (Farlati, *Illyricum Sacrum*). G. Fehér, 'Ungarns Gebietsgrenzen in der Mitte des 10. Jahrhunderts', *Ungarische Jahrbücher* 2 (1922), 37–69 (Fehér). B. Ferjančić, *Vizantiski Izvori za Istoriju Naroda Jugoslavije* (*S.A.N.*, Viz. Inst. 7, Belgrade, 1959) (Ferjančić). B. Grafenauer, 'Prilog kritici izvjestaja Konstantina Porfirogeneta o doseljenje Hrvata', *Historijski Zbornik*, 5 (Zagreb, 1952), 1–56 (Grafenauer, *Prilog kritici*). H. Grégoire, 'L'Origine et le nom des Croates et des Serbes', *Byzantion*, 17 (1945), 88–118 (Grégoire, *L'Origine*). K. Grot, *Izvjestija Konstantina Bagrjanorodnago o Serbach i Chorvatach* (St Petersburg, 1880) (Grot, *Izvjestija*). L. Hauptmann, 'Seobe Hrvata i Srba', *Jugoslovenski Istoriski Časopis*, 3 (1937), 30–61 (Hauptmann, *Seobe*). T. G. Jackson, *Dalmatia, The Quarnero and Istria*, 3 vols. (Oxford, 1887) (Jackson, *Dalmatia*). K. Jireček, 'Die Romanen in den Städten Dalmatiens während des Mittelalters', *Denkschriften der k. Akad. d. Wiss.*, phil.-hist. kl., 48–9 (Wien, 1902) (Jireček, *Die Romanen*). K. Jireček, *Die Handelsstrassen u. Bergwerke von Serbien u. Bosnien* (Prague, 1879) (Jireček, *Handelsstrassen*). K. Jireček, *Geschichte der Serben*, 1 (Gotha, 1911) (Jireček, *Geschichte der Serben*). K. Jireček and J. Radonić, *Istorija Srba*, 2nd ed. (Beograd, 1952) (Jireček, *Istorija Srba*). G. Labuda, *Pierwsze państwo slowianskie: Państwo Samona* (Poznań, 1949) (Labuda, *Pierwsze państwo*). J. Lucius, *De Regno Dalmatiae et Croatiae libri sex* (Amstelodami, 1668) (Lucius, *De Regno*). L. Niederle, *Slovanské Starožitnosti*, i–iii (Praha, 1902–21) (Niederle, *Slovanské Starožitnosti*). L. Niederle, *Manuel de l'antiquité slave*, i (Paris, 1923) (Niederle, *Manuel*). S. Novaković, 'Srpske Oblasti X, XI veka', *Glasnik srpskog drustva*, 48 (1880), 1–152 (Novaković). P. Skok, 'Iz srpskohrvatske toponomastike', *Južnoslovenski Filolog*, ii (1921), 311–18; iii (1922/3) 72–7; vi (1926/7), 65–95 (Skok, *Toponomastike* 1, 2, 3). P. Skok, 'Ortsnamenstudien zu *De administrando imperio* des Kaisers Constantin Porphyrogennetos', *Zeitschrift für Ortsnamenforschung*, 4 (1928), 213–44 (Skok, *Ortsnamenstudien*). P. Skok, *Dolazak Slovena na Mediteran* (Split, 1934; *Pomorska Biblioteka Jadranske Straze*, ii, 1) (Skok, *Dolazak Slovena*). P. Skok, *Slavenstvo i romanstvo na jadranskim otocima*, i, ii (Zagreb, 1950) (Skok, *Slavenstvo i romanstvo*). P. J. Šafařík, *Slovankské Starožitnosti*, 2nd ed. (Praha, 1862–3) (Šafařík, *Slovanské Starožitnosti*). P. J. Šafařík, *Slavische Alterthümer* (Leipzig, 1844) (Šafařík, *Slavische Alterthümer*). F. Šišić, *Geschichte der Kroaten*, 1 (Zagreb, 1917) (Šišić, *Geschichte der Kroaten*). F. Šišić, *Povijest Hrvata u vrijeme narodnih vladara* (Zagreb, 1925) (Šišić, *Povijest Hrvata*). V. N. Zlatarsky, *Istorija na B'lgarskata D'ržava prez srednite vekove*, i, 1 and 2 (Sofia, 1918, 1927) (Zlatarsky, *Istorija*). *Zbornik Kralja Tomislava* (Zagreb, 1925).

INTRODUCTORY NOTE

The chapters dealing with Dalmatia and the neighbouring Slav lands are particularly important because of the information they give on the early history of the Croats, Serbs and other Slav tribes on the Adriatic coast. Without this information our knowledge of the origin of the Croats and Serbs and of their history from the 7th to 10th cents. would be very scanty indeed. Documents issued by the first Croat and Serb rulers are very few; and the first native chronicler, the anonymous Priest of Duklja (Dioclea), wrote only in the second half of the 12th cent. His work, generally known as *Ljetopis popa Dukljanina*, is in any case of little worth. In the first part he gives some very confused and obscure accounts of the early history of the Croats and these are of doubtful value; while in the second part he confines himself to describing events which took place in Dioclea during the 11th and 12th cents. None the less, the first part of this chronicle, translated into Croat probably in the 14th cent., was the main source for Croat history down to the 17th cent.

More important, in spite of its bias toward the Croat nation, is the *Historia Salonitana* of the Archdeacon Thomas (†1268); but Thomas, naturally, was most interested in events directly connected with the city and church of Spalato.

Venetian and Italian chroniclers and Frankish annalists pay little attention to what was happening among the Croats and Serbs, and comment only briefly on the relations of their own countries with the Slavs from the 9th cent. onwards. The *Chronicon Venetum* of Dandolo (†1354) is more important, since the doge had at his disposal the archives of Venice concerning Venetian relations with Dalmatia. But his information adds little to what C. has to tell us about the early history of Croats and Serbs. The *Chronica Hungarorum* of the best Hungarian chronicler. Thuroczy de Szentmihály (†1490) is important only for the 14th and 15th cents. in Croat history. The other Greek sources are valuable only for the period of Slav migrations and for later periods of Serbian history.[1]

Owing to the scarcity of information about the early history of the southern Slavs and to the fact that many of C.'s statements cannot be directly confirmed by other evidence, his Slav chapters have been and still are the subject of lively controversy among historians of the southern Slavs. The first who tried to write their history on the basis of C.'s account and of other sources available in his day, was John Lucius. His work, *De Regno Dalmatiae et Croatiae libri sex*, published at Amsterdam in 1668, is a remarkable achievement, and its importance and usefulness were enhanced by the fact that he published in it for the first time the works of Thomas of Spalato and of the Priest of Dioclea, together with some other documents of less importance. But even this first Croat author, who is rightly called the 'father of Croat historians', though relying heavily on C.'s information, cannot abstain from criticizing (p. 45) what the emperor says about the migration of the Croats. His objections are similar to those later formulated by Slav philologists: how can C.'s account of White Croatia and White Serbia be reconciled with the fact that the dialects of the southern Slavs do not seem to have been influenced by those of the western Slavs, as we should have expected them to have been if Croats and Serbs had migrated southwards from modern Saxony and western Galicia, regions inhabited by western Slavs, in the 7th cent.? Lucius therefore wished to place C.'s White Croatia and White Serbia in eastern Galicia, down towards the former Sarmatia, where Pliny and Ptolemy had traced some Serbs.

Many historians accepted C.'s account at its face-value; *e.g.* D. Farlati and J. Coleti in their *Illyricum Sacrum* (Venice, 1751–1819), Du Fresne Du Cange (1746), the Serbs Julinać (1765) and Rajić (1793), the Croat J. Mikoczi (*c.* 1800), and especially the eminent German historian of Hungary and Croatia, J. Ch. Engel (1770–1814). But other scholars shared the objections of Lucius; *e.g.* Banduri (1711), Katančić (1798), the Czech philologist Dobrovský (1801), and the German specialist K. Zeuss (1837). These interpretations of C.'s account were further elaborated by the father of Slav archaeology, J. Šafařík (1795–1861), in his *Slovanské Starožitnosti* (Prague, 1837); and he was followed by the philologists Kopitar (*Glagolita Clozianus*, Wien, 1836) and Miklosić (*Vergleichende Lautlehre der slav. Sprachen*, Wien, 1879).

So far, scholars had only been trying to modify C.'s account in the light of facts known from elsewhere, without seriously doubting its reliability. But about the middle of the 19th cent. the first direct attack on the emperor's reliability was launched by the German scholar E. Dümmler[2], who regarded C.'s chapters on Dalmatia and the southern Slavs as a mechanical collection of items betraying 'vollkommene Geistlosigkeit'. The famous Croat scholar F. Rački (1828–94)[3] followed Dümmler, and his opinion was in turn confirmed by the authority of V. Jagić.[4] Jagić developed the philological argument already indicated by Lucius, and came to the conclusion that C.'s account of the origins of the

---

[1] *Cf.* Rački, *Rad Jugoslav. Akad.* 51 (1880) 140–207.
[2] *Älteste Geschichte.*
[3] *Književnik* I (1864), 36–77; *Rad Jugoslav. Akad.* 52 (1880), 141–89.
[4] *Archiv für slav. Philol.* XVII (1895), 47–87; *cf.* also Oblak, *ibid.* XVIII (1896), 228–34.

Croats and Serbs and of their migration during the 7th cent. should be rejected as a phantasy, which the Slavs belatedly invented and which was simply and naïvely reproduced by C.

Jagić's authoritative judgment halted the reaction in favour of C. which was beginning among some who had been impressed by the arguments of the young Russian scholar K. J. Grot. Grot devoted a whole work to the defence of C.'s chapters on Dalmatia[1]; and he was strongly supported by the Bulgarian scholar Brinov,[2] and by another Russian critic Florinskij.[3] But Jagić's authority was so great among Slav scholars that his opinion prevailed almost everywhere. All the most eminent historians of Dalmatia, Croatia and Serbia—C. J. Jireček, T. Smičiklas, Krek, Maretić, Kovačević, Jovanović, Stanojević and the historian of the reign of Heraclius, Pernice—followed the lead of Dümmler, Rački and Jagić in their interpretations of C.'s chapters. This scepticism influenced J. B. Bury also,[4] and was fully shared by the Czech archaeologist Niederle.[5]

F. Kos[6] and V. Klaić[7] made unsuccessful attempts at explaining C.'s puzzling account in the light of the Slav anti-Avar insurrection, led by the Frank Samo. Gumplowicz[8] identified the primitive Croats and Serbs with Goths. Only Nodilo[9] continued to defend the reliability of C., without however bringing forward any decisive arguments. The defence of Pavić[10] also made little impression.

A partial reaction against the general scepticism was to be observed after the publication of reports of 10th-century Arab travellers—Ibrahim ibn Jakub[11] and Mas'udi[12]—on White Croatia and White Serbia. At least, it seemed that the existence of a Croatia beyond the Carpathian Mountains and of a Serbia on the upper Elbe could not be doubted. This was acknowledged by L. Niederle[13]. But the rest of C.'s report continued to be rejected. Only in more recent years have there been signs of a return into favour of C., when the theory of a non-Slav origin of the primitive Croats and Serbs was put forward by the Slovenes N. Zupanić and L. Hauptmann (see on 30/61 ff.) and found some support among Slav philologists. However, the eminent Croat historian F. Šišić was not impressed by this new approach to the problem, and continued to refuse to accept C.'s statement as a secure basis for research into early Croat history. So the controversy goes on,[14] and it will take some time before a definite solution of these problems is reached. In the light, or in the shadow, of these contradictory appreciations C.'s account must here receive fresh examination and comment.

The basis for the study of C.'s chapters on Dalmatia and the Serbs, as for other parts of the treatise, is still J. B. Bury's important article 'The Treatise De Administrando Imperio' published in Vol. 15 of the *Byzantinische Zeitschrift* (1906), 517–77. Manojlović's thorough

[1] *Izvjestija Konstantina Bagrjanorodnago o Serbach i Chorvatach* (St Petersburg, 1880).
[2] *Zaselenie Balkanskago Poluostrova Slavjanami* (Moscow, 1872).
[3] *Žurnal Min. Nar. Prosv.* 214 (1881), 139–70; 215, (1881) 300–22.
[4] *A History of the Later Roman Empire* II (London, 1889), 275 f.; id., *BZ*, 15 (1906), 556–61.
[5] *Slovanské Starožitnosti*, part II, vol. I, 244–80.
[6] *Izvestja muz. dru. Ljubljana* VIII (1893), 206–11.
[7] *Povijest Hrvata* I (Zagreb, 1899), 30 ff.; id., *Rad Jugoslav. Akad.* 131 (1897), 11–16.
[8] *Chorwaci i Serbowie* (Warsaw, 1902); id., *Politischanthropologische Revue*, 1903, 779 ff.
[9] *Historija Srednega Vijeka* III (Zagreb, 1905), 433–45.
[10] *Cara Konst. Porfirogen. De adm. imp. glave 29–36* (Zagreb, 1906; 2nd ed. 1909; 3rd ed. 1913). In this little book Pavić, in order to 'save' the trustworthiness of C., allowed himself manipulations of the text which cannot be accepted by any serious student. He 'reconstructed' the text in such a way as to fit his theory that White Croatia was not north but south of Bavaria and that C.'s description of Croatia corresponded to that of the Priest of Dioclea, who divided Croatia into Alba and Rubea: see the critical reviews of his book by Jireček in *BZ* 17 (1908), 165–6, and Jagić in *Archiv für slav. Philol.* 31 (1910), 618–21.
[11] F. Westberg, *Zapisky imp. Akad. Nauk*, VIIIme série (St Petersburg, 1899); new ed. by G. Jacob, *Arabische Reiseberichte* (Berlin, 1927).
[12] Marquart 101 ff.
[13] *Slovanské Starožitnosti*, tom. cit., 262–74.
[14] A more detailed outline of the controversy down to 1925 is given by Šišić, *Povijest Hrvata*, 241–65; and down to 1949 by Dvornik, *The Making*, 268–304.

analysis of a great part of the treatise is of little use for the part of it in which we are interested here, because he was not able to finish his study and could not comment on the Slav chapters.

As regards cc. 29–36, Bury came to the conclusion that all of them were written in 948–9 with the exception of c. 30, which he regarded as an interpolation, composed after 950. The main argument for the latter dating is the mention of 'Otto the great king of Francia and Saxony', to whom the White Croats are said to be subject (30/71–5). Bury (523) was convinced by Westberg's[1] interpretation of this passage, 'who has shown that C.'s Βελοχρωβατία includes Bohemia, Moravia and the land of the Slovaks'. Therefore, continues Bury, 'the reference is to the Bohemian realm, and the ἴδιος ἄρχων of the time was Boleslav I. But Boleslav was reduced by Otto the Great in summer (May or June) 950 . . . We can say with probability that c. 30 was written after 950.'

Bury's dating was generally accepted.[2] But Hauptmann (*Jugoslov. Istoriski Časopis*, 3, 1937, 30–61) went further. He believed that c. 30 could not have been written before 955 (*cf.* below, p. 99, and on 30/75), and was more probably written after 962, when Otto I became emperor. Before 950 the Czechs and Magyars were enemies of the Germans. This situation changed after 955, when the Magyars were defeated by Otto and friendly relations between the Magyars and White Croats, whom, following Westberg, he places in Bohemia, became possible (30/75). Hauptmann's main argument is based on 30/73, Ὄτῳ τῷ μεγάλῳ ῥηγὶ Φραγγίας, which he punctuates with a comma after μεγάλῳ, and renders 'Otto the Great, king of Francia', noting that the epithet 'Great' was conferred on Otto in or after 962. This translation is obviously wrong; none the less, Hauptmann's punctuation may well be right, and with it his conclusion, if we render μεγάλῳ as 'elder' (*cf.* Manojlović IV, 147, note 2, and on 26/2, 46/3–4, 117, 151): for an 'elder' implies a 'younger', and Otto II was crowned king in 961. If therefore the text does really refer here to Otto I as 'Otto the Elder', and not as 'Otto the great king', this is proof positive that c. 30 must be dated after 961; *cf.* however 40/53, where Arpad is referred to as 'the *great* archon of Turkey'; and W. Ohnsorge, *Abendland u. Byzanz* (Darmstadt, 1958), 236, 245–6.

Hauptmann's rendering of μεγάλῳ as 'great' was rightly refuted by Labuda (*Pierwsze państwo*, 230–3); but Labuda thinks that c. 30 was written by C. in 944, when the emperor was at work on *De Them.*, and was added to *DAI* as a supplement to cc. 29 and 31. He tries to reconcile his thesis with the historical fact of Bohemia's submission to Otto, arguing that Boleslav of Bohemia was already tributary to Otto in 929.

Grafenauer (*Prilog kritici*, 18 ff.) rightly pointed out that the whole tendency and style of c. 30 differ from those of *De Them.*; and that the introductory ἰστέον, ὅτι, absent both from c. 30 and from *De Them.*, is absent also from several other chapters of *DAI*: so that its absence from c. 30 cannot serve as a decisive argument for Labuda's thesis. Grafenauer has, moreover, very convincingly shown (*ibid.*, 38 ff.) the impossibility of an hypothesis put forward by Budimir (*Glasnik Srpsk. Akad. Nauka*, I, 1949, 243–5) that C.'s account of the second migration of the Croats was only an adaptation of tales preserved by Herodotus (IV, 8–10, 33–6) about the origin of the Scythians and of the Delian story about the Hyperboreans. He also refuted the attempt of B. Bratanić (*Zbornik Radova*, Zagreb, 1951, 221–50) to show ethnographical arguments against the historicity of C.'s account of the migration of the Croats.

Grafenauer[3] regards c. 30 as an interpolation, composed by an unknown author after 955, or rather after 959, *i.e.* after C.'s death. The new chronological evidence which it gives on White Croatia (30/71–5) was, he believes, gathered in Venice. Cc. 29 and 31 show that in Byzantium there was little knowledge of countries beyond the Carpathians. Grafenauer regards c. 30 as the main source for early Croat history, since it reflects Croat

---

[1] *Op. cit.* 97–101.
[2] *Cf. Byzantinoturcica* I, 212.
[3] *op. cit.* 1–30. There is a short résumé in German *ibid.* 54–6.

national tradition. Cc. 29 and 31 should be used only with caution, as an auxiliary source, since they betray too much of the Byzantine spirit. Grafenauer therefore rejects the account of Heraclius' rôle in the migration and christianization of the Croats, and also the account in c. 32 of the migration of the Serbs, and of their settlement, first in Srbčište, then in Serbia proper.

Thus, Bury's thesis that c. 30 is an interpolation is still supported by most historians who do not reject the whole account as legendary. But there remains a great difference of opinion about the date of the composition of this chapter.

It should, however, be pointed out that there is one assumption in all these arguments which does not agree with the historical facts as they are known today. The starting-point in each case is the supposition that C. places White Croatia within Bohemia, and that this country was definitely subjected to Otto only in 950. It is true that Boleslav I of Bohemia had to acknowledge Otto's supremacy in 929, as did his predecessor St Wenceslas; but this date cannot be taken into consideration for dating the composition of c. 30, as did Labuda, because Boleslav I broke with Otto; and the Saxon chronicle of Widukind[1] speaks of a war between the German king and the Bohemian duke which lasted fourteen years and ended only in 950 with the submission of Boleslav.[2]

Again, why should it be taken for granted that C. is confusing White Croatia with Bohemia proper? Neither in 929 nor in 950 could Bohemia be described as being in good relations with Hungary. We have, moreover, to take into consideration the political situation as it really was in Bohemia. In the 10th cent. Bohemia was still divided into two independent dukedoms: the western and partly northern part of the country, with its centre at Prague, obeying the princes of Přemyslid dynasty; and the eastern and southern part, with its centre at Libice, ruled by the princes of the Slavnik dynasty. This latter part of Bohemia was still called Croatia in the Old Slavonic legend of St Wenceslas, written in Bohemia about 930. The Slavnik dynasty was of White Croat origin. This part of Bohemia had probably once been part of White Croatia; but, when the whole of Bohemia and the whole of White Croatia were incorporated by Svatopluk into the Moravian empire, the two Bohemian dukes came closer together and seem to have established a kind of common partnership: for we see the representatives of both dynasties recognizing in 895, after Svatopluk's death, the supremacy of Germany as represented by Bavaria.[3]

Part of White Croatia was thus really in Bohemia; and it might appear at first sight that Croatia and Bohemia could have been regarded as one country. However, a later date provides a still more plausible opportunity for this identification. Both dukes of Bohemia supported Otto I during his last campaign against the Magyars; and after Otto's great victory on the Lechfeld in 955, Boleslav and his Slavnik partner invaded Moravia and Slovakia, which were under Magyar domination. They became masters not only of those countries, but also of Silesia and Western Galicia with Cracow, the centre of C.'s White Croatia.[4]

If we wish to bring C.'s statement in c. 30 into accord with the historical facts, then we must conclude that this chapter was composed after 955, when White Croatia, annexed by the two rulers of Bohemia, was in fact, along with Bohemia itself, subject to Otto I. At this time even the title of 'great king' given to Otto in this chapter would be understandable (but see above, p. 97). Otto's destruction of the dreaded Magyar power on the Lechfeld in 955 made a profound impression everywhere in Europe, including Byzantium, where the Magyars were well known.

[1] *MGH* scr. III, 439, 454.
[2] Dvornik, *The Making*, 29–37.
[3] *Ibid.* 21 ff., 92 ff.
[4] *Ibid.* 33–4, 92–4. For Cracow as the centre of White Croatia, see T. Lewicki's article in *Sprawozdania* of the Polish Academy XLIX (Cracow, 1948), 24–34; *cf.* also V. Chaloupecký, *Český Časopis Historický* 48/49 (Prague, 1947/48), 241–47. For Bohemia in the 8th and 9th cents. see the study by V. Vaněček in *Slavia Antiqua* II (Poznań, 1949/50), 300–30, with résumé in English.

After this defeat friendly relations were established between the Magyars, the Germans and the lands of Boleslav I. Missionary activity among the Magyars started, not only from Bavaria but also from Bohemia. Moreover, it appears that the empire established by Boleslav I was a kind of federation of different Slav tribes, and that the conquered lands were governed by native princes. It is quite possible that the prince of White Croatia entered into matrimonial relations with the dynasty of Arpad. Géza's younger brother Michael seems to have married a Slav princess.[1] She may have been a daughter of the White Croatian ruler. As we shall see below (on 30/75), Christianity was not unknown in White Croatia, but in the middle of the 10th cent. it certainly could not have been called a properly Christian country.

The conclusion would therefore seem to be that c. 30 was written, not, as Bury thought, about 950–1, but after 955. It is certainly posterior to c. 29, and appears to be by a different author. But what of cc. 31–6? Are we to accept the general view that they are the continuation of c. 29, and were thus written, at least in their original form, in 948 or 949?

Macartney (138–9) doubted whether cc. 31–6 could have been composed at the same time as c. 29, and pointed to 31/75–82, a passage which seems to suggest a date later than 949. If we wish to determine the date at which this passage was written, we have of course to establish the date of Miroslav's reign. This is not easy, because the chronology of Croat rulers of this period is very uncertain. Most scholars have accepted the chronological sequence proposed by Šišić (*Geschichte der Kroaten*, 150): Mutimir 892–910 (?); Tomislav 910–28; Trpimir II 928–35; Kresimir 935–45; Miroslav 945–9; Pribounia 949; Kresimir II 949–69 (*cf.* on 31/42–52). If we accept this, then it follows that 31/75–82 cannot have been written before 950, but must be dated shortly after 950, during the reign of Kresimir II. Therefore, in order to save Bury's dating of this chapter, Runciman (*Romanus Lecapenus*, 208 ff.) reverted to the chronology of Croat rulers proposed by the first historian of Croatia, Farlati. According to this, Mutimir died in 900; he was succeeded, not by Tomislav, but by Trpimir's son, Kresimir, who died c. 908; then Kresimir's son Miroslav reigned four years and was deposed by Pribounia in 912. Then Tomislav appeared, deposed Pribounia, and reigned until c. 940.

This chronology has the advantage of explaining why in c. 31 C. does not mention the invasion of Croatia by Symeon of Bulgaria in 926. Not only does he not mention it, but he stresses on the contrary that the only unsuccessful invasion of Croatia by the Bulgarians took place in the reign of Boris-Michael, and that since then the two nations have maintained friendly relations (31/60–6). This dating would also explain why C. does not in this chapter mention the most powerful of the Croatian princes, Tomislav, of whose reign and of the military recovery which took place under it he seems to have no knowledge. It would also eliminate from the number of Croat rulers Trpimir II, whose existence seems problematic: see on 31/42–52, 71–82.

However, Farlati's chronology has also some weaknesses. It is not probable that before Tomislav's reign Croatia would have been able to muster such an imposing army and navy as that described at 31/71–4. But after the union of Pannonian with Dalmatian Croatia, which took place under Tomislav and was caused by the growing danger to which the Pannonian Croats were exposed when the Magyars were finally settled in the Danubian basin, Croatia's military importance increased considerably. In the same reign the Croats extended their supremacy over some important Adriatic islands also, which would explain the growth of the Croat navy.

On the other hand, at c. 32/151 C. represents Bosnia as belonging to Serbia. It is, however, most probable—and this is accepted by most historians of the period, *cf.* Šišić, *Geschichte der Kroaten*, 181 ff.—that the territory of Bosona, as C. calls it, formed part of Croatia at the end of the 9th and in the first half of the 10th cents. The Serbian ruler Časlav (*c.* 927–60) could have acquired this territory only when he had re-populated and

---

[1] B. Homan, *Geschichte des ungarischen Mittelalters* I (Berlin, 1940), 159.

re-established his country with the help of Romanus I, and when Croat power had declined. The best time for such an annexation would have been during the disorders which followed the assassination of Miroslav, dated by Šišić to 949 (*cf.* also Fehér 60). Časlav could hardly think of conquest at the beginning of his reign, since the restoration of his devastated country engrossed all his attention for at least a decade. Therefore the date of 949 would fit best for Časlav's expansion. Nor can we say that the Croat prince Kresimir II was a weak ruler: after having restored order in his country, he re-annexed Bosnia, profiting by the unrest in Serbia which followed the death of Časlav, *c.* 960: see Priest of Dioclea 324; Šišić, *Geschichte der Kroaten*, 155. Kresimir II also improved Croat relations with the coastal cities under Byzantine authority; which might explain why C. was so well informed about the military situation in Croatia during Kresimir's reign.

All this can be cited in support of Šišić's chronology for the sequence of Croat rulers. And it could also be concluded from the above that c. 32 could not have been written in 948 or 949, but only in or after 950, when news of the annexation of Bosnia by Časlav (*cf.* 32/151) had reached Constantinople.

As regards the rest of the information given in c. 32, it is to be noted that C. was drawing on two sources. 32/1–81 seems to have come from an older source, probably deposited in the archives of the reign of Leo VI. The rest of the chapter gives more recent information from the time of Romanus I (920–44) and the Serbian ruler Časlav (*c.* 927–60). It was in this more recent source that C. found the report of Symeon's attack on Croatia in 926 (32/126–8), about which nothing was recorded in his source on Croat history: see General Introduction p. 4.

It follows from all this that in composing the main part of c. 31 C. had at his disposal reports on Croatia dating only from the reign of Leo VI. He had no information about the reign of Tomislav; or, if he had any, it may be that he did not wish to divulge it because of the growth of Croat power during Tomislav's reign and the consequently independent behaviour of Croatia. At all events, the only information about this reign is the short passage on Croat military power at that time (31/71–4), and even here Tomislav is not mentioned. And the figures are revised at 31/81–2, the word ἀρτίως denoting the time of writing.

The solution of this tangled problem of composition and chronology would therefore seem to be that put forward in the General Introduction pp. 4–5: namely, that the Dalmatian and Slav συγγραφή, like other sections between cc. 14 and 42, was, as it now stands, not composed all at one time; but that it represents an earlier compilation with later insertions. The original narrative, compiled as part of an historical and antiquarian Περὶ ἐθνῶν, runs on directly in the following passages: 29/3–53, 217–95 (where 29/217 proceeds directly with the description of the places enumerated at 29/50–3); 31/3–70 (compiled before the reign of Tomislav, see above p. 99); 32/2–81, 146–50 (an historical account which ends at 32/81 with the early years of Peter of Serbia, 893–8, and proceeds to the usual list of place-names, 32/149–50); 33/3–15, 20–1; and all of cc. 34–6. The later insertions, which lie between these passages, all show the desire to bring the history up to date (often resuming it after several years of silence, as at 31/75 ff., 32/81), and almost all show the new *political* purpose of the book at work (so, 29/54–216, 30/119–42 mark the re-establishment of Byzantine hegemony over the Slavs by Basil I, and 32/81–146 follows the close relations of Byzantium with the Serbs in particular: *cf.* the style of c. 43). The General Introduction (p. 5) suggests that the date at which these later passages were inserted was 952, a date which would agree with C.'s knowledge of events after the death of Miroslav, and of the Serbian annexation of Bosnia (see above, p. 99). It may be, however, that c. 30 was added even as late as 955 or later (see above p. 98 and on 30/75).

C. 30 seems undoubtedly to have been compiled by a different author, and was added to the συγγραφή probably by C. himself, who, however, left it intact without taking the trouble to co-ordinate the new information with that contained in cc. 29, 31–6. This explains why the legendary story of the fall of Salona is told twice (see on 29/14–53).

though the second is the more consistent version. It may be that C. instructed the author of c. 30, who may have been a native of one of the Dalmatian cities, to collect information about the Slavs either by journeying to their countries or else in Venice. He seems to have been quite familiar with the history of Dalmatia, knew Slav, and was able thus to obtain accounts from the Slavs themselves. It must have taken him some time to collect his material, and his information is used independently of that contained in cc. 31–6. See also on 30/90–3.

29/1–2 Περὶ τῆς Δελματίας κτλ.
The Dalmatian-Croat-Serb συγγραφή, as originally composed, begins here: see Introductory Note above, p. 100, and on 29/54–8. The title given here is unusually apposite to the contents of the συγγραφή as a whole, since 29/3–53, 217–95 deals with Dalmatia, and cc. 31–6 with τὰ ἐν αὐτῇ παρακείμενα ἔθνη.

29/8 τὸ τοῦ Ἀσπαλάθου κάστρον. See on 29/237 ff.

29/10 φέρονται. The reading is right: cf. Cedrenus II, 274/25, 'his letters and other works . . . are preserved'.

29/11 Διόκλεια. See on 35/1–11.

29/14–53 Ἡ δὲ καί τῶν αὐτῶν Ῥωμάνων κτλ.
The story is repeated, in a slightly different and more logical form, at 30/14–61: see General Introduction p. 4, and below on 30/13. There is enough verbal correspondence between the two versions (e.g. 29/15, 30/10–11; 29/16, 30/25; 29/21, 30/28–30; 29/23, 30/47–8; 29/39–40, 30/44–5) to warrant belief in a common original. But the present version has been edited for the original scheme of a Περὶ ἐθνῶν, and edited also at Constantinople. The derivation of the place-name Κλεῖσα is given (29/30–1; cf. 29/218, 237 etc.); the Byzantine military terms κλεισοῦρα, ἀλλάγιον are used (29/22, 29; see on 50/94); the size of Salona is compared with that of Constantinople itself (29/27; cf. 9/68); and the story is rounded off with the usual list of place-names (29/50–3). This version, too, by a careless inference from the original (cf. 30/13), confuses the Avars with the Slavs (29/17, 33, 37), whereas the other version makes it clear that the Slavs came later to Dalmatia and expelled the Avars (30/65–71). This blunder, since it left 29/14–49 at variance with 31/8–20, was certainly helped by the insertion of the truer version found at 30/13–71. For the mythical character of both versions, see on 30/18 ff.; Ferjančić 11–12, note 11; and for the date, far from certain, of the historical capture, ibid.

29/30 Κλεῖσα.
Ancient Andetrium, modern Clissa, Klis: see J. Spon, Voyage d'Italie etc., I (Lyon, 1678), 108–10; A. Fortis, Voyage en Dalmatie, II (Berne, 1778), 61–4. On C.'s etymology of the word, see Skok, Starohrvatska Prosvjeta, n.s. I (1927), 76.

29/54–216 INTRODUCTORY NOTE
For Bibliography see above, pp. 87–8. This passage is an insertion into the original Dalmatian-Slav συγγραφή of the Περὶ ἐθνῶν. It is designed to emphasize by more modern instances the revived claim to Byzantine sovereignty over the West, both among the Lombards and the Slavs: cf. 29/213–16 with 32/141–5. In other words, the object of the passage is *political* rather than merely historical (see General Introduction p. 4).
The interpolation contains four separate items. 1. (29/54–84) is an admission that, despite the traditional subjection of the Dalmatian Slavs to Byzantium since the 7th

cent. (29/54–8; *cf.* 31/58–9, 32/146–8), they had in fact during the middle years of the 9th cent. been independent and pagan. This is followed by an account of their return to their political and religious allegiance in the time of Basil I (*cf.* Theoph. Cont. 84, 291–2, and 29/68–75). 2. (29/84–119) gives a Byzantine account of the relief of Dalmatia and the capture of Bari from the Saracens in 871. This again stresses Byzantine control over Dalmatia and the western Slavs, in conscious refutation of Frankish claims (see on 29/108–12); and claims for Basil I the initiative in the Bari campaign (see on 29/104). 3. (29/119–59) is an account of the Lombard revolt against the emperor Lewis in 871; and 4. (29/159–216) is a mythical account of the siege of Salerno by Abd-Allah in 871–2.

Items 3 and 4 are, as Bury (548–9) and Gay (170, note 1) saw, Lombard tales. The account of the revolt of Adelchis against Lewis is essentially Beneventan: it exonerates Adelchis, who is not mentioned by name, by putting the blame on the intrigues of Soldan; and it states that Lewis was merely excluded from, not imprisoned in, Beneventum (29/153). The Byzantines would naturally accept this version of the affair: they certainly approved, and may have inspired, the revolt of Adelchis (*cf.* Reginonis *Chronicon*, *MPL*, cxxxii, col. 103 A, ann. 871; but also Gay 102); and they certainly assisted him against Lewis two years later (*cf.* Hincmar 495/49–50, ann. 873). But the account is not by any means wholly fictitious: the character of Soldan is accurately sketched (29/130; *cf.* *Chron. Sal.*, 528/7; *Chron. Ahimaaz*, 74); Soldan was in touch with Adelchis both during and after the siege of Bari (29/127 ff.; *cf. Chron. Sal.*, 527/31–6; 528/2–8; W. 121/10–16, 122/7–16); and Lewis was in fact disposed to banish Adelchis (29/134; *cf.* Hincmar 492/44, ann. 871).

The account of the siege, on the contrary, is almost wholly apocryphal (see on 29/159–216). It appears to relate to the siege of Salerno by Abd-Allah in September 871, which was finally raised by the troops of Lewis in the following summer. The Byzantines took no part in this operation, and did not occupy Beneventum until 891 (see Gay 147). Soldan, so far from leading an African invasion, was still a prisoner at Beneventum (see Hirsch, *Byzantinische Studien*, 259). A 7th cent. version of the tale of the gallant messenger (29/172–211) is found in Paul the Deacon (v, cc. 7–8), which seems to confirm its Lombard origin; but a similar tale is told by Michael Syrus (iii, 122–3) of the capture of Melitene in 934. Whatever the source of the passage, the significance lies in the statement at 29/213–16, that since that time Capua and Beneventum have been subject to Byzantium (*cf. De Them.*, 98/42–4).

We must next glance at the passages parallel to 29/88 ff. which are found in Theoph. Cont. 289/3–290/24, 292/14–297/23, and *De Them.*, 97/18–98/44. Bury (550) and Moravcsik (*Atti del V Congresso internaz. di stud. biz.*, i, Rome, 1939, 519 and note 1) have shown that the versions of Theoph. Cont. and *DAI* derive independently from a common original. Pertusi (*De Them.*, 44–7) has tried to show that the version of *De Them.* is later than either of the other two; but *cf.* Ostrogorsky, *Byzantion*, 23 (1953), 38; in fact there is nothing to show why the versions of these passages in Theoph. Cont. and *De Them.* might not have been made by the same author from a common original. Bury advanced arguments tending to prove that the version of Theoph. Cont. was both earlier (573) and later (551) than that of *DAI*. Neither argument is conclusive; but since the version of *DAI* is an insertion, it is probable that its inclusion was not before 952 (see General Introduction p. 5).

29/54–8 Ὅτι ἀπὸ τῆς βασιλείας κτλ.

Cf. 31/58–60, 32/146–7, passages which must have been written before the present insertion; hence the lacuna after προσαγορευόμενοι must be filled up in the manner suggested by Grot and Bury (see Vol. I, 125). In fact the συγγραφή dealing with πᾶσα ἡ Δελματία καὶ τὰ περὶ αὐτὴν ἔθνη is cc. 29, 31–6 in their original form: see Introductory Note to cc. 29/1–53 etc., p. 100.

29/59 δια τὴν . . . νωθρότητα.   *Cf.* 22/41–4 for a similar attack on Amorian incompetence.

29/61–6 οἱ τὰ τῆς Δελματίας κτλ.
The coastal cities of Dalmatia were left to Byzantium by the Treaty of Aachen (812: see Dvornik, *Les Slaves*, 47; Dölger, *BES*, 326). The statement that they became independent in the reign of Michael II (820–9) and remained so until 868 (29/86 ff.) is found also at Theoph. Cont. 84/2–5, but not elsewhere corroborated. Their dependence on Byzantium even after Basil I's settlement was obviously loose: *cf.* 30/119 ff. The Dalmatian Croats, on the other hand, remained Frankish subjects until the revolt of Domagoj in 877: see on 30/78–88, and Dvornik, *Les Slaves*, 225–7. The passage at Theoph. Cont. 288/12–23 seems to refer to Michael III (288/14). For the foundation of the *thema* of Dalmatia see Ferluga, *Zbornik Filozofskog Fakulteta* (Belgrade), 3 (1955), 53–67, and *id.*, *Vizantinska uprava u Dalmaciji* (Belgrade, 1957), 68–86: the archontate of Dalmatia, administered by the chieftain of Zadar, was transformed into a *thema* by Basil I *c.* 870.

29/66–7 ἄρχοντας . . . ζουπάνους.
For the župans, see on 30/90–3. For the appointment of pro-Byzantine ἄρχοντες see 29/76–9, and *cf.* Leo, *Taktika*, cols. 968–9; Theoph. Cont. 292/5–13; Dvornik, *Les Slaves*, 228–9.

29/68–75 Ἀλλὰ καὶ οἱ πλείονες κτλ.
This is an exaggeration: see on 30/88–90. Theoph. Cont. 288/23–289/2, 291/9–11, suggests that those who required baptism were not only the pagan Narentans (29/79–84) but also relapsed Christians who had renounced the faith as a gesture of political independence: see Dvornik, *Les Slaves*, 228; A. Vogt, *Basile Ier* (Paris, 1908), 306–7. For the missionary work of Basil among the Dalmatian Slavs, see also Leo, *Taktika*, col. 969; Theoph. Cont. 291/20–292/4; Harun ibn Yahya, *ap.* Marquart 240, 242.

29/79 Οἱ δὲ Παγανοί.   *Cf.* on 36/1–13.

29/84–119 Ἐπεὶ δὲ κτλ.
The second section of this inserted passage now begins. It is clearly contemporary with the first (29/54–84), and picks up what was said at 29/54–60: see Introductory Note above. For the parallel passages in Theoph. Cont. and *De Them.*, see *ibid.* and *De Them.*, 44–5.

29/90 τοῦ τε Σολδανοῦ καὶ τοῦ Σάβα καὶ τοῦ Καλφοῦς.
For the chronological inaccuracy of the passage, see Hirsch, *Byzantinische Studien*, 255, and on 29/101–3. For Soldanos (Sawdan, Saugdan), emir of Bari 861–71, see Amari 513, note 2, 524, note 2; Vasiliev I, 264, note 2; Introductory Note above. For Kalfon, captor of Bari in 841, see Amari 498, 501. For Sambas, apparently a ruler, not of Bari, but of Taranto, *c.* 839, see *ibid.*, 496, note 2.

29/91 κατέλαβον ἐν Δελματίᾳ.
This passage, with its parallels, is our only source for the raid. Gay (92) and Bury (547, note 2) cite the *Cambridge Chronicle* (ed. Cozza-Luzi, 30), which records a second capitulation of Ragusa in ind. ⟨1⟩5 (866–7); but this is the Sicilian, not the Dalmatian Ragusa; see Vasiliev I, 263. The Dalmatian Ragusa, as our text shows, did not capitulate. But, confused as is the testimony, there is no reason to doubt the raid; see Gay 92. If the siege of Ragusa was raised in the spring of 868, after fifteen months (29/94), it must have been begun early in 867, when Michael III was still on the throne; *cf.* Theoph. Cont. 289/20–290/3.

8—D.A.I.

29/91-3 τὸ κάστρον τὸ Βούτοβα . . . τὰ κάτω.

That is, Budua, Porto Rosa (or, less probably, Risano: cf. J. G. Wilkinson, *Dalmatia and Montenegro*, I (London, 1848), 279, 394), and the city of Cattaro excepting the fort above it; see T. G. Jackson, *Dalmatia*, III (Oxford, 1887), 2, 3, and on 29/263.

29/97-8 Νικήτα . . . 'Ωορύφας.

See Bury, *ERE*, 143-4, note 7, 290, note 1; Vasiliev I, 214, note 3, 244 and note 1. He was admiral in 853 and *c*. 867-72; and eparch of Constantinople in 860 and again in (?) 878 (see Sym. Mag. 674/14, 687/13-15 and *cf. De Cer.*, 501/12, 503/2, 7). The Ooryphas of Theoph. Cont. 81/8 is probably not Niketas, for chronological reasons.

29/101-3 πολιορκήσαντες . . . τεσσαράκοντα.

For the chronological inconsistency of the passage, see Hirsch, *Byzantinische Studien*, 254. Bari was captured in 841 (or 842); see Gay 52; Vasiliev I, 209 and note 1. For Saracen constructions in Bari (not mentioned at Theoph. Cont. 290/20), *cf.* Gay 66 and note 1. For Saracen depredations in S. Italy as far as Rome, during the 40's to 60's of the 9th cent., see Theoph. Cont. 83/12-15; Genesios 116/1-2; Gay 53, 66-7; Vasiliev I, 210-12; and *cf.* on 27/63. 'Forty years' should be 'thirty years' (841-71); *cf.* John the Deacon 119: 'quam . . . civitatem . . . Sarracenorum gens per annos circiter triginta tenuerunt.'

29/104 ἀπέστειλεν.

For the date, 868, see Hartmann III/I, 283. There is no reason to doubt Basil's initiative: see Gay 91-3; Hartmann III/I, 306, note 25; Dvornik, *Les Slaves*, 218 (but also *Chron. Sal.*, 521/6 (W. 107/7-8); Hirsch, *Byzantinische Studien*, 257; Dölger, *BES*, 337-8, note 107). For the importance of Byzantine's sea-power in S. Italy at this time, see Engreen, *Speculum*, 20 (1945), 322-5.

29/105 ῥῆγα Φραγγίας . . . πάπα 'Ρώμης.

For the ῥῆξ Φραγγίας, see Ohnsorge 238-41; Dölger, *BES*, 315, 337. For the part played by Hadrian in the alliance, see Hartmann III/I, 283. For the political importance of the campaign, see Ohnsorge 219-25.

29/105-6 τῷ . . . ἀποσταλέντι στρατῷ.

The Byzantine fleet of Niketas appeared off Bari in 869, probably in the autumn (see Hartmann III/I, 306, note 25; *cf. Chron. Sal.*, 525/19 (W. 116/16)). It retired in the same year, *ibid.*, 525/9-10 (W. 116/3-4)), after quarrelling with the Franks. C. (29/98) gives the number of Niketas' warships as 100; Hincmar (481/23) as 'more than 200', and again (485/19) as 400. It is probable enough, as Gay (95) supposes, that the discrepancy is due to reinforcement of the Byzantine fleet by the Slav and Dalmatian detachments mentioned at 29/108-15; *cf.* also Bury, *Centenario della nascita di M. Amari*, II (Palermo, 1910), 33 and note 2. But that fleet took no part in the capture of Bari, which did not follow until more than a year after its withdrawal: see below, on 29/108-12.

29/108-12 τῷ παρὰ τοῦ βασιλέως . . . ἐπόρθησεν αὐτό.

Bari fell on the 2nd of February 871; *cf.* John the Deacon 119. But the Slav naval force which helped finally to reduce it was summoned by Lewis (see *Chron. Sal.*, 526/3-4 (W. 118/1-2)), and not by Basil: see Hartmann III/I, 289, 307, 308, note 27; and Dvornik, *Les Slaves*, 219-20, 224, who points out that the force in question consisted of Croats, who were in fact Lewis's subjects. In 870 the Byzantine navy was engaged in reducing the Slavs of the Narenta and others (*Chron. Sal.*, 525/48-526/3 (W. 117/24-32)), who were thus in no position to be serving in a Byzantine force against Bari. The discrepancy between the Byzantine and Frank accounts of the Bari campaign is therefore due to the fact that they refer to different years, the one to 869 (see preceding note), the other to

870–1. The Byzantine admiral George (*Chron. Sal.*, 521/9, 527/4 (W. 107/12, 120/6)) took only a small part in the final operation (see Dvornik, *Les Slaves*, 220), if indeed he took any at all, which Hartmann (*loc. cit.*) doubts; *cf.* also Amari 519–22. It is, however, only fair to the Byzantine sources to point out that there is one piece of evidence which may suggest that the fleet of Niketas, withdrawn late in the year 869, may have returned and taken part in the campaign of 870. We learn from *Chron. Sal.*, 525/48 (W. 117/24–5)) that Niketas went off to punish the Slavs 'Hadriano loci servatore cum classibus destinato'. This Hadrian was another of Basil's admirals (*cf.* Theoph. Cont. 309/22), and may have been left to command Niketas's (Byzantine, Dalmatian and Slav) fleets at Bari, while the commander-in-chief went off with a squadron against the Narentanes. This solution has the merit of making the Byzantine-Frank dispute more intelligible by referring it at least to the same year and campaign.

29/109 Χρωβάτῳ . . . Σέρβλῳ . . . Ζαχλούμῳ.
Supply ἄρχοντι in each case (not 'contingent', as the English version); *cf.* 29/113 'Σκλαβάρχοντας'. The Byzantine case is that these chiefs were their vassals (*cf.* 29/76); but this is probably anachronistic, and certainly untrue of the Croats at that time: see Dvornik, *Les Slaves*, 220. The use of the word κέλευσις is significant: see on 4/10, and Dölger, *BES*, 38, note 6.

29/113–15 Ἰστέον, ὅτι κτλ.
Cf. Chron. Sal., 536/3–4 (W. 118/1–2): 'eisdem Sclavenis nostris cum navibus suis apud Barim . . . consistentibus'. That is, in 870; see on 29/108–12. This Greek *scholion* may be quoted from the letter of Basil (Dölger, *Regesten*, 487) to which Lewis is here replying.

29/115–16 τὸ μὲν κάστρον . . . Ῥωμαίων.
This is inaccurate. After its capture, Bari was put in charge of a Lombard gastald, and not handed over to the Byzantines until Christmas 876; see Hirsch, *Byzantinische Studien*, 258; Gay 110 and note 3. What αἰχμαλωσία other than Σολδανὸς καὶ οἱ λοιποὶ Σαρακηνοί can have fallen to Basil is not clear.

29/119–59 Καὶ οὐδεὶς αὐτὸν κτλ.
Passage 3 of this section consists, not of serious history, but merely of a κατὰ παρέκβασιν διήγησις, as Theoph. Cont. 294/3–5 makes clear. Sources of the anecdote at 29/123–6 are noted in the Apparatus to Vol. 1, *ad loc*; *cf.* also Grecu, *Byzantinoslavica*, 13 (1953), 259. The few historical elements in the recital—the character of Soldan, his relations with Adelchis, and the design of Lewis to banish Adelchis—are noticed in the Introductory Note to the section. It remains to observe at 29/152–3 a verbal parallel to Liudprand, *Antapodosis*, 1, 40, where a similar story is told of the revolt of Adalbert the Rich against king Lambert: ὁ δὲ ῥὴξ ταῦτα πάντα ἀγνοῶν ἐξῆλθε πρὸς τὸ κυνηγῆσαι: 'Lambertus interea rex harum rerum inscius . . . venationibus occupatur'. For the imprisonment of Lewis at Beneventum, 13th August–17th September, 871, see *Chron. Sal.*, c. 109; Erchempert 252; *cf.* Gay 101–3; Hartmann III/I, 291–2, 308, note 29; Amari 523–5.

29/159–216 Μὴ ἐπιλαθόμενος δὲ κτλ.
In this passage the first paragraph (29/159–69), inaccurate as it is, has some historical basis. Though Soldan himself was not released by Adelchis until 876 (see *Chron. Sal.*, 533/51 (W. 134/1–2)), the African Saracens under Abd-Allah did invade Italy in September 871 and lay siege to Salerno; see *Chron. Sal.*, cc. 111–18; *MGH*, Poet. lat. III, 405, stanza 10; *cf.* Amari 526–9; Gay 102–6. This invasion procured the release of Lewis, who did in fact reject an appeal for help (29/163–9), not from Capua and Beneventum, but from Salerno (see *Chron. Sal.*, c. 117; Gay 104), although he subsequently defeated the Saracens near Capua (August 872).

For the mythical character and Lombard origin of the rest of the passage, see Introductory Note to this passage. It is just possible that the Byzantine relief of Beneventum here recorded (29/211–13) may be a confused recollection of the Byzantine intervention in aid of Adelchis against Lewis in 873 (see Hincmar 495/49, 50; ann. 873); but the statement that since that time Capua and Beneventum have been uninterruptedly subject to Byzantium is false; see Runciman, *Romanus Lecapenus*, 187–93.

29/217–95 ; 30–6   For Bibliography and Introductory Note to these sections see above, pp. 93–101.

29/217–21   τὸ κάστρον τοῦ 'Ραουσίου κτλ.

We now pick up the original version of the treatise, interrupted at 29/53: see above, p. 100. Ragusa, *lat.* Rhagusium, Rhacusa, gr. 'Ραούσιον, Croat Dubrovnik. C.'s etymology, repeated in the 12th-century Chronicle of the Priest of Dioclea (320), is inaccurate. The word 'lau', or 'lava' in the Latin idiom of Ragusa, does in fact mean a steep rock, and was preserved in the medieval topography of Ragusa. But the substitution of R for L, proposed by C., seems philologically inadmissible, since neither the vulgar Latin, nor the Latin idiom of Dalmatia, nor the language of the Illyrians, the primitive inhabitants of Dalmatia, preserves any instance of such substitution. The small island on which the city was built was called Ragousium in the pre-Greek and pre-Latin period by the primitive inhabitants of Dalmatia. When the island became a city, the name was latinized and the form Ragusa appeared. Later, the form Rausa, Raousion become common, the letter g disappearing according to a peculiarity of the Latin idiom of Ragusa. The name Dubrovnik was unknown to C. It designated at first a Slav suburb of Ragusa on the other side of the narrow canal separating the island from the coast; and was used by the Slavs to designate the whole city only when the suburb became part of Ragusa and when the canal separating the two was filled up. The word Dubrovnik derives from *dubrava*, a wood of oak-trees. The name was already known to the Priest of Dioclea. See Skok, *Slavia*, x (1931), 449–500; *cf.* also Jireček, *Handelsstrassen*, 10–15; Oberhummer in Pauly-Wissowa *RE*, n.s. I A, col. 130 (Ragusium); Šišić, *Povijest Hrvata*, 440 ff.; L. Villari, *The Republic of Ragusa* (London, 1904), 1–30.

29/223   Πίταυρα.

Pitaura, also called Epidaurus, 'Επίδαυρος, Ragusa Vecchia, and in Croat Cavtat (Captat, from Dalmatian Latin *civitate*). C. appears to give here the old Dalmatian form, Pitaura (civitas). It was an ancient Greek city, founded by the Dorians of Argos. Roman occupation (146 B.C.) did not interfere with its existence, and under Hadrian the city, now a Roman colony, flourished anew. From the 6th cent. A.D. onwards the city was a bishopric. It was destroyed about 615 by the Avars and the Slavs. Its last bishop, John, with a part of the population, took refuge near the coast, where Ragusa was founded. See Farlati, *Illyricum Sacrum*, VI, 4–35; Jireček, *Handelsstrassen*, 6–10; Patsch in Pauly-Wissowa, *RE*, VI, cols. 51–3 (Epidauros); Cons, *Province romaine*, 131, 173, 309 ff.

29/231–3   Γρηγόριος κτλ.

These names seem to be taken from a list of the oldest aristocratic families of Ragusa, which may have been kept in the city in C.'s time. C.'s information about Ragusa was obviously supplied by someone familiar with the local traditions. See Šišić, *Geschichte der Kroaten*, 161; and for the Latin names of citizens in the coastal cities, *cf.* Jireček, *Die Romanen*, I, 66 ff. The opinion of A. Pavić, *Cara Konst. Porf. 'De admin. imp.' glave*, 29–36 (Zagreb, 1906), 25, that this list was interpolated in the 13th or 14th cent. and that it contained names of prominent men from Split, is not substantiated.

29/233 πρωτοσπαθαρίου.

For the rank generally, see Guilland, *Byzantion*, 25–7 (1957), 649–95. The title was used at the time when Ragusa was founded: it is thus not an anachronism, as Bury (556, note 3) suggested.

29/233 Σαλῶνα.

Salona, the ancient capital of Roman Dalmatia, was destroyed by the Avars in 614. The surviving population took refuge on the islands and within the walls of Spalato. Others joined the refugees from Epidaurus and settled with them on the island of Ragousion. For Salona, see 29/25–53 and on 30/13, 14; *cf.* Novak, *Rad. Jugoslav. Akad.*, 270 (1949), 67–92.

29/234 ἔτη φ΄.

It may be that the original ms. of *DAI* read ἔτη τ΄, *i.e.* 300 years, and that φ΄, 500, is a copyist's error. To date the foundation of Ragusa to 649 would agree with historical fact, if we assume, as is suggested by Thomas the Archdeacon (c. 8), that the refugees spent some time in the islands reorganizing their navy and preventing the invaders from occupying the coast. See Šišić, *Geschichte der Kroaten*, 161; *id.*, *Povijest Hrvata*, 442.

29/236 ναῷ τοῦ ἁγίου Στεφάνου.

The church of St Stephen was a small edifice with an apse. It became an annex to a larger church constructed when Ragusa's importance had grown, and both churches were destroyed by the earthquake of 1667; see Jackson, *Dalmatia*, II, 324 ff. At a later period a church of St Stephen is mentioned in a part of the city called Posterula; but this can hardly be identical with the church erected, as C. tells us, in the old part of the city. Ragusan archaeologists have not yet solved this problem; *cf.* Skok, *Slavia*, x (1931), 452. A church of St Stephen in the old city, believed to be very ancient, is mentioned in 1440 by Philippus de Diversis (ed. Brunelli, *Programm d. k.-k. Obergymn. in Zadar*, 1879–80, 34). This document does not mention the relics of St Pancratius, but only those of SS. Petronilla and Domitilla and 'aliorum sanctorum copia grandis reliquiarum'. See Jireček, *Die Romanen*, I, 53; Šišić, *Geschichte der Kroaten*, 162, note 1, and *Povijest Hrvata* 442 (footnote 28).

29/237 ʿπαλάτιον μικρόνʾ.

C.'s etymology of the name Spalato (Croat *Split*) is based on popular imagination and cannot be accepted. The construction looks more like a large *castellum* than a 'little palace'. The suggestion of Thomas the Archdeacon (c. 4) that the name derives from Pallantheum, 'quod antiqui spatiosum dicebant palatium', is also unfounded. The true derivation is from Aspalathos, a place near Diocletian's residence. It is mentioned in the *Notitia Dignitatum* (ed. O. Seeck (Berlin, 1876), 150), and in the *Tabula Peutingeriana* (ed. K. Miller (Stuttgart, 1916), *segm.* VI, 3). Pliny, *Nat. Hist.*, XII, 52, describes a plant of this name, whose roots were used in the manufacture of perfumes. No doubt this Aspalathos and others in the Balkans and Asia Minor were called after the plant; *cf.* Wagler in Pauly-Wissowa, *RE*, II, cols. 1710 ff. (ʾΑσπάλαθος). M. Vasmer, *Abhandl. d. preuss. Akad.*, phil.-hist. Kl., 1944, no. 3, pp. 1, 3, derives the Slav form Split (Spljet) not from the Greek, but from the Latin word Spel(e)tum. *Cf.* Skok, 'Postanak Splita', *Anali histor. instituta* 1 (Dubrovnik, 1952), 23 ff.; *id.*, *Ortsnamenstudien*, 215.

29/238 ff. Διοκλητιανὸς τοῦτο ἔκτισεν.

Built by the emperor Diocletian during the years 293–305. The palace, an imposing quadrilateral structure (215 by 176 m.), was built in the style of a Roman residential villa, protected by strong fortifications. After Diocletian's death in 316, it became the property of the *fiscus*; and the northern part, called *Gynaecium Jovense* (*Notitia Dignitatum*, *ed. cit.*, 150), became a factory of cloth for the army. The imperial apartments were reserved to the use of personages of princely origin. The invasions of the 5th cent. do not seem to have done any considerable damage to the structure. The palace was, however, sacked by Totila, or his brother Ostroilus, during the war of Justinian against the Ostrogoths, then masters of North Italy and Dalmatia. After this it fell gradually into decay for lack of care by the imperial authorities. It was almost deserted when the inhabitants of Salona were forced to look for refuge in the islands and on the coast. According to Thomas the Archdeacon (cc. 9, 10), the inhabitants of Salona lived first on the islands and were persuaded to settle in the palace by Severus, a prominent citizen of Salona who was the first to take refuge at Spalato. G. Novak, *Actes du IIIme congrès int. d'ét. byz.* (Athènes, 1932), 145, advanced the theory that Spalato was a much older foundation, dating from the 3rd or 4th cent. B.C., and that the palace served as dwelling-place and haven for the inhabitants of Spalato during the invasions. The story of the foundation of Spalato by refugees from Salona was, he believed, invented later, in order to corroborate Spalato's claim to ecclesiastical supremacy over the whole of Dalmatia as heir of Salona. He expanded this theory in *Starohrvatska Prosvjeta*, n.s., II (1928), 30–6.

L. Karaman (*Strena Hoffilleriana* (Zagreb, 1940), 418–36) is also of opinion that the palace of Diocletian was never left completely abandoned. Part of it served as a refuge for the natives during the invasions before the destruction of Salona, and the number of its inhabitants gradually increased as refugees from destroyed cities settled in it. Karaman succeeded in finding some traces of Christian life in the palace during the 5th and 6th cents.: a cross on the architrave of the Porta Ferrea, two pilasters with rude crosses, and a column with a Corinthian cap in front of the palace temple. The last of these is regarded by Karaman as a remnant of a building which served as a church before the Mausoleum was converted into a cathedral, which he believes was done in the 8th cent. by Archbishop John of Ravenna. Novak's and Karaman's conclusions seem to be generally well founded.

For the palace, see R. Adam, *Ruins of the Palace of the Emperor Diocletian at Spalato in Dalmatia* (London, 1763); J. Niemann, *Der Palast Diokletians in Spalato* (Wien, 1910); E. Hébard, J. Zeiller, *Spalato, le palais de Dioclétien* (Paris, 1912); F. Bulić, L. Karaman, *Palaca cara Dioklecijana u Splitu* (Zagreb, 1927); F. Bulić, *Kaiser Diokletians Palast in Split* (Zagreb, 1929).

29/241   τοῦ ἁγίου Δόμνου.

St Domnus (Domnius), according to local legend a disciple of St Peter, who sent him to Dalmatia where he became bishop of Salona, and died a martyr's death under the emperor Trajan. In reality Domnus (Domnius), bishop of Salona, lived in the 3rd cent. and was martyred under Diocletian. His body, with that of another martyr, Anastasius, was buried in Salona; and both were brought to Rome by the Abbot Martinus, whom pope John IV, a native of Dalmatia, had sent thither in 641 with a large sum of money, in order to redeem captive Christians and to collect relics of saints from churches destroyed by Avars and Slavs in Dalmatia and Istria; see *Liber Pontificalis*, ed. Duchesne, I, 330. The pope deposited the relics in the oratory of St Venantius, built or restored by him near the Lateran Basilica of St John at the Lateran Baptistery. It may be that the inhabitants of Spalato obtained part of the relics from Rome, but the bodies of the two saints could not have been buried in the Church of St Domnus. The legend of the apostolic origin of St Domnus developed in Spalato during the period from the 7th to 10th cents., when Spalato began to claim ecclesiastical authority over the whole of Dalmatia as heir of Salona, presumed to be an ancient apostolic foundation. In order to reconcile historical and legendary traditions, it was supposed that there had been two bishops of the same name at Salona, Domnius the disciple of St Peter and Domnio, a martyr of the 3rd cent. Both had been buried in the Basilica of Salona, but the body of St Domnio had been brought to Rome by Martinus, while that of St Domnius had been discovered by the first archbishop of Spalato, John of Ravenna, in the 7th cent., and brought to Spalato; see Thomas the Archdeacon c. 12. In later tradition Domnio was again identified with Domnius, the legendary disciple of St Peter. See J. Zeiller, *Les origines chrétiennes dans la province romaine de Dalmatie* (Paris, 1906), 6–46; H. Delehaye, *Anal. Boll.*, xviii (1899), 393 ff.; *ibid.*, xxiii (1904), 13 ff. *Cf.* also the many studies on the controversy published by Monsignore Bulić in *Bullettino di Archeologia e Storia Dalmata* from the years 1896–1914 and 1922, and *id.*, *Vjesnik Hrv. arch. drustva*, n.s. xv (1928), 55–71; E. Dyggve, *History of Salonitan Christianity* (Oslo, 1951), 71 ff., 125 ff.

29/242   κοιτὼν τοῦ αὐτοῦ βασιλέως.
The church of St Domnus is to be identified with the mausoleum which Diocletian built for himself, and where his sarcophagus was deposited. This mausoleum was once thought to be a temple of Jupiter: a confusion arising from the facts that Diocletian regarded himself as the son or incarnation of Jupiter—Jovius—, and was deified after his death: see E. Hébard, J. Zeiller, *op. cit.*, 68 ff. The Greek word κοιτών corresponds to the Latin *cubiculum*, which however means not only a bed-room but also, in inscriptions, a tomb. A temple, not of Aesculapius but more probably of Jupiter, faced the mausoleum.

29/243   εἰλημaτικaὶ καμάραι.
C. means the crypt, which still exists and was for some time used as a chapel. It was never a prison: C.'s statement is based on a later, garbled tradition. The purpose of the crypt was to keep the upper part of the mausoleum dry: see E. Hébard, J. Zeiller, *op. cit.*, 96 ff.

29/245   ὁ ἅγιος ᾿Αναστάσιος.
St Anastasius, according to his short biographies, was a native of Aquileia, and, though wealthy, a fuller by trade. He went to Salona, where he was martyred, *c.* 304. His body seems first to have been hidden on the island of Lesina (also called Pharia, whence the confusion in the legend that he was first buried by the Christians of Africa), and then transferred by a noble lady to Salona. His relics were carried to Rome by abbot Martinus (see above on 29/241); but part of them may have been left in his sarcophagus and brought to Spalato. In order to explain the existence of relics in two different places, legend created another St Anastasius, a soldier of the class of *cornicularii* (soldiers decorated and promoted to adjutants), who was martyred under Aurelian. See J. Zeiller, *Les origenes chrétiennes dans la province romaine de Dalmatie* (Paris, 1906), 55–77; L. S. L. de Tillemont, *Mémoires pour servir a l'étude de l'histoire ecclés. des six premiers siècles*, v (Paris, 1702),148–9. For the Life of St A., see *AASS* 7th Sept., pp. 21–2, and Jelić's *Ephemeris Salonitana* (Jadera, 1894), 21–4. For A. Cornicularius, see H. Delehaye, *Anal. Boll.*, xvi (1897), 488–500.

29/246-55   τὸ τεῖχος τοῦ τοιούτου κάστρου κτλ.
The walls, originally in places 17 m. high and about 2·1 m. across, were constructed of stone blocks, often half a metre thick, from the quarries in Brazza and Traù. The method of construction described by C. was observed by Hébard and Zeiller (*Spalato, Le palais de Dioclétien* (Paris, 1912), 31) only in part of the interior of the palace, but it could have been seen on the walls in C.'s day. The 'rows of columns with entablatures above' derive from a legendary local tradition, and have no foundation in Diocletian's plan of construction.

29/256   οὔτε περίπατον . . . οὔτε προμαχῶνας.
This is inaccurate: guards could not have made a regular round of the walls had there been neither rampart nor bulwarks. The rampart was probably a flat terrace on top of the wall.

29/258–61 τὸ Τετραγγούριν.

The geographical description of Tetrangurin (Tragurium Traù, in Croat Trogir) is accurate, but the etymology a popular, and inaccurate, explanation. From 537, when Justinian's generals had ended Ostrogoth rule in Dalmatia, down to C.'s time the city was part of Byzantine Dalmatia. The Avar and Slav invasions did not interfere with it. The name Tetrangourion may derive from Troghilon, a place near Syracuse, the home of the Greek colonists of Lissa (Issa, in Croat Vis) who had founded the city. See Farlati, *Illyricum Sacrum*, IV, 303 ff.; Cons, *Province romaine*, 217 ff., 240 ff., 258; Egon Braun in Pauly-Wissowa, *RE*, n.s., VI A, col. 2076 (Tragurium). *Cf.* also J. Lucius, *Historia di Dalmatia et in particolare delle Città di Traù, Spalato e Sebenico* (Venice, 1674), 1 ff.; Mayer, *Bullettino di Archeologia e Storia Dalmata*, 50 (1928–9), 110–14, derives the name from τράγος and ὄρος ('goat's hill'), which does not seem satisfactory.

29/262 ὁ ἅγιος μάρτυς Λαυρέντιος.

The relics of St Laurentius must have been deposited in the cathedral church of Trogir, which was built in 503 to replace an older church dating, as local tradition says, from the time of Constantine the Great. The body of St Laurentius, Roman deacon and martyr, was buried in Rome, so that C.'s statement, based probably on local legend, is incorrect. There was a church of St Laurentius at Trogir, but it is mentioned for the first time only in a charter issued *c.* 1111; see Smičiklas, *Cod. dipl.*, II, 23. It is interesting to note that C. does not speak of a bishopric of Trogir. This suggests that in 949 the city had as yet no bishop. The bishopric must have been founded between 950 and 1000, because in the latter year the Venetian doge Peter II Orseolo is said to have been greeted in the city by bishop and citizens: see Dandolo, cap. x, pars 24, col. 229. *Cf.* Šišić, *Povijest Hrvata*, 444.

29/263 τὸ κάστρον τῶν Δεκατέρων.

Decatera, *lat.* Catharum, *gr.* τὰ Δεκάτερα, Croat Kotor. It was believed that Decatera was built on the site of the city of Acruvium, mentioned by Pliny, *Nat. Hist.* III, 22, as a Roman colony; an opinion which, according to Kiepert, *Formae Orbis Antiqui*, XVII, Beiblatt, 5, note 49, is unfounded, since Acruvium was situated at the entrance of the Bay of Kotor. Justinian, after the expulsion of the Goths from Dalmatia, rebuilt the castle of Κάτταρος. The fort survived the invasions and remained part of Byzantine Dalmatia. In *De Them.*, 97/21–2 C. speaks of τὰ κάτω Δεκάτερα, which suggests that he distinguished the acropolis from the settlement which grew round it. The settlement was sacked in 867 during the Saracen *razzia* described by C. (29/92), but the upper town seems to have escaped. See Tomaschek in Pauly-Wissowa, *RE*, I, col. 285 (Acruvium); Patsch, *ibid.*, IV, cols. 2246 f. (Decatera); Ferjančić 23, note 49.

29/263–5 ἑρμηνεύεται τῇ Ῥωμαίων διαλέκτῳ.

The ancient form must have been Cattaron or Cattaros, to which the Latin preposition 'de' was added. The change of the second 'a' into an 'e' is a peculiarity of the Dalmatian Latin dialect. In his attempt at an etymology C. may have in mind the word *catena*: the entrance to the Bay of Kotor still bears this name (Slav *verige*), and the bay is shaped like a chain; see Skok, *Ortsnamenstudien*, 216; Ferjančić, *ibid.*

29/266–8 τῷ δὲ χειμῶνι οὐδαμῶς.

Hardly an exaggeration, since in winter the inhabitants get only about three hours sunshine on sunny days, which are few. See Jireček, *Handelsstrassen*, 5 ff.

29/270–1 ὁ δὲ ναὸς . . . εἰλημaτικός.

The vaulted church of St Tryphon was built in 809 by a noble citizen of Kotor, Andreaccio Saracenis. It was partly destroyed by the Arabs in 841 and rebuilt 1123–66. St Tryphon was martyred at Nicaea during the Decian persecution; see P. Franchi de'

Cavalieri, *Haghiographica* (*Studi e Testi* xix, Rome, 1908), 45–74. His relics were appropriated by some Venetian merchants, who were afterwards forced by a storm to take refuge in the Bay of Kotor and persuaded to sell the relics to the city. The church still exists, and St Tryphon (Sveti Trifun) is the patron saint of the city. His feast-day is 3rd February. See Jackson, *Dalmatia*, iii, 38; U. Monneret de Villard, *L'architettura in Dalmazia* (Milan, 1910), 33.

29/272–5　τὸ κάστρον τῶν Διαδώρων.

Diadora, Croat Zadar, Italian Zara, the ancient city of Jader (Iadera, Ἰάδαιρα, Ἰάδερα), whose inhabitants, Ἰαδαστῖνοι, are mentioned for the first time in an inscription found on the island of Lesina, of the year 384 b.c. C. stresses the antiquity of the city in the popular etymology which he gives of its name. It became a Roman colony under Augustus. It survived the Gothic rule in Dalmatia and was restored to the empire in 540. After the fall of Salona (615), it became the chief city of Byzantine Dalmatia and a seat of the imperial military governor. Its importance increased considerably after the loss of Ravenna (751), and it became the capital of the archontate of Dalmatia, whose autonomy was recognized by Michael II (*cf.* 29/60–2). When the imperial sovereignty was restored in Zara in the second half of the 9th cent., the city retained its importance as the capital of the Dalmatian *thema* (*cf.* on 29/61–6), and in the 10th cent. its locally elected chieftains acted as imperial representatives in Byzantine Dalmatia. See Cons, *Province romaine*, 190 ff., 200 ff.; Vulić in Pauly-Wissowa, *RE*, ix, cols. 556 f. (Iader); A. Tamaro, *La Vénétie julienne et la Dalmatie*, ii and iii (Rome, 1919).

29/275–7　ἡ ἁγία Ἀναστασία.

St Anastasia, a noble Roman lady, was converted to Christianity by Chrysogonus. She helped Christians in Rome and Aquileia during the persecutions of Diocletian. She was executed at Sirmium by order of the prefect of Illyricum, Florus. She was buried in Sirmium, in the garden of a noble lady called Apollonia, who dedicated there a church to her memory. When Sirmium was occupied by the Huns in 447, Anastasia's relics were transferred to Constantinople and placed in a church dedicated to her. When in 804 Donatus, bishop of Zadar, and the doge of Venice Beatus came to Constantinople to negotiate the peace between Charlemagne and the Byzantines, the emperor Nicephorus I presented the relics to the bishop, who brought them to Zadar. St Chrysogonus was the patron saint of Zadar. A church of St Chrysogonus is mentioned in the testament of Andrew, prior of the Benedictine monastery in Zara, in 918. Prior Maius, in a document dated 986, says that the saint's body rested in the church dedicated to his memory. See *MPG*, cxvi, cols. 573–609; *AASS*, 3rd April, cols. 247 ff.; Farlati, *Illyricum Sacrum*, v, 34–5 (Translatio Constantinopoli Iaderam), reprinted by Rački, *Documenta*, 306–10. For St Chrysogonus see Rački, *Documenta*, 18, 21; Jireček, *Die Romanen*, i, 52; Šišić, *Geschichte der Kroaten*, 164, and *Povijest Hrvata*, 444; M. M. Vasić, *Architektura i skulptura u Dalmaciji* (Belgrade, 1922), 17, 120 ff.

29/278–9　Ὁ δὲ ναός.

The church of St Anastasia does not exist in the form described by C. It seems to have been rebuilt at the beginning of the 13th cent. Only some columns of the old basilica and some mosaics seem to have been preserved.

29/280　ἐξ ὑλογραφίας.

See Banduri's note, *MPG*, cxiii, cols. 269–70. The word means icon-paintings on wood, as distinct from mosaics. Theophanes (443/22–5) records that the iconoclast patriarch Niketas ordered the destruction of mosaics (εἰκόνας . . . διὰ μουσείου οὔσας) and wooden icons (ἐξ ὑλογραφιάς οὔσας); *cf.* also Cedrenus II, 497/20–1. Such pictures are referred to in the fourth session of the Seventh Oecumenical Council (Mansi xiii, col. 9 A-B).

29/282-4 ἡ Ἁγία Τριάς.

The church of the Holy Trinity, later called the church of St Donatus, is a round building with three apses, similar to San Vitale at Ravenna. The 'other church' above it is the gallery of the first, also with three apses superposed over those below, and accessible by a staircase round the outer wall. The church is now a museum. See Jackson, *Dalmatia* I, 250 ff.; G. Kowalczyk, *Denkmäler der Kunst in Dalmatien*, II (Berlin, 1909), 64 ff.; U. Monneret de Villard, *L'Architettura in Dalmazia* (Milan, 1910), 14–25; M. M. Vasić, *Architektura i skulptura u Dalmaciji* (Belgrade, 1922), 16 ff.

29/285-9 νησία . . . πάμπολλα.

The name ἡ Βέκλα, *ital.* Veglia, derives from the old Dalmatian word Vekla (*cl. lat.* vetula), adj. veklesun, a word which corresponds to Slav Starigrad, 'old city'. The Slav name of the island, Krk, used today, comes from the old form Curicum. The island was probably called Curica Vecla by the Latin population. The island and city of Arbe, originally Arba, are called Rab in Croat; see H. Krahe, *Die alten balkan-illyrischen geographischen Namen* (Heidelberg, 1925), 15, 77, 80. Opsara, Croat Osor, *ital.* Ossero, derives probably from old Dalmatian Apsarus. Lumbricaton, Croat Vergada, possibly from rubricata (*sc.* insula), an island with reddish soil; see Skok, *Ortsnamenstudien*, 216–7; *id.*, *Slavenstvo i romanstvo* I, 21–34.

29/290-5 τὰ ὀνόματά εἰσιν οὕτως κτλ.

Katautrebeno (or Katangrebeno, as Skok reads) in fact designates two islands, today called Pasman and Kornat. On Pasman (possibly from *lat.* Postumiana) is a place called Tkou, Kun, in documents of 1070–8 Kutono (see Rački, *Documenta*, 170), which recalls C.'s form Katan. Kornat derives from Grebeno, and Greben means 'hilly country'. Pizouch is today Dugi otok ('long island'), *ital.* Isola lunga; but Πιζύχ is still preserved in the place-name Čuh on the island. Župančić sees in this word a name given to the island by the Pelasgians, akin to the Etruscans, who were superseded in the Balkans by Greeks, Illyrians and Thracians. He derives the name from the Caucasian root č'voχ, which means 'long'; it would thus mean the same as the present Slav name, 'long island'. Suić, *Starohrvatska Prosvjeta* 4 (1955), 135–40 derives from Greek ἀπίδιο-ὀχός, 'a field with pears'. Selbo, from Latin silva, 'forest', is today Silba in Croat and Selva in Italian. Skerda, from the Illyrian root skard or skerd, lies between Premuda and Ist, and is called Skarda vela ('big Skarda') in Croat and Scarda in Italian. Aloëp, in Croat Olib (Ulib), *ital.* Ulbo, is called in medieval documents Allubium, probably from Latin alluvium. The name Skirdakissa covers two islands: Skirda, called by the Venetians Scherda parva, now Croat Skerda mala; and Kissa, now Croat Pag, *ital.* Pago. The name Kissa, of Greek origin, is still preserved in Caska, a place on the island of Pag. Pyrotima is the Croat and Italian Premuda. Meleta is the Croat Melata, and the Italian Melada. Estiounez covers two islands: Sestrunj, probably from old Dalmatian estrun, *cl. lat.* extraneus; and Ez, now the small island of Iz, *ital.* Eso. See Tomaschek, *Sitzungsber. d. Akad. Wien*, 113 (1886), 339–48; H. Kiepert, *Lehrbuch der alten Geographie*, Berlin (1878), 360 ff.; Jireček, *Geschichte der Serben*, I, 116–22; Šišić, *Geschichte der Kroaten*, 158 ff.; *id.*, *Povijest Hrvata*, 445; Skok, *Ortsnamenstudien*, 213–20; N. Župančić, *La signification de quelques vieux noms géographiques et ethniques de la péninsule balkanique* (Ljubljana, 1933); *id.*, *Atti del V Congresso internaz. di studi bizantini*, I (Rome, 1939), 333–7; Skok, *Slavenstvo i romanstvo* I, 78–103; Strgačić, *Starohrvatska Prosvjeta* (1949), 87–102; Ferjančić 25–6.

30/1-5 Διήγησις κτλ.

For this interpolated chapter, see Introductory Note above pp. 97–9 and for the short preface (30/2–5), *cf. De Cer.*, 456/4–5. The difference in style between c. 30 and cc. 29, 31–6 speaks against the assumption of Bury (525) that all these chapters are the work of one author, c. 30 having been added later; and against that of Fehér (66) who regards c. 30 as the introduction to the συγγραφή promised at 29/56. The title reveals that the author was particularly interested in the history of Dalmatia; and he may himself have been a Dalmatian from one of the coastal cities: *cf.* Introductory Note p. 101; Fehér 60; Macartney 136–138.

30/6–12   Τοῖς οὖν καὶ τῆς Δελματίας κτλ.

The author of this chapter gives only a very short description of Dalmatia under the Romans, for which see G. Zippel, *Die römische Herrschaft in Illyrien bis auf Augustus* (Leipzig, 1877); P. O. Bahr, *Der Ursprung der römischen Provinz Illyrien* (Grimma, 1876); Cons, *Province romaine*; Patsch, Pauly-Wissowa, *RE*, iv, cols. 2448–55 (Delmatae); Mommsen, *The Provinces of the Roman Empire* (ed. Haverfield, i, London, 1909), c. vi; Jireček, *Geschichte der Serben*, i, 1–59; Šišić, *Geschichte der Kroaten*, 21–34; *id.*, *Povijest Hrvata*, 41–174; Vulić in Pauly-Wissowa, *RE*, ix, cols. 1085–8 (Illyricum); G. Cardinali, *Enciclopedia Italiana*, xviii, 835–8. Five Roman emperors, Claudius, Aurelian, Probus, Diocletian and Maximinian, were of Illyrian peasant stock: *cf.* E. A. Freeman, *The Illyrian Emperors and their Land* (*Historical Essays*, 3rd series, 1879), 32 ff.

30/13   παρελήφθη παρὰ τῶν Σκλαβικῶν ἐθνῶν.

See on 29/14–53. The Slav occupation of Dalmatia is not recorded in detail by C. The Slavs started migrating from their original habitat, which was situated probably in what is now Poland down to the river Bug, through the Moravian Gates and the Carpathian Mountains into Hungary. They were on the move in the direction of the Danube and the Roman frontiers already by the beginning of our era. Certain places in Croatia, between the Sava and the Drava and in the so-called Banat between the lower Tisza and the Danube, have borne Slav names from the 2nd cent. onwards: *e.g.* Vuka, Vrbas, Vučica. Slavs (Venedi) are mentioned in the 3rd and 4th cents. in former Dacia and in Bessarabia. These Slav settlements survived the Hunnic invasion, and were strengthened by new Slav contingents during the 5th cent. Slav settlements in modern Wallachia on the Danube were the first to come into contact with the Byzantine empire; and after 517 they started to cross the Danube with the object of raiding Macedonia, Thessaly and Epirus. Justinian forced the Antes, the most powerful Slav group, to become *foederati* of the empire. At the beginning of the 6th cent. Slav tribes entered Illyricum and started to push in the direction of Dalmatia, passing by Salona and reaching the shores of the Adriatic in 536. In 548 they were before Dyrrhachium. Procopius (*B.G.*, iii, 38, 40; iv, 45) and Theophanes (233) speak at length about the Slav invasions of Illyricum in 549, 550 and 559. In spite of the violent character of these Slav incursions, the Byzantines might have been able to settle some of the Slavs in Illyricum and, in time, to pacify, civilize and assimilate them, as they did the Antes. However, the appearance of the Avars in Europe made this impossible. The Avars, Turkish tribes who had accepted the name of their masters (the Avars of Tunguz race), moved towards Europe after the destruction of the Avar empire in Asia. About the middle of the 6th cent. they crossed the lower reaches of the Volga, defeated the Turkish Bulgars who controlled the region between the Kuban and the Don, and accepted the invitation of the Lombards of Pannonia to attack the German Gepids in former Dacia. They annihilated the Gepids; and, when the Lombards abandoned Pannonia to conquer northern Italy, became masters of the whole Danubian basin. The Slavs in Hungary, Wallachia, Pannonia, Noricum, Illyricum, Moravia and Slovakia had to acknowledge Avar supremacy; while the Slavs of Bohemia and Poland allied themselves with the Avars against the Franks. The Antes who opposed Avar rule were annihilated by the khagan Apsich in 602. Under Avar leadership Slav attacks on Illyricum and Dalmatia increased. A permanent Slav settlement on Byzantine soil is mentioned for the first time in 581 (Dvornik, *Les Slaves*, 4 ff.), but Slavs must have settled in parts of Dalmatia even before that date. The capture of Sirmium by the Avars and their Slav allies during the reign of Maurice (582–602) opened the way to new penetration. The Byzantine generals Priscus and Peter defeated the Avars, but the death of Maurice made it impossible to exploit the victory. During the reign of Phocas (602–10) Dalmatia was again repeatedly invaded; and during the 7th cent. the whole country was occupied by numerous Slav tribes. Meantime, Slavs established in Noricum and Pannonia penetrated into Istria and Venetia, pushing towards the shores of the Adriatic, towards Tagliamento in Italy, and deep into the Alps. The struggle with the Persians prevented the Byzantines from concentrating on the defence of Illyricum. It was only by a miracle that Thessalonica was saved; and the year 626, when the Persians allied themselves with Avars and Slavs and laid siege to Constantinople, was one of the most critical in Byzantine history. See Lucius, *De Regno*, 40 ff.; Dümmler, *Älteste Geschichte*, 353–429; Klaić, *Povijest Hrvata*, I (Zagreb, 1899), 25 ff.; Jireček, *Die Romanen*, I, 21 ff.; Niederle, *Slovanské Staro žitnosti*. I (oddil II histor.), 174 ff.; *id.*, *Manuel*, I, 88 ff.; Šišić, *Geschichte der Kroaten*, 41–60; *id.*, *Povijest Hrvata*, 177–235; Jireček, *Geschichte der Serben*, I, 81–109; Dvornik, *Les Slaves*, 1–63; A. A. Vasiliev, *Justin the First* (Harvard, 1950), 302–12; Labuda, *Byzantinoslavica*, 11 (1950), 167–73; Dvornik, *The Slavs*, chapters I, II, pp. 3 ff.

30/14   Σαλῶνα.

Salona was not built by Diocletian. Its foundation probably dates from before the Celtic invasion of Dalmatia, since the name does not seem to be Celtic. However, the building of the imperial palace at Aspalathus (see on 29/237 ff.), where Diocletian lived after his abdication, naturally contributed to the growth of Salona also. For the history of Salona, see Cons, *Province romaine, passim*; Vulić, in Pauly-Wissowa, *RE*, I (Zweite Reihe, 1920), cols. 2003–6 (Salona); Modestin, *Narodna Enciklopedija*, IV (Zagreb, 1929), 273–6.

30/18 ff.   Ἠθροίζοντο οὖν κτλ.

See on 29/14–53. C.'s account of the capture of Salona is legendary. Thomas the Archdeacon (cc. 7–11) gives a different version; and though he confounds Avars with Goths and is too prone to moralizing, his narrative seems nearer to the truth. According to him, the enemy surrounded the city, overwhelmed the defenders with projectiles, and, when panic seized the citizens, entered Salona, which they sacked and burnt. Most of the citizens escaped by boat to the islands of Solta, Brazza, Lesina, Lissa and Curzola. The exact date is not known. The last dated inscriptions found in the ruins are from 612. The city may have been captured *c.* 614 by the Avars, who may or may not have been supported by allied or subject Slavs. See Jireček, *Geschichte der Serben*, 95 ff.; Bulić, *Bullettino di Archeologia e Storia Dalmata*, 29 (1906), 268–304; Ostrogorsky[2] 76.

30/61 ff.   Οἱ δὲ Χρωβάτοι κτλ.

The account of the arrival of the Croats in Dalmatia is given in two versions, in cc. 30 and 31. The version given in c. 30 is more detailed, and must have been gathered on the spot, somewhere in Dalmatia, in one of the Latin cities, where C.'s reporter could easily have met with Croats familiar with their own national traditions. C. 30 is therefore the Croat version of the Croat migration from White Croatia to Dalmatia. When C. wrote his short description of the settlement and expansion of the Slavs in Dalmatia (29/54–88 and cc. 31, 32), these details were not known in Constantinople. The account in cc. 29, 31 and 32 seems to be based on information found in the archives of the Foreign Ministry.

It is interesting to note that in this Croat version there is no mention of the part played by Heraclius in settling the Croats in Dalmatia. This may be taken as confirming the hypothesis that the report comes from the Croats themselves: they would not be anxious to stress the rôle of Heraclius in their *Landnahme*. Moreover, in c. 30 details are given which could have been learned only from a Croat source. The other account (31/1–25) seems to betray a Byzantine source, probably the records kept in the archives of the

Foreign Ministry. One can see in 31/1–25, as also in 31/33 and 58 ff., the tendency to emphasize Byzantine claims to suzerainty over the lands of the Croats, which had belonged to the empire. Thus the emphasis laid on the rôle of Heraclius in Croat history becomes understandable. This rôle was well known to C., and he has made a clear allusion to it already at 29/54.

It has been said in the Introductory Note to this section (p. 96) that the account of the Croat migration in the 7th cent. (the date is implied also at 30/61 ff., where it is stated that the Croats left their homeland while Dalmatia was occupied by the Avars) has been and still is the subject of controversy. But recently this controversy has taken a new turn. The philological argument put forward by Jagić (above, p. 95), whose authority seemed overwhelming, has ceased to convince Slav philologists. A. Meillet, *Le Slav commun* (Paris, 1924), 2 ff., states that the differentiation of the primitive Slav idiom into distinct languages started only in the 7th or 8th cents. N. van Wijk, *Les langues slaves: De l'unité à la pluralité* (Paris, 1927), 53 ff., applied this new philological finding to C.'s account of the late migration of the Croats and Serbs: he says ,'Quant au récit de Constantin le Porphyrogénète sur l'origine septentrionale des Serbes et Croates, il nous semble être d'autant plus plausible qu'il place la migration de ces deux tribus à une époque où la différenciation linguistique était encore très faible, ce qui facilitait la fusion de leurs dialectes avec ceux de leurs nouveaux voisins'. Vaillant, *Conférences de l'Institut de Linguistique de l'Université de Paris*, VIII (1949), 29, justly observes that the Slavs 'were still conscious of speaking the same language' at the end of the 9th cent. R. Jakobson, quoted by Grégoire, *L'Origine*, 90, thinks that there are some important similarities between the languages of the northern and of the southern Slavs which could be adduced as an argument for, rather than against, C.'s version of the Croat migration.

The fact that the name 'Croat' cannot be derived from a common Slav root has suggested to many historians and philologists that the primitive Croats may not have been of Slav origin. N. Županić sees in them and in the Serbs brothers of the Pelasgians and Etruscans. L. Hauptmann argues for a Sarmatian origin of the primitive Croats. Philological arguments brought forward by M. Vasmer have proved the Iranian origin of at least the name of the Croats. S. Sakać thinks that he has discovered the name 'Croats' in inscriptions of Darius dating from the 6th cent. B.C., in which are mentioned a Persian province and people called Harahvaiti, Harahvatis, Horohoati. It is however difficult to imagine why this people, when it left its homeland on the frontiers of modern Afghanistan under Indian pressure, should be supposed to have crossed the whole Iranian plateau in order to settle between the Caucasus and the Sea of Azov, where the name 'Choroatos' can be traced in two inscriptions of the 3rd cent. A.D.; see V. Latyšev, *Inscr. Ant. Orae Septent. Pont. Eux.*, II (Petropoli, 1890), nos. 430, 445. If the name is Iranian, it may have been that of another tribe, akin to the Harahvatis, which, at the time of the great Indo-European migration, instead of following other Iranian tribes to Iran, moved south-west towards the Caucasus. It should be noted that *De Cer.*, 688/11, 13 mentions two tribes, Krevatades and Sarban, in the Caucasus near the river Terek; and in these A. Rambaud, *L'Empire grec au Xme siècle* (Paris, 1870), 510, 525 ff., saw the Croats and Serbs. The Krevatades cannot be identified with the Czerkess Gabardinci (see Grégoire, *La Nouvelle Clio*, IV, 1952, 323; V, 1953, 466–7), because the latter moved into this region only in the 14th or 15th cents. It is thus possible to surmise that the Croats and Serbs, surprised by the Huns, who wrought such havoc among the Sarmatian tribes in S. Russia and between the Caucasus and the Sea of Azov, were cut in two parts, one of which looked for security in the Caucasus, and the other and greater fled towards the Carpathians and settled among the Slavs in modern Galicia and modern Saxony. If this theory could be more decisively proved, we should see in it a phenomenon analogous to the Turkish Bulgars among the Slavs of Macedonia and Thrace, and to the Germanic Varyags in Russia. Although to a large extent assimilated by their Slav confederates and subjects, the Croats and Serbs still preserved Sarmatian military traditions, and probably formed a kind of standing-army of cavalry among the Slavs. This would explain why in his plight Heraclius accepted their help against the Avars who were destroying prosperous Byzantine provinces; see further on 31/7–8, 22–5. See Jagić, *Archiv für slav. Philologie*, XVII (1895), 47 ff.; Klaić, *Povijest Hrvata*, I, 30; Niederle, *Slovanské Starožitnosti*, II, 277; *id.*, *Manuel*, I, 88 ff.; Gumplowicz, *Politischanthropologische Revue*, I (1903), 779 ff.; Županić, *Etnolog* (Ljubljana), 1–5 (1926–33), and *Narodna Starina*, II (1922) (studies in Slovene, with French *résumés*); Hauptmann, *Strena Buliciana* (Zagreb, 1924), 515–46; *id.*, *Jugoslov. Ist. Časopis*, III (1937), 30–61; M. Vasmer, *Untersuchungen über die ältesten Wohnsitze der Slaven: Die Iranien in Südrussland* (Leipzig, 1923); Vernadsky, *Journal of the Amer. Orient. Soc.*, 65 (1943), 257–9; Sakać, *Orientalia Christiana Periodica*, XV (1949), 313–40; Grégoire, *L'Origine*; Dvornik, *The Making*, 268–305 (complete bibliography with quotations from all available sources); *id.*, *The Slavs*, 26 ff., 52.

30/61–3   ἐκεῖθεν Βαγιβαρείας κτλ.

The existence of Croats beyond the Carpathian Mountains is attested by Mas'udi (Marquart 101 ff.), by the Persian Geographer of the 10th cent. (*ibid.*, 466–73), by king Alfred in his Anglo-Saxon translation of Orosius' *History of the World* (tr. Bosworth, London, 1855, I, c. I, para. 12), and by the foundation charter of the bishopric of Prague (Cosmas, *Chronica*, MGH scr., n. s. II, 134–40). In view of this evidence almost all historians accept the existence of Croats at least in north-eastern Bohemia during the 10th cent., and it is attested by other Czech sources also. Since the Scandinavian *Hervarar Saga* (ed. S. Bugge, Christiania, 1865) calls the Carpathian Mountains 'Harvadja', that is, 'mountains of the Croats', and since the *Russian Primary Chronicle* (ed. Cross and Sherbowitz-Wetzor (Cambridge, Mass., 1953), 65, 119) also speaks of Croats in modern Galicia, the existence of what C. calls White Croatia beyond the Carpathians should not be doubted. The information of Mas'udi and the Persian Geographer should also be interpreted in this sense. The location of the White Croats 'beyond Bavaria' (30/62) can be reconciled with historical facts. The Croats of Bohemia, with their dynasty of Slavnik princes, formed a common state with the Czechs, led by their princes of the Přemyslid dynasty; and, after the defeat of the Magyars on the Lechfeld in 955, Boleslav I of Bohemia, with the Slavniks, occupied the western part of modern Galicia with Cracow, and Silesia (see Introductory Note to this section pp. 98–9). Thus White Croatia, belonging to the Czech state, could be located 'beyond Bavaria', the neighbour of Bohemia. See V. Minorsky, *Ḥudūd al-'Alam, ' The Regions of the World' ; A Persian Geography* (London, 1937); J. Widajewicz, *Studie nad relacją o Słowianach Ibrāhīma ibn Jakūba* (Krakow, 1946); *id.*, *Państwo Wislan* (Krakow, 1947); T. Kowalski, *Relacja Ibrāhīma ibn Ja'kūba z podróży do krajów słowianskich* (Krakow, 1946); T. Lewicki, *Sprawozdania* of the Polish Academy, XLIX (Cracow, 1948), 24–34; *id.*, *Slavia Antiqua*, II (Poznań, 1949–50), 349, 356, 359; Labuda, *Pierwsze państwo*, 207 ff.; Grafenauer, *Prilog kritici*, 34 ff.; Dvornik, *The Making*, 36 ff., 92 ff., 271 ff., 283 ff.

30/64–6   ὅ τε Κλουκᾶς κτλ.

The etymology of the names of the Croat chiefs is still a matter of controversy among specialists. Mikkola's suggestion (*Archiv für slav. Philol.*, 41, 1927, 157 ff.) that we should see in them the names of Avar chiefs was generally rejected. Oštir (*Etnolog*, I, 1927, 1–35) saw in them traces of the language of the primitive population of modern Galicia, before the Indo-European period. The theory of Gumplowicz (*Politischanthropologische Revue*, I, 1903, 779 ff.) that the Croat chiefs were the descendants of Goths who had fled into modern Galicia after the Hunnic onslaught, was unsuccessfully defended and developed by J. Rus (*Kralji dinastije srevladicev* (Ljubljana, 1931); *id.*, *Etnolog*, V–VI (1933), 31–43; see the critical review of his ideas by Hauptmann, Mayer and Segvić in *Nastavni Vjestnik*, XLI (1932–3), 76–92). The theory of Howorth (*Journal of the Anthropological Institute of*

Great Britain and Ireland, XI (1882), 224 ff.) was recently revived by Grégoire (*L'Origine*). He (p. 93) gives the following etymologies for the names: 'Lovelos rappelle Lublin, Kosentzes Kosice, Bouga le fleuve Bug. Je laisse de côté ici les autres noms, bien que Kloukas fasse songer à Cracovie ou à Glogau.' These are ingenious and daring suggestions, but they are not conclusive; and they have been rejected by Labuda, *Pierwsze państwo*, 250–5, and by Grafenauer, *Prilog kritici*, 45 ff. The most disputed etymology has been that of the name Kosentzes. Hauptmann (*Seoba*, 60) derives the name from the Sarmatian Kasagos; others regard it as Gothic, and think that a Gothic tribe joined the Croats on their migration to Galicia after the Hunnic onslaught. Skok (*Etnolog*, VII, 1934, 80 ff.) favours the Avar origin of the names Mouchlo and Kosentzes, which seems hardly plausible. All these theories show that up to the present no Slav etymology of the names has been found; and this seems to support the hypothesis that the primitive Croats were not of Slav origin; see on 30/61 ff., and Dvornik, *The Making*, 273 ff., 289 ff. For bibliography of Croat tribes, see Ferjančić 30–1, note 84; and of Kosentzes, *Historija Naroda, Jugoslavije* I (Belgrade, 1953), 174.

30/66–71, 76–8 ἦλθον εἰς Δελματίαν κτλ.
The description of the attack on the Avars corresponds well with what is said in this chapter about the origin of the Croats (30/60–2). The Croats took the easy route, following the course of the Pruth or Sereth towards the lower Danube and the territory of the Bulgars, themselves allies of Heraclius and hostile to the Avars; they reached Thrace, and were thence directed to the Byzantine possessions bordering Dalmatia on the Adriatic. With the help of the imperial navy, of the native Slavs and perhaps also of Latin refugees on the islands they were able to start a successful offensive against the Avars in Dalmatia. C. rightly points out (30/75–7) that only after conquering Dalmatia and settling there did some of the Croats continue the offensive in Pannonia and Illyricum. The success of the Croats in Dalmatia may have encouraged the Greek prisoners concentrated by the Avars in the land between the lower Sava, Drava and Danube, to revolt under their leader Kuver and to reach Byzantine territory, an exploit which is recalled in the *Miracula S. Demetrii* (*MPG*, CXVI, col. 1365). Grégoire (*L'Origine*, 104 ff.) has rightly connected this event with the difficulties which the Avars had met with in Dalmatia. All this resulted in a considerable weakening of the Avar power, and allowed the Croats to free the Slavs between the Sava and Drava, and to found there the so-called Pannonian Croatia, ruled by an independent Croat prince who was on friendly terms with the Croats of Dalmatia (30/77–8). From the military point of view C.'s account of the Croat campaign seems logical. His statement that remnants of Avars still lived in Dalmatia in his time is supported by Dalmatian toponymy. The Slavs called the Avars 'Obri'. Place-names deriving from this word (Obrov, Obrova, Obrovo, Obrovać) are still numerous in the north of Dalmatia and in the Croat district Lika-Krbava: see Šišić, *Geschichte der Kroaten*, 55 ff.

Labuda (*Pierwsze państwo*, 259) thinks that the Croats moved southwards between 622 and 627. Grafenauer (*Prilog kritici*, 44) dates their migration from the year 622/3, and brings it into connexion with the revolt of the Moravian Slavs under Samo. Both think that the Croats reached Dalmatia through the Moravian Gates, Pannonia and former Noricum. This is highly improbable. The Avars would hardly have permitted a large contingent of warriors with families to cross their territory and settle down in Dalmatia, which they regarded as subject to themselves. A much easier and safer way was along the great rivers behind the Carpathians towards the lower Danube, whence Byzantine territory could be reached. It also seems more likely that the migration took place *c.* 626: see on 31/8–9. For the liberation of the Slovenes of Carinthia from the Avar yoke by the Croats, see Dvornik, *The Making*, 289 ff.; *cf.* also S. Antoljak, 'Hrvati i Karantanij', *Godišen Zbornik* of the Faculty of Philosophy of the University of Skopje, kn. 9 (1956), no. 2.

30/73-4   τῷ μεγάλῳ ῥηγὶ Φραγγίας.

See Introductory Note above, p. 97. If μεγάλῳ here means 'elder', as at 26/2 etc., then Otto II was already crowned, and c. 30 must be dated after 961. We have in any case historical reasons for dating it after 955: see next note.

30/75   μετὰ τοὺς Τούρκους καὶ ἀγάπας ἔχοντες.

Friendly relations between the White Croats and Magyars could have existed after the Magyar conquest of Great Moravia (c. 906). White Croatia had been subject to Svatopluk since c. 880. We may suppose that Croatia recovered its independence after 906, and that the prince of White Croatia, in order to save himself from the fate of Moravia, made an agreement with the Magyar prince Arpad, which may have been sealed by a marriage alliance between the two. This may have taken place after some fighting between Croats and Magyars mentioned by C. at 31/86-7. But this passage is more fittingly explained in accordance with historical facts after 955; see Introductory Note to this section (p. 98). In particular, C.'s statement that the White Croats are subject to 'Otto the great (or elder) king of Francia' would reflect the situation after 955, when Boleslav I and his Slavnik partner had conquered Moravia with Slovakia and western Galicia with Cracow, that is, the former White Croatia. Before that date only the Croats of Bohemia were subject to Otto. It is however not quite accurate to say that the White Croats were not baptized in the 10th cent. (30/74). It is true that, according to the *Vita Methodii* (Dvornik, *Légendes*, 389), the Croat prince refused to be baptized when he was independent; but, after the annexation of the country by Svatopluk, Christianity penetrated to the region of Cracow. It was however a rude form of Christianity, although the disciples of Methodius who fled to Cracow after the disaster (Dvornik, *The Making*, 250 ff.) may have continued to work among the White Croats. Christianity was reintroduced in Cracow after 955; but it can hardly be thought that in C.'s time the whole country could be called truly Christian.

30/78-88   Μέχρι δὲ χρόνων τινῶν κτλ.

It is interesting to note that the source of this information—probably native Croat tradition—says nothing of the submission of the Croats to Byzantium, which is so much stressed in c. 31 (*e.g.* 31/58-60). The native tradition forgot that the Croats had once been nominally under Byzantium, but well remembered their subjection to the Franks. However, this subjection did not, as the narrative suggests, date immediately from the expulsion of the Avars from Dalmatia and from lower Pannonia between the Sava and the Drava. The Croats of Dalmatia and Pannonia enjoyed almost complete independence, although nominally under Byzantium, until the Frankish expansion under Charlemagne. When the Duke of Bavaria submitted to Charlemagne in 788, Istria was lost to Byzantium, and the Slavs on the Istrian coast and in Noricum became Frankish subjects. Charlemagne then turned against the Avars, whom he annihilated in two campaigns (791 and 795/6). The Croats of lower Pannonia were at that time ruled by prince Vojnomir, who, according to the *Annals of Lorch* (*MGH*, Scr. I, 182), joined the Franks in their campaign. He had, however, to acknowledge Frankish supremacy, and his territory, with Noricum and Istria, was added to the March of Friuli. The attempt of the Margrave Erich to bring the Dalmatian Croats also under Frankish rule miscarried, and Erich died while besieging Rjeka, the ancient Tarsatica (Fiume), in 797. The Dalmatian Croats came under Frankish suzerainty only after the Peace of Königshofen (803), ending the war between Franks and Byzantines which had broken out when Charlemagne had taken the imperial title. The Byzantines kept only Venice and the Latin coastal cities with some islands. This settlement was confirmed by the Treaty of Aix-la-Chapelle (812). The first recorded prince of the Dalmatian Croats was Vyšeslav; and his successor Borna (c. 810-21) is mentioned in 814, together with Ljudevit, prince of the Pannonian Croats, as paying homage to Lewis the Pious. The Pannonian Croats were the first to revolt against the Franks, and Ljudevit made an attempt to unite all Croats and Slovenes of Istria and former Noricum. He defeated Borna of Dalmatia, established himself in Sisak (former Siscia), and overcame several Frankish armies. But when, in 822, an immense army invaded Croatia, he fled the country and was murdered in 823. Pannonian and Dalmatian Croatia became a Frankish dominion once more; but the Dalmatian Croats were granted the right to choose their own princes. The Bulgars, profiting by the troubles which followed the partition of the Carolingian empire, annexed a part of Pannonian Croatia, the region of Sirmium; and for a time they extended their sovereignty over the whole of Pannonia, which, however, reverted to the Franks at the conclusion of the Treaty of Paderborn (845).

Dalmatian Croatia, under its princes Vladislav, who probably succeeded Borna, and Mislav (c. 835–45), continued under Frankish supremacy; and had to build a small navy against Arab incursions, which brought the Croats into a short conflict with Venice. Mislav and his successor Trpimir (845–64) are known to have been in friendly relations with Byzantium. The final revolt of the Dalmatian Croats against the Franks took place under Domagoj (864–77), who usurped the throne and forced Trpimir's son Zdeslav to take refuge at Byzantium. When Carloman, son of Lewis the German, who, besides Bavaria, Bohemia, Pannonia and Carinthia with Pannonian Croatia, had inherited also Italy and Dalmatian Croatia, tried, on the death of his father (876), to strengthen his authority in Dalmatia, the Croats revolted; and though the attacks of their flotilla against the Istrian coast were thrown back by the Venetians, they managed to defeat Carloman's army and to regain complete independence.

It is most likely this event that is recorded here in our text. Some historians still think that we have here to do with Ljudevit's revolt; and see in Kotzilis (30/87) the Margrave of Friuli Cadolah, whose despotic rule, hinted at by C.'s source, was responsible for Ljudevit's uprising. It is, however, more likely that we should identify Kotzilis not with Cadolah but with Kocel, the Slav prince of upper Pannonia, a Frankish vassal who may, like his father Pribina, have governed Pannonian Croatia also: we do not hear of any prince of Pannonian Croatia after the conclusion of the peace with Bulgaria which restored Pannonian Croatia, minus the region of Sirmium, to the Franks; see Šišić, *Geschichte der Kroaten*, 70.

L. Hauptmann (*Razprave* of the Academy of Ljubljana, 1 (1923), 321 ff.) believes that Kocel wished his territory to be subject ecclesiastically to the diocese of Sirmium, created for St Methodius in 870 by Pope Hadrian II; and that for this reason the Franks expelled him and gave his territory to Gazwin (Chozwin), who is mentioned c. 874. But this Gazwin is described merely as 'comes' and may have administered a part of Kocel's territory. In fact, Kocel was not deprived of his territory by the Franks because of his sympathy with Methodius. In 873, three years after Methodius' imprisonment by the Frankish bishops, pope John VIII addressed a letter to Kocel (*MGH*, Ep. VII, 282–3). He was thus still alive at that time, but is mentioned as dead in a document issued between 876 and 880. As a Frankish vassal he was ordered to suppress the revolt of the Dalmatian Croats in 876, and lost his life in battle. See Šišić, *Geschichte der Kroaten*, 95 ff.; id., *Povijest Hrvata*, 357 ff.; Dvornik, *Les Slaves*, 226 ff. For Franks, Byzantines and Croats in the 9th cent., see Manojlović, *Rad Jugoslav. Akad.*, 150 (1902), 102.

Grafenauer, *Zgodovinski Časopis*, 6 (1952–3), 171–90, rejected Šišić's thesis and tried to prove that Kotzilis should be identified with Cadolah and that the passage should be referred to Ljudevit's revolt. Even if we admit that Šišić's main argument (97 note 1; *Ann. Bert.*, ann. 876) has its weakness, it does not mean that there was no military clash between the Franks and the Croats in 876. We have no proof that Kotzilis-Kocel had disappeared in 874. It is quite possible that C. is here telescoping three events: the revolt under Ljudevit, baptism under Borna, and the final fight for freedom in which Kocel had perished in 876.

9—D.A.I.

30/88–90 ἐξητήσαντο τὸ ἅγιον βάπτισμα κτλ.

It is again to be noted that the source used here does not speak of the rôle played by Heraclius in the christianization of the Croats, though this is emphasized in c. 31; but it remembers the name of the prince who came to the agreement with Heraclius. The account in c. 30 contains an echo of Heraclius' attempt to convert the Croats, but it is a confused echo. Porinus was identified by Grégoire (*L'Origine*, 94) with Kocel's father Pribina. This can hardly be accepted, even if Pribina was governing, not only his principality round Lake Balaton, but also Pannonian Croatia. Rački suggested (*Documenta*, 291) that Πόρινος should be Βόρινος, Slav Bor'na, Borena, Borin, Borna; and this suggestion, already made as early as 1859 by Dümmler in the first edition of his *Geschichte des ostfrankischen Reiches*, is nowadays generally accepted. Dümmler (*Älteste Geschichte*, 391), on the basis of this text, dated the insurrection of the Croats to the reign of Porinus. This would appear to be wrong, since the text implies that Porinus came *after* the revolt against Kocel. There seems however to be a confusion in the passage. As will be shown on 31/22–5, we cannot date the christianization of the Croats after the revolt. We have therefore to assume that the author of this chapter is telescoping two or three separate accounts, that of the insurrection and that of the conversion. He does indeed mention Porinus after the revolt; but it is only the conversion which he dates to Porinus' reign. This being so, we may perhaps compare the account of the same event given at 31/21–5 with the present account, and see in Porinus and Porga the same prince, the two variants of whose name correspond to the two different traditions, the native Croat and the Byzantine.

When the Croats revolted in 875–6 they already had their own national bishopric at Nin, founded in the early part of the 9th cent.; so that our passage cannot be brought into chronological relation with that revolt. But even if we suppose that our text refers to the revolt of Ljudevit, we should bear in mind that even in his time the Croats were already Christians. Their first recorded prince of this period, Vyšeslav, was a Christian; although, admittedly, the progress of christianization was much accelerated when the Franks became masters of Dalmatian Croatia. All this seems to suggest that in 30/87–90 we have a reference to the first attempt, that of Heraclius, to christianize the Croats under their prince Porinus/Porga, which even the Croat national tradition remembered, though for national reasons it forgot the initiative of Heraclius. For Porinus see the thorough study of F. Šišić, *Genealoški prilozi o hrvatskoj narodnoj dinastiji* (Zagreb, 1914; first published in *Vjesnik arheoloskago drustva*, n.s., XIII), 18–48, 'Hrvatski arhont Porin'.

S. M. Prvanović ('Ko je bio hrvatski knez Borna?', *Rad Jugoslav. Akad.* (1957), 301–5) regards Borna as the ruler over two South-Serbian tribes, the Timočans and the Guduščans, who had separated themselves from the Bulgarian rule and joined the Franks. Borna refused to join Ljudevit's revolt and went with the Guduščans to Croatia. According to the author, the Franks settled Borna's people in the region between Velebit and Mala Kapela, and Borna became ruler of Dalmatia and Croatia under Frankish suzerainty. He regards Vyšeslav only as ruler of a part of this country, which became a political unit only under Borna and his successors. Lack of more reliable documentary evidence prevents us from giving a definite solution to this problem. *Cf.* Dvornik, *Les Slaves*, 47–9, 226 ff.

30/90–3 εἰς ζουπανίας ια'.

The word 'župania', county, with 'župan', count, is often taken for Iranian, which would agree with the attribution of an Iranian or Sarmatian origin to the Croats (see on 30/61 ff.). The dignity of 'župan' existed only among the Croats, southern Serbs and Sorbs (Sorabs, Serbs) in modern Saxony, whence the southern Serbs are said to have originated; and this is in favour of the Iranian hypothesis. However, the Iranian or Sarmatian origin of the word is not proven. It is true that the Czechs and the Poles did not know these terms, but they had the word 'pan', meaning master, petty ruler. It seems therefore more probable that the word 'župan' derives from a common Indo-European root; cf. Hujer, Listy Filologické, xxxi (Prague, 1904), 104–7. Skok, however (Jugoslov. Istor. Časopis, ii (1936), 1–15), thinks that the word is Turkish, and came to the Slavs through the Avars.

The names of the Croat counties in C.'s Greek transliteration end not, as might be expected, with an -ia but with an -a stuck on to the Slav terminations. Skok (Ortsnamen-studien, 225) explains this by the fact that the names of the counties are mostly identical with names of towns: 1. Chlebiana is the Slav Hlev'no, in Bosnia; 2. Tzenzina is Cetina, on the river of the same name (which however C., 30/105, 113, calls Zentina); 3. Emota is Imota, a place-name and district in present-day Dalmatia (today Imotski, s.c. 'grad'); 4. Pleba is Pliva in the valley of Vrbas, today only the name of a river; 5. Pesenta is Pseta, north-east of Pliva, comprising the territory of the upper Una and Sana rivers in north-western Bosnia, with a centre probably somewhere near Petrovac; 6. Parathalassia is the župania on the sea between the rivers Cetina and Krka, with its centre at Klis, from which the county was later called the župania of Klis. Its župans seem to have been called 'morsticus', from mor'st', mor'sk', deriving from the word more, sea. Skok (Južnoslov. Filolog, vi, 65) thinks that C. is here translating the Slav name of the župania, Primorje; 7. Breberi, north of the lower Krka river, is identical with Breber, today Bribir near Skradin (old Scardona); 8. Nona is Nin in north Croatia; as early as c. 800 the župan Godeslav, a Christian, is mentioned in an inscription over the entrance to the Chapel of the Cross at Nin, which he had founded; 9. Tnena, Tnina is Knin (Tenenum in Croat documents), on the upper Krka, with centre at the castle of Knin; 10. Sidraga, north-east of the župania of Bribir, with centre at Belgrad on the coast. The etymology of the word is not known: perhaps from s'draga, convallis; 11. Nina, a name not traced in documentary evidence; the župania may have lain between those of Knin, Nin, Sidraga and Bribir. Skok (Ortsnamenstudien, 226) thinks that this župania is identical with Nona, Nin, ancient Aenona: Nona is the Romano-Dalmatian form, Nin the Slav, and both derive from the ancient city name Aenona, though C. thought that they designated two separate županias. These eleven županias were governed by župans. North of the Velebit Mountains were situated three županias governed not by a župan, but by a ban. The first of these, Kribasa, should be identified with Krbava. Its political centre was a place of the same name, known today as Udbina. The Greek transliteration of the name was faulty. The second, Litsa, in Slav Lika, lay in the valley of the river Lika, and its centre in the middle ages was the castle of Počitelj. The third, Goutziska (Gadska, Gačka), lay in the valley of the river of that name, with its centre at Otočac; for the Greek transliteration of the name, see Skok, Ortsnamenstudien, 227. The ban, who according to our text governed in the 10th cent. these three županias only, later on became the most important functionary in Croatia, representing the king and giving orders to all the župans. The office was introduced into Hungary also during the 12th cent. Šišić (Geschichte der Kroaten, 56) thinks that the Croats inherited the term from the Avars, whose traces survived principally in these very three županias governed by the ban. It is said to derive from bajan, which recalls the name of the famous 6th cent. Avar khagan; (cf. also B. von Arnim, Zeitschr. für slav. Philol., ix (1932), 406). See Rački, Documenta, 413 ff.; Grot, Izvjestija, 98–101; Šišić, Geschichte der Kroaten, 166 ff.; id., Povijest Hrvata, 444–51; Skok, Starohrvatska Prosvjeta, n.s., 1 (1927), 60–76, 161–96; id., Ortsnamenstudien, 226 ff.; Barada, Nastavni Vjesnik, 43 (1933–4), 172–9, 250–7; Skok, Južnoslov. Filolog, vi (1926–7), 65–95; id., Zeitschr. für Ortsnamenforschung, xi (1935), 157–83.

The description of Croatia given in c. 30 is incomplete. In north-western Croatia there were two more županias, Vinodol and Modruše, mentioned first in 1163 (Smičiklas, Cod. Dipl., ii, 96); our author omits these, although he says himself (30/8–10) that Dalmatia extended north-westwards to the boundary of Istria. There is no mention of županias north of the three which were governed by the ban. In C.'s time Pannonian Croatia was already united to Dalmatian Croatia, but our author does not say so. Nor is there any mention of the territory north of the župania of Pseta and between the župania of Pliva and the Bosna river, although all these lands belonged to 10th cent. Croatia. These omissions enable us to determine more precisely whence the author of this chapter derived his information. In view of the fact that he pays most attention to the central part of the coast of Croatia and its immediate interior, we may gather that he got his material on Croatia from Spljet (Spalato). A native of Zara (Zadar) would probably have paid more attention to north-western Croatia, from the Adriatic coast to the upper Kupa river.

30/95-7 ἡ δὲ Διόκλεια κτλ.

For Dioclea see c. 35: here only the geographical extension of the country is given. Dyrrhachium (*ital.* Durazzo, Slav and Turkish Drač), another name of the Greek colony Ἐπίδαμνος, founded 627 B.C. by Greeks from Corinth and Corcyra. It seems that the Illyrian word Dyrrhachion denoted the peninsula on which the colony was founded, and that both names were used for the city. The name Dyrrhachium prevailed during the Roman period. The city reached the apex of its importance as the capital of the Roman province of Epirus Nova and later of the *thema* of Dyrrhachion, and as an ecclesiastical metropolis. It survived Gothic, Avar and Slav invasions, and was coveted in vain by the Bulgars under Symeon the Great. See Philippson in Pauly-Wissowa, *RE*, v, cols. 1882-7 (Dyrrhachion).

Elissus (Lissus, *ital.* Alessio, Slav Ljes), a place on the Drini near Scodra, is mentioned as a see under the metropolis of Dyrrhachium in the *Notitiae Episcopatuum*, a survey of bishoprics as they existed in C.'s time; see Gelzer, *Abh. d. bay. Akad. Wiss.* 21 (Munich 1901), 558. *Cf.* Anna Comnena, ed. Reifferscheid, II, 171/20-30.

Antibari (*ital.* Antivari, Slav and Turkish Bar, Albanian Tivari), opposite to the Italian city of Bari, was founded probably at the beginning of the 7th cent. A.D., by Latin refugees from Doclea (Dioclea), destroyed in the Avar and Slav invasions. It was soon coveted by the Slavs; and, as the residence of a bishop, became an important missionary centre for the conversion of the Slavs of Dioclea; see Barada, *Rad Jugoslav. Akad.*, 270 (1949), 93-113; Dvornik, *The Slavs*, 279 ff.

Helcynium (formerly Olcinium, *ital.* Dulcigno, Slav Ucinj), a coastal city between Antibari and the river Bojana. Founded by Greeks of Colchis, it later belonged to the Illyrian kingdom, and, after the Roman capture of Dalmatia, was exempted from payment of tribute. Under Byzantium it belonged to the *thema* of Dyrrhachion, and is listed, from the 9th cent. onwards, as the see of a bishop. See Cons, *Province romaine*, 101, 258; Nani in *Enciclopedia Italiana*, XIII, 264 (Dulcigno); Jireček, *Handelsstrassen*, 65.

30/97 μέχρι τῶν Δεκατέρων. For Decatera see on 29/263.

30/99 Τερβουνίας. For Terbounia (Trebinje, later Travunia), see on 34/1.

30/101 τῶν Ζαχλούμων. For the *archontia* of the Zachlumi, see on 33/1-15.

30/101 τοῦ Ὀροντίου ποταμοῦ. Orontius (*ital.* Narenta), the present-day Neretva, from the Illyric Narona; see Skok, *Ortsnamenstudien*, 238.

30/104 ἡ Παγανία. For Pagani, Pagania see on 36/1-13.

30/105 τρεῖς ἔχουσα ζουπανίας. See on 30/90-3.

30/106 τὴν Ῥάστωτζαν καὶ τὸν Μοκρὸν καὶ τοῦ Δαλέν.

The župania Rhastotza is identified with Rastok. Barada (*Starohrv. Prosvjeta*, n.s., II, (1928), 41) sees in the word a slavized form of a non-slav name. Mokros corresponds to the Slav form Mokro, today Makar, a mountain near Makarska, a name deriving from Makar. Dalen is identified by Šišić (*Geschichte der Kroaten*, 169) with Dolje. Skok (*Ortsnamenstudien*, 229 ff.) thinks that C. here confuses the Illyrian name Dalma (Slav Duvno, ancient Delminium) with the Slav name Dolje.

30/110 τὰ Μέλετα κτλ.

Meleta (*ital*. Meleda), modern Mljet, is given at 36/17 the alternative name Malozeatai, and identified with the Melite of *Acts* 28, 1–5. Malozeatai must be an *ethnikon*, 'inhabitants of Meleta'.

Kourkoura (*ital*. Curzola), modern Korcula, is called at 36/16 'Kourkra or Kiker'. It is the old Corcyra, the name having been latinized by the substitution of 'u' for 'o'. Kiker is a Greek transliteration of old Slavonic Krkar.

Bratza (at 36/21 Bratzis, *ital*. Brattia) is modern Brač; it was Brazza in the Latin dialect of Dalmatia. But C. seems here to give the Slav locative form 'na Braci', or Bratzis.

Phara (see also 36/20) appears in medieval documents as Farra or Quarra. The feminine form indicates that the original masculine Pharos had changed under the influence of the Dalmatian Latin idiom to (*sc*. insula) Phara. The same change is found in the names of other islands. The masculine reappears in the Croat name of the island, Hvar, since the masculine substantive 'grad' is understood. The Italian name of the island, Lesina, derives from Slav ljesno, 'wooded' (*sc*. ljesno ostrovo, 'wooded island') See Skok, *Ortsnamenstudien*, 231; *id.*, *Slavenstvo i romanstvo*, I, 171 ff., 181 ff., 198 ff., 209 ff.; Ferjančić 34–5; and 36/15–21.

30/115 τοῦ κάστρου Ἀλβούνου.   Albunum, in Croat Labin, an Ancient Roman city, called Alvona by Pliny, *Nat. Hist.*, III, 21, and in the *Tabula Peutingeriana*.

30/116 τὴν Τζέντινα καὶ τὴν Χλέβενα.

For Tzentina (Cetina) and Chlebena, see on 30/90–3. For the θέμα Ἰστρίας *cf.* 30/10, 114: an anachronism, since Istria was lost to Byzantium by *c.* 800 (see on 30/78–88).

30/122 τῶν Παγανῶν.

The Slavs on the river Narenta (Neretva), called Pagani by C. (36/1), became dangerous pirates. From their bases on the islands they also attacked Venetian vessels. The Venetians sent an expedition against them, and in 830 a *modus vivendi* was concluded between the Narentan chief and the doge John Parteciacus. But the agreement was not kept by the Slavs; and John the Deacon speaks of renewed Slav piracy in 834, 835 and 846 (ed. Monticolo (Rome, 1890), 112, 115). See Dvornik, *Les Slaves*, 52, 54.

30/125-41 πάντα . . . τῷ στρατηγῷ ταῦτα παρεῖχον κτλ.

Basil I re-established Byzantine prestige on the Dalmatian coast when he forced the Arabs to raise the siege of Ragusa in 868 (see on 29/91). C. records (29/58–66) how the Latin cities of Dalmatia and the Slavs of the coast and the interior had become independent of Byzantium in the reign of Michael II (820–9). Basil restored Byzantine sovereignty in the area, and the *thema* of Dalmatia seems to date from his time; see *De Them.*, 41–2. Posedel (*Historijski Zbornik*, III (1950), 217 ff.) would like to date its foundation between 842–8. Ferluga's date of *c.* 870 is more probable: see on 29/61–6. At all events it was not founded before 842, and the opinion of Barada (*Rad Jugoslav. Akad.*, 270 (1949), 93 ff.), that it existed already in the second half of the 8th cent., is without foundation. Basil I compelled the Slavs on the coast also to recognize Byzantine supremacy (870–1; see on 29/108–12); and this was no doubt the occasion for regularizing the relations between the cities of the Dalmatian *thema* and the Croats and other Slavs, as C. describes (30/127 ff.). See Radonić, *Izv. Russk. Archeol. Inst. v Konstantinopole*, 6 (1900), 418–17; Jireček, *Handelsstrassen*, 3–19; Dvornik, *Les Slaves*, 217 ff.; Ostrogorsky[2] 190, note 3.

31/1-6 *Περὶ τῶν Χρωβάτων κτλ.*

We now resume the original Dalmatian and Slav συγγραφή interrupted at 29/295. The information on the Croats supplied in this chapter has a strongly Byzantine bias, which suggests that it was derived from the imperial archives (see on 30/61 ff.). What is said in this passage about White Croatia corresponds to what is said at 30/61-3. Turkey is Hungary; and when we take into consideration that White Croatia from *c.* 880-906 belonged to Great Moravia, and that Bohemia, which after 955 became the heir of Moravia, was under Frankish suzerainty, we can see why emphasis is laid on White Croatia's proximity to Francia. The Serbs in question (31/6) can only be the Sorabs of modern Saxony (see on 32/1-6). *Cf.* Barada, *Nastavni Vjesnik*, 42 (1933-4), 172-9, 250-7.

31/7-8 '*οἱ πολλὴν χώραν κατέχοντες*'.

C.'s etymology of the name of the Croats is still a puzzle. There is certainly no justification for it in Slavonic. Probably C. or his informant saw in the name some real or fancied similarity to a Turkish or other foreign word of this sense. See however B. von Arnim, *Zeitschr. für slav. Philol.*, IX (1932), 137: 'Mir ist nicht klar, welcher mitteltürkische, zufällig anklingende Ausdruck die Etymologie verschuldete'.

31/8-9 *πρόσφυγες παρεγένοντο.*

The statement that the Croats had asked Heraclius for his protection is not supported by any other evidence. It is possible that, on the contrary, it was Heraclius who took the initiative and offered the Croats Dalmatia if they could wrest it from the Avars. We know that the emperor was looking everywhere for allies against the Avars. He made an alliance with Kuvrat the khagan of the Bulgars in the Don region, and sent embassies to the Franks, undoubtedly with the same aim. The most probable moment for his *pourparlers* with the Croats seems to be the year 626, when Constantinople, besieged by Persians, Avars and Slavs, was in great danger. The Croats may have accepted the emperor's offer in or about that year. The prestige of the Avars had suffered by reason of their defeat at the walls of Constantinople; and the successful revolt of the Moravian Slavs under the leadership of the Frank Samo made it easier for the Croats to expel the Avars from Dalmatia. It is hard to determine whether our author is right in stating (31/9-10) that the Croats got into touch with Heraclius before the Serbs did so. It may be that Heraclius opened negotiations with the Croats before the small detachment of Serbs appeared on the imperial frontier. Although a Croat request for settlements on imperial lands cannot be excluded as impossible, it is more probable that Heraclius invited their migration, and that the Byzantines reversed the truth in order to strengthen claim to sovereignty over Dalmatia, after the expulsion of the Avars. See Dvornik, *The Making*, 286 ff.; and on 30/66-71 etc.

31/11-14 *τοὺς Ῥωμάνους . . . οὓς κτλ.*

The Latin inhabitants of the *thema* of Dalmatia are here called 'Romani' to distinguish them from the 'Romaioi', or Greek-speaking citizens of the empire in general. The rôle of Diocletian is again exaggerated (*cf.* 31/26-30); but the emphasis laid on it illustrates the importance of Diocletian's memory in the minds of the Dalmatians, and shows that the Latins of the coastal cities were very conscious of their tie with ancient Rome. See Jireček, *Die Romanen*, I, 44 ff.

31/21 *τοῦ Πόργα.*

For Porgas, see on 30/88-90. Sakać (*Osoba i Duch*, IV (1952), 24) rejects the common interpretation of the name, Borko, and sees in it the old Iranian form Pouru-gâo, 'rich in cattle'.

31/22-5 ἀπὸ ʽΡώμης ἀγαγὼν ἱερεῖς.

Jireček, *Geschichte der Serben*, 1, 104, rejected the statement that Heraclius asked Rome to send priests to Dalmatia; and historians have accepted his opinion. But his scepticism was unjustified. Heraclius was on excellent terms with pope Honorius, who went so far in his efforts to reconcile the emperor's monothelistic ideas with orthodox doctrine that he was himself suspected by many of heresy. Moreover, the whole of Illyricum was until 731 under the jurisdiction of the Roman patriarchate, and this jurisdiction was fully respected by the Byzantines; so that it was quite natural for the emperor to apply to the pope in the religious affairs of that province. Very little information is available on the progress of Christianity among the Croats at that period. The words of our text certainly cannot be taken as meaning that the Croats had their own hierarchy in the 7th cent. On the other hand, there must be some historical basis for C.'s statement. He perhaps had in mind the ecclesiastical re-organization of the coastal cities which had remained under Byzantine sovereignty but which, with the rest of former Illyricum, were ecclesiastically subject to Rome. Any changes in the religious organization of those cities had therefore to be made with the co-operation of the popes. If we could trust the local tradition of Split (Spalato), we should conclude that Heraclius promoted this city, heir to the ancient Salona, to a metropolis, and founded bishoprics in some other cities. Local tradition ascribes the foundation of an archbishopric in Spalato to this period, and calls the first archbishop John of Ravenna; see Thomas the Archdeacon, c. 11. But this tradition is late and partial. John of Ravenna is commonly regarded as a legendary figure, created out of a confusion with pope John IV, a native of Dalmatia, or else with pope John X, who reorganized the Dalmatian and Croatian hierarchy and subjected the whole country to Spalato in *c.* 925. However, Grba (*Etnolog*, v-vi (1933), 113-15) thinks that John of Ravenna lived at the beginning of the 9th cent., in the reigns of Nicephorus I and of his son Stauracius (801-11). And more recently L. Karaman (*Strena Hoffilleriana* (Zagreb, 1940), 427-33) republished a sarcophagus which, according to its inscription, contained the body of an archbishop John. Karaman, who dates the sarcophagus to the second half of the 8th cent., thinks that the archbishop John can only be the John of Ravenna mentioned by Thomas the Archdeacon, and that the re-organization of the church of Spalato should be dated to this time; he also believes that this reorganization coincided with that of the *thema* of Dalmatia under a military governor at Zara, but this latter hypothesis we have already seen reason to reject (see on 30/125-41). While admitting that John of Ravenna also worked for the christianization of the Croats, Karaman ascribes the conversion of that nation solely to Frankish missionaries. But the fact that the first Croat bishopric was founded, not near Spalato, but at Nona (Nin), nearer to Frankish territory, cannot be invoked in favour of his thesis and against the assumption that the coastal cities did much for the conversion of the Croats. Nona is indeed far from Spalato, but it is near to Zara, which remained untouched by the invasions and always had its bishops.

C.'s account of the christianization of the Croats under Heraclius is no doubt exaggerated. Heraclius may have planned their conversion and the foundation of bishoprics, and naturally asked the pope to put these plans into practice. His request may have been recorded in Byzantine archives; but it was never fully executed. In spite of that, we are entitled to presume that the christianization had started from the coastal cities—it was in their own interest to establish peaceful relations with the newcomers—and that Rome must have played some part in it. We learn from the *Liber Pontificalis* (ed. Duchesne 1, 330; *cf.* Rački, *Documenta*, 277) that soon after Heraclius' initiative, pope John IV (640-2), himself a Dalmatian, sent in 641-2 the abbot Martin to Dalmatia and Istria, to recover relics of saints from the destroyed churches (see on 29/241). Jireček, *Geschichte der Serben*, 1, 104, quoted this incident as a proof that the Croats were still pagans, and that the initiative of Heraclius should be regarded as legendary. But the fact that the abbot was able to travel freely over the whole country without hindrance from the newcomers, and to ransom many Christian captives from the conquerors, seems rather to indicate a considerable change of heart among the new masters of the country, brought about probably by the initiative of Heraclius and the work of the first missionaries. In any case, the incident shows that peaceful relations between the coastal cities and the Croats had been established by c. 641, and that Rome had not lost interest in the country. This interest appears to have continued after 641: for pope Agathon, writing in 680 to the emperor Constantine IV (*MPL*, LXXXVII, col. 1226A), mentions that Roman missionaries are working among Slavs, which can only mean among the Croats.

Although it is impossible to follow the progress of Christianity in Dalmatia, we can suppose that already during the 8th cent. churches were built for the new converts. Vyšeslav, prince of Dalmatia, who is mentioned c. 800, was probably Christian before he had to recognize Frankish supremacy. Under the Franks Christianity naturally took firm root in Croatia; but two facts show quite clearly that the beginning of Christianity in Croatia was not due exclusively to the Frankish clergy. First of all, the Croat Church did not know the Frankish system of proprietary churches, which was introduced into all lands in which Frankish missionaries worked. Secondly, the Croat Church was not attached to the Frankish provinces of Aquileia or Salzburg, but had its own national bishopric at Nin. This bishopric is mentioned for the first time only in 852, but it must have existed some time before that date. It was subject directly to Rome, which shows that Rome was anxious to reserve for herself the fruits of her missionary activity among the Croats. The foundation of an independent Croatian bishopric was perhaps hastened by Rome when the Franks got political control over Dalmatian Croatia. It is not known whether the first attempts at christianization reached Pannonian Croatia. It is logical to suppose that the activity of Frankish missionaries was more systematic in Pannonian Croatia, and that the conversion of Vojnomir, the first Pannonian prince whose name is known, should be attributed to them. See F. Bulić, J. Bervaldi, *Bogoslovna Smotra*, III (1912), 141 ff.; Segvić, *Anal. Boll.*, 33 (1914), 265 ff.; Dvornik, *Les Slaves*, 71 ff.; id., *Légendes*, 256 ff.; Skok, *Dolazak Slovena*, 143 (Latin Christian terminology in Croat), 173 ff. (symbiosis of Roman and Slav elements); Dvornik, *The Slavs*, 76 ff.

31/28-9 τοῦ βασιλέως Διοκλητιανοῦ κτλ.

For the repeated mention of Diocletian, see on 31/11-14. The amphitheatre, the ruins of which are extant, was probably built by Diocletian, since the site of it was not yet part of the city at the end of the 2nd cent. A.D. See E. Dyggve, *History of Salonitan Christianity* (Oslo, 1951), XI ff. for complete bibliography of the antiquities of Salona and of their excavation; cf. also Leclercq, *Dict. d'Arch. chrét.*, XV (1949), cols. 602-24 (Salona).

31/32-42 χρησμὸν γάρ τινα καὶ ὁρισμόν.

This account of a special pact concluded by the Croats with the pope, in spite of its legendary aspect, seems to combine two events in Croat history: first, the establishment of friendly relations between Croats and Christians in the Byzantine coastal cities, as a result of the work of Latin missionaries sent by popes Honorius, John IV and Agathon; and second, the exchange of messages between prince Branimir and pope John VIII in 879. The second event took place after the overthrow of the pro-Byzantine prince Zdeslav, when the pope seized the occasion to bind the Croats more firmly to St Peter and Rome. The following passage from the papal letter shows that the fidelity of the Croats to St Peter was stressed by the pope (*MGH*, Ep. VII, 152): 'Quia Deo favente quasi dilectus filius sancto Petro et nobis, qui per divinam gratiam vicem eius tenemus, fidelis in omnibus et obediens esse cupias et humiliter profiteris, tuae nobilitati dignas valde gratias his nostri apostolatus litteris agimus paternoque amore utpote karissimum filium ad gremium sanctae sedis apostolicae matris tuae ... redeuntem suscipimus et spiritualibus amplectimur ulnis atque apostolica volumus benignitate fovere, ut gratiam et benedictionem Dei sanctorumque Petri et Pauli apostolorum principum et nostram super te habens diffusam, a visibilibus et invisibilibus hostibus . . . salvus semper et securus existas optatamque de inimicis victoriam facilius possis habere.' Another letter, addressed to Branimir in 881 (*ibid.*, 258), shows that the pope had in mind a kind of pact to be concluded between St Peter's successor and the Croat people: Quapropter mandamus, ut revertente ad vos dilecto episcopo vestro idoneos legatos vestros praesentaliter ad nos dirigere non praetermittatis, qui pro parte omnium vestrum nos et sedem apostolicam certificent de his quae mandastis, ut et nos cum illis missum nostrum dirigamus ad vos, quibus secundum morem et consuetudinem ecclesiae nostrae universus populus vester fidelitatem promittat. There is no evidence to date this pact from the time of Heraclius or from the reign of pope Agathon. See S. Sakać, *O krštenju i ugovoru* in *Iz slavne hrvatske prošlosti; Ugovor pape Agatona i Hrvata proti navalnom ratu* (Zagreb, 1931); Dvornik, *Légendes*, 257 ff., 272 ff.; Sakać, *Život*, VII (1936), and critical review in *Jugoslov. Istor. Časopis*, II (1936), 169. For the meaning of ὁ τῶν Χρωβάτων θεός, see B. Imhof, M. Perojević and S. Sakać in *Obzor* (1936), reviewed in *Jugoslov. Istor. Časopis*, II (1936), 280 ff.

31/42-52 ἀνήρ τις . . . Μαρτῖνος ὀνόματι.

According to Rački, *Documenta*, 399, who is followed by other Croat historians (*cf.* Šišić, *Geschichte der Kroaten*, 153 ff.; *Povijest Hrvata*, 430 ff.), the visit of Martin should be dated to the 10th cent. Prince Trpimir (31/43) is not, they maintain, Trpimir I, but Trpimir II (*c.* 928-35), and his son is his successor Kresimir II (*c.* 935-45). But this solution presents difficulties. First, we know nothing about any Trpimir II, whose reign has to be invented to suit this theory. Second, if we accept the existence of Trpimir II in the 10th cent., followed by Kresimir and Miroslav, we are forced to suppose that during the few years between 928 and 949 the Croat throne was occupied successively by a grandfather, a father and a grandson; which seems rather improbable. V. Klaić therefore suggested (*Nastavny Vjesnik*, XXXIII (1925), 275-82, reprinted in *Zbornik Kralja Tomislava*, 212-14) that we should date Martin's visit to the reign of Trpimir I. If he is right, we should give to the reigns of Trpimir I and Kresimir I the span of about twenty years, *c.* 845-64. This is quite reasonable, the more so since we do not know when Trpimir died: documentary evidence about his reign is confined to one 'Paginula privilegialis et donatio', decreed by him on 4th March, 852 in Biać, for the benefit of the church of Spalato; see Rački, *Documenta*, 3-6. It is therefore quite possible that he died earlier than is generally supposed, and that the Kresimir mentioned at 31/44 is his son and successor Kresimir I, who died or was dethroned *c.* 864. The story of Martin would in any case agree better with the circumstances of the reign of Trpimir I. During this reign the activity of Roman missionaries in Croatia must have increased because of the dangerous competition of Frankish clergy. About that time, if not earlier (see on 31/22-5), the bishopric of Nin was founded for the Croats by Rome, and subjected directly to the Holy See. The holy man Martin seems, however, to have been a Frankish missionary from the patriarchate of Aquileia (*cf.* 31/44-5, and the remarks of Skok, *Dolozak Slovena*, 141-9, on the activities of Frankish missionaries among the Croats). However, he cannot be identified with the Saxon Gottschalk who had stayed at Trpimir's court, as L. Katić (*Saksonac Gotšalk na dvoru kneza Trpimira* (Zagreb, 1932), 29 ff.) pretends. His mission may have brought about better relations between Croats, Franks and Venetians. The peaceful policy of the Croats resulting from Martin's preaching (31/49-52) seems to suggest this. (An alternative is to suppose that the whole story of Martinus is a late echo of the mission of abbot Martin in 641; see on 31/22-5.) If Klaić's interpretation is accepted, we may trace the history of Dalmatian Croatia as follows: about the year 864 Trpimir's dynasty was dethroned, and Domagoj became ruler (*c.* 864-76), followed by his son Ilkjo (876-8). Trpimir's son Zdeslav returned to the throne with Byzantine help in 878, but was dethroned in 879 by Branimir, probably one of the high Croat aristocracy (879-92). Only after Branimir's death did Trpimir's youngest son Mutimir become prince (892-*c.* 910), and was followed by his son Tomislav (*c.* 910-28). Tomislav's successor was not Trpimir

II, his supposed brother but of whose existence we know nothing, but Kresimir II (928–45), who is mentioned at 31/76. We do not know whether Kresimir II was Tomislav's son or nephew; all we can deduce from C.'s account is that he was a member of Trpimir's dynasty.

Klaić's proposed interpretation of C.'s story was criticized by G. Manojlović (*Zbornik Kralja Tomislava*, xi ff.), who tried to show that C. was interested primarily in events which happened during the reign of his grandfather Basil I and of his father Leo VI and would provide useful lessons for his son, for whose education his book was written. On this supposition Manojlović built up his theory that the Croat princes Trpimir, Kresimir and Miroslav were all C.'s contemporaries. Trpimir he identified with Tomislav; and the new pact concluded between the pope and the Croats (31/49–52) he thought to be an echo of the Synod of Spalato (925), which finally decided the submission of all Croat lands, including the Latin cities, to the Holy See. C. had made a point of this event because the Byzantines had themselves made peace with Rome in 923, when all traces of the schism caused by Rome's approval of Leo VI's fourth marriage were erased: *cf.* V. Grumel, *Les Regestes* 1/2, no. 712. However, Manojlović's arguments are themselves not without some weaknesses. First, there is no evidence for the supposition that the first name of Tomislav was Trpimir. If we eliminate the fictitious Trpimir II (and Manojlović himself suppresses him, and regards Kresimir as Tomislav's son), then no other prince of the national dynasty except the 9th cent. Trpimir was called by this name. It was not Trpimir but Kresimir which seems to have become the name most characteristic of the dynasty: four Croat princes bore this name, perhaps even five, if we adopt the interpretation of Klaić. Second, it seems that the author of this chapter is, as Klaić suggested, telling his tale in chronological order: first, the settlement of the Croats on imperial soil and their baptism; next, an event which occurred under Trpimir in the first half of the 9th cent.; next, the attack on Croatia by Boris of Bulgaria; next, the peak of Croat military power under Kresimir's father Tomislav, whom the author however does not mention; and last, the decline of Croatia under Miroslav, C.'s contemporary. Third, Manojlović lays too much emphasis on the 'schism' between Rome and Constantinople owing to Leo VI's tetragamy. The whole of this controversy over chronology shows once again how poor is our information on early Croat history, and how much we have to rely for our knowledge of it on correctly interpreting cc. 30 and 31 of *DAI*.

It is interesting to notice the Greek transliteration of the names Trpimir, Kresimir: Τερπημέρη, Κρασημέρη. These forms could be genitives of Latin nominatives Terpimerus, Krasimerus. This may throw light on the origin of C.'s information, which may thus have been a Latin document read by C.'s informant in one of the Latin coastal cities or deposited in imperial archives.

It is odd that C. does not mention here the name of the most powerful Croat prince, Tomislav I, who took the royal title. This may be due to Byzantine political mentality. It was not in the Byzantine interest to glorify a prince who became too powerful, one who united Dalmatian and Pannonian Croatia, who extended his sway over many Adriatic islands, who gave his protection to the Serbs, and to whom Byzantium had to surrender her suzerainty over the Dalmatian *thema*. It was customary at Byzantium to ignore where possible events and exploits which were contrary to the interests of the empire. Or, the explanation may lie in the process by which *DAI* was compiled: see General Introduction p. 4, and above pp. 99–100.

31/61–7   εἰ μὴ Μιχαὴλ κτλ.

The statement is contradicted by 32/126–8: for the significance of this, see above p. 99, and General Introduction p. 4. The account of a conflict between Croats and Bulgars under Boris seems to be based on an unknown Croat source. Šišić (*Geschichte der Kroaten*, 80 ff.; *cf.* Dvornik, *Les Slaves*, 54) dates this conflict between the years 854 and 860. Runciman (*First Bulgarian Empire*, 91 ff.) thinks that Boris invaded, not Dalmatian, but

Pannonian Croatia, and combines C.'s account with that of *Annales Bertiniani* (*MGH*, Scr. I, 448, ann. 853), where there is mention of a Bulgarian attack, with the help of local Slavs, on the territory of Lewis the German. This explanation would be plausible were it not that C. emphasizes that Croatia has never been subject to the Bulgars (31/60). This is true only of Dalmatian Croatia: Pannonian Croatia was for some time under Bulgarian supremacy (see on 30/78-88). Moreover, it appears that the whole of the rest of c. 31 is concerned with Dalmatian Croatia only. It is therefore more likely that our account deals with an attack on Dalmatian Croatia and its prince Trpimir by Boris of Bulgaria between 854 and 860. The account in *Annales Bertiniani* refers to another incident, Boris's attack on Pannonian Croatia with the help of some local Slav tribes. But Runciman is right in rejecting the suggestion of Zlatarsky (*Istorija*, I/2, 7) and Bury (*ERE*, 383) that the Slavs mentioned by the *Annales* were Moravians. The Annalist seems to have in mind a local Pannonian Croat tribe, whose help was however of no avail. These two Bulgarian attacks were followed by an attack on the Serbs, also unsuccessful (32/45-8).

31/68-70 κάστρα οἰκούμενα κτλ.

Nona, *ital.* Nona, Croat Nin, the ancient Roman city of Aenona in Liburnia, north of Zara. It was the residence of the first Croat princes, and the see of the first Croat bishops; see on 30/90-3. Belgrad ('white city'), a new Croat foundation on the coast south of Zara, often served as a residence for Croat princes; now a small town called Biograd. Belitzin, transliterated by C. from the Slav locative form 'v' Beliči,' τὸ Βελίτζιν, now Belica. Skordona, former Scardona, capital of the Roman province of Liburnia; we have no information about its destruction by the invaders (see Jireček, *Die Romanen*, 28-9); it is the modern Skradin. Chlebena is Hljevno, in the župania of Χλεβίανα (30/91). Stolpon is Stupin, the Stulpini of Pliny, *Nat. Hist.*, III, 139, and the Stluppi of Ptolemy, *Geograph.*, II, 16, 9, a Liburnian city on the coast; it is mentioned as Stilbiza in documents of 1080 and 1097 (see Rački, *Documenta*, 131, 179; and *cf.* Fluss in Pauly-Wissowa, *RE*, n.s., III A, col. 2552 (Stluppi), and Skok, *Slavenstvo i romanstvo*, I, 156-7). Tenin is Knin, north of Skradin, in the župania of ἡ Τνήνα (30/92). Kori is Karin, on the coast near the mouth of the river Zrmanja; Ptolemy, *Geograph.*, II, 17, 3, calls it Κοράνιον, and Pliny, *Nat. Hist.*, III, 140, Corinium, a station on the road Burnum–Hadra–Nedinum (now Gradino by Nadin)–Iader (Zara); see Patsch in Pauly-Wissowa, *RE*, IV, cols. 1231-2 (Corinium). Klaboka is Klobuk, where there is mention of a church in a document of 1078 (Rački, *Documenta*, 114). See on 30/90-3; and for C.'s transliterations Skok, *Toponomastike*, I, 317 f., and *id.*, *Slavenstvo i romanstvo*, I, 86, 89.

31/71-82 ἡ βαπτισμένη Χρωβατία ἐκβάλλει κτλ.

On the significance of the whole passage see above pp. 4, 100. This prince Kresimir (31/76) is, according to Klaić (see on 31/42-52), Kresimir II, who succeeded Tomislav in 928 and reigned until 945. He was most probably Tomislav's son. If so, we must eliminate from the list of Croat rulers Trpimir II, for whose existence there is no documentary evidence, and who has been 'created' in modern times to explain C.'s story. Though C. does not mention Tomislav (*c.* 910-28) by name, his information about the considerable military power of Croatia before the reign of Kresimir II is most valuable, as it gives us our only tangible evidence on the Croat expansion under Tomislav, who brought his realm to the peak of its power. Even if we suppose that the high numbers of cavalry and infantry include all men capable of military service in an emergency, the military strength of Croatia was still imposing. This account can be taken at its full value if we suppose with the majority of scholars that under Tomislav Pannonian Croatia was definitely united with Dalmatian Croatia to form one powerful state, which reached from the Adriatic coast to the Drava river, and included the territory between the Vrbas and lower Bosna rivers. The large number of Croatian ships makes it probable also that Croatia possessed the important islands of Vis, Brač and Hvar, and perhaps even the territory of the Narentans; see Šišić, *Geschichte der Kroaten*, 131. In order to preserve their possessions in Dalmatia the Byzantines, at war with Symeon of Bulgaria, placed the Dalmatian *thema* under Tomislav's protection. This situation lasted until the death of Kresimir I (or II, according to Klaić). Under his son Miroslav a civil war broke out, and the ban Pribina (Πριβουνία) murdered Miroslav, whose brother Michael Kresimir II (949-69) (or III, according to Klaić) he placed on the throne. Pribina governed the županias of Lika, Krbava and Gadska (30/93-4), and he is the first Croat ban whose name is known to us. The civil war weakened Croatia's prestige, and resulted in a heavy territorial loss. The Narentans regained complete independence, and the islands of Brač and Hvar joined them. The Serbian prince Časlav occupied Bosnia, together with the territory adjoining Bulgaria; and the Byzantines resumed direct control over the Dalmatian *thema*. All this explains why the military power of Croatia sank so low under Kresimir III, and why its navy was so much diminished. C.'s estimate of the reduced military power after 950 (31/79-82) was therefore probably accurate, though unfortunately the actual figures are not preserved to us. See Šišić, *Geschichte der Kroaten*, 154 ff.; and for the boundary between Croatia and Hungary see *id.*, *Povijest Hrvata*, 405 ff.; τὰ ὄρη which, according to 13/7, separate Croatia from Hungary are the hills of Mačely, Ivančica, Kalnik and Bilogorje, near the Drava river.

31/72-3 σαγήνας . . . κονδούρας.
From A. Dain, *Naumachica* (Paris, 1943), 41, 101 it would appear that σαγῆναι were heavy ships of burden, which is clearly not the meaning here. For Croat sea-power from 7th to 11th cents., see B. Poparić, *O pomorskoj sili Hrvata za dobe narodnih vladara* (Zagreb, 1899), 40-82.

31/83-91 ἡ μεγάλη Χρωβατία κτλ.
For the progress of Christianity among the White Croats see on 30/75. The author had apparently little information about the military potential of White Croatia; nor does he say anything definite about Byzantine pretensions to sovereignty over that country. The Croats who were subject to attack by the Franks may be those of eastern Bohemia, who probably belonged to White Croatia; and, in trying to subjugate the Slav tribes of Bohemia, the Franks may have drawn the Bohemian Croats into the conflict. When the Czechs and the Croats of Bohemia made their submission in 895, the Bohemian part of White Croatia was attached to the Frankish empire. For the relations between the White Croats and the Magyars after the destruction of the Moravian empire (*c*. 906), see on 30/75. We do not know of any armed conflict between White Croats and Magyars (Turks); but, in spite of the friendly relations subsisting between the two (30/75), Magyar raids into Croat territory through Moravia, then in Magyar hands, were not impossible. As regards the Pechenegs C. is no doubt right: the Pechenegs were masters of southern Russia, and it appears that White Croatia included the territory of the upper Dniester, where we must probably locate the Croats mentioned in the *Russian Primary Chronicle* (ed. Cross and Sherbowitz-Wetzor, 64, 119; ann. 6412-15, 6500). The sea mentioned at 31/89-91 does not seem to be the Black Sea, though it would appear natural to think so. C. however calls the Black Sea 'Pontus' (42/6, 91; 53/524); and the Greeks in general called it 'Pontos Euxeinos'. The 'dark' sea (31/91) is therefore probably the Baltic, so called because of its geographical position and climate. We may see in this an indication that C.'s information was based on some native account. Cracow was an important centre on the Vistula of trade with lands on the Baltic coast, a fact that has often been overlooked. See Dvornik, *The Making*, 296-304.

32/1-6 Περὶ τῶν Σέρβλων κτλ.
The country 'beyond Turkey (Hungary)', neighbour to Francia and to White Croatia, should be modern Saxony, where remnants of Serbs (Sorbs) are still living. The name 'Boiki' has been much disputed over by specialists (*cf.* Niederle, *Slovanské Starožit-*

nosti, II, 1, 250 ff.; Werchratskij, *Arch. f. slav. Phil.* 16 (1894), 591-4), but Skok (*Orts-namenstudien*, 223 ff.) has proved that the 'place called Boïki' can only be Bohemia. Grégoire (*L'Origine*, 98) rejects Skok's proposal to read 'Boioi', and suggests 'Boimi'. C.'s account contains one serious inexactitude: namely, the statement that the Serbs lived 'in a place called by them Boïki'. Although we have documentary proof of the existence of Croats in Bohemia, we have none to suggest that Serbs lived there. Bohemia was in fact another neighbour of White Serbia.

The White Serbs were certainly unbaptized in the time of Heraclius, and even in C.'s time they could hardly be called Christians, although the Christian faith was not unknown to them. Their hostility towards the Franks from the beginning of their history prevented their receiving the Christian faith preached by Frankish missionaries. Their *symbiosis* with Christian Moravians and Czechs in Great Moravia (*c.* 882-900) was too short to allow a deep penetration among them of Moravian Christianity with its Slav liturgy. When, after their separation from Great Moravia, the Serbs had once more to recognize Frankish supremacy, their hostility to Frankish institutions did not abate. King Henry I, the Fowler, conquered their territory in 928, and Otto I consolidated the German hold over the whole country between the Saale, Elbe and Bober rivers. Although Otto I founded a bishopric for the Serbs at Meissen, the latter continued stubbornly to refuse baptism from their conquerors; and the Germans had to bring German colonists into the country in order to fill the churches built for, but carefully avoided by, the Serbs. See Dvornik, *The Making*, 27 ff., 291 ff.; *id.*, *The Slavs*, 293 ff.

32/7-11 εἰς Ἡράκλειον . . . προσέφυγεν.

It is not impossible that the Serbs learnt of Heraclius, and of his search for allies against the Avars, from the Franks, to whom Heraclius had sent embassies. The Chronicle of Fredegarius (*MGH*, Scr. rer. Merov., II, 151, 153, 155) records that Dagobert, king of the Franks, and the emperor Heraclius exchanged embassies and concluded a treaty of friendship. The chronicler dates the treaty to the year 629; but we are entitled to date the embassies to *c.* 626, when Heraclius was looking everywhere for help against the Avars (see on 31/8-9), if not earlier. The Franks were also interested in the Avars: we learn from the same Chronicle that they helped the Moravian Slavs to revolt against their Turkic masters. It may be that Byzantine diplomacy had something to do with this revolt. Samo, who led the rebels, and became the head of their new political formation (*c.* 625), was a Frank sent to them by Dagobert *c.* 622-3. We know that the Serbian prince Dervan voluntarily joined the state of Samo in 632, after Samo had successfully defended the independence of his new realm against Dagobert. It is therefore quite possible that the incident described at 32/7-9 took place about this time, and that the leader of the Serb detachment which migrated to Byzantine soil was Dervan's brother. Mas'udi, who gathered some information on the Slavs in northern Europe during his travels in 943, suggests that the political organization of the Serbs was very powerful. He calls them 'Surbin, a people feared by the Slavs for reasons too long to enumerate, owing to characteristics which it would be too discursive to explain, and also because they have no religion to submit to'; see Marquart 102. Mas'udi must have been citing some historical records of the northern Slavs, since in the 10th cent. the Serbs were by no means such as he describes them. We may suppose that the migration here reported by C. considerably weakened the Serb state, and that this induced Dervan to join the new Slav realm of Samo, in order to resist growing pressure from the Franks. See Dvornik, *The Making*, 270 ff., 286 ff., 289 ff.; Labuda, *Pierwsze Państwo*, 194 ff., 321 ff.; Chalou-pecký, *Byzantinoslavica*, 11 (1950), 223-39, a review of Labuda's book.

32/11-12 ἐν τῷ θέματι Θεσσαλονίκης.

It appears that the Serbs took the easy way, following the Oder, upper Vistula, San and one of the waterways (Dniester, Pruth or Sereth) behind the Carpathians leading to the Black Sea and the lower Danube, whence they could easily reach Byzantine territory. It is difficult to imagine them travelling through Hungary and former Roman provinces in the Balkans, which were still controlled by the Avars; see on 30/66–71, 76–8. The former route is indicated also by the fact that Heraclius settled them first in the *thema* of Thessalonica where they founded a colony at Serbia (Srbčište), north of Mt. Olympus. See Županić, *Etnolog*, II (1928), 26–35; *id.*, *Byzantion*, 4 (1927–8), 277–80; M. Vasmer, *Die Slaven in Griechenland (Abhandl. d. preuss. Akad.*, phil.-hist. kl., 12, 1941), 187 (*Σέρβια*). For the *thema* of Thessalonica see on 32/16–20.

For the Serb settlement in C.'s 'Serblia', see Skok's exhaustive study in *Glas Srpsk. kral. Akad.*, 176 (1938, drugi razred), 243–84. It appears that this place was of considerable strategic importance, guarding the approach to Thessaly and Greece proper. The fact that Heraclius settled the Serbs there shows that he must have been impressed by their military qualities. If we recall what Mas'udi says about the White Serbs (see on 32/7–11), and if we accept the plausible theory that there were among them Iranian (Sarmatian) elements, Heraclius' decision will appear understandable. Iranians had a good military record. The strategic importance of the place was tested in the Byzantine war against Samuel in the year 1000 (Cedrenus II, 452/20), and during the campaigns of Stephen Dušan against Byzantium. The Turks too were aware of the strategic value of the area, since they settled Turkish colonists in it. The many Slav names of places in the neighbourhood may indicate that some Slav tribes had penetrated thither even before the Serbs; but some of these names may date from a later period. The name *Σέρβλια-Σέρβια* corresponds to the Slav name Srblje—Srb—Srbica.

32/12–15 'δοῦλοι' προσαγορεύονται κτλ.

For the many attempts at derivation of the name 'Serb', see Niederle, *Slovanské Starožitnosti*, II, 486 ff. C.'s popular etymology has been rejected by most philologists. It was resuscitated, though unsuccessfuly, by Grégoire (*L'Origine*, 117); *cf.* Ostrogorsky[2] 85, and see the remarks of Skok on the word τζερβουλιανός, in *Glas Srpsk. kral. Akad.*, 176 (1938, drugi razred), 246–8. Niederle thought that the name 'Serb' might be Slav, but could point to no Slav root for it. The main reason for doubting this is that Pliny already knew a tribe of the name settled in the region of the river Don (*Nat. Hist.*, VI, 7, 19; Maeotici, Vali, Serbi, Arrecchi); and Ptolemy (V, 9, 12) also places his *Σέρβοι* in this region. Moreover, as we have seen (on 30/61 ff.), *Σαρβᾶν* were living in the Caucasus in C.'s time. It should further be noted that Serb and Croat settlements were intermingled in the old White Serbia and White Croatia, which suggests that the two tribes had always been closely connected. All this makes it quite reasonable to assume that the Serbs, like the Croats, were originally Iranian, although the name 'Serb' has not yet been discovered in the Iranian vocabulary. If this theory is accepted, then the settlement of the Serbs among the Slavs in modern Saxony, between the rivers Saale, Elbe and Bober, should be dated to the same period as the migration of the Croats beyond the Carpathians, that is, after the invasion of the Huns. See Županić, *Narodna Starina*, I (1922), 107–18; *id.*, *Zbornik J. Cvijić* (Belgrade, 1924), 555; *id.*, *Etnolog*, II (1928), 74–9; Dvornik, *The Making*, 268 ff.

32/16–20 Μετὰ δὲ χρόνον τινὰ κτλ.

It is extremely difficult to date this migration of the Serbs with any accuracy. We learn from 31/8–10 that the Croats applied to Heraclius before the Serbs did so, which may be explained as in the note on 31/8–9. But from the same passage (31/10–11) it is clear that the application of both Croats and Serbs should be dated to the time when the Avars were still masters of the greater part of Roman Illyricum. However, C. speaks only of the Croats as having fought against the Avars and having expelled them. The Serbs meantime had been settled at Serbia (Srbčište). Dissatisfied with the lands allotted them, they asked the emperor to let them return home, and he consented; but possibly some of them stayed behind in Srbčište. Curiously enough, this time the Serbs did not turn north-east and go back the way they had probably come, but marched towards the confluence of the Sava and Danube rivers, as if meaning to cross Avar territory on their way home. They perhaps chose this route because the Croats were at that time fighting the Avars. We know from 30/67 that the Croat-Avar war lasted some years. We may therefore conclude that the Serb prince with his retinue and warriors, learning of Croat successes against the Avars, decided to seize the opportunity to settle on the liberated territory. By the emperor's order the military governor at Belgrade directed them to the country now called Serbia. Although our account says nothing of any fighting between Serbs and Avars, it may be that the Serbs helped the Croats by attacking the Avars from the north, and thus enabled the Croats to push further along the coast and into the interior of Dalmatia. In order to stress Byzantine rights over the reconquered lands, C. represents the whole incident (32/16–27) as having taken place by permission of Heraclius, following a request of the Serbs themselves. But we may detect in it the experienced hand of Byzantine diplomacy. It would have been foolish to allow a well disciplined, if small, body of seasoned fighters to leave imperial territory when every effort was being made to combat the Avar danger. It may have been the governor of Belgrade who, from this strategic position on the Danube, directed the newcomers into the interior of modern Serbia.

The mention of Belgrade (32/20) is interesting. We know almost nothing of Singidunum after 600. It is generally supposed that the city succumbed to the attacks of the Avars. But it is possible that the Byzantines were able to recover this important strategic point after the defeat of the Avars in 626, or perhaps as a result of the Croat offensive in Dalmatia.

It is also interesting to note that C. here uses the Slav name of the place, and not the old Roman name of Singidunum. The term 'strategos' should here be understood in its original sense of 'commander', and not as governor of a province, since in Heraclius' time *themata* (*cf.* 32/11) hardly as yet existed in the west. What was left of Byzantine possessions in these parts—Macedonia, Thessaly, Hellas, Peloponnesus—continued to be governed by the Praefectus praetorio Illyrici, who resided at Thessalonica. The first European *thema*, that of Thrace, was created by Constantine IV (668–85). Hellas was made into a *thema* by Justinian II (685–95). A Praefectus praetorio Illyrici is mentioned as late as 796 (*MPG*, xcix, col. 917C). A *thema* of Thessalonica was probably created only at the beginning of the 8th cent. (*cf.* P. Lemerle, *Philippes et la Macédoine Orientale*, Paris, 1945, 129): so that when the term is used at 32/11, the reference is to the old prefecture of Illyricum under a title more familiar to the 10th cent. (*cf.* 30/116). But what C. says of the settlement of the Serbs at Srbčište near Olympus is true, since the region was in fact administered in Heraclius' time by the Praefectus resident at Thessalonica: see Dvornik, *Légendes*, 3–9; Ostrogorsky² 108; *id.*, *Zbornik Radova S.A.N.*, 21 (1952), 65.

32/27-8 πρεσβύτας ἀπὸ ῾Ρώμης.
The first attempt to christianize the Serbs must have coincided with the attempted conversion of Croats (31/21-4), after the liberation of this part of Illyricum from the Avars. Here again Heraclius, respecting the ecclesiastical organization of his time, had to approach the Patriarch of Rome in this matter; see on 31/22-5. We know nothing of the results of this first missionary work among the Serbs. Christianity no doubt penetrated among the Slav tribes on the coast from the Latin and Greek coastal cities; but almost nothing was done in Serbia proper. See Runciman, *First Bulgarian Empire*, 283; and for a more recent bibliography of the Serbian pagan religion, see Jireček, *Istorija Srba*, 91 ff.

32/30 τοῦ ἄρχοντος τοῦ Σέρβλου.
The name of this first ruler of the Serbs in their new land was unknown to C. But the passage (32/29-31) tells us an interesting detail about the time of his death. In spite of a lacuna in the text, it seems clear that C. dates his death to a time when Bulgaria was still

a Byzantine province. Byzantine rule over provinces occupied by the Bulgars ceased *c.* 680. It is unlikely that this first Serb prince ruled all the time from *c.* 626–30 until *c.* 680; but at least we may conclude that when he died the Byzantines were still masters of the lands which were to become the new state of Bulgaria. Our author does not know the names of his immediate successors. These princes ruled over a small area centring round the valleys of the upper Drina river and its affluents (Piva, Tara, Lim, Uvac) and of the upper Morava with Raška and Ibar. It was separated from the coast by the territory of the Zachlumi and that of Dioclea, which were originally governed by their own rulers. Serbia had access to the sea only through Trebinje (see on 34/1). The first Serbian princes mentioned by name in this chapter (32/34–5) are Vyšeslav, Radoslav and Prosigois (Prosigoj), who governed under Byzantine supremacy in the second half of the 8th and the beginning of the 9th cents. The first prince whose name introduced the Serbs into the annals of history was Vlastimir (32/35), who seems to have ruled between 835 and 860. The Bulgarian invasion of Serbia (32/39) should be dated 839. Presiam is here called 'prince of Bulgaria'; and Zlatarsky (*Istorija*, I, 1, 346) accepts him as such. But Bury (*ERE*, 481–4) thought him identical with Malamir; and Runciman (*First Bulgarian Empire*, 87 f., 292–7) suggests that Presiam, probably a scion of the reigning house, was only the commander of the invading army under Khagan Malamir; the Serbs took him for the khagan, and our author repeated the Serb version of the incident. The chronology of Malamir's reign is very uncertain, which makes it difficult to establish the succession on the Bulgarian throne at this time.

32/45–6 Μιχαήλ . . . Πρεσιάμ, τοῦ πατρὸς αὐτοῦ.

If we accept the supposition that Presiam was not a khagan but only the relative and general of khagan Malamir (see preceding note), then we must assume that Malamir reigned until 852, and was then succeeded by Boris, his nephew, son of Svinitse.

32/52–60 Μουντιμήρου παιδία κτλ.

Rasi, now Raška, near Novi Pazar, is on the frontier between Bulgaria and Serbia. It should be noted that one of Mutimir's sons had a Christian name, Stephen (32/52), as had also his nephew, Peter (32/61); this shows that by this time Christianity had made progress in Serbia proper. Boris's unsuccessful invasion of Serbia (32/44 ff.) should be dated *c.* 860. Mutimir is probably the Slav prince to whom pope John VIII addressed a letter in 873, inviting him to place his land under the jurisdiction of the metropolitan see of Sirmium, which had been created for St Methodius, the Apostle of the Slavs. The recipient of this letter can hardly have been a prince of Pannonian Croatia (Rački, *Documenta*, 368), since Pannonian Croatia seems at that time to have been governed by Kocel, prince of upper Pannonia under Frankish suzerainty (see on 30/78–88), to whom John VIII had addressed another letter about the same time (873). As Mutimir seems to be sole ruler of Serbia in 873, the expulsion of his brothers must be dated before this year. See Jireček, *Geschichte der Serben*, 195; Dvornik, *Les Slaves*, 54 ff., 260 ff.; Runciman, *First Bulgarian Empire*, 92.

32/65 ὁ Τζεέσθλαβος. I.e. Časlav.

32/67 ᾽ μετὰ τὸν αὐτοῦ θάνατον κτλ.

Mutimir died *c.* 890, and his son and successor was deposed by his cousin Peter *c.* 891. Peter reigned until 917, and his reign was most prosperous for Serbia. He started to expand his realm towards the Adriatic. He forced the Narentans to recognize him as overlord (32/84). During the first period of Symeon's struggle with Byzantium, Peter, though nominally subject to Byzantium, remained neutral and indeed was in very close relations with Symeon. We may suppose that during his long reign religious influences began to penetrate into Serbia from Bulgaria. The Serbs profited also by the spread of

Slav culture then flourishing under Symeon. Peter was thus able to defeat two pretenders to his throne, Bran, son of Mutimir (*c.* 894; 32/72–4), and Klonimir, son of Strojimir (*c.* 896; 32/74–7). His expansion into the valley of the Naretva (Narenta) should be dated between 896 and 910.

32/76 τὴν Δοστινίκαν.
  This is the Δεστινίκον of 32/150. It was probably situated near the upper Uvac river, and was later called Sjenica. See Šišić, *Povijest Hrvata*, 459; Skok, *Ortsnamenstudien*, 234.

32/81 Μετὰ δὲ τὸν καιρὸν κτλ. The later section of c. 32 begins here: see above, pp. 4–5, 100.

32/83–6 Λέων ὁ ῾Ραβδοῦχος.
  Leo Rhabduchus is mentioned by Leo Grammaticus (258/21), Theodosius of Melitene (ed. Tafel, München, 1859, 181) and Cont. Geo. Mon. (845/8) as military governor of Dyrrhachion in 880, at the time of the Byzantine expedition against Calabria which resulted in the recapture of Tarentum from the Arabs. If this information, which derives from the Chronicle of the Logothete, is reliable, then we have to suppose that Leo was military governor of Dyrrhachion from at least 800 until 917, which, though not impossible, seems improbable. On the other hand, Leo Choerosphactes, writing probably before 911 to a son of the patrician Nicetas Monomachos, requests his correspondent to approach his (Choerosphactes') brother-in-law Leo Rhabduchus, magister and *logothetes tou dromou*, through whose intercession Choerosphactes hopes to be pardoned by Leo VI; see G. Kolias, *Léon Choerosphactès, magistre, proconsul et patrice* (Athens, 1939), 128–9. C.'s statement (32/83–4) that Rhabduchus became a magister and logothetes only after 917 is therefore inaccurate. Lascaris (*Revue historique du Sud-Est Européen*, xx, 1943, 202–7) is therefore inclined to think that the mission of Rhabduchus to Peter must date from the first war between Symeon and the Byzantines (894–6), when Symeon had occupied thirty fortified places in the *thema* of Dyrrhachion and when Rhabduchus was military governor of that *thema*. If this were right, we should have to re-date the reigns of all Serbian princes of this period, whose chronology has so far been based solely on C.'s account.
  However, apart from this one inconsistency, C.'s chronology, which may be based on a lost Serbian chronicle, seems to be pretty accurate (see Ostrogorsky, *Istoriski Časopis*, 1–2, 1948–9, 24–9, who however does not notice the conclusions of Lascaris); so that it would be rash to date the occupation of Serbia by Symeon (32/91–9) to 894–6 rather than to 918. It seems more reasonable to suppose, either that C.'s informant made a slip of the memory in stating that Rhabduchus was the military governor who was charged with the mission to Peter; or else that Rhabduchus undertook the mission, not in the capacity of military governor of Dyrrhachion, but in that of *logothetes tou dromou*. In either event, C.'s error would be quite understandable. See Ostrogorsky[2] 216 f. (though again he does not cite the stimulating observations of Lascaris). Most recently, however, Ostrogorsky (*Zbornik Radova S.A.N.*, 44, Viz. Inst. 3 (1955), 29–36) has concluded that the letter of Choerosphactes should itself be dated after 917. See Ferjančić 54, note 178.

32/87 Μιχαήλ, ὁ ἄρχων τῶν Ζαχλούμων. See on 33/16.

32/90–1 κατὰ τὸν καιρὸν ἐκεῖνον κτλ.
  Symeon's campaign against Peter of Serbia is dated by Runciman (*First Bulgarian Empire*, 163) to the year 918. This dating would explain why Symeon did not exploit his decisive victory at Anchialos in 917 by an attack on Constantinople, which would have been the logical step. It is noteworthy that the Bulgarian generals mentioned in this chapter (32/93, 117–18, 127) still bear non-Slav names and titles. This indicates that the old

privileged class of Turkic boyars still held important posts in the Bulgarian state under Symeon, and that the slavization of the Turkic upper class was not yet complete in the first quarter of the 10th cent. The names mentioned at 32/117-18, 127 are perhaps not personal names but Turkic titles. See Grot, *Izvjestija*, 134, 146, 193-5, 204; Zlatarsky, *Istorija*, 1/2, 421, 475, 501. For C.'s account of the Bulgaro-Byzantine wars, see Grot, *Izvjestija*, 192 ff.; Jireček, *Geschichte der Serben*, 199 ff.; Šišić, *Geschichte der Kroaten*, 123-30; *id.*, *Povijest Hrvata*, 405 ff.; Zlatarsky, *Istorija*, 1/2, 401-73; Runciman, *First Bulgarian Empire*, 162-7.

32/99-111 Παῦλος, ὁ υἱὸς Βράνου.
Scholars disagree about the date of Paul's reign. Jireček (*Geschichte der Serben*, 199), Runciman (*First Bulgarian Empire*, 166 f.) and Ćorović (*Prilozi za kniževnost, jezik, istoriju i folklor*, 14 (1934), 6-16) think that it was in the third year of his reign that Paul was attacked by Zacharias, and that he ruled three more years after his victory over the pretender; they thus date his reign from 917 to 923. But Ostrogorsky (*Istoriski Časopis*, 1-2, 1948-9, 27) has convincingly shown that C. allots only three years to the whole of Paul's reign, and that the unsuccessful attempt of Zacharias happened during those three years. The emperor's informant followed the account of a lost Serbian chronicle, and for medieval chroniclers the reign of a prince formed a chronological unit. Ostrogorsky thus confirms the conclusions of Zlatarsky (*Istorija*, 1/2, 461) and Šišić (*Povijest Hrvata*, 409), both of whom allowed only three years to Paul's reign. There is however an objection to this solution. The first, unsuccessful attempt of Zacharias to dethrone Paul was inspired by the emperor Romanus I (32/100-3), who was not crowned until December 920; therefore this attempt can hardly be dated to the same year. If we accept Ostrogorsky's thesis that C. allots only three years to Paul's reign, then we must date that reign 918-21/2. It is probable that Symeon's attack on Serbia took place in 918, after the battle of Anchialos (see on 32/90-1), and that Paul was replaced on the throne about the middle of the same year. He may have reigned until the middle of 922. We have also to suppose that the defeat of Zacharias, his dispatch to Bulgaria, the change in Serbian policy and the victorious return of Zacharias to Serbia all took place between January and December 921, unless we can add the first half of 922.

32/112, 117-18, 127 τοῦ Μαρμαῆμ κτλ. See on 32/90-1. Himnikos (32/118) is the Minikos of Theoph. Cont. 401/4.

32/126-45 Κατὰ τὸν καιρὸν οὖν ἐκεῖνον.
The Bulgarian attack on Croatia (see Theoph. Cont. 411/13-16) is datable to 926; see Šišić, *Geschichte der Kroaten*, 140, and *id.*, *Povijest Hrvata*, 422. The date of Časlav's return from Bulgarian captivity is disputed. Some scholars count the seven years (32/128) from the destruction of Serbia, and date Časlav's escape from Preslav to 931 or 932; so Grot, *Izvjestija*, 196; Zlatarsky, *Istorija*, 1/2, 540; Šišić, *Geschichte der Kroaten*, 152; Jireček, *Geschichte der Serben*, 202; P. Mutafčiev, *Istorija na b'lgarskija narod*, 1 (Sofia, 1943), 246; Gruber, *Zbornik Kralja Tomislava*, 335. Others date his escape to 933 or 934; so Runciman, *First Bulgarian Empire*, 185; see bibliography in the study of Ćorović, *Prilozi za kniževnost, jezik, istoriju i folklor*, 14 (1934), 6-16. But neither of these dates explains why Časlav did not profit by the complete change in Bulgarian policy which followed the death of Symeon (27th May, 927) and waited to escape until 932 or 934; although it was obviously in Byzantium's interest to establish Serbia as a state independent of Bulgaria at the earliest possible moment. We must therefore accept the suggestion of Ostrogorsky (*Istoriski Časopis*, 1-2, 1948-9, 29) that the seven years in question are to be counted from the beginning of Zacharias' reign, which is probably datable to 921-2 (see on 32/99-111). Časlav will thus have escaped to Serbia in 928 or 929. See also V. Ćorović, *Chistoria Bosne* (Belgrade, 1940), 140ff.

32/149-51 κάστρα οἰκούμενα.

For Destinikon, see on 32/76. Tzernabouskeï is regarded by Šišić (*Povijest Hrvata*, 459) as an adjectival form of the common Slav place-name Crni Vrh (Black Hill). Megyretous is a Greek transliteration of the Slav locative form v' Med'ureci (between the rivers), a place between the rivers Tara and Piva, the modern Sokol. Dresneïk is identified by Šišić (*Povijest Hrvata*, 459) with Bresnik, the medieval name of Plevlje in the country of Novi Pazar; the name derives from the Slav word brest (elm-wood). Lesnik was identified by Šafařík (*Slovanské Starožitnosti*, 652) with Ljesnica, on the Drina; the name derives from Slav ljeska (hazel-nut); Rački (*Documenta*, 415) also cites a Lesnik near Prizren. Salines is Soli (salt), the modern Tuzle, which is a Turkish translation of the Slav word Soli; it is possible that in C.'s time the old Roman form was still current, though the Roman population had long disappeared. Bosona derives from the name of the river Bosna; see Jireček, *Handelsstrassen*, 29–36. Katera is a Roman name, Catera, and the place is identified by Šišić (*Povijest Hrvata*, 461) with Kotorac, near Ilidze by Sarajevo and the sources of the river Bosna. Desnik is probably Desngrad, a castle on the right bank of the upper Bosna. See Novaković 137 ff.; Jireček, *Handelsstrassen*, 31–5; *id.*, *Geschichte der Serben*, 120 ff.; Skok, *Ortsnamenstudien*, 233–6; Jireček, *Istorija Srba*, i, 67 ff.; V. Ćorović, *Chistoria Bosne* (Belgrade, 1940), 120 ff.; Ferjančić 58.

33/1-15 Περὶ τῶν Ζαχλούμων.

The 'country of the Zachlumi' (*cf.* 30/100-4) lay on the Adriatic coast from Ragusa to the river Narenta, and extended into the interior about the whole course of the upper Narenta. It was called Hlm in the old Serbian language, and Hum or Humska zemlja during the Middle Ages. Its Latin names were Chelmania, Chulmia, Zachulmia and Terra de Chelmo. It got its modern name of Hercegovina (land of the duke) in 1448, when Stephen Vukčić, a grandee of Bosnia, detached it from Bosnia and governed it with the title of Herceg (from German Herzog). Hlm or Hum means 'hill' or 'mountain'; and the Greek form given by C. seems to be a rendering of the Old Slav locative plural, v' Zachl'ml'achъ, 'in behind the hills': see Skok, *Ortsnamenstudien*, 222; Novaković 30 ff.

33/13-15 τὸ Βόνα.

Bona is probably the castle of Blagaj on the hill Hum, about twenty miles south-east of the modern capital of Herzegovina, Mostar, which was founded after 1483, at the beginning of the Turkish occupation. Blagaj is probably a Slav translation of a Latin name (blag = bonus). Stephanus of Byzantium (ed. Meineke, Berlin, 1849, i, 182) knew of a city called Bunnos, which he placed in Illyria; and this may be C.'s Bona. The river (33/14-15), which rises under the rocks of Hum, is still called by its Roman name, Bona. See Jireček, *Geschichte der Serben*, 118.

33/16 Μιχαήλ, τοῦ υἱοῦ τοῦ Βουσεβούτζη.

Michael, prince of the Zachlumi (*c.* 910–30, or ?950), was jealous of the Serbian expansion under prince Peter and of his subjugation of the Narentans (see on 32/67); he therefore did not follow the pro-Byzantine policy of Peter, but on the contrary whole-heartedly embraced the cause of Symeon of Bulgaria (32/86–90). His first move against the Byzantines is recorded by the historian of Venice, John the Deacon (ed. Monticolo, Rome (1890), 132): probably in 913, Michael learnt that Peter, son of Ursus the doge of Venice, was returning from Constantinople with rich presents and the title of proto-spatharius; he took Peter prisoner, impounded his presents, and sent him to Symeon of Bulgaria, to whom the Venetians had to pay a large sum for his ransom. Michael's next step against Byzantium, described at 32/86–99, cost Peter of Serbia his throne (918). Jireček (*Geschichte der Serben*, 199 ff.; *id.*, *Istorija Srba*, 114) thinks that Michael continued to be hostile to Byzantium, and that in 926 his fleet attacked Byzantine possessions in Apulia, where he occupied Siponto; the attack is recorded by *Annales Barenses*, *Annales*

Beneventani and Lupus Protospatharius (*MGH*, Scr. III, 175; V, 52, 54; Rački, *Documenta*, 393). But it does not follow from these vague accounts that Michael was acting in this instance against Byzantine interests: the *Annales* speak only of Michael's occupation of Siponto, but make no mention of any plundering by 'Michael rex Sclavorum'. *Annales Barenses* give a detailed though inaccurate date for the event: 'mense Julio, die sanctae Felicitatis (*i.e.* 10th July), secunda feria, indictione XV', or Monday (*sic*) the 10th July, 927. The event was thus clearly remembered by the annalist; and if Michael had caused the citizens of Siponto any considerable loss, he would probably not have omitted to say so. On the other hand Michael is said to have been present at the Synod of Spalato in 925, when pope John X addressed a letter to Tomislav of Croatia and Michael of Zachlumje (Rački, *Documenta*, 187–94). This would suggest that in 925 Michael was on good terms with Tomislav at a time when the latter was himself on the best of terms with the Byzantines. It is true that the authenticity of the Acts of the Synod of Spalato, preserved only in two mss. of the 16th cent., is questioned by some scholars, though other documents in the same two mss. have been accepted as genuine. Jireček denied the authenticity of the Acts mainly because Michael is said to have been present, which, Jireček thought, was impossible since Michael was still an enemy of Byzantium and in 926 attacked Siponto. But this objection is not in itself decisive: on the contrary, the very fact that the Acts record the presence of a prince so little known to posterity is an argument for their authenticity. It is indeed possible that the Acts and the papal letter have received later additions, since they contain the interdiction on the use of the Slav liturgy, a step which is more likely to have been taken during or after the reign of pope Gregory VII than in the 10th cent. But even if we accept this possibility, this does not mean that the Acts and the letter are wholly spurious. Nor is it impossible that the original Acts and letter did in fact contain the interdict on the use of the Slav liturgy, and that a later Croat national assembly, an echo of which may be preserved in the confused account of the Priest of Dioclea (c. VIII, 300 f.), revoked the two unpopular decrees which forbade the use of the Slav liturgy and suppressed the Croat bishopric of Nin. At all events, the Slav liturgy continued in use side by side with the Latin, and the bishopric of Nin lasted until the 16th cent.; see Manojlović, *Zbornik Kralja Tomislava*, LXII ff.

From all the above, then, it seems more logical to conclude that Michael of Zachlumje changed his policy after 921, when Paul of Serbia, the successor of Peter, turned to Byzantium and was replaced by Symeon's protégé Zacharias (32/105–8). Byzantine diplomacy then tried to counter the Bulgarian threat by making overtures in the Balkans: Tomislav of Croatia was given the protectorate over Byzantine possessions in Dalmatia, Zacharias of Serbia went over to the Byzantine side (32/108–11), and everything suggests that Michael followed suit *c.* 922–3. This will be the date of his being made 'pro-consul and patrician' (33/16). His alliance with Croatia saved him from the fate of Zacharias, who in 924–5 was ousted by the Bulgarians and fled to Croatia (32/117–20). In these circumstances, it would be natural that Michael should have attended the Synod of Spalato in 925. His expedition against Apulia was, on this hypothesis, a result of his alliances with Croatia and Byzantium: it was undertaken at the request of Byzantium against the Arabs, who in 926 had renewed their raids on Byzantine possessions; see Hartmann, *Geschichte Italiens im Mittelalter*, III/2 (Gotha, 1911), 161 ff.; Vasiliev II, 223 f. It may be that from their nest on Mt. Gargano the Arabs had attacked and seized Siponto, and that the Slav expedition expelled them.

Two theories have been advanced to explain why *Annales Barenses* call Michael 'rex Sclavorum'. Šišić (*Povijest Hrvata*, 425) suggested that the expedition was sent out by king Tomislav, and that Tomislav's Christian name was Michael. Gruber (*Zbornik kralja Tomislava*, 337–41) believed that since Michael of Zachlumje could not by himself have provided a sufficient number of ships and men for such an expedition, he was therefore only the commander of an expedition for which the Croat king had provided the greater number of the forces dispatched. Even if we reject Gruber's theory, supported by

Manojlović (*ibid.*, xlix), that Zachlumje actually became a part of Croatia, it should be emphasized that the Zachlumians had a closer bond of interest with the Croats than with the Serbs, since they seem to have migrated to their new home not, as C. says (33/8–9), with the Serbs, but with the Croats; see below, on 33/18–19.

33/17 Βουσεβούτζη. Greek transliteration of the Slav name Vyšević.

33/18–19 Διτζίκη.
For the many attempts at interpreting this name, see Niederle, *Slovanské Starožitnosti*, II, 276 f. Skok (*Ortsnamenstudien*, 239 f.) seems finally to have solved the problem: he thinks that the word is erroneously transliterated, and that we should read Λ for Δ and ν for τ, Λινζίκη for Διτζίκη. If this is right, it is only a Greek rendering of the name attached to the Poles in the *Russian Primary Chronicle* (ann. 6539; ed. Likhačev (Moscow, 1950), 101) where they are said to inhabit a country called 'Ljazh'skaya zemlja'. At 9/10 (see note *ad loc.*) and 37/44 C. refers to Λενζανῆνοι, Λενζενίνοι, who are Polish Slavs. The old Russian form Lęžaninъ, meaning a Pole (*cf.* also the form Lędjaninъ), survives in the old Hungarian name for the Poles, Lengyen, and in the modern name Lengyel. This name was known also to Thomas the Archdeacon (c. vii, p. 25), who however latinized the form Lęžaninъ, identifying it with the name of the Celtic tribe Lingones, which he placed in Poland. We must thus recognize the word Λινζίκη as an adjective qualifying the river Visla as a 'Polish' river. The reading Λιτζίκη is adopted by Grégoire (*L'Origine*, 98 ff.), who however retains the reading τοὺς ἐπονομαζομένους (33/18) and refers it to the prince's folk rather than to the river Visla. This emendation throws new light on the origin of the Zachlumian dynasty and of the Zachlumi themselves. C.'s informant derived what he says about the country of Michael's ancestors from a native source, probably from a member of the prince's family; and the information is reliable. If this is so, we must regard the dynasty of Zachlumje and at any rate part of its people as neither Croat nor Serb. It seems more probable that Michael's ancestor, together with his tribe, joined the Croats when they moved south; and settled on the Adriatic coast and the Narenta, leaving the Croats to push on into Dalmatia proper. It is true that our text says that the Zachlumi 'have been *Serbs* since the time of that prince who claimed the protection of the emperor Heraclius' (33/9–10); but it does not say that Michael's family were Serbs, only that they 'came from the unbaptized who dwell on the river Visla, and are called (reading *Litziki*) "Poles"'. Michael's own hostility to Serbia (*cf.* 32/86–90) suggests that his family was in fact not Serb; and that the Serbs had direct control only over Trebinje (see on 32/30).

C.'s general claim that the Zachlumians were Serbs is, therefore, inaccurate; and indeed his later statements that the Terbouniotes (34/4–5), and even the Narentans (36/5–7), were Serbs and came with the Serbs, seem to conflict with what he has said earlier (32/18–20) on the Serb migration, which reached the new Serbia from the direction of Belgrade. He probably saw that in his time all these tribes were in the Serb sphere of influence, and therefore called them Serbs, thus ante-dating by three centuries the state of affairs in his own day. But in fact, as has been shown in the case of the Zachlumians, these tribes were not properly speaking Serbs, and seem to have migrated not with the Serbs but with the Croats. The Serbs at an early date succeeded in extending their sovereignty over the Terbouniotes and, under prince Peter, for a short time over the Narentans (see on 32/67). The Diocleans, whom C. does not claim as Serbs, were too near to the Byzantine *thema* of Dyrrhachion for the Serbs to attempt their subjugation before C.'s time. See the short study of Hauptmann, *M. Rešetarov Zbornik iz Dubrovačke Prošlosti* (Dubrovnik, 1931), 17–24.

33/19 Ζαχλοῦμα. The river Zachluma is the same as the river Bona (33/15): see Jireček, *Istorija Srba*, I, 66.

33/20-1 κάστρα οἰκούμενα.

Stagnon, lat. Stamnum, Stamum, is the castle of Stagno, Slav Ston, which defended the approach to the long peninsula now called Sabbioncello, Serbian Peljesać, and the isthmus called Prevlaka, a term corresponding to the Greek δίολκος and the Russian 'volok'; see Jireček, *Geschichte der Serben*, 118. Mokriskik is Mokr'sko or Mokr'ski grad, castle of Mokr'ski, probably situated near Mokro, west of Mostar, on the right bank of the Narenta; see Skok, *Jugoslov. Istor. Časopis*, 3 (1937), 92–106. Iosli is the modern Ošlje, north-east of Ston, on the road from Dubrovnik to Metković; the Greek transliteration should more correctly have been ᾿Οσλιή, since the word is an adjectival form from os'l', an ass; see Skok, *Toponomastike*, 3, 70. Galoumaïnik perhaps means Glumaivi c(astrum), identified with Glumive in Popovo Polje, on the left bank of the Narenta, north of Ošlje. Dobriskik is D'br'sk' c(astrum), today the region of Dabar, in the hills east of Stolac. See also Novaković 40 ff.; Jireček, *Handelsstrassen*, 25–7; Skok, *Toponomastike*, 3, 67.

34/1 Περὶ τῶν Τερβουνιωτῶν.

See 30/98-100, and *cf. De Cer.*, 691/10. The country was also called Tribunium, Tribunia, and later Tribigna. Although the Slav name is Trebinje, the country always appears in the titles of Serbian kings in one of its Greek forms: Travunia, Trebunia, Trovunia. The name is probably of Illyrian origin, but the Slavs adapted it to their own language as though deriving from Slav 'trebiti', clearing, or 'tvr'd'', firm; the latter derivation is given at 34/12–14.

The region of the Kanalites, now Konavle, derived its name either from the aqueduct (canalis) of Roman Epidaurum, or else from *lat.* canabulae, ditches dug to drain the fields; see Skok, *Dolazak Slovena*, 203. Either derivation would witness the survival of Roman elements in the country at the coming of the Slavs. The Slavs once more adapted the name to their own language, deriving it from the word 'kola', a waggon-load, and this was accepted by C. (34/16–17). B. von Arnim, *Zeitschr. f. slav. Phil.*, IX (1932), 137, wrongly derives the word from Turkish 'ganly', a two-wheeled cart.

According to 34/4-6, Trebinje and Konavle were occupied by Serbs; this may mean that some of the followers of the anonymous Serbian prince who arrived in the time of Heraclius moved on from Serbia proper, reached the coast and became župans of Trebinje/Konavle under Serbian supremacy; but see on 33/18–19.

34/6-11 ὁ ἄρχων Βλαστίμηρος.

For Vlastimir see also 32/35. The marriage between his daughter and Kraïna may have taken place *c.* 850. Phalimir is Hvalimir, and Tzouzimir Čučimir, who was perhaps the archon in C.'s time. See Šišić, *Geschichte der Kroaten*, 173–4; *id.*, *Povijest Hrvata*, 455.

34/19-20 κάστρα οἰκούμενα.

Terbounia is Trebinje, former political centre of the country, situated on Lake Trebinje, through which flows the river Trebistica. Ormos is Vrm; the Priest of Dioclea (c. xxx, p. 325) mentions a župania Vrmo in Trebinje, and ruins of a fort Vrono are still to be seen on the right bank of the Trebistica, between Trebinjo and Bileć: this was undoubtedly the site of C.'s Ormos/Vrm. Rhisena is the Illyrian city called ῾Ρίζων, ῾Ριζούς, Rhizinium, on the Roman road from Decatera to Epidaurum, on the Gulf of Cattaro (see Oberhummer in Pauly-Wissowa, *RE*, n.s., 1 A, cols. 937 f., ῾Ρίζων); the Priest of Dioclea (*loc. cit.*) knew the župania of Ressena, and the name survives in the modern Risan. Loukabetai is a name perhaps derived from Luka: several places and a hill have names derived from this word, but it is not possible to identify the one mentioned here. Zetlibi has also not been identified. For attempts to localize Loukabetai and Zetlibi, see Novaković 23–5; *cf.* also Grot, *Izvjestija*, 166; Jireček, *Handelsstrassen*, 22–5; Skok, *Dolazak Slovena*, 177–86.

35/1–11   *Περὶ τῶν Διοκλητιανῶν.*

The country is called after the ancient Illyrian city of Doclea, which was occupied by the Romans in 168 B.C. The legendary tradition, here cited by C., that the city was founded by Diocletian originated from the false assumption that he had been born at that place. It was this tradition also which changed Doclea into Dioclea. The city was the capital of the Roman province of Praevalis. It is not known when it was destroyed by invading Avars; but from letters sent by pope Gregory I (590–604) to its bishop, we deduce that it ceased to exist at the beginning of the 7th cent. The land was called in Greek *Διόκλεια*, in Latin Dioclia and in Serb Dioklitija. The Adriatic Sea was also often called by the Serbs Dioklitijsko More, and the Lake of Scutari Dioklitijsko Jezero. From the 11th cent. onwards the old name of Dioclia was gradually replaced by Zeta (in Latin Zenta, or Genta), the name of an affluent of the river Morača. The extent of the country is given at 30/95–8. The population was not purely Slav: a part of the original Illyrian population survived the invasions, and a number of Roman elements found security in the coastal cities. The Byzantines had thus no difficulty in maintaining control over the coastal region, called Maritima in Latin and Primorje or Pomorje in Slav. This region formed part of the *thema* of Dyrrhachion, and the metropolitan of that city exercised jurisdiction over the coastal cities. The rechristianization of Dioclea started from Dyrrhachion. In the period after the invasions the metropolis of Dyrrhachion counted only four bishoprics; but by the end of the 11th cent. it had beneath it five additional sees, Dioclea, Scutari (Skadar), Drivasto, Palati and Antibari, which profoundly influenced the life of the local population. In spite of Byzantine control, it was in Dioclea that began in the 11th cent. the first attempt to form a Slav state which should unite all the Slav peoples from Croatia down to the *thema* of Dyrrhachion, including Serbia proper. However, the kingdom of Dioclea, founded by prince Michael and his son Bodin, was of short duration, and *c.* 1090 Alexius I restored Byzantine supremacy over all the Slav principalities. See Sticotti, *Schriften der Balkankommission*, vi (Wien, 1913), 1 ff., 209 ff.; Jireček, *Geschichte der Serben*, 115 ff.; Šišić, *Geschichte der Kroaten*, 174; *id.*, *Povijest Hrvata*, 456; Dvornik, *The Slavs*, chapters vi, x, pp. 116 ff., 279 ff.; *cf.* Patsch in Pauly-Wissowa, *RE*, v, cols. 1251 f. (Doclea).

35/13   *μεγάλα κάστρα οἰκούμενα.*

These three cities have not yet been certainly identified. Jireček believes that Gradetai stands for Starigrad, which may have been the older name of the city of Budva (Butoba; 29/92), on the coast. Novigrad is perhaps Prevlaka, which guards the peninsula on the south of the Bay of Cattaro. Lontodokla remains a mystery. See Jireček, *Handelsstrassen*, 19–21; Skok, *Toponomastike*, 67 ff.

36/1–13   *Περὶ τῶν Παγανῶν.*

The Pagani are also mentioned at 29/65 and 30/102–12, 122, where additional historical and topographical information about them may be found. The Narentan Slavs differed in many respects from the other Slavs of Dalmatia. The Venetians tried hard to convert them, hoping that Christianity might curb their piracy; but the Narentans were obdurate, and were the last of the southern Slavs to accept Christianity (see 29/81–4). In the 9th cent. the operations of Narentan and Arab pirates hindered communications between Venice and Constantinople; see F. Dvornik, *The Photian Schism* (Cambridge, 1948), 140, 157–8. Moreover, the Narentans were not governed by an archon or župan, as were the other Slavs; they seem to have been subject to a kind of oligarchic régime, in which the direction of political affairs was in the hands of tribal chiefs. John the Deacon speaks of a Narentan chief surrounded by numerous nobles (*MGH*, Scr. vii, 31–3; Rački, *Documenta*, 425, 427), forty of whom were taken prisoner by the Venetians. The Narentan system seems thus to have been similar to that of the Polabian Slavs. The Narentans were scarcely influenced by Croats or Serbs, and seem to have been settled on the coast before the latter entered Illyricum. For C.'s statement that the Pagani are 'descended from the unbaptized Serbs' (36/5–6), see on 33/18–19. It is obvious that the small retinue of the Serbian prince could not have populated Serbia, Zachlumia, Terbounia and Narenta.

36/14–15 κάστρα οἰκούμενα.

Mokron is the old Roman town of Mucru, Muicurum, the ruins of which, now called Makar, may be seen near the port of Makarska; see on 30/106; Farlati, *Illyricum Sacrum*, III, 172; Skok, *Ortsnamenstudien*, 229; Fluss in Pauly-Wissowa, *RE*, XVI, cols. 450, 492 (Muicurum, Mucru). Beroullia is Vrulja, a name still preserved in the Bay of Vrulja. Ostrok, or Ostrog, was situated on a plateau near the mountain called Viter; it is not identical with the village of Zaostrog, on the coast south of Makarska; see Skok, *Topono-mastike*, 3, 70; Banović ('Gdje se je zaprava nalazio srednovjecni neretvanski grad Ostrog?') in *Serta Hoffilleriana* (Zagreb, 1940), 395–9. For Slavinetza (*Σλαβίνετζα*) Skok would read *Λαβίτζανε*, and identify the place with Labčanj, modern Gradac, on the coast between Brist and the Narenta. See Jireček, *Handelsstrassen*, 28; Šišić, *Geschichte der Kroaten*, 170; id., *Povijest Hrvata*, 452; Skok, *Ortsnamenstudien*, 230.

36/15–21 ταύτας τὰς νήσους. See on 30/110.

36/22–3 τὰ Χώαρα κτλ.

For Choara Šišić (*Geschichte der Kroaten*, 170) would read Choaza (*Χόαζα*), and identify it with Sušac-Cassa, which belonged to the Zachlumians. Iës is the ancient Greek colony of Issa, Italian Lissa, now the island of Vis; in C.'s time it belonged to Croatia. Lastobon is Lastovo, belonging to Zachlumia; the island's ancient name was Ladesta, but it was called Lagosta, Lagusta or Langusta in the middle ages, which gave rise to the corruption Insula Augusta; the Serbs called it Lasta in the medieval period; see Jireček, *Handelsstrassen*, 29. See further, Barada, *Starohrvatska Prosvjeta*, n.s., II, 1–2 (1928), 37–54; for the Greek colonization of Issa and Pharos, see Novak, *Strena Hoffilleri-ana* (Zagreb, 1940), 111–28 (with German resúmé); Skok, *Dolazak Slovena*, 119–31; id., *Slavenstvo i romanstvo*, I, 181–97.

Cc. 37–42

BIBLIOGRAPHY

Gy. Czebe, 'Turco-byzantinische Miszellen, 1: Konst. Porph., De Administrando Imperio 37 Kapitel über die Petschenegen'; *Kőrösi Csoma-Archivum*, 1 (1921–5), 209–19 (Czebe). K. Czeglédy, 'A IX századi magyar történelem föbb kérdései', *Magyar Nyelv*, 41 (1945), 33–55 (Czeglédy 1). K.Czeglédy, 'A kangarok (besenyök) a VI. századi szir forrásokban', *A Magyar Tudományos Akadémia nyelv és irodalomtudományi osztályának közleményei*, 5 (1954), 273–6 (Czeglédy II). J. Deér, 'Le problème du chapitre 38 du D.A.I.', *Mélanges H. Grégoire*, IV (Brussels, 1953), 93–121 (Deér). G. Fehér, 'Ungarns Gebietsgrenzen in der Mitte des 10. Jahrhunderts', *Ungarische Jahrbücher*, 2 (1922), 37–69 (Fehér). H. Grégoire, 'Le nom des Hongrois', *Byzantion*, 12 (1937) 645–50 (Grégoire 1). H. Grégoire, 'Le nom et l'origine des Hongrois', *Zeitschr. d. deutsch. morgenländischen Gesellschaft*, 91 (1937), 630–42 (Grégoire II). H. Grégoire, 'L'habitat "primitif" des Magyars', *Byzantion*, 13 (1938), 267–78 (Grégoire III). M. Gyóni, *A magyar nyelv görög feljegyzéses szórványemlékei (Die Streudenkmäler der ungarischen Sprache in gr. Texten)* (Budapest, 1943) (Gyóni). Gy. Györffy, 'Besenyök és magyarok', *Kőrösi Csoma-Archivum*, 1 Erg.-Bd (1939), 397–500 (Györffy 1). Gy Györffy, 'Kurszán és Kurszán vára. A magyar fejedelemség kiala-kulása és Óbuda honfoglaláskori története (Kurzan und Kurzans Burg. Angaben zur Frage des Doppelkönigtums u. zur Geschichte von Óbuda zur Zeit der Landnahme)', *Budapest régiségei*, 16 (1955), 9–40 (Györffy II). J. Harmatta, 'Szines lovú népek', *Magyar Nyelv*, 42 (1946), 26–34

(Harmatta). G. Kuun, *Relationum Hungarorum cum Oriente gentibusque orientalis originis historia antiquissima*, I, II (Claudiopoli, 1892–5) (Kuun). J. Markwart, 'Kultur- und sprachgeschichtliche Analekten', *Ungarische Jahrbücher*, 9 (1929), 68–103 (Markwart). K. H. Menges, 'Etymological Notes on some Päčänäg Names', *Byzantion*, 17 (1944–5), 256–80 (Menges). Gy. Németh, 'Zur Kenntnis der Petschenegen', *Kőrösi Csoma-Archivum*, I (1921–5), 219–25 (Németh I). Gy. Németh, 'Die Petschenegischen Stammesnamen', *Ungarische Jahrbücher*, 10 (1930), 27–34 (Németh II). Gy. Németh, *A honfoglaló magyarság kialakulása* (Budapest, 1930) (Németh III). H Schönebaum, 'Zur Kenntnis der byzantinischen Geschichtsschreiber von der ältesten Geschichte der Ungarn vor der Landnahme', *Ungarische Bibliothek*, Erste Reihe, 5 (Berlin-Leipzig, 1922), 33–49 (Schönebaum). A. Zeki Validi Togan, ' "Ibn Faḍlān's Reisebericht" ', *Abhandlungen für die Kunde des Morgenlands*, XXIV, 3 (Leipzig, 1939) (*Ibn Fadlans Reisebericht*). G. Vernadsky, M. de Ferdinándy, *Studien zur ungarischen Frühgeschichte*, I. Lebedia, II. Álmos; *Südosteuropäische Arbeiten*, 47 (Munich, 1957) (Vernadsky-Ferdinándy).

37 INTRODUCTORY NOTE

This chapter is composed of six sections, relating partly to the history of the Pechenegs (37/2–14, 19–25, 50–7) and partly to their organization (37/15–19, 25–49, 58–71). C. attributed great importance to the Pechenegs (see General Introduction p. 7 and Introductory Note to cc. 1–8, p. 12), and therefore makes a point of explaining in great detail the organization of their clans and the territories occupied by them. The whole of this information appears to come from Pecheneg sources. C. himself tells us how it was obtained, since we read (1/18–20) that every year imperial agents were sent to the Pechenegs for the purpose of maintaining good relations with them. These envoys approached the Pechenegs sometimes by sea to the mouths of the rivers Danube, Dniester and Dnieper (8/5–9), and sometimes invited them to the fort of Cherson (7/3–8), whither the Pechenegs themselves came for trade or to perform some service or other (6/3–5). We also know that Pecheneg hostages were detained, not only at Cherson (7/5–6), but also at Constantinople (1/20–2).

The information in c. 37 cannot be exactly dated, but there is no reason to doubt that all of it is of C.'s own time (*cf.* 37/13–14).

37/2 Πατζινακῖται. See on 1/17.

37/2–3 Ἀτήλ ... Γεήχ.
Turkish names for the Volga and the Ural; see *Byzantinoturcica*, II, 80, 109 (2nd ed., 78, 109); Menges 259, 260. For the original homeland of the Pechenegs, see *Ibn Fadlans Reisebericht*, 140–7.

37/4 Χαζάρους.
See *Byzantinoturcica*, I, 44–6 (2nd ed., 81–6); II, 280–2 (2nd ed., 335–6); M. I. Artamonov, *Ocherki drevneyshey istorii Chazar* (Leningrad, 1936); A. Zajączkowski, *Ze studiów nad zagadnieniem chazarskim* (Kraków, 1947). P reads Μαζάρους; but, despite Macartney 32, this seems to be a slip, since at 37/5 the same ms. gives Χαζάρων. For the form Μάζαροι, see *Byzantinoturcica*, II, 158 (2nd ed., 179).

37/4 Οὔζους. See on 9/114.

37/5 πεντήκοντα. See on 37/13–14.

37/11 Τούρκους.
The invasion and defeat of the Turks by the Pechenegs is also recorded by Regino, ann. 889 (*MGH*, Scr. I, 599–601; *cf. Annales Mettenses* in Duchesne, *Hist. Franc.*, Scr. III, 324–5; both texts also published by A. Gombos, *Catalogus fontium historiae Hungaricae*, I (Budapest, 1937), 156–7, and III, 1938, 2038–9). Regino's words are: 'Anno 889 gens Hungarium (= Hungarorum) ... a Scythicis regnis et a paludibus, quas Thanais sua refusione in

immensum porrigit, egressa est. . . . Ex supradictis igitur locis gens memorata a finitimis sibi populis, qui Pecinaci vocantur, a propriis sedibus expulsa est.' That is to say, according to Regino's information, the Pechenegs drove the Hungarians from the district of the river Don (Thanais): *cf.* Macartney 69–70. For the chronology, see on 37/13–14.

37/13-14   ἔτη πεντήκοντα πέντε.

The number is different from that given above at 37/5. Scholars have made various attempts to explain the discrepancy. Bury (567), like others before him, assumed that the figure πέντε had dropped out of the previous passage, and that 'fifty-five' should be read in both places. Manojlović (IV, 58) thought that originally 'fifty' stood in both passages, but that a copyist added 'five' to the second, with an eye to the year in which he was copying. In the Apparatus of my edition (Vol. I, p. 167) I suggested the possibility that the second passage is corrupt, that the number of years has dropped out after ἔτη, and that the cypher N̄ε stands not for 55 but for Indiction 5; (this conjecture might derive support from the fact that a similar misunderstanding of a numerical cipher is seen at 40/53-4, where P reads δ̄ (τέσσαρας), but the later V and F read δέ.) If this were the case here, the fifth indiction would correspond to 931/2 or 946/7.

But all this is mere conjecture. There is no evidence to provide an accurate dating. None the less, the author's words σήμερον (37/10) and μέχρι τὴν σήμερον (37/13) show that, here as elsewhere, the text refers to C.'s own time; though Manojlović (IV, 95–6) believes that this part of the work was compiled during the reign of Leo VI. It is of the first importance to determine to what event C.'s text here refers: that is to say, where and when did the Pechenegs defeat the Hungarians, and from what place did they expel them? As is well known, C. elsewhere describes *two* attacks by the Pechenegs (38/19–26 and 38/55–60, 40/25–7). The first attack by the Pechenegs, who had been defeated by the Chazars, fell on the Hungarians in their original homeland of Lebedia; the second fell on them in Atelkuzu, where they lived until the Graeco-Bulgarian war of 894–6; (for Grégoire's theory of a single attack by the Pechenegs, see on 38/56–60). Fehér (61–2) maintained that at 37/8–14 the reference is to the *first* Pecheneg attack; but Thúry (*Századok*, 30 (1896), 798) long ago emphasized that the words τὴν σήμερον παρ' αὐτῶν διακρατουμένην γῆν (37/10) and δεσπόζουσι τὴν τοιαύτην χώραν (37/13) must refer to the *second* Pecheneg attack, since in C.'s time the Pechenegs had already possessed themselves of *all* the territory right up to the Danube (*cf.* 5/6; 8/5; 42/20–1). Macartney (83–6) maintains that the figure 50 at 37/5 comes from the original Pecheneg account, and represents Pecheneg memory of the event; whereas the figure 55 at 37/14 was calculated by C., and gives an accurate date for the Graeco-Bulgarian war (894–6), following which the Hungarians were expelled from their seats north of the Danube by the Pechenegs (*cf.* 40/19). If this is so, the composition of C.'s narrative (supposing the figure 55 to be authentic) will date to the years 949–51, which does in fact correspond with the time at which the book was written.

We have still to note the discrepancy, that Regino dates his account to the year 889, and says definitely that the Hungarians were expelled by the Pechenegs from the area of the Don; while C.'s text alludes to the occupation of the Hungarian homeland by the Pechenegs, an event which took place after the Graeco-Bulgarian war, when the Hungarians were living near the mouth of the Danube; see Cont. Geo. Mon. 853/22; Leo, *Taktika*, col. 956 D. We may thus suppose that our passage (37/2–14), which derives from a Pecheneg source, gives only a brief résumé of events relating to the Pechenegs, and therefore speaks of only one Pecheneg attack on the Hungarians, omitting details of history not important to the Pechenegs themselves; and similarly Regino ascribes to the year 889 all the events which took a long period of time to develop, that is, the journey of the Hungarians from the Don up till their conquest of their present territory. C.'s text here, therefore, is not inaccurate, as some scholars have supposed: he is simply quoting the account of his Pecheneg informant.

37/15 θέματα.

This is of course the technical term which connotes a *province* of the Byzantine empire (*cf.* 50/92–166 and on 50/93). It is clear from the following account (37/32–6) that the word means here the territory or homeland of the various Pecheneg clans.

37/16 μεγάλους ἄρχοντας.

The phrase is used elsewhere in the book only with reference to the great prince of the Hungarians and Moravians (40/53; 41/6). The μέγαλοι ἄρχοντες of the Pechenegs are contrasted with the ἐλάττονες ἄρχοντες (37/33). For the formula of imperial γράμματα dispatched to the Pecheneg chiefs, see *De Cer.*, 691/4–7, and *cf.* on 4/10.

37/16–19 τὰ δὲ θέματά εἰσιν ταῦτα κτλ.

The names of the Pecheneg clans are repeated in the same forms at 37/21–4; but at 37/34–45, 68–71, they appear in compound forms. Németh (1) was the first to point out that these compound forms are made up of two elements, the first being the colour of a horse, the second the title of a dignitary. See reference to supplementary notes of Györffy, Harmatta and Moravcsik in *Byzantinoturcica*, II, *s. vv.*; and Menges 260–70. For the constitution of Pecheneg clans in the 11th cent., *cf.* Cedrenus II, 581/23–582/1.

37/20–4 εἶχον ἄρχοντας κτλ.   For the names of the Pecheneg chiefs, see *Byzantinoturcica*, II, *s. vv.*; Menges 265–7.

37/34–45 αἱ τέσσαρες . . . γενεαί κτλ.   For the geographical location of the various Pecheneg clans, see Czebe; G. Fehér, *Kőrösi Csoma-Archivum*, 1 (1921–5), 133.

37/44 τοῖς τε . . . Λενζενίνοις.   See on 9/10 and 33/18–19.

37/46 Μορδίας.

If the reading of P is right, this must refer to the territory of the Mordvinians, a Finno-Ugrian people; but see A. Zeki Validi Togan, *Kőrösi Csoma-Archivum*, 3 (1940), 58–60.

37/51–7 θελήσει τινὲς ἐξ αὐτῶν κτλ.   This is confirmed by Arabic sources: see *Ibn Fadlans Reisebericht*, 144–7; Grégoire, *Byzantion*, 17 (1944–5), 412.

37/59–64 ἐρημόκαστρα κτλ.   For the names of these cities, see Németh 1; Menges 272–3; *Byzantinoturcica*, II, *s. vv.* For Aspron, see on 9/91.

37/68–71 καὶ Κάγγαρ ὀνομάζονται κτλ.

This statement, which derives from a Pecheneg source, is confirmed by 38/20–1, 25. Its correctness is corroborated by the etymology of the word: see *Byzantinoturcica*, II, 132 (2nd ed., 145); Menges 270–1. It is highly significant that the name, in the forms *hangār* and *kangār*, is found in Syrian sources applied to a people who fought with the Persians in the middle of the 6th cent.; see Czeglédy II. For Grégoire's hypothesis (Grégoire 1, 648–50; II, 639–40) that Κάγγαρ is a corruption of Βάγγαρ, which itself is identical with Κάβαροι (39/2–14; 40/1–7), a corrupt form of Βάκαροι (= *Vengry*), see on 39/2. For the significance of the phrase ὡς ἀνδρειότεροι καὶ εὐγενέστεροι, see Czeglédy II, 269–72.

38 Introductory Note

This chapter is in two main sections, 38/3–65, 38/66–71. Various opinions are held as to the sources, especially of the former section. Some think that part of the narrative derives from a Slav source, on the ground that the words βοέβοδος (38/5) and ζάκανον (38/52) are of Slav origin. However, Vernadsky has recently demonstrated the infiltration of these and several other common Slav words into the speech of the Hungarians themselves (Vernadsky-Ferdinándy 21-6). It is moreover to be noted that the word ζάκανον is used also in connexion with the Pechenegs (8/22), and even occurs in 'Suidas' (ed. Adler, II, 9, *s.v.* δατόν): so that it can be regarded as a common locution even in Middle Greek. The word βοέβοδος (see Gyóni 33-4) may have been used by C.'s informant merely to distinguish the earlier Hungarian 'chiefs' from their later 'princes'; though Vernadsky sees in its use an indication of Slavonic influence in the Hungarian ruling class at an early date (Vernadsky-Ferdinándy 24). Macartney (98-9) distinguishes two sources of information, a Slavonic for 38/3-23, and a Hungarian for 38/31-60. Grégoire (II, 632-3) thinks that the first section consists of two parts (38/3-19, 38/19-65) which are versions of the same events and constitute 'doublets' one of another: see on 38/56-60. More recent research has led to the conclusion that 38/3-65 derives from Hungarian sources; see Deér 103-6.

We know that Byzantium was in close touch with the Hungarians and that Byzantine envoys were often sent to their country. In 894, that is even before the Hungarian conquest of their present territory, Niketas Skleros was sent to them by Leo VI, and met their chiefs somewhere near the mouth of the Danube in order to conclude with them an alliance against the Bulgarians; see Cont. Geo. Mon. 853/20-854/1; Theoph. Cont. 358/7-10. The mission of the cleric Gabriel is an important instance of contact at a later date (see on 8/23, 30); and C. himself relates (40/63-5) how the great-grandson of Arpad, together with the third prince of the Turks, visited the Byzantine court. That court therefore had several opportunities for obtaining information about the Hungarians. Bury (565) believed that the report of the cleric Gabriel (8/23-33) might have served as the source of this chapter, though this cannot be established with certainty. See further Bury 564-6; Manojlović IV, 117-26; Macartney 98-103. Our own opinion (*cf.* Deér, 107, 113-14) is that 38/3-65 derives from one or more *Hungarian* sources: that is to say, it is compiled from notices written down at the imperial court from accounts given by various Hungarian informants. At all events it is remarkable that C. had at his disposal more detailed information about early Hungarian history than he had about the early history of any other nation; *cf.* Vernadsky-Ferdinándy 48, note 21.

38/3-65 "Ὅτι τὸ τῶν Τούρκων ἔθνος κτλ.

Some details about the life of the Hungarian people prior to their conquest of modern Hungary are preserved in Islamic sources, whose notices relate to the years 870-89; these notices are published in the collection *A magyar honfoglalás kútföi* (Budapest, 1900), 139-284; and *cf.* Czeglédy 1. Scholars have noted that the information of these Islamic (Arab and Persian) writers does not agree with that of C., and have made various attempts to explain apparent discrepancies. According to one theory (Czeglédy 1) the accounts of C. (38/3-65) and of the Islamic sources do not refer to the same domicile of the Hungarians, and the latter are describing a period of Hungarian history not mentioned by C. since he knew nothing about it. A second theory (Deér) maintains on the contrary that C.'s narrative reproduces a Hungarian dynastic tradition which was communicated to him by his Hungarian guests. On this second hypothesis, 38/3-65 is a medley of folk-tale and historical elements of the Hungarian past, beginning with Lebedias, who, as Deér believes, lived as long before as the 8th cent., and going down to Arpad, the famous hero of the *Landnahme*. More recently another theory (Györffy II) has been put forward, according to which Arpad's great-grandson, from whom C. derived the information in 38/3-65, gave the Byzantine court a deceptive account of events preceding the *Landnahme* in order to convince the emperor of the legality of Arpad's dynasty, omitting to mention that Arpad, as Györffy thinks, after the death of his co-ruler Kursan (Cont. Geo. Mon. 854) in 904, seized the supreme power without opposition. In this way Györffy reconciles the contradiction that the Islamic sources speak of a double princedom among the Hungarians, whereas C. makes no mention of this. It will thus be seen that the problems connected with c. 38 are as yet far from being satisfactorily solved.

38/4 Λεβεδία.

The form of the name is no doubt Greek (*cf.* Ἀλανία, Τουρκία, Χαζαρία etc.); but it is quite possible that the Hungarians themselves called the place *Levedi*, as C. says. after their voivode Levedi, since in Old Hungarian personal names are also used as territorial determinatives; see Gyóni 81–2; *Byzantinoturcica*, II, 157 (2nd ed., 177). The precise location of Lebedia is not stated. We are told at 38/8–9 that 'there runs a river Chidmas, also called Chingilous'; but the names are not found elsewhere, and hitherto no sure identification has been made with any known river. Some identify it with the river Συγγούλ (?Ὕγγουλ: 42/58); but the Syngoul itself is unknown to other sources. The Chidmas/Chingilous has been sought by scholars in the following rivers: Kodyma, Inchul or Inchulets, Orel, Molotchnaya, Donets and Don: see Schönebaum 34, 42; Macartney 91; while Lebedia itself has been located on the Dnieper, between the Dnieper and the Don, near the Don and Donets, and on the banks of the Meotis and the Kuban. Of late, the majority of scholars incline to the view that Lebedia lay west of the Don. In C.'s day the eastern frontier of Patzinacia was the Don, whereas C. says (37/9–14) that the Pechenegs took the land of the Hungarians. See finally Vernadsky-Ferdinándy 14–17, where the boundaries of Lebedia are suggested on the evidence of existing place-names.

38/5 τοῦ πρώτου βοεβόδου.

Cf. 38/12, 16, 33, 37; the expression 'first voivode', despite the passage 38/43–4, is ambiguous. It may mean first in chronological order, or else first in rank. The words ὡς καὶ οἱ λοιποὶ μετ' αὐτόν (38/6–7) are especially difficult. At 40/48 πρώτην indicates rank; but 'after him', both here and elsewhere in Middle Greek texts, may be used either in respect of rank (*cf.* Kinnamos, 262/22; Cedrenus II, 405/19) or in respect of time (*cf.* 44/9; Menandros, *Excerpta de Legationibus*, ed. de Boor, 195/14). Schönebaum (38) understands οἱ λοιποί as the 'successors' of Lebedias; but see Deér 93–7. It may be that the Byzantine official who transcribed the account of his Hungarian informant was not very clear as to what was meant.

38/6 Λεβεδίας.

The name is not found in other sources. Hungarian scholars see in it the Hungarian form *Levedi*; see on 38/4. Manojlović (IV, 96–7) regards Lebedias as a mythical figure; but Deér (101–2) believes him to have existed, but to have lived in the middle of the 8th cent. Vernadsky derives the name from Slav *lebed'*, a swan (Vernadsky-Ferdinándy 17–21).

38/8 Χιδμάς . . . Χιγγιλοὺς.   See on 38/4 and 42/58–9.

38/9 Σάβαρτοι ἄσφαλοι.

See 38/28. The name is variously interpreted: see Gyóni 112–14; *Byzantinoturcica*, II, 223–4 (2nd ed., 261–2); Grégoire III, 276–7. It is in all probability related to the name of the Savirs and means 'invincible Savartians'. Armenian and Arab sources mention a people called 'Sevordi' which in the 8th cent. lived near the river Kour, on the northern border of Persarmenia; scholars believe this people to be identical with C.'s Savartians. See also *De Cer.*, 687/13–14 (Σερβοτιῶν τῶν λεγομένων Μαῦρα παιδία); Macartney 87–8; Németh III, 316–18; Deér 97; Czeglédy II, 272–6.

38/10–11 γενεαὶ ὑπῆρχον ἑπτά.

Cf. 39/10–12; 40/3–6. The tradition of seven clans is preserved also in Hungarian sources; *cf.* Simonis de Keza, *Gesta Hungarorum*, cap. 26 (*Scriptores rerum Hungaricarum*, I, 165). See also Leo, *Taktika*, col. 957 B.

38/11–12 ἄρχοντα . . . οὐκ ἐκτήσαντο.   *Cf.* 38/53–4; Deér 119–20.

38/13–14 ἐνιαυτοὺς τρεῖς.

Most scholars believe that the text is corrupt here, and that for τρεῖς one should read 300 (Grégoire II, 636; Deér 108, note 2; Vernadsky-Ferdinándy 14), or 200 (c for Γ, Moravcsik), or 20 (Marquart 33). In the Apparatus to Vol. I, p. 171, I proposed the correction συμμαχῶν τε for συμμαχοῦντες, which, if right, would refer not to the Turks in general, but to Lebedias. But it is only a bold guess.

38/15 Χαγάνος. See *Byzantinoturcica*, II, 280 (2nd ed., 333).

39/19–23 Οἱ δὲ Πατζινακῖται κτλ. *Cf.* 37/5–14.

38/20, 25 Κάγγαρ. See on 37/68–71.

38/26–31 Καὶ τὸ μὲν ἕν μέρος κτλ.

Cf. 38/61–5. But the eastward migration of the Savartoi asphaloi cannot have been precipitated by the Pecheneg attack, which had taken place, according to Regino, as recently as 889 (see on 37/11). It must have happened much earlier than this, because the Savartians lived on the north border of Persarmenia as early as the 8th cent.: see on 38/9. Perhaps C.'s informant confused the Hungaro-Pecheneg war of 889 with an earlier war between Kangars (Pechenegs) and Savartians: see Czeglédy II, 274–6.

38/30 Ἀτελκούζου.

The name occurs again at 40/24, in the form Ἐτὲλ καὶ Κουζοῦ. It no doubt represents the Old Hungarian Etel-küzü, which means 'between the rivers' or 'Mesopotamia'; see Gyóni 23; *Byzantinoturcica*, II, 79 (2nd ed., 77). However, since the first element of the compound (Ἀτελ-, Ἐτέλ) may also be the name of a specific river, it is possible that the meaning is 'the territory of, or about, a specific river' (the Volga, 37/2; or the Don or Dnieper). The question is still not finally solved. C. gives no details as to the location of Atelkuzu; we may only conclude that it lay west of Lebedia. It was formerly held that the position was accurately defined at 38/66–71; but, as we know, the τῶν Πατζινακιτῶν τόπος in C.'s time stretched from the Don to the Danube, and this area obviously cannot be identical with Atelkuzu, since it comprehended Lebedia as well. Some scholars have in fact tried to identify Atelkuzu with Lebedia (*e.g.* Macartney 90–6; Grégoire II, 635) but this hardly agrees with 38/3–4, 30–1, where both territories are mentioned in accurate chronological order. Vernadsky places Atelkuzu mainly west of Lebedia, though partly overlapping it on the east (Vernadsky-Ferdinándy 14).

38/33 Λεβεδία. An obvious correction for the meaningless χελάνδια of P.

38/40–6 Τὴν περὶ ἐμὲ κτλ. The words of Lebedias, if authentic, appear to be the earliest instance of Hungarian speech translated into Greek; *cf.* 8/29–33.

38/43 Ἀλμούτζης.

He appears in Hungarian sources as Almus (= Álmos); see *Scriptores rerum Hungaricarum*, I–II (Budapest, 1937–8), Index, *s.v.*; *cf.* Gyóni 16–18; *Byzantinoturcica*, II, 69 (2nd ed., 63). That Álmos was in fact the first prince, and not his son Arpad, is maintained by Deér 109–10, 114–15. For his semi-legendary origins and historical importance, see Vernadsky–Ferdinándy 26–8, 35 ff.

39/44 Ἀρπαδήν.

In Hungarian sources Arpad (= Árpád); see *Scriptores rerum Hungaricarum*, I–II, Index, *s.v.*; *cf.* Gyóni 19–20; *Byzantinoturcica*, II, 74–5 (2nd ed., 71).

38/53 εἰς σκουτάριον.
This usual method of proclaiming a sovereign was already in existence in Roman and Byzantine ceremonial; see Treitinger, 20–3; Ostrogorsky, *Historia*, 4 (1955), 252–6.

38/53–5 Πρὸ δὲ τοῦ ᾿Αρπαδῆ κτλ. *Cf.* 38/10–12.

38/56–60 ἐπιπεσόντες οἱ Πατζινακῖται κτλ.
See 40/13–22. This second attack of the Pechenegs (896) compelled the Turks to settle in the land where 'they now live to this day'; *cf.* 40/7–27; 13/6–7; 41/19–27; 51/103–20. Grégoire (II, 633, 635), believing that in this chapter we have a 'doublet', or two accounts of the same incident, concludes that the Pechenegs attacked the Turks once only; see the Introductory Note to this chapter. But this is at variance with C.'s statements that the Turks have *often* (πολλάκις) been attacked by the Pechenegs, although not since their migration to modern Hungary; see 3/2–5; 8/23; 38–60–1.

38/58 Μοραβίαν. *Cf.* 13/5; 41/1.

38/62–5 εἰς τὰ τῆς Περσίδος μέρη. See on 38/26–31.

38/66–71 ὁ τῶν Πατζινακιτῶν τόπος κτλ. See on 38/30.

38/68 Βαρούχ. Probably the Pecheneg name for the Dnieper; see Marquart 33, 190, 505; Manojlović IV, 65; Schönebaum 44; Macartney 54.

38/69 Κουβοῦ. Pecheneg name for the Bug (Βογοῦ, 42/59). See Marquart 33, 505; Manojlović IV, 65; Schönebaum 44.

38/70 Τροῦλλος. In later sources Turla; a Turkish name of the Dniester; see Marquart 33, 190; Manojlović IV, 65; Schönebaum 44; Macartney 54.

38/70 Βροῦτος. The modern Pruth; see Marquart 33; Manojlović IV, 4; Schönebaum 44.

38/71 Σέρετος. The modern Sereth; see Marquart 33; Manojlović IV, 4; Schönebaum 44.

39/2 Κάβαροι.
The name is of Turkish origin: see Gyóni 61–82; *Byzantinoturcica*, II, 132 (2nd ed., 144); Menges 274. Grégoire, who believes that the Pecheneg name Κάγγαρ (37/68–71) is a corruption of Βάγγαρ, thinks that the name Κάβαροι is similarly corrupted from Βάκαροι, and identifies the latter with the Slavonic form of the Hungarian name Vangar (*Vengry*): see Grégoire I, 648–50; II, 639–40. But the form Κάβαροι occurs several times in *DAI* (see Index to Vol. I, p. 298), and it is hard to think every instance corrupt. Moreover, the authenticity of the form is witnessed by the fact that the name 'Cowari' is found in a western source in connexion with events of the year 881: see *Annales ex Annalibus Juvavensibus antiquis excerpti*, ed. Bresslau, *MGH*, Scr. xxx, 2, 742; *cf.* Shünemann, *Ungarische Jahrbücher*, 2 (1922), 221; Macartney 76. Schönebaum (*Aus der byz. Arbeit d. deutsch. demokrat. Republik*, 1 (1957), 142–6) will identify the Kabaroi with the people of Choresm, in Central Asia ('Chwār, Chowār, die aus Ch⟨w⟩oresm Stammenden'), a people of mixed stock and judaïzing religion; they joined the Chazars, he believes, after their expulsion from Choresm by the Arabs in 712; and in 780 revolted against the Chazar government (the πρώτη ἀρχή of 39/4), by whom they were again expelled and joined up with the Turks.

39/6 κατεσκήνωσαν μετὰ τῶν Τούρκων. In 780, according to Schönebaum, and certainly before 881 : see the preceding note.

39/7–10 Ὅθεν καὶ τὴν τῶν Χαζάρων γλῶσσαν κτλ.
A disputed passage, since the wording, as in other parts of the chapter, is not at all clear. The following solutions are possible: (a) that οἱ Κάβαροι is the subject of all three clauses; (b) that οἱ Κάβαροι is the subject of the first clause, and οἱ Τοῦρκοι of the second and third; (c) that οἱ Κάβαροι is the subject of the first clause, οἱ Τοῦρκοι of the second and οἱ Κάβαροι again of the third: see Marquart 53; Manojlović IV, 119; Schönebaum 39, 45; Németh III, 17, 234; Ibn Fadlans Reisebericht, 200. But, however we take it, the passage testifies to the fact that the Hungarians, owing to their association with the Kabaroi, became bilingual.

39/10–12 Διὰ δὲ τὸ . . . πρῶται γενεαί. See 40/3–4

39/11 τῶν ὀκτὼ γενεῶν. Contrast 38/10–11, which probably refers to a time when the Kabaroi had not yet united with the Turks.

39/13 ἐν ταῖς τρισὶ γενεαῖς. That is to say, the Kabaroi were divided in three clans of their own, but in the Hungarian clan organization they formed one single clan, the first.

39/13–14 μέχρι τὴν σήμερον ἔστιν.
This must mean that the *principle* of a single Kabaran prince is in force at the time of writing. An individual prince appointed before 881 could not have been still alive in 951 : still less one appointed, according to Schönebaum's theory (see on 39/2), in the late 8th cent.; ἔστιν here is therefore not parallel with ἔχει; at 50/120.

40/1–3 Περὶ τῶν γενεῶν κτλ. For the connexion of the heading, or title, with what follows it, see General Introduction p. 8.

40/3–4 Πρώτη . . . γενεά. See 39/3–7, 12.

40/4–6 δευτέρα . . .Κασῆ.
The text gives the impression that these names appearing in the genitive case (τοῦ Νέκη . . . τοῦ Μεγέρη) are forms of personal names (ὁ Νέκης . . . ὁ Μεγέρης); but there is no doubt that it is the Hungarian tribal names that are given. The construction in all probability corresponds to the Old Hungarian mode of expression. For the etymology of these names, the first and second of which are Finno-Ugrian and all the rest of Turkic origin, see Németh III, 241–73; Gyóni 96, 90, 70–2, 128, 40–1, 66–8; Byzantinoturcica, II, 182, 164, 150–1, 253, 104, 139–40 (2nd ed., 210, 186, 169–70, 299, 109, 154–5).

40/6–7 Καὶ οὕτως . . . γῆν. See 39/6–7.

40/7–12 Μετὰ δὲ ταῦτα . . . ὑπέστρεψαν.
Details about the Bulgaro-Byzantine war of 894–6 are found in many other sources: see 51/110–24; Leo, *Taktika*, col. 956 C–D; Cont. Geo. Mon. 853/1–855/16 (see ed. Moravcsik, *Antik Tanulmányok* 4 (1957), 285–8); Theoph. Cont. 357/12–360/17; *Chronika Georgiya Amartola v drevnem slavyanorusskom perevode*, II (ed. Istrin, Petrograd, 1922), 27–8; *Annales Fuldenses* (*MGH*, Scr. 1), 412; *Chudo svyatogo Georgiya o Bulgarine* (ed. Loparev, *Pamyatniki drevney pismennosti*, 100 (St Petersburg, 1894)). Abstracts are collected in *A magyar honfoglalás kutfői* (Budapest, 1900), 317, 355–61, 373. For the modern literature, see Macartney 177–88; also G. Kolias, *Léon Choerosphactès, magistre, proconsul et patrice* (Athens, 1939), 24–34; Ἀρχεῖον τοῦ Θρακικοῦ Λαογραφικοῦ Θησαυροῦ 7 (1940–1), 348–9; Ostrogorsky² 205–6; Zlatarsky, *Sbornik za narodni umotvorenija, nauka i knižnina*, 24 (1908), 90–101.

40/8–9 προσκληθέντες διεπέρασαν. Marquart (52–3, 522) thought that the subject of the sentence was not the Turks but the Kabaroi; see however Bury 563 and note 1.

40/10 Πρεσθλάβου. The Bulgarian city of Preslav.

40/11 Μουνδράγα. Bulgarian locality, identified with the present day Madara; cf. Cont. Geo. Mon. 855/7.

40/12 Λιούντικα. It is to be noted that this person is not mentioned among the sons of Árpád in the genealogy of the royal house (40/53–55). Németh III, 286, identifies him with Tarkatzous (40/54), believing that he had two names. Grégoire I, 647, identifies him with the Lebedias of 38/6.

40/13–19 Μετὰ δὲ τὸ πάλιν κτλ.
Symeon's alliance with the Pechenegs and the Pecheneg attack on the Turks are not mentioned in other sources, but cf. 38/55–60. The expression τὰς αὐτῶν φαμιλίας παντελῶς ἐξηφάνισαν (40/17–18) seems to be an exaggeration.

40/19–22 Οἱ δὲ Τοῦρκοι κτλ.
For the conquest by the Turks of their present country, see also 13/6–7, 38/57–60, 40/25–7, 33–4, 41/21–3. The facts that Symeon incited the Pechenegs against the Hungarians and that the latter, as a result of their defeat, began to occupy their present territory, are not elsewhere recorded.

40/22 ἀνωτέρω, ὡς εἴρηται.
There has previously been no mention of this, but see below 40/37–8; we must therefore conclude that these words are a mistaken insertion by a copyist; see Manojlović IV, 110; Macartney 142; Fehér 48.

40/24 Ἐτὲλ καὶ Κουζοῦ.
Cf. on 38/30. The text is not clear. Some scholars understand the reference to be to two rivers (Ἐτὲλ and Κουζοῦ) and have proposed to correct the text as follows: τῶν ἐκεῖσε διερχομένων ποταμῶν (e.g. Marquart 33, note 3). But if the designation Ἀτελκούζου (38/30) is 'river-country', 'the country of a particular river', the reference is to one river only. If this is so, we can understand the sentence in one of two ways: (a) the river flowing there is called Etel and Kouzou (in this case Ἐτὲλ καὶ Κουζοῦ is a mistake for Ἐτελ-κούζου); or (b) the river Etel which flows there is also called Kouzou. Of these two interpretations (b) gives unsatisfactory sense; so that probably καὶ has been inserted in error between the two halves of the word Ἐτελ-κούζου.

40/28 Τραϊανοῦ γέφυρα. Its remains, opposite Turnu Severin, are to be seen today.

40/29 ἡ Βελέγραδα. See Index to Vol. I, p. 292. It is the modern Beograd, and the ancient Singidunum.

40/31 κατὰ τὴν τοῦ ποταμοῦ ἀναδρομήν.
The expression may derive from the ancient belief that the Danube joined the Adriatic Sea along the Save, which was regarded as a kind of 'turning back' of the Danube: cf. Pliny, Nat. Hist., III, 127–8.

40/33 ἡ μεγάλη Μοραβία. See 13/5, 41/2.

40/34 Σφενδοπλόκος. See 41/2.

40/37-8 τῶν ἐκεῖσε ῥεόντων ποταμῶν. See 40/22.

40/38 Τιμήσης. The modern Temes; see Gyóni 134-5.

40/38 Τούτης. Unknown river; see Gyóni 138.

40/39 Μορήσης. The modern Maros; see Gyóni 92.

40/40 Κρίσος. The modern Körös; see Gyóni 75-6.

40/40 Τίτζα. The modern Tisza; see Gyóni 136; Szádeczky-Kardoss, *Acta Ant. Acad. Sci. Hung.*, 2 (1953), 89.

40/41-4 Πλησιάζουσι δὲ τοῖς Τούρκοις κτλ.
Cf. 13/3-8. For the problems arising, see Bury 564; Manojlović ıv, 116; Fehér 44-69. *Cf.* on 13/5, and General Introduction p. 7.

40/44 ὀκτὼ γενεαί. *Cf.* 39/11, 40/3-6.

40/46 εἰς τοὺς ποταμούς.
There is no need to emend. The meaning is that the Hungarian clans, joined together in a still loose confederation, will when attacked unite to defend themselves upon the *rivers*, along the two banks of which the territory of each clan extended. Rivers played a large part in the life of the Hungarians, as in that of all nomads; see 38/8, 66-71; 40/22-4, 37-40; and *cf.* Fehér 48.

40/47-8 Ἔχουσι δὲ κεφαλὴν κτλ. See 38/53-5.

40/49 γυλᾶν.
See Glossary to Vol. ı, p. 318; *cf.* 40/51-2. Old Hungarian dignity, and also a proper name, the modern Gyula: see Gyóni 43-5; *Byzantinoturcica*, ıı, 109 (2nd ed., 115).

40/49 καρχᾶν. See Glossary to Vol. ı, p. 322; *cf.* 40/51-2. Old-Hungarian dignity: see Gyóni 60-1; *Byzantinoturcia*, ıı, 139 (2nd ed., 155).

40/53-65 Ἰστέον, ὅτι ὁ Ἀρπαδῆς κτλ.
For this genealogical tree of Arpad, see Bury 563; Manojlović ıv, 124; Schönebaum 49; Macartney 109. It is noteworthy that C. gives no such details about any other royal house. See also on 40/12.

40/54 Ταρκατζοῦν. Perhaps identical with Λιούντικα (*cf.* on 40/12). See Gyóni 129-30; *Byzantinoturcica*, ıı, 253 (2nd ed., 300).

40/54 Ἰέλεχ. See Gyóni 58; *Byzantinoturcica*, ıı, 125 (2nd ed., 136).

40/55 Ἰουτοτζᾶν. See Gyóni 60-1; *Byzantinoturcica*, ıı, 128 (2nd ed., 140).

40/55 Ζαλτᾶν. See Gyóni 54-5; *Byzantinoturcica*, ıı, 119 (2nd ed., 129).

40/57 Τεβέλη. See Gyóni 131; *Byzantinoturcica*, ıı, 256 (2nd ed., 303).

40/57 Ἐζέλεχ. See Gyóni 48-9; *Byzantinoturcica*, ıı, 114 (2nd ed., 121).

40/58 Φαλίτζιν. See Gyóni 139; *Byzantinoturcica*, ıı, 278 (2nd ed., 331). He is the same as Φαλῆς (40/61).

40/59 *Ταξίν.* See Gyóni 128–9; *Byzantinoturcica*, II, 252 (2nd ed., 298); Liudprand, *Antapodosis*, V, 33.

40/61 *Φαλῆς.* See on 40/58.

40/61 *Τασῆς.*
His parentage is not clear, as he is not mentioned in the list of Árpád's grandsons at 40/56–9; see Gyóni 130; *Byzantinoturcica*, II, 253–4 (2nd ed., 300).

40/64 *Τερματζοῦς.* See Gyóni 132–3; *Byzantinoturcica*, II, 258–9 (2nd ed., 306).

40/64 *Βουλτζοῦ.*
See Gyóni 36–7; *Byzantinoturcica*, II, 102 (2nd ed., 107). Termatzous who 'came up' to the imperial court is not mentioned by other sources; but Skylitzes (Cedrenus II, 328/3–20) has a detailed account of the visit of this other chief, whom he calls Boulosoudis (*Βουλοσουδής*): see Moravcsik, *American Slavic and East European Review*, 6 (1947), 136–7. The term *φίλος* indicates that Árpád's descendant had received from the imperial court the honorary title of 'friend', for which see on 8/18. The visit of the Hungarian chiefs must have taken place in or about the year 948.

40/66 *Καλῆ.* See Gyóni 64–6; *Byzantinoturcica*, II, 134 (2nd ed., 147).

40/67 *Καλῆ.* C. here cites the name in the genitive case, as it had stood in the previous line.

41/2 *Μοραβία.*
See 13/5, 38/58; *cf.* Bury 566; Marquart 115–22; Manojlović IV, 106–14; Macartney 147–51; F. Dvornik, *Légendes*, 235–47; *id.*, *The Making of Central and Eastern Europe* (London, 1949), 19–22.

41/2 *Σφενδοπλόκος.* The ruler of Moravia, *Svetoplъkъ (†894). See Melich, *Magyar Nyelv*, 18 (1922), 110–14.

41/3–19 *"Εσχεν δὲ ὁ αὐτὸς κτλ.*
For ancient versions of this tale, see Apparatus to Vol. I, 180. *Cf.* also Tille, *Revue des Etudes Slaves*, 5 (1925), 82–4; Lambrev, *Istoricheski Pregled*, 3 (1947), 350–9. It forms a characteristic element in the matter of the original *Περὶ ἐθνῶν*: see General Introduction p. 3.

41/19 *Μετὰ δὲ τὴν τελευτὴν κτλ.*
Svatopluk died in 894, and the civil war among his sons therefore broke out in 896: see Bury 566. How soon after this the Turks came, and by what stages, are still matters of dispute. 41/19–25 are of course historical notices, to be distinguished from the legendary matter of 41/3–19; although, if *Annales Fuldenses* (ann. 894) is to be trusted, 'Zwentibaldus, dux Maravorum' did in fact close his life 'hortando suos'. With *ἔριδος καὶ στάσεως* (41/20), *cf. ibid.*, ann. 898, 'dissensio atque discordia'.

41/21–3 *ἐλθόντες οἱ Τοῦρκοι.* See 13/6–7; 38/57–60; 40/25–7, 33–4.

42 INTRODUCTORY NOTE
This chapter falls into two main divisions: 42/15–23, 55–110; and 42/23–55. The former is taken from an Itinerary of the northern border of the empire from Belgrade to the Caucasus, fragments of which appear also at 40/27–34 (*cf.* Macartney 140–3), and

perhaps again at 37/58–67. The latter, dealing with the foundation of Sarkel and the incorporation of Cherson as an imperial province (*cf.* Manojlović IV, 128), is an inserted historical narrative which appears in another version at Theoph. Cont. 122/19–124/5: see on 42/22–55, and Introductory Note to 29/54–216. We have here an interesting instance of the patchwork composition of *DAI*; and it is important to note that the two elements are not separated by any paragraph or ἰστέον, ὅτι.

The date of composition of c. 42 is uncertain. If Macartney (143) is right in thinking that 42/62–4 implies a knowledge of c. 37, we may date c. 42 to 951/2. 42/18–22 at least makes clear that the Itinerary was compiled after 906; and the use of the Thessalonica–Belgrade route as a normal post-road seems to imply a date after 927: see on 42/17.

42/15 Δανουβέως. See Gyóni 45–6.

42/16 Βελέγραδα. See on 40/29.

42/17 ἡμερῶν ὀκτώ.
For this route, see Manojlović IV, 9–10. There is no need to emend 8 to 18, with Marquart (241): a mounted man on a post road could 'comfortably' cover 450 miles in eight days, and the imperial 'swift post' would probably have covered them in four. The route could hardly have been open to imperial traffic till after the death of Symeon of Bulgaria (927): *cf.* Jireček, *Die Heerstrasse von Belgrad nach Constantinopel* (Prague, 1877), 76–7; Marquart 241.

42/19 Μοραβίας. See on 41/2 (Μοραβίας).

42/20 Σάβα. The modern Sava: see Gyóni 117.

42/21 Δίστρας. The Bulgarian city of Dristra, ancient Dorostolum.

42/22–55 μέχρι τοῦ Σάρκελ κτλ.
Cf. Theoph. Cont. 122/19–124/5, where we find the same story in a much more literary style. It seems that both accounts derive from the same source: see Moravcsik, *Atti del V Congresso internaz. di stud. biz.*, I (Rome, 1939), 519, and Introductory Note to c. 29/56–216.

42/24 Σάρκελ.
Cf. 11/8. For ἄσπρον ὀσπίτιον Theoph. Cont. has the more literary λευκὸν οἴκημα: see *Byzantinoturcica*, II, 229 (2nd ed., 268–9). For the name Sarkel, see Menges 257–9; Czeglédy, *Magyar Nyelv*, 48 (1952), 79–86 and 49 (1953), 175–8; Harmatta, *ibid.*, 178–83.

42/24–5 ἐκτίσθη παρὰ . . . Πετρωνᾶ.
For the date of this construction (*c.* 833), see Bury, *ERE*, 416. It is not clear whether this Petronas is to be identified with the famous brother-in-law of Theophilus, for whom see Theoph. Cont. 946, *s.v.*, and *Anal. Boll.*, 18 (1899), 252; 62 (1954), 187 ff.; also *De Cer.*, 647/22. Bury, *ERE*, 524, distinguishes the two. It may be significant that a 9th cent. seal found at Cherson has the inscription of a Πετρωνᾷ ἀνθυπάτῳ πατρικίῳ βασιλικῷ καὶ γενικῷ λογοθέτῃ (Vishnyakova, *Vestnik Drevney Istorii*, I, 6 (1939), 123, 129). It is possible that this Petronas was father of Basil I's eparch Marian (Cont. Geo. Mon. 839/5–6), and grandfather of Basil Camaterus (*ibid.*, 863/22). For the Camaterus family, see *BZ*, 34 (1934), 352–8; Schlumberger, *Sigillographie*, 629; Βυζαντίς I (1909), 476.

42/27 χαγάνος . . . πὲχ. See *Byzantinoturcica*, II, 214, 280 (2nd ed., 333, 250); *cf.* Bury, *ERE*, 404–5.

42/29 ᾐτήσαντο.

Why this fort was constructed is disputed. Some think it was a defence against the Pechenegs (see Theoph. Cont. 122/23–4; Cedrenus II, 130/1–3); but at that time the Pechenegs still lived far from the Don: cf. 37/2–3. Others have thought that it was built against the Russians: cf. Bury, ERE, 417. But most scholars believe it to have been built against the Hungarians, and indeed one Arab source hints that this was so: see Marquart 28–9; Manojlović IV, 28–9; Ostrogorsky² 169, note 1.

42/45–6 ὁ τὰ πάντα . . . πρωτεύων.

For the pre-thematic administration of Cherson, see Bréhier, Institutions, 209–10. The πρωτεύων was still an imperial official in the 10th cent.: cf. Cedrenus II, 372/8–9.

42/54–5 ἡ τοῦ Σάρκελ . . . καθέστηκεν.

The site of Sarkel was discovered by Russian excavators near the village of Tsimliansk on the left bank of the Don: see M. T. Aramonov, Srednevekovye poseleniya na nizhnem Donou (Leningrad, 1935); id., Voprosy Istorii 1949, no. 10, 138–43; 1951, no. 4, 147–51; and id., Acta Arch. Acad. Sc. Hung., 7 (1956), 321–41. For the date, see on 42/25.

42/58–9 Συγγοὺλ . . . Βογοῦ.

Of these rivers the Syngoul (?Yngoul) is unknown, but has been identified with the Chidmas/Chingilous: see on 38/4. The Hybyl and the Almatai are likewise unknown. The Kouphis has been identified with the Κοῦφις mentioned by Theophanes (356/27, 357/9, 434/11); cf. Nicephorus, ed. de Boor, 33/15, who calls it Κῶφις. However, Theophanes is perhaps confusing two rivers, since in other sources we find Κωφήν as a name for the Kuban, whose ancient name was the same as the ancient name of the Bug, i.e. Hypanis. The Bogou is the modern Bug: see Manojlović IV, 3. Marquart (505) proposed to read ὁ Κοῦφις ὁ καὶ Βογοῦ. For the Syngoul, see most recently the study of Fehér, noticed in BZ, 53 (1960), 459.

42/63 Σαράτ, Βουράτ. The Sarat and the Bourat seem to be the same as the Sereth and the Pruth of 38/70–1.

42/65 Δανάστρεως.

The distance given forces us to correct the Δανάπρεως of P to Δανάστρεως: see F. Westberg, Die Fragmente des Toparcha Goticus (Mém. de l'Acad. imp. de S.-Péterbourg, V, 2, (1901), 97–8). For the Gold Coast, cf. Manojlović IV, 4, note 5.

42/68 τὰ Ἀδαρά. See Duchesne-Guillemin, Byzantion, 12 (1937), 737–9.

42/69 τὰ Νεκρόπυλα.

Cf. Theophanes 357/1, 373/21, 434/12; Nicephorus, ed. De Boor, 41/24. It is the ancient Karkinitic Gulf: see Westberg, op. cit., 98–9.

42/72 τὰ κάστρα τῶν κλιμάτων. See on 1/28.

42/76 πρὸς μὲν τὸ ἀρκτῷον κτλ. See Westberg, op. cit., 99.

42/77 μαύρην Βουλγαρίαν. See on 12/1.

42/78 Συρίαν. See M. V. Levchenko, Ocherki po istorii russko-vizantiiskikh otnoshenii (Moscow, 1956), 192.

42/80 σοῦδαν . . . ποιησάμενοι.

This operation is often mentioned in antiquity; see Herodotus IV, 3; Ptolemy, Geogr., III, 6, 5; Steph. Byz. s.v., τάφροι. For the word σοῦδα, see Index to Vol. I, p. 329, s.v.; and for its especial usage here see Grégoire, Byzantion, 12 (1937), 295–7.

42/88 *Χαράκουλ.*   Unknown river: see *Byzantinoturcica*, II, 285 (2nd ed., 340); Menges 276.

42/88 *βερζήτικον.*
See *Byzantinoturcica*, II, 88 (2nd ed., 89); Menges 276; Koukoulès in *EEBΣ*, 20 (1950), 346; Vasiliev, *Justin the First* (Cambridge, Mass., 1950), 357, note 27.

42/89 *Βὰλ . . . Χαδὴρ.*
None of these rivers is known. See *Byzantinoturcica*, II (2nd ed.), 85, 334; Menges 277–8. Marquart (530, note 1) proposed to read *Βὰλ ὁ καὶ Βουρλίκ.*

42/92 *Ταμάταρχα.*   The Tmutorokan of the Old Russian sources: see *Byzantinoturcica*, II, 251 (2nd ed., 297); Vernadsky, *For Roman Jakobson* (1956), 590–1.

42/95 *Ἀτέχ.*   See *Byzantinoturcica*, II (2nd ed.), 77; Menges 278.

42/96 *Οὐκρούχ.*   Most probably the Kuban: see *Byzantinoturcica*, II (2nd ed.), 229; Menges 279.

42/97 *Ζιχίαν.*   See on 6/5.

42/97–8 *Νικόψεως . . . κάστρον.*   For the river, see also *De Cer.*, 794/2; for the town, see F. Brun, *Chernomor'e*, II (Odessa, 1880), 259.

42/100 *Παπαγία.*
Cf. 53/496, 499. The place is not mentioned elsewhere: see F. Kulakovsky, *Alany po svedeniyam klassicheskich i vizantiyskich pisateley* (Kiev, 1899), 53.

42/101 *Κασαχία.*   The country of the Circassians, whom the Russian chronicles call Kosogi: *see* Kulakovsky, *Alany*, 53; Marquart 2, 479.

42/102 *Ἀλανίας.*   *Cf.* 10/4; Runciman *Romanus Lecapenus* 172–3.

42/105–7 *Τουργανὴρχ . . . Πτελέας.*   See *Byzantinoturcica*, II (2nd ed.), 309, 319; Menges 278–9. Spatalon and Pteleai are unidentified.

42/109 *τῆς Ἀβασγίας.*   See Zonaras, ed. Dindorf, III, 333–5. *Cf.* Marquart 173–8; Runciman, *Romanus Lecapenus*, 170–1; Toumanoff, *Le Muséon*, 69 (1956), 73–82.

42/110 *Σωτηριουπόλεως.*   This place has been identified with the ancient Pityus and the modern Pitsunda: *see* Brun, *op. cit.*, 245.

Cc. 43–46/165

BIBLIOGRAPHY

I. MEDIAEVAL ARMENIAN AND GEORGIAN SOURCES

Ardzrouni, Thomas: *Patmout'ioun Tann Ardzrouneats (History of the Ardzrouni Family)*, ed. K. Patkanov (St Petersburg, 1887); French translation: M. E. Brosset, 'Histoire des Ardzrouni', in *Collection d'historiens arméniens*, I (St Petersburg, 1874) (Thomas Ardzrouni).   Asoghik, Stephen, of Taron: *Histoire Universelle*, livre III; ed. and tr. F. Macler (Paris, 1917: this edition supersedes the Armenian edition by Chahnazarian, Paris, 1859, and that of Malkhasiants, St Petersburg,

1885) (Ạsoghik). John VI, Catholicus: *Patmout'ioun Hayots* (*History of the Armenians*), ed. M. Y. Emin (Moscow, 1853: the French translation by Saint-Martin, published posthumously in Paris in 1841, is unreliable) (John Catholicus). Kaghankatouatsi, Moses: *Patmout'ioun Aghovanits Ark'ayits* (*History of the Kings of Aghovania*), ed. M. Y. Emin (Moscow, 1860) (Moses Kaghanka-touatsi). Orbelian, Stephen: *Patmout'ioun Tann Sisakan* (*History of the House of Sisakan*) (*Siounia*)), ed. M. Y. Emin (Moscow, 1861) (Orbelian). Vardan, Vardapet: *Havak'oumn Patmout'ian* (*Universal History*); Armenian Text (Venice, 1862) (Vardan). The Georgian Chronicle: *Khartlis T'zovreba*, ed. and tr. M. Brosset, *Histoire de la Géorgie*, 1 (St Petersburg, 1849) (*Georgian Chronicle*).

2. MODERN WORKS

N. Adontz, 'Les Taronites en Arménie et à Byzance', *Byzantion*, 9 (1934), 715–38; 10 (1935), 531–51; 11 (1936), 21–42 (Adontz I, II, III). W. E. D. Allen, *A History of the Georgian People* (London, 1932) (Allen). M. Brosset, *Additions et éclaircissements à l'histoire de la Géorgie* (St Petersburg, 1851) (Brosset). M. Canard, *Histoire de la dynastie des H'amdanides*, 1 (Paris, 1953) (Canard). R. Grousset, *Histoire de l'Arménie des origines à* 1071 (Paris, 1947) (Grousset). E. Honigmann, *Die Ostgrenze des byzantinischen Reiches* (A. A. Vasiliev, *Byzance et les Arabes*, tom. III, Brussels, 1935) (Honigmann). H. Hübschmann, 'Die altarmenischen Ortsnamen', *Indogermanische Forschungen*, 16 (1904), 197–490 (Hübschmann). J. Laurent, *L'Arménie entre Byzance et l'Islam* (Paris, 1919) (Laurent). J. Markwart, *Südarmenien und die Tigrisquellen* (Vienna, 1930) (Markwart, *Südarmenien*). M. J. Saint-Martin, *Mémoires historiques et géographiques sur l'Arménie*, 2 vols. (Paris, 1818, 1819) (Saint-Martin, *Mémoires*). C. Toumanoff, 'The Early Bagratids', *Le Muséon* 62 (1949) 21–54 (Toumanoff, *Bagratids*). *Id.*, 'Chronology of the Kings of Abasgia', *ibid.* 69 (1956) 73–90 (Toumanoff, *Abasgia*).

INTRODUCTORY NOTE

With these chapters, written or compiled in 952 (45/39–40), we leave behind that part of the book originally composed as a Περὶ ἐθνῶν (cc. 14–42), and embark on material inserted with the new, diplomatic purpose of *DAI* in view: see General Introduction pp. 2–4.

The chapters deal with the Armenian and Georgian princes and their vassals whose territory marched with the north-east frontier of the empire in Asia. C. does not mention, except incidentally, the Armenian and Georgian princes further to the east, though he gives a list of them, as imperial vassals, in *De Cer.*, 687, 688. He assumed that his readers were aware of the general, contemporary situation.

The land of Armenia was possessed by a number of hereditary princes, whose title of Ishkhan was translated by the Byzantine chancellery as ἄρχων. The head of the greater families was known as Grand Prince (Medz Ishkhan), but the family territory was often divided up between junior members. Occasionally one prince would establish a rough hegemony over his colleagues, and would be elected, apparently by their general consent, as Prince of Princes (Ishkhan Ishkhanats); he was recognized at Constantinople as ἄρχων τῶν ἀρχόντων. The Mamikonian family had held this hegemony from the 5th to 8th cents., but in the course of the 9th cent. it had been displaced by the Bagratids, whose chief, Ashot the Great (see 44/6), had been recognized as Prince of Princes in 862. The Arabs invaded Armenia during the latter half of the 7th cent., but had never established more than a suzerainty over the country. It was their practice usually to appoint a leading Armenian prince as their viceroy, and to call upon him to supply troops to aid them in their campaigns in the north. But the emperor always considered the Armenians as his vassals; and the Armenians themselves realized the value of being able to play off one suzerain against the other. Except during periods of persecution by the Arabs, it is probable that the Armenians preferred Arab to Byzantine suzerainty. This was due to the influence of the Armenian Church, which had been separated from the Orthodox Church since the Council of Chalcedon (451), and to which Islam was less objectionable than a powerful and proselytizing rival form of Christianity. The head of the Armenian Church was the Catholicus, whose residence during the 9th cent. was the town of Dovin (see on

44/4) in the Araxes valley, and whose dignity often passed from uncle to nephew in the family of St Gregory the Illuminator. At the same time Armenia had many intimate connections with Byzantium. The Armenian race was always too prolific to be contained in the wild and narrow valleys of Armenia. While many emigrants settled in Moslem countries, often abjuring their faith, the vast majority moved westward into the empire where, once they adopted Orthodoxy, they became a dominant element in Byzantine society, playing a rôle not unlike that of the Scots in English history during the last two centuries. Many soldiers and civil servants were of Armenian origin, and the imperial throne was open to them. Heraclius is said to have been an Armenian, and Leo V. The 'Macedonian' dynasty, to which C. himself belonged, claimed a high Armenian origin; and C.'s father-in-law, Romanus Lecapenus, was the son of an Armenian. These immigrants all retained an interest in their native country.

It was the policy of the empire to prevent as far as possible Arab domination of Armenia, for it was from Armenia (as was proved in the late 11th cent.) that Asia Minor was most vulnerable to invasion (cf. 44/125–8). In particular, the emperor was anxious to keep loyal buffer-states on his actual frontier.

The decline of Arab power in the mid-9th cent. gave more independence to Armenia, under the leadership of the Bagratid dynasty. The main branch of the family now owned the central Araxes valley, including the metropolis of Dovin and the future capitals of Ani and Kars; and their dominion stretched from Lake Van to the Kour valley, close to Tiflis. Another branch owned the district of Taron, on the Byzantine frontier. A third had spread into Georgia, where it possessed the provinces of Karthli and Tao. Further south, the land between the Araxes, Lake Van and Lake Urmiah was owned by the family of the Ardzrouni, who claimed descent from the Assyrian king Sennacherib. The third great family of the time, the Orbelians, owned the province of Siounia, to the east of the Bagratid territory.

North of Armenia were the various Georgian or Iberian princes, of whom the Bagratids of Karthli were the most important till the end of the 9th cent., after which, in about 908, they lost most of their lands to the king of Abasgia. The branch of Tao was considered of less importance, but it owned lands of great strategic value, commanding the roads from the empire into northern Armenia and the Caucasus. The Georgians and their princes were Orthodox, but they frequently intermarried with the Armenians: and it seems that the Prince of Princes Ashot established some sort of suzerainty over his Georgian cousins. The Caucasian nations to the north and east, of which Mas'udi says that 'God alone knows the number', played little part in Armeno-Georgian politics.

Apart from petty wars between the princes, which were endemic in Armenia, Ashot's reign was one of peace. He was punctilious towards the Arabs, who left him alone. In 886 he took the title of King (T'agavor), with the consent of the princes, and was crowned by the Catholicus. The caliph confirmed the title (as Shahanshah), and sent him a crown. This revival of the royal title, which had been in abeyance for four centuries, seems to have roused the attention of Byzantium, and Ashot thought it tactful to visit Constantinople. He was received there with great honour by the emperor Leo. On his return, in 890, he died as the result of a fall. It may be remarked that, while the Armenian historians declare that Ashot was recognized as king by the emperor, the Byzantine chancellery continued to call him ἄρχων τῶν ἀρχόντων. Perhaps the similarity of this title with the alternative Armenian word for king, Ark'ah,—a title regularly now given to Ashot in Armenia—softened the snub. Ashot further established his influence over his rivals by a policy of judicious marriages, which made him a kinsman to all the chief Armenian families.

Ashot, then, died in 890. His eldest son and successor, Sembat, lacked his father's personality and influence. The office of *generalissimo* of the Armenian forces, Sparapet, was, it seems, reserved for a cadet of the royal house. Sembat's uncle, brother and nephew, who in turn enjoyed the office, were all disloyal to him. His nephew, the prince of Vaspurakan, turned against him with most of the other princes. Their motive was. largely a dislike of the pro-Byzantine policy that he inaugurated. This policy involved him also in wars against the Arabs: in particular against Ahmed ibn Isa ibn Sheikh,. governor of Diyarbekir, who conquered most of the lands of the Bagratids of Taron in 870, and against the brothers Afshin and Youssouf, Turks of the Sadjid dynasty who were in turn governors of Azerbaijan. Afshin, who died in 901, occupied Dovin and took Tiflis from the Georgian Bagratids. His brother Youssouf, annoyed at Sembat's refusal to aid him in a revolt against Baghdad, denounced him as a traitor to the caliph; and was ordered to punish him and give the title of king to Gagik Ardzrouni of Vaspurakan, his. nephew. Deserted by almost all the Armenian princes, and receiving no help from Byzantium, Sembat was eventually captured by Youssouf in 912, and was put to death (see 44/7, 26–7). He is known in Armenian history as Sembat the Martyr. Of his sons, Ashot, the elder, fled to Constantinople, and the younger, Abas (see on 44/9–10), to Abasgia.

This disaster roused Constantinople to action, and in 915 an expedition was sent by the empress-regent Zoë under the domestic Leo Phocas to place Ashot on his father's throne and to restore his lands to him. It was, on the whole, successful, though the Bagratids did not recover Dovin and their easternmost possessions. Ashot reigned till 929, in comparative prosperity, despite intermittent civil wars, largely due to the disloyalty of his brother Abas. Abas succeeded him, and reigned till 951. While Ashot on the whole favoured a pro-Byzantine policy, Abas reverted to the Bagratid tradition of friendship with the Arabs, though he had to face Arab invasions in 931 and 936. He did not exercise much authority over the other princes, and managed to avoid civil war with them. Gagik Ardzrouni of Vaspurakan (see on 43/111) was reconciled with the Bagratids, probably through Byzantine mediation, but he retained the title of king, and his prestige was enhanced by the fact that the Catholicus, after the fall of Dovin, had settled in Ardzrouni territory, first at Tzoroy Vankh and later at the island monastery of Agthamar.

Thus by 950 Armenia was enjoying a period of comparative peace and prosperity. Byzantium was encroaching on the west, but the main principalities were for the moment left in a state of independence. The Arabs were no longer a serious menace, but were of value as a counter to use against the empire. In Georgia the chief power was still the orthodox kingdom of Abasgia, which was regarded at Constantinople as a satisfactory vassal state. See further Canard 462–71.

C. tells us at 45/39–40 that he is writing in the year 952. It is probable that all the chapters 43–6 date from the same time. His sources of information, apart from the records of the Byzantine chancellery, were the embassies that the empire periodically sent into Armenia and Georgia, and the Armenian and Georgian embassies to Constantinople. On the whole, his information is borne out by Armenian and Georgian sources. His only major inexplicable error concerns the geography of the river Araxes (45/158–64).

43/1 Περὶ τῆς χώρας τοῦ Ταρών.
The province of Taron (in Armenian Taron or Taroun) occupied the valley of the southern branch of the upper Euphrates, west of lake Van, with its capital at Moush (Canard 186–7). The name is found in classical writers such as Tacitus (Ann., XIV, 24, regio Tauraunitium, a false derivation from the Taurus Mts.); and occurs frequently in early Armenian history (the historian Zenob wrote a history of Taron, published in French in Langlois, Collection d'historiens de l'Arménie, I, 333–55). It had been the cradle of Armenian Christianity; St Gregory the Illuminator built his first church at the old capital Ashtishat, near Moush (Agathange, Histoire du Règne de Tiridate, tr. Langlois, Collection d'historiens de l'Arménie, I, 173). In the course of the 8th cent. the Bagratid family had taken over the province from the Mamikonians; but on the death of Ashot the Carnivorous (772–826), the prince who established Bagratid hegemony in Armenia, the Arabs obliged his sons to divide his dominions. Bagrat was established as prince of Taron

in 830, while his brother Sembat received the older Bagratid lands on the Araxes. It is probable that Bagrat was the elder brother, and for that reason later Armenian historians, who derived their information from sources favourable to Sembat's line, the later Royal Bagratids, never mention the relationship, which is known to us only from Arab sources (see Laurent 105, 106 and note 2). Bagrat was recognized by the Arabs as Prince of Princes, but in 851 they took him with all his family into captivity at Samarra. His sons, Ashot and David, were released in about 858.

Ashot had some difficulty in recovering his lands, owing to the intrigues of his cousin Ashot the Brave, son of Sembat; and part of them temporarily passed to an Ardzrouni prince Gourgen, who had the support of Byzantium. After Basil I's annexation of Tephrice in 872 Ashot adopted a pro-imperial policy, and was recognized as Prince of Princes and Curopalate by Byzantium. In 878 he was defeated by an alliance between his Bagratid cousins, the Ardzrouni and the Arabs, and replaced by his brother David, whom the Arabs recognized as Prince of Princes (for a *résumé* of this complicated history, see Laurent 272-4, and Adontz I, 721-31). David reigned from 878 to 885 or 895; (Thomas Ardzrouni III, § 20, 221, says that David reigned seven years, but Adontz I, 724, note 3, suggests that seven is a mistake for seventeen, as the prince of Taron whom Thomas (III, § 22, 231) says died two years after the earthquake of 893, must be David). He was succeeded, not by his son Ashot, but by his nephew Gourgen, who soon afterwards was killed by an Arab general, Ahmed ibn Isa, who overran his country (see Thomas Ardzrouni, *loc. cit.*, who calls Gourgen 'son of the Curopalate', that is, of Ashot). Sembat vainly wrote to Ahmed to ask him to restore the territory to the rightful heir Ashot (see Thomas Ardzrouni III, § 23, 236; John Catholicus 96).

It was probably about now (900) that Leo VI annexed the district of Tekis and established the *thema* of Mesopotamia (see 50/111-32, with notes *ad loc.* and on 45/44) thus bringing the imperial frontier up to the borders of Taron. But at this point Armenian sources cease to give us information about Taron; and we begin C.'s story with a gap which prevents an absolutely certain identification of his characters. The genealogical tree on the facing page gives the probable relationships (names mentioned by C. are given in capitals).

43/7 Κρικορίκιος.

The name is 'Gregory', in Armenian Grigor, with Armenian diminutive '-ik' attached. The suffix may have been used by the Armenians to distinguish the bearer from some older Gregory unknown to us. At 43/35 C. uses the form Γρηγόριος for the same person. This Gregory was probably the son of the pro-Byzantine prince of Taron, Ashot, son of Bagrat, for whom see preceding note and genealogical tree p. 161. Gregory must have obtained the principality about 896, perhaps as the candidate of the Moslem general Ahmed. His political conduct, as described by C. (43/7-26), was typical of all the Armenian princes of the time; and the geographical position of his principality was suitable for the selling of information to either side. Gregory is only once mentioned in Armenian sources, when, in about 910, he went on an unsuccessful mission on behalf of his cousin king Sembat to the emir Afshin: John Catholicus, describing this (127), calls him 'the great, wise and judicious ishkhan of the Armenians'. His choice as an envoy suggests that he was friendly with the Arabs. He already had the Byzantine title of Patrician. See Canard 466-7; Laurent, *Ech. d'Or.*, 37 (1938), 128.

43/11 διαφόρως. *Cf.* Cedrenus II, 681/22.

43/18 ἀπέστελλεν ἀεὶ δῶρα. For the significance of this exchange of presents, see Treitinger 202; Dölger, *BES*, 16-17.

43/21 διὰ γραμμάτων. *Cf.* 43/50-1, and see on 4/10. Contrast 43/65, with note *ad loc.*

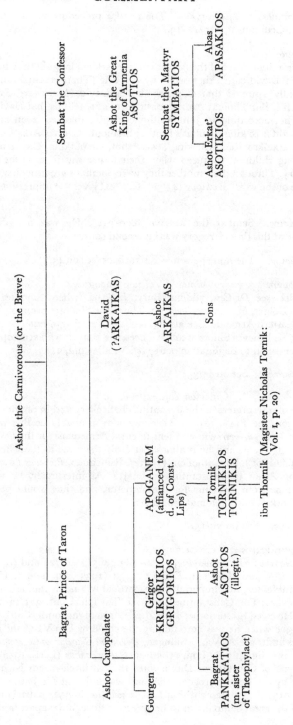

43/22–3 θεάσασθαι . . . μετασχεῖν. The regular procedure at the visits of clients to the capital: cf. Cedrenus II, 615/12–13.

43/28 'Αρκάϊκα.
This name is a diminutive of the Aι menian title Ark'ah, king. Both Ashot son of Bagrat and his brother David called themselves by this title (Thomas Ardzrouni III, § 20, 219–20). It is usually assumed that C.'s Arkaïkas is David (Markwart, *Südarmenien*, 324; Adontz I, 723 ff.). But Thomas Ardzrouni III, § 20, 221, tells us that David had only one son, Ashot, who, according to John Catholicus (96), married, soon after his father's death, the daughter of king Sembat's brother Shapouh. C. gives Arkaïkas two sons. It is probable that Arkaïkas, the 'little king', was Ashot, son of 'king' David, and that his two sons were young children, captured when their father was fighting for his inheritance against Gregory. Through their mother they were Sembat's great-nephews, which would justify C.'s use of the word ἀνεψιούς (43/32). C.'s text gives the impression that they were young.

43/30 Συμβάτιος. Sembat the Martyr (890–912). He was on good terms with Constantinople at this time. Gregory was his second cousin.

43/35 Γρηγόριος. The same person as Krikorikios (see on 43/7).

43/36–7 Σινούτην . . . χαρτουλάριον . . . ὀξέως δρόμου.
For the office, see *De Cer.*, 788/22; Bury, *IAS*, 92 (where Sinoutes is mis-printed Sinartes); also Dölger, *Finanzverwaltung*, 62. The name Sinoutes probably means a native of Siounia, in eastern Armenia. See also G. Kolias, *Léon Choerosphactès* (Athens, 1939), 55, 56, note 2, 59; K. believes Sinoutes to have been the eunuch who accompanied Choerosphactes on his mission to Baghdad in 906–7 (cf. Vasiliev II/2, 21).

43/39 'Αδρανασήρ. See on 45/35.

43/41–2 Θεοδώρου . . . 'Αρμενίων ἑρμηνευτοῦ.
For the rôle of interpreters in the Byzantine chancellery and in providing the emperor with information, see Bury, 540–1. Theodore may probably be the πρωτοσπαθάριος Θεόδωρος ὁ τοῦ Παγκράτη who was sent to enrol Armenians for the Cretan expedition of 911 (*De Cer.*, 657/21); and he is almost certainly the same as the Theodore Basilikos (T'edoros Vaslikos) of John Catholicus (154; cf. Runciman, *Romanus Lecapenus*, 131) who conducted king Ashot to Constantinople in 914. As interpreter, he would translate reports that came from Armenia for the emperor, and thus would be able easily to sabotage the work of any diplomat sent there.

43/43 βασιλικὸς. See on 22/15.

43/43–5 Κωνσταντῖνος . . . ἑταιρειάρχης.
For the δομέστικος τῆς ὑπουργίας, see *De Cer.*, 463/8–464/21 and cf. Theoph. Cont. 397/12; Bury, *IAS*, 126; Laurent, *Ech. d'Or.*, 32 (1933), 39, note 1. He was a palace official responsible for the imperial table, probably under the minister known as ὁ ἐπὶ τῆς τραπέζης. For Constantine Lips, see Theoph. Cont. 371/13–18; 384/15–16; 389/9, 17–19. He owed his surname, ὁ τοῦ Λιβός, 'son of the south wind', to a gale which arose in June 908 when he was entertaining the emperor Leo VI at the dedication of a church he had built: see A. Van Millingen, *Byzantine Churches in Constantinople* (London, 1912), 122–7, 131, fig. 42; R. Janin, *Constantinople byzantine* (Paris, 1950), 354. He took part in the revolt of Constantine Dux against the patriarch-regent Nicholas (913), but was pardoned by the empress-regent Zoë, and was killed at the battle of the Acheloüs (20th August, 917). C.'s statement that Lips is *now* (*i.e.* in 952) patrician proconsul and commander of the great company must be an error: since, quite apart from the fact of his

having been killed in 917, a man who was a trusted diplomat and had a nubile daughter in Leo VI's reign could hardly be in active service fifty years later. Adontz II, 533–5, attempts to solve the problem by postponing the events in our passage to the year 909, but even that does not rejuvenate Constantine Lips sufficiently. It seems clear that C. has made a careless mistake, and probably meant to say 'the *father* of the present patrician proconsul, etc.'. The patrician was perhaps Bardas Lips, who took part in a conspiracy in 961 (Cedrenus II, 341/21–342/6). The name Bardas suggests that the family had Armenian blood (*cf.* Adontz *loc. cit.*). See, however, Pseudo-Codinus, in Preger, *Scriptores Originum Constantinopolitanarum* (Leipzig, 1907), II, 289/5–9: τοῦ δὲ Λιβὸς ἡ μονὴ ἐν τοῖς χρόνοις ʽΡωμανοῦ τοῦ γέροντος καὶ τοῦ πορφυρογεννήτου Κωνσταντίνου υἱοῦ Λέοντος (i.e. 922–44) ἀνηγέρθη παρὰ (κωνσταντίνου A2) πατρικίου τοῦ Λιβὸς τοῦ γεγονότος δρουγγαρίου τῶν πλωΐμων, which, if the reading of the Paris ms. is correct, testifies to the existence of a lord admiral Constantine Lips in the reign of Romanus I (*cf.* Guilland, *BZ*, 44 (1951), 217); but no such admiral is otherwise known, and there may be a confusion with Constantine Gongyles (see on 46/50). See also Janin, *Mémorial L. Petit* (Bucharest, 1948), 225–6; and Schlumberger, *Sigillographie*, 673, for the seal of Κωνσταντῖνος ὁ Λιβής. For the grand hetaeriarch, see Guilland, *Byzantinoslavica*, 19 (1958), 68.

43/53 πρωτοσπαθαρίου τιμήσας ἀξίᾳ. For the rank, see Guilland's article cited on 29/233. For imperial titles given to foreign potentates, see Treitinger 191–5.

43/55 ʼΑπογάνεμ.
Abu Ghanim. Many Armenian notables were given Arabic surnames or nicknames, by which they were commonly known: see Laurent 181, note 4. Apoganem's Christian name is not known.

43/64–5 Εἰσελθόντος . . . Κρικορικίου.
At *De Cer.*, 137/16–139/20 there is a description of the Feast of St Basil, on the 1st of January in the 3rd indiction, during which the 'Magister and Prince of Taron', supported by the foreign minister, is presented to the emperor, and is given ceremonial gifts. He is followed by the Bulgarian embassy staff, and then by his own staff. This may allude to the visit of Gregory mentioned in our passage which, since it took place in the reign of Leo VI, could thus be dated to 1st of January, 900 (see Bury, *English Historical Review*, 22 (1907), 420–1); and the events previously recorded in c. 43 would then belong to the years 896–9. Adontz I, 175–6, accepts the identification of this Prince of Taron with Gregory; but later, II, 533–5, in order to rejuvenate Constantine Lips (see on 43/43–5), he says that the 3rd indiction must be a misprint for the 13th, and that Gregory's visit took place in 909–10. But, in fact, there is no reason for supposing that the emperor mentioned in this chapter of *De Cer.* is Leo VI. There is a reference at the end of the chapter (*De Cer.*, 139/20) to τοῖς βασιλεῦσι (*cf. ibid.*, 137/20) which suggests the existence of co-emperors. These might be Leo and Alexander, but equally well Romanus I, his sons and his son-in-law; and the phrase τοὺς φίλους Βουλγάρους (*ibid.*, 139/1) fits better into the years after 927 (*cf.* however *BZ*, 47 (1954), 9). In that case, the visit of a Taronite prince took place in 929–30, and refers probably to Gregory's son Bagrat (see 43/150). As the events described by C. as happening between Gregory's accession (896, at the earliest) and his visit to Constantinople seem likely to have occupied more than three years, it seems better to assume that his visit took place about 906; (910 would be too late, as Apoganem visited the capital, and later Gregory proposed to revisit it, while Leo was still alive). Vogt, *Commentaire*, I, 153–4, opts for the later dating of *De Cer.*, I, c. 24 (= 33 in his edition); but he thinks that it was Gregory who came to Constantinople in 929–30, 'comme il semble que seul de tous les Taronites, Grégoire ait été magistros et que, par ailleurs, nous savons qu'il mourut en 930'.

43/65 στρατηγοῦ.

The use of this title, military governor of an imperial province, suggests that Taron was now considered as forming an integral part of the empire (cf. 43/153), though it was not formally annexed till 966/7: see on 43/185, 187–8; and cf. on 43/21; Laurent, *Ech. d'Or.* 37 (1938) 128.

43/66–7 οἶκος . . . Βασιλείου τοῦ παρακοιμωμένου.

The gift of a palace at Constantinople was sometimes a reward for good vassal princes: see *Ep. Romani Lecapeni, Δελτίον τῆς Ἱστ. καὶ Ἐθνολογ. Ἑταιρίας* 2 (1887), 409, where the emperor offers a palace and estates to an eastern prince (see on 43/111). The house of Constantine Barbaros 'in Arcadianis' (near the Forum of Arcadius) is mentioned at *AASS*, 26th March, p. 669 F (cf. *Byzantion*, 24 (1954), 147). For Basil the chamberlain, see on 50/233–4.

43/76 χρυσοβουλλίου.   See on 45/101.

43/80 Κρικορίκιος . . . ἐξῃτήσατο.

Gregory's recent submission was perhaps due to fear of the emir Youssouf, who launched an attack on Armenia in 909. From the context it appears that Gregory did not visit Constantinople on this occasion, though he obtained possession of the House of Barbaros and, as appears from 43/91, was responsible for its upkeep.

43/92 προάστειον . . . Κελτζηνῇ . . . Τατζάτου.

For προάστειον, see C. Neumann, *Die Weltstellung des byzantinischen Reiches vor den Kreuzzügen* (Leipzig, 1894), 59, note 2; Dölger, *Finanzverwaltung,* 127–8; Ostrogorsky, *Vierteljahrschrift für Sozial- und Wirtschaftsgeschichte,* 20 (1927), 20–2; Každan, *Viz. Vrem.,* 11 (1956), 100–1. For Keltzini, see on 50/116; Cedrenus II, 682/7–11: it was a *tourma* of Mesopotamia on the north branch of the upper Euphrates, with its chief town at the modern Erzincan. The context implies that it was, by this time (c. 928), considered safe from Moslem incursions. This was probably a result of the campaigns that the imperial general John Kourkouas inaugurated in 926 (see Vasiliev II/2, 148 ff.; Runciman, *Romanus Lecapenus,* 137). For Tatzates (Tadjat in Armenian), see Theoph. Cont. 404/4–16: he was a rich Armenian who joined the military governor of Chaldia, Bardas Boïlas (a fellow Armenian, as his name shows), in a revolt against Romanus I in 923. As a result, his property had been confiscated. Adontz (1, 735–6) dates this revolt and the campaign of John Kourkouas, Domestic of the Scholars, against Dovin (cf. on 45/56) to 921, basing his date on Asoghik. It seems better to keep to the date suggested by Theoph. Cont., since John probably did not become Domestic till 922: see on 45/56.

43/98 τοῦ Γρηγορᾶ.

Adontz 1, 735, suggests that this Grigoras was Grigoras Iberitzes (Theoph. Cont. 372/15; 384/4–7), the father-in-law of Constantine Dux, with whose revolt in 913 he had been associated. But as Iberitzes thereupon retired into a monastery and there is no proof that he had estates in Keltzini, the identification is unsubstantiated. There is no other Grigoras known with whom this Grigoras can be identified.

43/100 ὁ Τορνίκης.

This is the Armenian name Thornik (T'ornik), or Teranik. At 43/136, C. calls him Tornikios. Thornik was the son of Apoganem by an earlier marriage, as it seems that Apoganem's marriage with the daughter of Constantine Lips was never completed (43/78–9).

43/111 Κακικίου τοῦ ἄρχοντος Βασπαρακά.

Gagik Ardzrouni, prince of Vaspurakan and anti-king of Armenia, ruled from c. 908 until 936 or 943 (see Canard 469, note 214). His mother was a daughter of Ashot the Great. He was made king of Armenia by the emir Youssouf in about 910; and he was recognized as ἄρχων τῶν ἀρχόντων by Byzantium, probably after the death of Ashot Erkat' (929), when Ashot's brother and successor was in disfavour with the emperor (see on 44/9-10). This transfer of the title to the prince of Vaspurakan is marked at *De Cer.*, 687/4-5, where Gagik or his successor is ὁ νῦν τιμηθεὶς ἄ. τῶν ἀ.; contrast *ibid.*, 686/22-3. This title Gagik was holding at the time when Romanus I wrote a letter (now wrongly superscribed, see Dölger, *BES*, 39, note 8) to an unknown rival potentate, offering to transfer the title from Gagik to him, and to subject to him both Gagik himself and the magister Abas, king of Armenia: see Δελτίον τῆς Ἱστ. καὶ Ἐθνολογ. Ἑταιρίας 2 (1887), 407-9; Dölger, *Regesten*, 631; Runciman, *Romanus Lecapenus*, 159-60. Until the time of Kourkouas' campaigns, Gagik had little contact with the empire; but in 926 or 927 he started abortive negotiations with Constantinople about Church Union (see C. F. Neumann, *Versuch zur Geschichte der armenischen Literatur* (Leipzig, 1836), 126). His démarche to Romanus over Gregory's salary may have been made at the same time. His successor was Derenik, who reigned till 953.

43/111 Ἀδρανασήρ. See on 45/35.

43/112 Ἀσωτικίου, τοῦ ἄρχοντος τῶν ἀρχόντων.

Ashot Erkat' (erkat' = 'iron'), 915-29. The diminutive form '-ik' was doubtless used by the Armenians to distinguish him from his grandfather, Ashot the Great (or Elder). See Adontz, *Ann. de l'Inst. de Phil. et de l'Hist. Orientales*, 3 (1935), 13-35.

43/128-9 τὴν δὲ ῥόγαν . . . ἐκκοπῆναι αὐτήν.

The English translation is incorrect, as is that of Adontz (I, 719). The meaning is that Gregory 'demanded either that he should receive his stipend *gratis* (προῖκα) . . . or else that it should be cut off': cf. Leo Diac. 100/11: προῖκα τὴν ῥόγαν ἐπηύξησε, that is to say, the emperor raised the rate of interest without demanding an increase of 'invested' capital. See on 50/242-3.

43/132 Ἀσώτιον. The illegitimate son of Gregory, who had already been created a protospatharius (43/51-3).

43/135 Κρικορικίου . . . ἀπολιπόντος.

Gregory's son Bagrat probably visited Constantinople as soon as possible after his father's death, to be recognized as his heir (cf. on 43/64-5 and 43/150). Gregory therefore probably died early in 929.

43/136 Τορνίκιος. Cf. gloss at Vol. I, 20/2-3.

43/137 τὸν πρωτοσπαθάριον Κρινίτην.

Adontz II, 535-9, derives this surname from the castle of Krni in Digisini, the Tekis of 50/115 (see Markwart, *Südarmenien*, 40-1; and Honigmann 69). Adontz mentions the other known members of the family, none of whom can be certainly identified with the interpreter (see also on 50/34); who may, however, be that Krinitis of Chaldia, appointed governor of Calabria by C. at the time of the African civil war (945-6), and then recalled for extortion: see Cedrenus II, 357/20-358/7; Gay 212-13; cf. Vasiliev II/2, 158 and note 2. Adontz II, 537, is clearly wrong in identifying this person with Paschalios.

43/150 Παγκράτιος. Bagrat (or Bagarat), a frequent name in the Bogratid family. His visit may be dated to December 929-January 930 (see on 43/64-5).

43/155 τοῦ μαγίστρου Θεοφυλάκτου.

Adontz II, 539–40, convincingly identifies this Theophylact with the patrician who was host in 919 at the dinner-party where C.'s tutor was arrested: see Theoph. Cont. 397/14. *Cf.* also *Vita Euphrosynae Junioris* (*AASS*, November, III), 887. For the close alliance of Taronite and Lecapenid houses, see Laurent, *Ech. d'Or.*, 37 (1938), 127–35.

43/176 Μιχαήλ . . . κομμερκιαρίου Χαλδίας.

Michael, whose house, or monastery, seems to have been confiscated by the crown, was perhaps concerned in the Chaldian revolt of 923 (see on 43/92). For the office of κομμερκιάριος, see *De Cer.*, 717/8 = Bury, *IAS*, 140/9, with *ibid.*, 88; Dölger, *Finanzverwaltung*, 62. For the κομμέρκια of Chaldia, *cf. De Cer.*, 697/1–2, with Reiske's note at II, 821.

43/177 τὴν τοῦ Ψωμαθέως μονήν.

The monastery is referred to by ownership (monastery of the protospatharius Michael) and by locality (monastery of Psomatheus, or in Psomathia); *cf.* Theoph. Cont. 9/10–11: βασιλικὸν οἶκον τοῦ Ζήνωνος καὶ τὸν Δαγισθέα. Psomathia or Psamathia was a quarter of Constantinople on the Sea of Marmora, between the Wall of Constantine and the Church of St John Studius. It contained a palace and a home for old men, attributed to St Helena, and a sea-gate: see Preger, *Scriptores Originum Constantinopolitanarum* (Leipzig, 1907), II, 216/1, where the name is τὸν Ψωμαθέαν. The name may originally allude to the sand (ψάμμος) thrown up against the walls here. See further *Vita Euthymii*, ed. De Boor (Berlin, 1888), 155–6 and 211 *s.v.*; R. Janin, *Constantinople byzantine* (Paris, 1950), 384, PSAMATHION.

43/183 Οἰκείᾳ δὲ ἀγαθότητι ὑπείξας. A quotation from the bull of Romanus; *cf.* 45/117–18.

43/185 Οὐλνούτιν.

The Armenian Oghnout or Eghnout, and modern Ognut, in the north-west of Taron (see Honigmann 148; Canard 467). T'ornik must have possessed an appanage in the centre or east of Taron, which his cousin Bagrat was anxious to recover. Though C. implies that the empire took over the whole of T'ornik's inheritance, it is clear from 43/188 that T'ornik's heirs retained a considerable amount of land. It is also clear from this passage that although Taron might now rank as an imperial *thema* (see on 43/65), the governorship remained in the family of Gregory: *cf.* Canard 467.

43/187–8 τὸ μὲν ἥμισυ . . . οἱ τούτων ἐξάδελφοι.

Gregory's sons were Bagrat and the illegitimate Ashot (43/164). The date of Bagrat's death is unknown. In the list of princes who submitted to Saïf ad-Daula in 940 is Ashot b. Grigor, some of whose land was confiscated: see Canard 481, 485, and on 44/17–115. It is probable that Bagrat was dead by then, and that Ashot was prince of Taron (Canard 467, 484–5). Ashot died in 966–7 (Asoghik 44), and the Byzantines took Taron. Cedrenus II, 375/1–4 says that the land was ceded by the brothers Gregory and Bagrat, who were in fact Ashot's sons. Their descendants played a considerable part in Byzantine domestic history (see Adontz III, 21 ff.). By the 'sons' of Apoganem, whose only recorded son was T'ornik, C. probably means his descendants. Arab sources tell us of an Armenian prince Ibn-Thornik, who was living in 936 and whose town of Moush was sacked by Saïf ad-Daula in the spring of 940 (G. Weil, *Geschichte der Califen* (Mannheim, 1848), II, 674–5; Markwart, *Südarmenien*, 463; Canard 481); and Adontz II, 541, assumes that Ibn-Thornik is a mistake for Ibn-Grigor. Moush was the chief city of Taron and its possessor must have been the reigning prince. But there is no reason for accusing the Arabs of inaccuracy. If Bagrat died in about 935, when Byzantine influence was strong in western Armenia

(Melitene had been captured in 934: Vasiliev II/2, 154), the Byzantines may well have helped T'ornik's son, who had been living in Constantinople, to become prince, as a more legitimate heir than the bastard Ashot; Ashot therefore appeared in 940 in Saïf ad-Daula's camp, ready to cede territory in return for Saïf ad-Daula's support, with which he managed to obtain the throne. C.'s reference to Gregory as 'father of Ashot' (43/28–9) may be explicable by the fact that Ashot was reigning while C. was writing.

44/1–5 Περὶ τῆς χώρας τοῦ Ἀπαχουνῆς κτλ.

This chapter deals with the history of the Kaïsite emirs of Manzikert. The Kaïsites were a clan from Arabia, settled in Syria and Iraq under the caliph 'Umar. The first of the clan to appear in Armenia was el-Asat ibn Kaïs, governor of Armenia and Azerbaijan about the year 650 (see Laurent 322–6, who gives a *résumé* of the known facts about the history of the Kaïsites). It is probable that the subsequent Kaïsite emirs in Armenia descend from him. We next hear of them a century later, when the Kaïsite Djahap, already established in the country round Manzikert, married a Mamikonian princess who brought him as dowry the land of Apahounik', in about 775. Djahap became one of the leading potentates in Armenia, and even captured Dovin in 813, but probably died in that year. His attempt to conquer Taron had been foiled by the contemporary Bagratid prince Ashot the Carnivorous, who had the support of the caliph. Djahap's son, Abd al-Malik (813–20), unsuccessfully attacked Bardas in Aghovania in 813, and was evicted from Dovin by Ashot's brother Shapouh (Marquart 405–6, 452). Abd al-Malik's son, Sawada (820–30), conquered Khelat' and tried to invade Siounia; his wife was a Bagratid, called Arouseak (John Catholicus 64). Sawada was succeeded by another Djahap, who was defeated in 863 by Ashot the Great, acting on behalf of the caliph. It is probable that the Apelbart of C.'s narrative (44/17) was his son. Laurent (*loc. cit.* and 345) cites the Moslem general Ali Dovaphi (*i.e.* ?Djahap), son of Hussein, son of Siba el-Kaïsi, whom the Armenians wished to keep as their governor in 841, as a member of this family. Thomas Ardzrouni (II, § 6, 111) calls him Ala, and later (112) Opha. Vardan (109) mentions a son of Djahap called Apelhert, who invaded Siounia in about 849. See Canard 473, notes 226, 227.

44/1 Ἀπαχουνῆς.

Apahounik' was a district comprising the upper valley of the southern branch of the Euphrates, north of lake Van: see Honigmann 147 and map IV; Canard 187. It was of great strategic importance as it controlled the route from the Bagratid possessions in Taron to those in central Armenia.

44/2 Μανζικίερτ.

Manzikert, later famous as the site of the defeat of Romanus IV by Alp Arslan (1071), was one of the oldest towns in Armenia; it was known originally as Manavatzkert, and later Mandzkert or Manatskert, in Syriac Manazgerd, and in Arabic and Old Turkish Melaskjird or Melaskerd. It is situated close to the Euphrates (Murad-Cay). See Honigmann map IV; Canard 187.

44/2 Περκρί.

Perkri, the Armenian Berkri, was close to the north-east tip of lake Van: see Honigmann map IV; Canard 184, map VI; 188, note 283. Till the early years of the 10th cent. it was held by Arab emirs of the 'Uthman dynasty: see Canard 473 and note 226. Some time after 903, perhaps in 912 (44/50–4), it was annexed by the Kaïsite emir of Manzikert.

44/3 τοῦ Χλιὰτ καὶ τοῦ Χαλιὰτ.

Two names for the same town (*cf.* 44/11, 20), Khelat' in Armenian and Akhlath in Arabic (τοῦ καὶ Χαλιὰτ). It was situated on the north-west corner of lake Van: see

Honigmann map IV; Canard 184, map VI. It had been in Bagratid possession for a short time about 750, but had been occupied by the Kaïsites early in the 9th cent.: see Laurent 101, note 6.

44/3 '*Αρζές.*
Armenian Ardjesh, on the north-east shore of lake Van: see Honigmann map IV; Canard 184, map VI; 188, note 283. It seems to have been in Kaïsite ownership since the end of the 8th cent.

44/4 *Τιβί.*
Armenian Dovin or Dvin, Arabic Dabil; the older Greek form was *Δούβιος* (Procopius, *Bell. Pers.*, II, 24-5). It was situated east of the Araxes, a few miles south-east of Erivan: see Honigmann map IV; Canard 183, and map VI. The Arabs had made it the seat of their government in Armenia, and under their rule it was a prosperous city. The Catholicus of Armenia had had his reisdence there since before the Arab conquest: see Introductory Note p. 157. In the later 9th cent. it formed part of the Bagratid lands, though it still contained the Arab governor's court. It was re-occupied by the Arabs during the reign of Sembat (890-912), and remained in Arab hands. John Kourkouas temporarily occupied the town in 927: see on 45/56.

44/4 *τοῦ Χέρτ καὶ τοῦ Σαλαμᾶς.*
The canton of Her and its chief town Salamas were situated on the east of Vaspurakan, and north-west of lake Urmiah: see Canard 192-4 and map V. At the end of the 9th cent. Her was disputed between the Ardzrouni princes and Moslem emirs. Derenik Ardzrouni, Ashot the Great's son-in-law, was killed there by a treacherous Moslem emir in 886 (Thomas Ardzrouni III, § 20). It can never have formed part of Ashot's possessions, though he may for a time have maintained suzerain rights over it.

44/5 *Τζερματζοῦ.*
This could be Tjermatzor in Mokk', south of lake Van (Honigmann 147, 197); but is more probably Sermantzou, north of Taron (Markwart, *Südarmenien*, 305; Canard 475, note 230).

44/6 '*Ασωτίου.*   Ashot the Great (862-90): see Introductory Note pp. 158-9.

44/8 '*Αποσάται.*   Youssouf Abû Kasim ibn Abû Sâdj, governor of Armenia and Azerbaijan for the caliph, *c.* 905-20: see Introductory Note p. 159.

44/9 '*Ασώτιον.*   Ashot Erkat', the Asotikios of 43/112.

44/9-10 '*Απασάκιον . . . μάγιστρον.*
Abas, king of Armenia from 929 until 951 (Canard gives 953 on p. 465, and 958 on p. 466). C. uses the diminutive form perhaps because Abas was a younger brother. Magister as a title ranked below curopalate (Bury, *IAS*, 29-35), the title given to the head of the Iberian Bagratids (45/2-3). The wording of the passage suggests, especially if Abas died in 951 before it was written, that Abas was never recognized as Prince of Princes by Byzantium, though his brother Ashot Erkat' had been so: see on 43/111, and the letter of Romanus I there cited. The prince of princes at the time of this latter document was Gagik of Vaspurakan; and if Byzantium had had in mind to transfer the title from Gagik, it would not, as the emperor's words make clear, have been to the 'magister Apasakios'. Abas was out of favour with the Byzantine government, no doubt because of his pro-Arab policy: see Introductory Note p. 159; Runciman, *Romanus Lecapenus*, 159-60.

44/13-14 τὴν μεγάλην 'Αρμενίαν.

Great Armenia was traditionally the country from the Euphrates to the Caspian. According to Moses of Khorene, this was the territory conquered by Aram, eponymous founder of the race.

44/14 Κάρς. C. is wrong here. Kars only became the capital of Armenia under Abas. Till his time the Bagratid capital had been Erazgavor or Bagaran.

44/17-115 "Οτι 'Απελβὰρτ κτλ.

See Canard 471-84. The Greek version is supplemented by Armenian and Arabic documents. The Saracen emir Apelbart I (Abu'l-Ward, rather than Markwart's 'Abd al-Barr) is here stated to have held Manzikert, together with Chliat and Arzes and Perkri, as vassal of Ashot, prince of princes (862-90); but cf. on 44/19-21. Apelbart I was succeeded by his son Abelchamit ('Abd al-Hamid), and he in turn by his son Aposebatas (Abu Sawada). On the death of the prince of princes Sembat (912), Aposebatas made himself independent in Manzikert; his younger brother Apolesphouet (Abu'l-Aswad) and Apolesphouet's cousin (ἀνεψιός, 44/56, rather than nephew) Achmet or Achamet (Ahmad) administered Chliat, Arzes and Altzike; and the third brother Aposelmis (Abu Salim) occupied Sermantzou. All these territories were ravaged and put under tribute to Byzantium by Kourkouas between 928 and 931 (Canard 739-40). Aposebatas was succeeded in Manzikert by his son Abderacheim ('Abd ar-Rahim). Abderacheim was succeeded, not by his infant brother Apelmouze (Abu'l-Mu'izz), but by his uncle Apolesphouet; and he by his younger brother Aposelmis. The son of Aposelmis, Apelbart II, is the emir at the time of writing (952); he has murdered his cousin Achmet, who till then had retained control over Chliat, Arzes and Altzike, and has annexed those cities, for which he refuses to pay to Byzantium the tribute imposed in 931: the empire must therefore reassert its suzerainty over them.

Some evidence about the Kaïsite dynasty between 868 and 914, which at least does not conflict with C.'s account, is found in Thomas Ardzrouni (III, §§ 19, 20; cf. Markwart, Südarmenien, 300, 505; Canard 475-6). But three Arabic texts relating to the 'assize' held by the Hamdanid Saïf ad-Daula near lake Van in the spring of 940 give information not quite consistent with that of c. 44 (Canard 480-4). The text of Ibn al-Azraq states that among those who presented themselves on that occasion were 'Ahmad b. 'Abd ar-Rahman; Abu'l-Mu'izz, Lord of Khelat', Dhat al-Jauz (sc. Altzike), Ardjesh and Perkri; 'Abd al-Hamid, lord of Manzikert'. Markwart, by suppressing the conjunction between the first two persons named, identifies these as a single person, Ahmad b. 'Abd ar-Rahman Abu'l-Mu'izz, who is the Achmet of 44/56, 76: and this identification seems to be proved by the facts that (i) the places here assigned to Abu'l-Mu'izz are exactly those assigned to Achmet at 44/100-2, 108-9; and (ii) in the same text Ahmad is not referred to again, but only Abu'l-Mu'izz. The Abu'l-Mu'izz of Ibn al-Azraq is therefore not identical with C.'s infant Apelmouze (44/74-5, 82-4, 90-1), who was passed over in favour of his uncle Apolesphouet (44/95-7).

We have next to note that whereas Ibn al-Azraq calls the lord of Manzikert 'Abd al-Hamid in 940, C. calls him Aposelmis (Abu Salim; 44/99-100). But a second Arabic text, that of Abu Firas, relating to the same epoch, does refer to Abu Salim, who should therefore, it seems, have been described by Ibn al-Azraq, not as 'Abd al-Hamid, but as ibn 'Abd al-Hamid, that is, 'son of Abelchamit' (cf. 44/24-31). The various accounts are therefore quite consistent, so long as we do not confuse Ahmad Abu'l-Mu'izz (whose father 'Abd ar-Rahman is not mentioned by C.) with his first cousin once removed, the infant Abu'l-Mu'izz (Apelmouze). The subsequent history of the dynasty is clear. Aposelmis/Abu Salim of Manzikert was succeeded by his son Apelbart/Abu'l-Ward II shortly after 940 (44/106-7), who murdered his cousin Achmet/Ahmad and seized Khelat', Ardjesh and Dhat al-Jauz some time before 952 (44/112-14).

44/19-21 Δέδωκεν δὲ ⟨τῷ⟩ αὐτῷ 'Απελβὰρτ κτλ.

It is to be noted that C.'s claim to Khelat', Ardjesh, Dhat al-Jauz and Perkri (44/115) rests not only on their subjugation by Kourkouas (see preceding note), but also on the pretext that they were, until 912, held by the Kaïsite emirs as vassals of the prince of princes, himself a vassal of the emperor (44/45-9). Canard (476) doubts the truth of this vassalage to the prince of princes.

44/41 τοῦ Κορὴ καὶ τοῦ Χάρκα.

Khorkhorounik' and Hark', the two districts lying north-west and west of Manzikert: see Canard 184, map VI.

44/45-9 ἐπεὶ ⟨δὲ⟩ ὁ ἄρχων τῶν ἀρχόντων κτλ. See on 44/19-21: the claim to suzerainty over Armenia was nominal rather than real, even in C.'s time.

44/57 τὸ 'Αλτζικέ. Armenian Ardzke, Arab Dhat al-Jauz: a castle on a hill overlooking lake Van, between Khelat' and Ardjesh: see Canard 184, map VI.

44/115 ὀφείλει ὁ βασιλεὺς ἀναλαβέσθαι.

For the significance of this directive, see General Introduction p. 4; and Manojlović III, 125 ff. The subsequent paragraph suggests that Apelbart II, after murdering Achmet, refused to continue paying the tribute to the empire (see on 44/17-115). Apelbart was killed in 964 (Canard 483); Manzikert was captured and destroyed by Bardas Phocas in 968 (see Asoghik 44; cf. Honigmann 96). Khelat', Arzes and Perkri passed in about 980 to the emirs of Mayyafariqin of the Kurdish Marwanid dynasty, who, during the civil wars of Basil II's reign, occupied Manzikert also. They were driven out by the Iberian Bagratid David the Curopalate, on whose death Manzikert and the lake Van cities were annexed by Basil II, in 1001 (see Honigmann 150-7).

44/128 ἀπλίκτα. Cf. Leo, Taktika, cols. 792 D ff.

45/1 Περὶ τῶν 'Ιβήρων.

In these chapters, 45 and 46, C. describes the dealings of the imperial government with the Iberian or Georgian branch of the Bagratid family, whose possessions lay along the imperial frontier from Taron to the Black Sea. The *Georgian Chronicle* tells us of a Bagratid Gouaram who was king of Georgia from 575 to 600, and who had the title of Curopalate; his son Stephen succeeded him and reigned from 600 to 619, without assuming the title of king (see *Georgian Chronicle*, 135-9; cf. Marquart 393-4; Goubert, *Mém. L. Petit* (Bucharest, 1948), 114-18). But there is no external confirmation of their existence. The authentic Bagratids of Georgia descend from Ashot the Bagratid, Patrician of Armenia, blinded in 748, for whose ancestry see Toumanoff, *Bagratids*, 37-9. His younger son Vasac had been prince of Taron, but had been obliged to migrate northward and had settled in Klardjeth, just east of the Byzantine frontier on the river Chorokh (see Ghevond, *Histoire des guerres et des conquêtes des Arabes en Arménie*, tr. Chahnazarian (Paris, 1856), 141; *Georgian Chronicle*, 149-50, which makes Adarnase I a nephew of 'Adarnase the Blind', who is otherwise unknown, cf. Marquart 415). Vasac's son Adarnase and his grandson Ashot, called The Great by the Georgian chroniclers, extended their domains southward into Tao (the Greek 'land of Taokhoi', the Armenian Tahots) and north-eastward into Karthli, in the heart of Georgia, in the valley of the Kour. At some time the family adopted the Orthodox faith, abandoning the separatist Church of their Armenian cousins, and professed a loyal vassalage towards Constantinople: cf. Goubert, *op. cit.*, 119. Both Adarnase and Ashot the Great seem to have received the title of Curopalate (see *Georgian Chronicle*, 154; we are told that Ashot was specifically made Curopalate by the emperor, sc. Leo V: cf. Marquart 392). On Ashot's death (830) Karthli was conquered by the Arabs; but his second son Bagrat I (830–76), who was a child when he succeeded, recovered the province and reigned from Tiflis, with the title of Curopalate, but as vassal of the Arabs. Ashot the Great's eldest son, Adarnase, inherited Klardjeth and Tao, with his capital at Ardanoudj. Adarnase's two younger sons, Gourgen and Sembat, divided the territory, Gourgen taking Tao and Sembat Klardjeth with Ardanoudj. The Karthli branch, which was continually at war with the Abasgians and the Arabs for the possession of Karthli, seems to have held a long strip of territory stretching south-west of Karthli, east of Klardjeth and Tao, down to the upper valley of the Araxes. See *Georgian Chronicle*, 155–65.

C.'s narrative deals with both the Karthli and the Ardanoudj branches of the family. It is a confusing account, but in fact the genealogical details that he gives are confirmed, apart from minor errors, by the *Georgian Chronicle*. In the genealogical tree overleaf, based on Armenian and Georgian sources (*Georgian Chronicle*, esp. 159–61, 165; Ghevond 141), the characters mentioned by C. are given the chapters and lines in which he refers to them. See also Marquart 391–465, esp. 427–35; and, most recently, the authoritative study of Prince C. Toumanoff (now printing in *Le Muséon*), whose stemma is accompanied by an exhaustive genealogical commentary. The work appeared too lately for use here.

45/2–42　ʼΙστέον, ὅτι ἑαυτοὺς κτλ.

This is the only passage in cc. 43–6 which preserves the scheme of a Περὶ ἐθνῶν underlying cc. 14–42: see General Introduction pp. 3–4. C.'s account of the origin of the Bagratids is uncorroborated elsewhere, and is actually unfair to the antiquity of the family, though presumably he obtained it from Iberian and Bagratid sources, and his dates fit in with Georgian legend. According to his version, the founders of the family were David and Spandiatis, descendants of king David and Bathsheba (Marquart 392 seems to be wrong in calling them actual *sons* of D. and B.); David and Spandiatis left Jerusalem in about A.D. 450 and came to Iberia, where the Iberians carved out a kingdom at the expense of the Persians, and afterwards increased their power through the help of the emperor Heraclius. Spandiatis, who was reputed invulnerable, was childless; but David had a son Pankratios, who had a son Asotios, whose son Adarnase was made Curopalate by the emperor Leo VI. After stating that his own father's contemporary Adarnase was David's great-grandson, C. then states that David's migration from Jerusalem took place five hundred years before (*cf.* Marquart 392). 'Spandiatis' is unknown. The name is perhaps a variation of Sembat or Shambath, the founder of the Bagratids according to Armenian legend (see below); or it may have some connection with the Armenian 'Spand' (= 'sacrifice'), and refer to some 'Spandounig', *i.e.* Grand Master of the Sacrifices (see also Marquart 428–30). The genealogy is incorrect though the names given are all frequently found in the Bagratid family. But the Jewish origin of the family appears in the Georgian and Armenian legends. The Georgian legend emphasizes the relationship to the Virgin Mary, to which C. refers (45/7). Indeed, in Tsarist Russia, before the revolution, at the great Court festival that took place on the day of the Assumption of the Virgin, the prince Bagration always appeared in full mourning, as it was a family affair. *Cf.* Toumanoff, *Le Muséon* 65 (1952) 244–6.

According to the *Georgian Chronicle* (136–7), the Bagratids descend from Cleopas, the brother of St Joseph. In the middle of the 6th cent. A.D., twenty-eight generations later (an unnecessarily large number to cover five and a half centuries), the family was represented by a certain Solomon, whose seven sons left Palestine for Armenia. Though they lived in Palestine, their mother was a Chosroïd princess. In the province of Ekletz (= Ekegheats-Gavar, just east of Erzincan: see Saint-Martin, *Mémoires*, I, 45; = Keltzini: see on 43/92, 50/116) they were baptized by the local queen Rachel, and one of them married her daughter. Four of the brothers, Gouaram, Sahac, Asam and Warazward, went on into Iberia, where Gouaram became king and Curopalate, and was the ally of the emperor (*sc.* Maurice). He reigned from 575–600. His son Stephen (600–19) was the ally of Heraclius (*cf.* 45/22–8; Marquart 393–4). Subsequent Bagratids descend from Gouaram. The 18th cent. Bagratid prince Wakhoucht, feeling the story inadequate, introduced the name Bagrat by giving it to that son of Solomon who married Rachel's daughter, and saying that Gouaram's son was given his uncle's name, and that king Gouaram was his son.

The fifth-century Armenian historian Moses of Khorene quotes the earlier Syriac writer Mar Abas Catina as mentioning as unworthy of belief a popular theory that the Bagratids descend from the eponymous king of the Armenians Haïk. On the contrary, he says, their ancestor was a Jew called Shambath, who had been taken into captivity by king Nebuchadnezzar and been given by him to the Armenian king Hratchea. In the time of king Vagharsak (A.D. 192–207) the Bagratids, descendants of Shambath (or, according to Moses of Khorene, who is vague about dates, Shambath himself) obtained the hereditary right to crown the king, the rank of Master of the Horse (aspet) and of commander of the western frontier. Thenceforward their name appears with growing frequency in Armenian history. According to the family legend, they remained steadfast in the Jewish faith in spite of persecution, till their conversion to Christianity was brought about by the apostle St Thaddeus, a few years after the Crucifixion (see Moses of Khorene, ed. in Armenian by Abeghian-Harout'unian (Tiflis, 1913), I, § 22, 68–9, II, §3, 105, § 8, 108; John Catholicus 14, 16–17; Asoghik 7–8; Brosset 141–3; *cf.* Marquart 391 ff.). Moses says nothing of the kinship with the Virgin, but by the time of John Catholicus (17) this is accepted.

In contrast to all this legendary material, Marquart (436–9) and, in more detail, Toumanoff (*Bagratids* 35–54) have been able to trace the historical origins of the Bagratids at least as far back as the Conversion of Armenia (end of the 3rd cent.), at which time the office of 'aspet' was already attached to the head of their house. We need not doubt their Jewish origin: large numbers of Jews from the Assyrian captivity—Israel rather than Judah—settled in Armenia, where, as in Babylonia, there were hereditary chiefs who claimed descent from David, known as the 'Princes of the *Diaspora*', till the high Middle Ages (see Brann-Chwolson, *Entsiklopedicheskiy Slovar* XI, St Petersburg, 1893, 440–1). The Bagratids may well have been of their number, like the family of Amatounis, who also claimed Jewish origin. But Toumanoff (*Bagratids* 22–5) believes that they were more probably of 'Urartian or Hurrian-Subarean' stock.

45/20 εἰς τὰς δυσκολίας. *Cf.* Cecaumenus 25/23, and Βασίλειος Διγενὴς Ἀκρίτας, ed. Kalonaros II (Athens, 1941), 6/90.

45/29-33 Διὰ δὲ τὸ . . . Χριστιανοῖς.
The connection of the Iberians with Jerusalem dates from before Bagratid times. A late tradition said that the first Christian king Miriam made a pilgrimage there. King Wakhtang, with his mother and sister, visited the City in about A.D. 470 (see *Georgian Chronicle*, 114). According to tradition, Miriam founded the Monastery of the Cross, on the site where Lot planted the tree from which the Cross was made. Probably Wakhtang was the founder, for the building was amongst those restored by Justinian (see Procopius, *De Aed.*, V, 9, 6), after its destruction in the Samaritan rebellion. Prince Constantine of Iberia, martyred by the Arabs in the late 9th cent., visited Jerusalem and made many gifts there. During the Crusading kingdom travellers tell of Iberian establishments; and under the caliphs in the later Middle Ages the Georgians, who were then the only Christians allowed to bear arms in Jerusalem, obtained possession of the Chapel of Golgotha (see *AASS*, November, IV, 557; Jacques de Vitry, *History of Jerusalem*, tr. Stewart, in *Palest. Pilgr. Text Society* (1896), 83; *cf.* H. T. F. Duckworth, *The Church of the Holy Sepulchre* (London, 1922), 261–71). In the mid-18th cent. they still maintained fourteen establishments in or near Jerusalem, but soon afterwards, owing to the taxes

FAMILY TREE OF THE IBERIAN BAGRATIDS

Ashot the Blind, 'Patrician of Armenia' (†761)

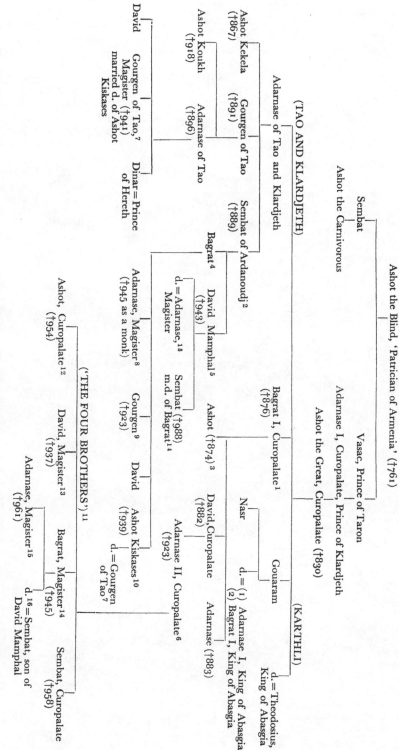

1. Bagrat I, Curopalate c.45/34
2. Sembat of Ardanoudj c.46/4
3. Ashot c.45/34. 35
4. Bagrat, c.46/3,5,6
5. David Mamphal, c. 46/3,5,29,36,38+1
6. Adarnase II, Curopalate, c.43/39.47,111; c.45/35; c.46/36,83,85,147,164 (Called son of Ashot, c.45/35)

7. Gourgen of Tao, Magister: c.46/11,18,20,22,25,30,52,58, 66,87,90,92,94,107,121,126,129,154
8. Adarnase, Magister, c.46/6
9. Gourgen, c.46/719
10. Ashot Kiskases, c.46/7,10,13,19,23,31,57,64,70,98,106, 109,117,124,125,150,162

11. 'The four brothers', c.45/70-1; c.46/89
12. Ashot, Curopalate, c.46/25,37,80,130,146,154,163
13. David, Magister, c.46/79,95,96,117,151,154
14. Bagrat, Magister, c.45/147,153; c.46/27,39
15. Adarnase, Magister, c.45/126; c.46/40,41
16. daughter of Bagrat, Magister, c.46/39

demanded by the Ottoman authorities, they sold everything to the Greek Orthodox community (see Brosset 197 ff.). For Georgian pilgrims to Jerusalem in the 9th cent., see Theoph. Cont. 119/15–16, and *cf.* on 46/54–5.

45/35 Ἀδρανασή.
Elsewhere, Ἀδρανασέ, Ἀδρανασήρ: Curopalate, reigned 881–923, son of David, not Ashot (see genealogical table, and Marquart 392). He played a large part in Ibero-Armenian history. He was obliged to acknowledge the suzerainty of king Sembat the Martyr (see Introductory Note to this section, p. 159) in about 899, and was rewarded by coronation as king of Iberia by Sembat (see John Catholicus 101–2). Besides Karthli and Gougark, he owned land in Tao (*ibid.*, 102, 119). In later life he turned against the Armenians, but was reconciled and performed the coronation of Ashot Erkaṭ' after Sembat's death (*ibid.*, 146–7). About the end of his reign, he lost Karthli to the Abasgians (see *Georgian Chronicle*, 159). His sons were therefore keenly interested in extending their lands in the south, and in expanding from Tao into the Araxes valley; and therefore were concerned with the fate of Theodosioupolis.

45/39–40 ἔτη ν′ κτλ.
A. M. 6460, 10th indiction, is A.D. 952. The year 552 (400 years previously) would roughly correspond to the time of the entry of the Bagratids of the branch of king Gouaram according to the Georgian legend (see on 45/1, *init.*, and Marquart 393); but C. seems uncertain whether the figure should be 400 or 500.

45/43–175 Ἰστέον, ὅτι ὁ φιλόχριστος κτλ.
The rest of c. 45 is purely political and diplomatic, being designed to make good Byzantine claims on the territory of Theodosioupolis: see General Introduction p. 3.

45/44 Φασιανὴν.
See Honigmann 151, 196 and note 8. C.'s Phasis is the river Araxes (see 45/130), and Phasiane is a district in the upper valley of the Araxes, immediately to the east of Theodosioupolis (see Canard 184, map VI). The Armenians called the district Basean or Basen, and the Byzantines seem to have derived the name falsely from the Phasis, which they therefore identified with the Araxes instead of the Rion, the original Phasis. Earlier, in Menander (*Excerpta de Legationibus*, ed. de Boor, Berlin, 1903) 202/8, it is called Βασσιανή. Two campaigns are described in this passage: the first under Lalakon, the second under the domestic Katakalon. Evidence from two orations of Arethas (*BZ*, 47 (1954), 13–15) suggests that the first was undertaken in 901 (at least it cannot be earlier than 900: *ibid.*, 15 and *cf.* on 50/111–32), and the second, which may not only have reached but also captured Theodosioupolis (Leo, *Taktika*, col. 981 A), in 902. Vasiliev II, 101 rightly connected *Taktika loc. cit.* with 45/52, as against A. Rambaud, *L'empire grec au X siècle* (Paris, 1870), 426, note 2, and Honigmann 79, note 2. *Cf.* on 45/143–4, and Mitard, *BZ*, 12 (1903), 590.

45/47 Λαλάκωνα.
Schlumberger, *Sigillographie*, 296, published a seal of 'Leo Lalakon, Curopalate and Duke of the Armeniakoi'. See also *MPG*, cv, col. 513 B for Λέων ἐκεῖνος ὁ Λαλάκων who was τῶν Νουμέρων δομέστικος in January 859; this is not likely to be C.'s Lalakon, but may have been his father or uncle. Nothing else is known of C.'s Lalakon, or of his unnamed fellow governors, excepting that the governor of Mesopotamia was presumably Orestes (50/127).

45/51 Κατακαλὼν.
The magister Katakalon was Leo Katakalon, who was defeated by the Bulgarians in 896 at Bulgarophygon (Theoph. Cont. 359/23, 360/8–13). The date of this campaign

(902, see on 45/44) shows that Katakalon was still domestic six years after Bulgarophygon. For Katakalon, see further *De Cer.*, 456/17–457/8; *Vita Euthymii*, ed. De Boor (Berlin, 1888), 5/24–5, 16/7–8, 140–2; Bănescu, *Acad. Roumaine, Bull. Sect. Hist.*, 11 (1924), 3–4; Zlatarsky, *Sbornik za narodni umotvorenija, nauka i knižnina*, 24 (1908), 143, note 2.

45/52 Θεοδοσιουπόλεως.
Called Karin by the Armenians, and Qâlîqualâ, later Arzan ar-Rûm (modern Erzerum), by the Arabs. It had been re-founded and strongly fortified under Theodosius II, but had been in Arab hands since the middle of the 7th cent.: see Saint-Martin, *Mémoires*, 66–8; Honigmann 10, 79–80; Canard 244–5.

45/56 Ἰωάννης ὁ Κουρκούας.
See Theoph. Cont. 277/8, Cont. Geo. Mon. 847/16 (? his father); Theoph. Cont. 397/17–18 (drungarios of the watch, 920); *ibid.*, 404/8 (domestic, 922; *cf.* on 43/92); *ibid.*, 415/10–417/2 (*cf.* Vasiliev II/2, 154); *ibid.*, 426/3–428/2 (*cf.* 45/143); *ibid.*, 429/3–16; 443/5–6 (*cf.* Vasiliev II/2, 157). For his eastern campaigns, see Canard 731–53. He was domestic, or commander-in-chief, continuously for twenty-two years and seven months (Theoph. Cont. 426/13–14; *cf. ibid.*, 415/11–12): if, as Theoph. Cont. 426/12–13, suggests, he was retired in late December 944, then his appointment will date from June 922, after the defeat of Pothos Argyros at Manglava two months earlier (Theoph. Cont. 401–2). He died some time after 946: see Theoph. Cont. 443/6–7; Vasiliev II/2, 157, 407. His campaign against Dovin (Tibi) took place in 927: see on 43/92; Vasiliev II/2, 150; Canard 739.

45/59 Θεόφιλος.
Brother of John Kourkouas and grandfather of the emperor John I Tzimiskes: see Theoph. Cont. 428/3–20; Cedrenus II, 318/9–12; Canard 731. He was appointed military governor of Chaldia in 923 or 924, after the revolt of Bardas Boïlas (see on 43/92); and his first tenure of the post (45/59–60) probably lasted at least until 940: see on 45/143–4.

45/62–3 χώραν . . . χωρίον.
Where these words are used in distinct and technical senses, χώρα denominates (as here and at 43/181, 182, 184; 44/40 etc.) a tract of country en bloc; and it may imply the tract surrounding or subordinate to a large town (χωρόπολις, 46/43), in which case it is the equivalent of ἡ περίχωρος, ἡ ἐπικρατεία (43/186; 44/107; 44/67). χωρίον on the other hand is the equivalent of κώμη (see Dölger, *Finanzverwaltung*, 66, and *cf.* Cedrenus II, 577/7–13, where κωμόπολις is contrasted with the μεγίστη πόλις of Theodosioupolis), and was the technical name for an agricultural community or 'village': that is, a collection of houses with adjoining plots or farms, treated as a unit or commune for purposes of taxation (*Steuergemeinde*): see Ostrogorsky, *Vierteljahrschrift für Sozial- und Wirtschaftsgeschichte*, 20 (1927), 15–17, 42–6; Dölger, *Finanzverwaltung*, 66, 126, 134–5; Constantinescu, *Acad. Roumaine, Bull. Sect. Hist.*, 13 (1927), 168–74; A. P. Každan, *Agrarnye Otnosheniya v Vizantii*, XIII–XV vv. (Moscow, 1952), 54–5; Dendias, Πεπρ. τοῦ θ' διεθν. βυζαντ. συνεδρίου II (Athens, 1956), 358. As however χωρίον is often used in a non-technical and purely territorial sense (*e.g.* 25/26, 45/66), when the word 'village' would be inappropriate, it is better to translate χωρία as 'territories' except where, as here, the *buildings* of a commune are specifically implied (see Vol. I, p. 332 *s.v.* χωρίον).

45/63 Ἀβνίκου.
The modern village of Avnik, situated south of the Araxes, on the watershed between it and the southern branch of the Euphrates, about 40 miles east of Theodosioupolis: see Honigmann 80. It was an Arab emirate (45/130–2).

45/68 ἡ βασιλεία ἡμῶν. For the formula, see Dölger, *BZ*, 33 (1933), 445; and *id.*, *BES*, 22.

45/68 Κετζέον.
This city is unidentifiable. It was already part of the Iberian Bagratid domains. It is perhaps the village of Hindakh (Honigmann 193, ᾿Ανδάκων), on the road running north-east from Theodosioupolis into Tao; or a castle, in the pass of this road, called by the Georgians Kartlis Qeli, the 'Throat of Karthli', and by the Turks Gurgi Bogaz, the 'Throat of Georgia'. For these operations against Theodosioupolis, see on 45/143–4.

45/69 σιταρχεῖσθαι *Cf.* Cecaumenus 26/29.

45/70–1 τὸν κουροπαλάτην καὶ τοὺς ἀδελφοὺς αὐτοῦ.
Ashot, son of Adarnase, and his brothers David, Bagrat and Sembat (see genealogical tree p. 172). Ashot became Curopalate after his father's death (46/162–5).

45/77–8 τὸν Βασπαρακανίτην. Gagik Ardzrouni of Vaspurakan (908–36); see on 43/111.

45/81–2 τουρμάρχην.
The *tourma* was a sub-division of the *thema*, the provincial army-corps and, like the *thema*, became associated with the district occupied by the division; see Leo, *Taktika*, cols. 708–709, and *cf.* on 50/94. The turmarch was thus both lieutenant-general and governor of a sub-province.

45/83 διὰ κελεύσεως. See Dölger, *Regesten*, 614.

45/101 χρυσοβούλλια.
That is to say, χρυσόβουλλοι λόγοι or γραφαί, a type of document dating from the reign of Leo VI. For the *form*, see Dölger, *BD*, 39–43; and for the *purpose*, as patents of gifts to a subject (*e.g.* 43/87, 96, 99; *Vita Euthymii*, ed. De Boor (Berlin, 1888), 29/1; Cedrenus II, 642/16–17), and hence as vehicles for treaties with foreign powers regarded as Byzantine subjects, *ibid.*, 42. *Cf.* also Treitinger 212, 213; Dölger, *BES*, 16, 21; and on 45/105–6.

45/101–2 τοῦ κυροῦ ῾Ρωμανοῦ. See Dölger, *Regesten*, 615.

45/103 Ζουρβανέλη . . . ἀζάτου.
A ms. note on the Paris ms. (P) of *DAI* (see Vol. I, 20/5–6) says that this Zourvanelis is the father of Tornikis 'now syncellus'. John Thornik the Syncellus, co-founder of the Iviron monastery on Mt. Athos, who left his cell to take service under Basil II, was a well known figure later in the 10th cent. St Euthymios the Iberian was his nephew. In the *Life of St John and St Euthymios* (*Anal. Boll.*, 36–7 (1917–19), 18 and note 3) we are told that Thornik's father was called Abugharb, evidence confirmed by Asoghik (133, 146, 151, 165). The *Life* also says (*loc. cit*) that Abugharb was an old friend of the Byzantine court. We may therefore assume that the Zourvanelis of 45/103 is in fact Abugharb Tchordvaneli. The name Tchordvaneli is a Georgian surname, which occurs among Abugharb's descendants, used almost as a Christian name. The family also employed Armenian names such as Thornik and Bagrat, like many of the Georgian nobility, amongst whom Armenian influences were strong; but there is no need to assume that it was therefore an orthodox Armenian family, as Adontz (II, 544) patriotically claims. St Euthymios's father, Abugharb's son-in-law, was a Meshkian noble, and Abugharb was probably the same. A late tradition (see Brosset 190) says that he came from Ksani

(in central Georgia), but that is improbable. For details of the family, see Adontz II, 543 ff.; *id.*, *Byzantion*, 13 (1938), 143 ff.; and, more reliably, the *Life of St Euthymios* (see Peeters, *Anal. Boll.*, 50 (1932)), 358 ff. The word 'azat' (*cf. De Them.*, 75/7) is an Armenian word, = 'free' or 'noble', which passed early into Georgian usage (the Georgian 'Asat' = free or noble, and 'Azni' = the nobility). Its use does not give corroborative evidence (as Adontz II, 544, thinks) that Tchordvaneli was an Armenian.

45/105-6 περιέχει ὑποσχέσθαι τὸν αὐτὸν κουροπαλάτην.
For the χρυσόβουλλος λόγος *embodying* the reciprocal promises of the other contracting party, see Dölger, *BES*, 21: 'Der Schwierigkeit, dass die Urkunde die vorher in harten Kämpfen ausgehandelten Versprechungen des Vertragspartners möglichst genau enthalten muss, wird dadurch begegnet, dass man *die entsprechenden Eidesurkunden des Vertragspartners in Form von Inserten in den Verleihungstext hereinnimmt*' (our italics).

45/117-18 αὐτοῦ τοῦ στρατοπέδου. The word αὐτοῦ shows that C. is here quoting the bull *verbatim*.

45/124 τὸ δὲ τῆς βασιλείας ἡμῶν. See Dölger, *Regesten*, 649. It must be dated 945-9: see on 45/143-4.

45/125 ὅσους ἂν τόπους κτλ. Apparently a common formula in such agreements: *cf.* Cedrenus II, 558/18-21, 559/9-11; Anna Comnena x, 9 (ed. Reifferscheid II, 91/17-21).

45/125-6 ὁ μάγιστρος 'Αδρανασέ.
Son of the Curopalate Ashot's brother Bagrat (†945: see genealogical tree p. 172). As Ashot was apparently childless, he may have regarded his nephew Adarnase as his heir, though in fact he was succeeded as curopalate by his brother Sembat. The Index to Vol. I, p. 289, refers to him incorrectly here as Adranase 2. He is in fact the same as Adranase 3, except for the reference at 46/6, which is to his cousin, son of Bagrat of the Ardanoudj branch.

45/129 Μαστάτον. The position of Mastaton is unknown, but presumably it was near Avnik: see Honigmann 80, 164.

45/133 'Ιωάννης . . . ὁ 'Αρραβωνίτης.
Not elsewhere known, but may be referred to by Yahya-ibn-Saïd (Vasiliev II/2, 97): *cf.* ed. Kratchkovsky and Vasiliev (*Patrologia Orientalis*, 18 (1924)) 774, note 2.

45/143-4 ἐπολιόρκησεν τὴν Θεοδοσιούπολιν.
The chronology of these operations against Theodosioupolis (45/67-154) is very doubtful, and the city seems to have changed hands more than once during the first half of the 10th cent. The evidence of Thomas Ardzrouni (III, § 22; *cf.* Adontz I, 724), with which we may connect Leo, *Taktika*, col. 956 C (καὶ γὰρ . . . ἀσχολουμένων), suggests that it was besieged by the Byzantines in 895. It was probably captured by Katakalon in 902 (see on 45/44), but was certainly not in Byzantine hands when Kourkouas began his eastern campaigns twenty years later (Vasiliev II/2, 147). According to Michael Syrus, it was taken by the Byzantines about or shortly after 934-5 (Honigmann 79, note 2). But it was probably not in Byzantine hands in the autumn of 939, when Saïf ad-Daula dislodged the Byzantines from Hafjij (Vasiliev II/2, 122). It was certainly not in Byzantine hands in 945, as 45/124-8 makes clear. It was finally captured by the Byzantines in 949 (Asoghik II, 37-8; *cf.* Honigmann *loc. cit.*; and 45/134, where Theophilus is described as 'now', in 952, governor of the province). The siege here described (45/143 ff.) cannot therefore be dated with certainty. The terminus ante is the date of the death of Bagrat

Magister, 945 (see 45/147). The most probable date is April to October 939, after which the Byzantines were compelled to evacuate Hafjij and Theophilus' own province of Chaldia was invaded: see Canard 744-5.

45/146-7 Πετρωνᾶν τὸν Βόϊλαν . . . κατεπάνω Νικοπόλεως.
For the Boïlas family, see Theoph. Cont. 404/5, 411/3-4: they were friends of the emperor Romanus I (*cf.* Romanus Boïlas, Zonaras, ed. Dindorf, IV, 176/31), but Petronas does not occur elsewhere. The *thema* of Nikopolis was in Epirus (*De Them.* 92); it was a naval *thema*, and may have maintained a force of Mardaïtes under a katepan (*cf.* C. N. Sathas, *Bibliotheca graeca medii aevi*, II (Venice, 1873), νγ′), as did the naval *thema* of the Kibyrrhaiotai (50/169; *cf. De Cer.*, 659/16). But it is hard to see what a western naval officer should be doing at a military siege in the Far East; and in view of the connexions of the Boïlas family with the nearby province of Chaldia, it seems far more likely that Petronas was katepan of an Armenian force stationed at Nikopolis in the *thema* of Koloneia, for which see *De Them.*, 74/8; Cedrenus II, 625/11; Canard 248, map IX. For the office of katepan, see on 50/169-70; for katepans of small districts or (as here) cities, Cedrenus II, 494/23; 702/3; 727/12; Glykatzi-Ahrweiler, *Bull. Corr. Hell.*, 84 (1960-1), 64-5; and on 27/69-70.

45/147 Ὁ δὲ μάγιστρος Παγκράτιος. This Bagrat is the brother of the curopalate Ashot, and the father of the magister Adarnase (see on 45/125-6).

45/155 διότι. Means here διὰ ταῦτα or ὥστε: see on 51/20.

45/157 δοῦλος καὶ φίλος.
The terms are diplomatic: as δοῦλος καὶ φίλος (see on 4/10), the curopalate receives a κέλευσις (*De Cer.*, 687/16-17; *cf.* on 8/24). See Dölger, *BES*, 41, note 10, who, however, seems to confuse the Iberian curopalate with Ashot Erkat': see on 43/111.

45/158-64 ἵνα γένηται σύνορον κτλ.
C.'s geography is at fault. The Araxes flows eastward: hence the *left* bank is the north bank, the side on which Theodosioupolis lies, while Avnik is beyond the *right* or south bank. It is however possible that C. conceived every road and river as going towards Constantinople, and used 'left' and 'right' from the point of view of someone facing the capital. Ἰλλυρία is the Armenian province of Aghori, south of Theodosioupolis (see Hübschmann 444). Theodosioupolis had been annexed to the empire in 949 (see on 45/143-4), only three years before C. was writing. The question of the frontier was therefore highly topical.

45/174-5 ἀρκεῖσθαι . . . ἐπιζητεῖν. Cf. *MPG*, CXI, col. 57 B: ἀρκεῖσθαι . . . καὶ μηδὲν πλέον ἐπιζητεῖν. Both are quotations from documents.

46/3-4 Ἰστέον, ὅτι . . . τοῦ Ἴβηρος.
See genealogical tree p. 172, Ardanoudj branch. The 'great' or 'elder' (see on 26/2, 46/117, 151) Sembat died in 889, Bagrat in 909, and David as a monk in 943: see *Georgian Chronicle*, 165. They all had the title of Mamphal, which does not mean 'all-holy' but 'ruler' ('Mamphali' in Georgian). *Cf.* Marquart 186.

46/6-10 Ὁ δὲ Παγκράτιος . . . Κισκάσῃ.
Of Bagrat's sons Adarnase died as a monk in 945, Gourgen in 923 and Ashot Kiskases in 939. The *Georgian Chronicle*, *loc. cit.*, gives a fourth son, David, who died in 908, and gives Gourgen a posthumous son Gourgen, who lived on to 968. His uncle Ashot presumably seized his inheritance before he was born, and C. is technically correct in saying that

Gourgen died childless (46/9). Kiskases is the Georgian 'kiskasi', 'nimble', rather than 'kaskasi', 'merry' as Brosset (154, note 5) suggests.

46/11   Κουρκένην.
This Gourgen must be Gourgen of Tao, head of the senior branch of the Iberian Bagratids. He died in 941. His quarrels with his father-in-law must have taken place about 930 to 935, and the events described in 46/22-34 about 941-2, certainly before 945, when Bagrat, brother of the curopalate, died (see 46/27, and on 45/143-4; 45/147).

46/14   Τυρόκαστρον.
'Cheese-castle' has the same name in Georgian (Kveli-tzihe). It is about forty miles north-west of Ardanoudj (see Honigman 148 and note 4; map IV).

46/14-15   'Ατζαρά . . . Κώλωριν.
See *De Cer.*, 688/1. The river Atzara or Adjara flows into the Chorokh or Akampsis a few miles above its mouth, which marked the imperial frontier on the Black Sea (see Honigmann 54 and map IV). Kolorin is presumably the name of this frontier district. Ashot's new territory therefore marched with Abasgia.

46/16-17   Γεωργίου . . . 'Αβασγίας.   See Toumanoff, *Abasgia*, 81. George ruled 915/6-959/60.

46/22   Τελευτήσαντος . . . Κουρκενίου.
Gourgen (†941) was the last of his branch (apart from a sister Dinar, who was princess of Hereth). His territories were therefore divided. The Abasgians presumably took Azaria, the curopalate and his brother the lands of Tao itself, and Sembat son of David Mamphal (46/29) Ardanoudj. Sembat was next heir to the Ardanoudj branch (as Adarnase, Ashot Kiskasis's brother, was probably already a monk, and Gourgen, posthumous son of Gourgen, was only 18), if a woman was excluded from the succession.

46/36-8   Τοῦ Δαυὶδ . . . ἐξαδέλφαι.
David's and Adarnase the Curopalate's mothers may have been first cousins; but so were their fathers, Sembat and David the Curopalate (see genealogical tree p. 172).

46/38-41   Εἶχεν . . . τοῦ Δαυίδ.
Sembat's wife was the sister of the Magister Adarnase (see on 45/125-6) and niece of the Curopalate Ashot. It was probably to avoid marrying within the prohibited degrees (though the Bagratids from family pride were careless of this, see 45/8-10) that Adarnase only married his brother-in-law's sister after his own sister's death.

46/42   'Αρδανούτζιν.
Ardanoudj, on a tributary of the Chorokh, is still a considerable village, though its importance as a road-junction (46/43-5) has been taken by Ardvin, on the Chorokh some fifteen miles to the west; see Marquart 183-4; Allen 58; Honigmann map IV.

46/43   ῥαπάτιν . . . χωρόπολιν.
See Honigmann, *Byzantion*, 10 (1935), 148-9 (ῥαπάτιν = προάστειον); P. K. Hitti, *Origins of the Islamic State*, 1 (Columbia, 1916), 256. For χωρόπολιν, cf. on 45/62-3.

46/47   'Αρζῦν. This is the Arabic word 'Ardhun', which means 'territories' (an old plural): see G. W. Freytag, *Lexicon Arabico-Latinum*, 1 (Halle, 1830), 26.

46/48   τῶν Μισχιῶν.   Meshkia, alternatively Samtzkhé or upper Karthli, is the historic name of south-west Georgia including Klardjeth and Tao: see Allen 17.

46/49–165 "Ὅτι ὁ μακάριος βασιλεύς κτλ.

It is important to note that these events took place *before* those related at 46/22–34 (see Runciman, *Romanus Lecapenus*, 169, note 1), that is to say, *before* Ashot Kiskasis had been ejected from Ardanoudj by his son-in-law Gourgen. A terminus ante is supplied by the death of David Magister (†937: see 46/79). But Kiskasis inherited Ardanoudj as early as 923, on the death of his brother Gourgen (46/9–10); and it appears from 46/82–3, 162–5 that the curopalate Adarnase, who died in 923, had not long been dead. Romanus I began to interest himself in the eastern frontier as early as 922, and with increasing intensity after 924 (Canard 725–7): it therefore seems likely that the events here described fall between 923 and 930. This being so, it may be wondered whether the visit of an Iberian curopalate to Constantinople (Theoph. Cont. 402/12–21) may not be the visit of Ashot mentioned at 46/163–5; it is true that the chronicler appears to date his visit to 922, but may have misplaced it by a year or two.

46/50 πατρίκιον Κωνσταντῖνον καὶ δρουγγάριον.

The description of this Constantine as admiral of the fleet makes possible one of two identifications: first, he may be the one-time admiral Constantine Lips mentioned in Preger, *Scr. Orig. Const.*, II, 289/5–9 (see on 43/43–5), who in turn *may* be identical with the C. Lips who 'is now (952) patrician proconsul and grand hetaeriarch' (43/44–5; *cf.* Guilland, *BZ*, 44 (1951), 217); but this is improbable, since C. makes no mention of the latter's ever having been admiral. The second identification is more probable: namely, that he is Constantine Gongylios or Gongyles, whom we know to have been admiral in 949 (Theoph. Cont. 386/5–6, 390/13, 395/5, 436/8–9; Leo Diac. 7/3–7; Cedrenus II, 336/8–11; *cf.* Grégoire, *Byzantion*, 24 (1954), 147–8; omitted from Guilland's list of admirals but see *id.*, *Rev. Et. Byz.*, 13 (1955), 70); and who, though 'now' admiral, was at the time of his mission to Ardanoudj (between *c.* 923–30, see preceding note) protospatharius and manglavite (46/50–1, 140–4). It is true that Theoph. Cont. 390/13 describes Gongyles as already πατρίκιος in 917; but this may be an anticipation. Gongyles was one of two eunuch brothers who were friends of the empress Zoë; and though he interceded to prevent the blinding of Romanus Lecapenus in 917, he joined the revolt of Leo Phocas in 919. The present narrative, with its evident bias against Romanus (46/135–48) and its citation from actual documents (46/139–48), is presumably Constantine's own account of his mission, which he seems to have mishandled. This Constantine was perhaps identical also with the 'spatharocandidate and proximus' who conveyed a letter from Romanus I to the unknown rival of Gagik of Vaspurakan (see on 43/111); but here again there is a difficulty: for that letter cannot have been written before Ashot Erkat''s death in 929, and yet Constantine is still only spatharocandidate. Either therefore 45/50 ff. must be dated after 930 (which is not very probable, see preceding note), or else the envoys are different men. For μαγγλαβίτης, see on 51/72–3.

46/52 ἱμάτιον μαγιστράτου.

For the significance of an embassy sent with robes, see Treitinger 194, 195; Dölger, *BES*, 16 and note 19. The himation of the magistracy was the *sticharion*, a long, close-fitting tunic (see *De Cer.*, 144/8, 23/2). *Cf.* also *MPG* cxi, cols. 236 C, 308 D.

46/54–5 ὁ μοναχὸς ... Κυμινᾶ.

For Georgian pilgrims to Jerusalem, see on 45/29–33. For the use, or misuse, of pilgrims as secret and confidential agents, see Theoph. Cont. 119/12–19, and *cf.* Lopez, *Byzantion*, 18 (1948), 151. The monasteries on Mt. Kyminas are often referred to (see Mercati, *Byz.-Neugr. Jhrb.*, 4 (1923), 9–10), but its location is disputed (see Bury, *ERE*, 150, note 1).

46/67 πιττάκιον. For the πιττάκιον, see Dölger, *BD*, 46.

46/68 Συμεών, τοῦ πρωτοασηκρῆτις.

It is possible that this person was none other than Symeon the Logothete, whose chronicle is the basis of the chronicles of this period (see Bury 536–7). For πρωτοασηκρῆτις, see Bury, *IAS*, 97–8; Dölger, *BD*, 62–3; Bréhier, *Institutions*, 167.

46/84–6 οἱ τοῦ ᾿Αδρανασὲ . . . ἐξαδέλφου αὐτῶν. See genealogical tree, p. 172.

46/87 πρῶτον ἄνθρωπον . . . κανισκίου.

For πρῶτος ἄνθρωπος, 'prime minister', 'vizier', *cf. MPG*, cxi, col. 317 A. For his dispatch with a κανίσκιον, *cf. De Vel. Bell. (ap.* Leon. Diac.) 196/14. For the word κανίσκιον, see Vogt, Commentaire I, 154.

46/109–15 φλάμμουλα . . . εὐφημήσας.

φλάμμουλον is the usual word for a national or regimental banner (see 29/39, 30/46 and on 50/94; Bréhier, *Institutions*, 378), with the same significance as a standard nowadays. For the procedure here adopted, *cf.* Anna Comnena XI, 2, 6 (ed. Reifferscheid II, 107/2–5).

46/117 ὁ μέγας. See on 46/3–4.

46/119 τοῦ ᾿Ακαμψῆ καὶ τῇ Μουργούλῃ.

The Akampsis is the Chorokh and the Mourgouli the Murgul Su, its last tributary from the west. These two districts formed the extreme east corner of the province of Chaldia (see Honigmann 54 and map IV). David's lands were therefore situated between Ardanoudj and Atzaria and the Abasgian frontier, whereas his brother's lands were further south, towards Basean. This explains why David, rather than the curopalate his brother, was interested in the fate of Ardanoudj; while Ashot and Bagrat were interested in Theodosioupolis: see on 45/70–1, 147.

46/128 ὁ δομέστικος. John Kourkouas: see on 45/56.

46/139–48 Οὐκ ἔγραψα κτλ.

These are quotations from the actual documents (see on 46/50), as may be seen from 46/139–40, which gives Constantine his correct contemporary rank. But with what degree of truth Constantine's account lays all the blame on the emperor, it is not now possible to say: it all depends on the genuineness of the document cited at 46/68–76.

46/151 τὸν μέγαν. See on 46/3–4; and Manojlović III, 149: magistru Davidu staromu. For the sequence of events, see on 46/49–165.

Cc. 46/166–169; 47–48

INTRODUCTORY NOTE

Cc. 47, 48 contain the single item of history which the author includes under the second part of his third heading (P/21–3; *cf.* 46/166–7). This item concerns Byzantine-Saracen negotiations over Cyprus in 698 (47/15–25), the remainder of the two chapters being irrelevant (*cf.* General Introduction p. 2). The interest of the passage and of its position in C.'s work lies in its constituting a further proof that between the 7th and middle 10th cents. Cyprus was not regarded as a part of the Byzantine empire, except during seven years of the reign of Basil I: see *De Them.*, 81/20–3, and *cf.* Canard, *Bulletin d'Etudes orientales de Damas*, 13 (1949–51), 62; Jenkins, *Studies presented to D. M. Robinson*, II (1953), 1006–14 (modified in some particulars by Hatzipsaltis, *Kypriakai Spoudai* 20 (1956), 15–29 and Dikigoropoulos, *Report of the Department of Antiquities Cyprus 1940–1948* (1958), 94–114, who believe that Cyprus was re-occupied by Byzantium under Michael III and Theodora). Although in the treaty of 688–9 Armenia and Iberia were classed with Cyprus as areas in which Byzantines and Saracens exercised joint authority (Theophanes 363/11; *cf.* on 22/9–14), yet by C.'s time the first two were already regarded as Byzantine spheres, and their rulers as Byzantine vassals: *cf.* 44/45–7, 45/156–7. Cyprus on the other hand had been regarded as a neutral condominium since 688, or even since 648: see G. Hill, *History of Cyprus*, I (Cambridge, 1940: cited in the following notes as 'Hill'), 284, 287; and was still so regarded in C.'s time. It could therefore form a fit subject for negotiation between Byzantium and the Saracen *ethnos*. The source of 47/15–25 is not known; it is our only evidence for the resettlement of the Cypriots in 698. The passage, wholly diplomatic in content, was probably added to the book in 952: see General Introduction pp. 5–6.

46/166-7 μεταξὺ 'Ρωμαίων καὶ διαφόρων ἐθνῶν.
This is an intentionally vague phrase, designed to slur over a compromise which Byzantium had agreed to in times of weakness two and a half centuries before, but which was now felt to be discreditable. The position of Cyprus was by this time an anomaly: and indeed only thirteen years later (965) it was re-incorporated into the empire by Nicephorus II.

47/3-5 τῆς νήσου . . . καταλαβόντος.
The date of this removal of the Cypriots by Justinian II (Theophanes 365/9–13) is 691 (Theophanes A. M. 6183; *cf.* Mich. Syr. II, 470). The Trullan Synod, which confirmed the rights of Nova Justinianopolis (47/6, 48/11–12), sat from winter 691 to spring 692; see Hill 287, note 2. The motive for Justinian's act was not, however, a Saracen capture of Cyprus (*cf.* Mich. Syr. *loc. cit*); the migration formed part of a much larger policy of mass migrations undertaken by the emperor in various parts of the empire: see Ostrogorsky[2] 107–8. The removal of the Cypriots was a breach of the treaty of 688 (see on 22/9–14), and led to war with the caliph in 691 or 692; see Ostrogorsky[2] 107.

47/5-14 ἐγένετο οἰκονομία. For this οἰκονομία, see J. Hackett, *History of the Orthodox Church of Cyprus* (London, 1901), 37–41; Hill 288–9.

47/9-11 καὶ γὰρ καὶ αὐτὸς κτλ. For this quite baseless tradition, see Hill 280, note 5.

47/15 Μετὰ δὲ ἑπτὰ ἔτη.
That is to say, in 698; see Dölger, *Regesten*, 261. The emperor was no longer Justinian II but Tiberius III Apsimarus (see on 22/6–9), who, as ex-drungarios of the Kibyrrhaiote *thema* (Theophanes 370/24), was naturally interested in a spot which vitally concerned the sea-defences of southern Asia Minor. Hill 289, note 2, accuses C. of stating that the re-settlement of the Cypriots was also the work of Justinian; in fact, C. merely says ὁ βασιλεύς.

47/16-19 ἀπέστειλεν πρὸς τὸν ἀμερμουμνῆν κτλ.
The procedure of sending a letter by the hand of a professional diplomat (βασιλικός, see on 22/15), accompanied by a delegation of Cypriots, seems to have been followed closely by the patriarch Nicholas in 913: see Jenkins, *Mélanges H. Grégoire*, I (Brussels, 1949), 268. For the Phangoumeis, a word of unknown origin, see Hill 289, note 3, who also points out the anachronism of sending a delegation to 'Baghdad' (47/16) at this date: see on 25/63–4.

47/19   τὸν ἐν Συρίᾳ ὄντα λαόν.

It is not clear how or when these Cypriots had been transported to the Saracen empire. 47/3–4 suggests that they had been removed as a result of a Saracen capture of the island in 691; but there is no evidence for any such capture. It may be that the Cypriots in question were taken prisoner by Mu'awiyah in 653/4; cf. Hill 285.

47/24–5   τοὺς ἐν Ῥωμανίᾳ κτλ.   See Hill 288 and note 3.

48/1 ff.   Κεφάλαιον λθ' κτλ.

This chapter is merely the source from which 47/3–14 is taken. Its inclusion was probably not intended by C.: see General Introduction pp. 1–2.

48/15–16   τὸ γὰρ ἐν ἑκάστῃ ἐκκλησίᾳ κτλ.

The reference is to the 8th Canon of the 3rd Oecumenical Council at Ephesus (Rhallis-Potlis II, 203–4): σώζεσθαι ἑκάστῃ ἐπαρχίᾳ καθαρὰ καὶ ἀβίαστα τὰ αὐτῇ προσόντα δίκαια ἐξ ἀρχῆς καὶ ἄνωθεν. See Hill 275–6.

48/22–32

We now reach C.'s fourth section (P/23–4; 48/23–5), which deals with internal reforms and covers the rest of the book: see General Introduction pp. 6–7. The material is divisible under three heads: (a) provincial organization and administration (49–50/168; 51/192–204; 53/512–35); (b) naval administration (60/169–221; 51/5–191; with passages on Greek Fire, 48/28–32, 53/493–511); (c) civil policy (50/222–56). Cc. 52 and 53/2–492 are unedited source material. The whole section shows traces of hasty selection and arrangement, which are in keeping with the fact that it was one of the last sections added to the book, in 952, when its new, diplomatic and administrative, purpose had been resolved on (General Introduction p. 5). It is to be noted that the provincial section (a) deals with recovered territories now inside the imperial frontiers, just as the contemporary cc. 43–6 deal with efforts to recover territories still outside them: cf. 43/65; 44/115–24; 45/156–75; 46/113–19.

48/28–32

Ἰστέον, ὅτι ἐπὶ Κωνσταντίνου κτλ.   For Greek Fire, see on 13/73. Manojlović I, 54 attributes the juxtaposition of the migration of the Cypriots and the Greek Fire to their connexion with Cyzicus (48/20, 31). If this is not fanciful, it would suggest that both notices came from the same file.

Cc. 49, 50/1–82

BIBLIOGRAPHY

TEXTS

Τὸ Χρονικὸν τῆς Μονεμβασίας,, ed. Bees, Βυζαντίς I (1909), 37 ff.; but the parts relevant to the 9th cent. were re-edited by St. P. Kyriakides, (see below, 'Modern Works'), and references in the following notes are to his text.

Scholion of Arethas of Caesareia on Dresden MS. of Chronicle of Nikephoros; text and Engl. tr. in P. Charanis, Chr. Mon. (see below, 'Modern Works'), 152–3.

Συνοδικὸν γράμμα τοῦ ἁγιωτάτου καὶ οἰκουμενικοῦ πατριάρχου κυρίου Νικολάου: MPG cxix, cols. 877, 880.

MODERN WORKS

A. Bon, Le Péloponnèse byzantin jusqu' en 1204 (Paris, 1951) (Bon).   P. Charanis, 'Nicephorus I, the Saviour of Greece from the Slavs', Byzantina-Metabyzantina, I, 1 (1946), 75–92 (Charanis, Nicephorus).   P. Charanis, 'The Chronicle of Monemvasia and the Question of the Slavonic Settlements in Greece', Dumbarton Oaks Papers, 5 (1950), 141–66 (Charanis, Chr. Mon.).   F.

Dvornik, *Les Slaves, Byzance et Rome* (Paris, 1926) (Dvornik, *Les Slaves*). F. Dvornik, *Les Légendes de Constantin et de Méthode vues de Byzance* (Prague, 1935) (Dvornik, *Légendes*). B. Ferjančić, *Vizantiski Izvori za Istoriju Naroda Jugoslavije*, II (*S.A.N. Posebna Izdanja*, Viz. Inst. 7, Belgrade, 1959), 66–74 (Ferjančić). R. J. H. Jenkins, 'The Date of the Slav Revolt in Peloponnese under Romanus I', *Late Classical and Mediaeval Studies in Honor of A. M. Friend, Jr.* (Princeton, 1955), 204–11 (Jenkins). St. P. Kyriakides, *Οἱ Σλάβοι ἐν Πελοποννήσῳ: Βυζαντιναὶ Μελέται* VI (Thessalonike, 1947) (Kyriakides). G. Ostrogorsky, 'Postanak tema Helada i Peloponnes (Die Entstehung der Themen Hellas und Peloponnes)', *Zbornik Radova S. A. N.* 21, Viz. Inst. 1 (1952) 64–77 (Ostrogorsky, *Entstehung*). Dion. A. Zakythinos, *Οἱ Σλάβοι ἐν Ἑλλάδι* (Athens, 1945) (Zakythinos).

INTRODUCTORY NOTE

C. begins his account of provincial reforms and administration with narratives of three revolts and reductions of Slavs in Peloponnesus, the first between 802–11, the second in 841–2 and the third in 921. The semi-legendary story of the repulse of the Slavs from Patras (c. 49) is brought by Charanis (*Nicephorus*, 83–4; *Chr. Mon.*, 150, 156, note 53) into relation with a series of events narrated in the *Chronicle of Monemvasia*. This *Chronicle* describes the defeat of the 'Slavene nation' of Peloponnese in 805 by the strategos Skleros, and the consequent re-founding of Patras and its re-peopling by the descendants of its old inhabitants, who had been expelled to S. Italy 218 years previously. Charanis suggests that the victory of Skleros was followed two years later, in 807, by the siege of newly refounded Patras, of which our c. 49 tells; and in fact K. Hopf (*Geschichte Griechenlands* (Leipzig, 1867), 99) long ago suggested 807 as a date for the events of this chapter, in view of the presence of a Saracen fleet in Byzantine waters in that year; *cf.* 49/8–9. But the evidence is fragile, as Bon (46) observes; *cf.* Kyriakides 27, and on 49/4. Nor is it at all certain that the *Chronicle of Monemvasia*, despite the exactitude of the dates which it gives, is worthy of the confidence which has sometimes been placed in it. This has been shown by Kyriakides (esp. 50 ff.), who regards the document as based on a 'pious fraud' put out by the metropolitan of Patras in the reign of Leo VI and datable, since Nicholas Mysticus was patriarch (pp. 30–2), to the years 901–7, perhaps 901–2, if this is the date of Leo's διατύπωσις: see the reply of Charanis, *Byzantinoslavica*, 10 (1949), 254 ff.); and also Setton, *Speculum*, 27 (1952), 358–60, and Zakythinos 44. It is not relevant to discuss the question at length here. It is sufficient to say that Kyriakides (19) has shown very good reason to believe that the source of C.'s narrative about Patras was the preamble of the bull issued by his father Leo VI (49/71–5; *cf. MPG*, CVII, cols. 657–8 A), which in turn rested on information supplied by oral tradition (49/60–1) to the metropolitan of Patras in the early tenth century; *cf.* Manojlović II, 54–5. The original bull of Nicephorus I, which assigned the defeated Slavs to the Church of St Andrew (49/59), must by then have been lost, otherwise there would have been no need to resort to oral tradition (Kyriakides 25). This is not to say that C.'s narrative, even if we cannot postulate a written source for it earlier than the 10th cent., is unhistorical from start to finish: on the contrary, the survival in the 10th cent. of a colony of Slavs devoted to the Church at Patras is good evidence for the truth of their story of a Byzantine victory over them in the time of Nicephorus I. But it is not at all clear that we can work C.'s narrative in with the *Chronicle of Monemvasia* to make a coherent series of historical events; or that we can use what is avowedly a 10th cent. narrative, based on contemporary oral tradition, to prove what was or was not the administrative status of Peloponnesus at the turn of the 8th and 9th cents. (see on 49/13–14). For the relation of the Synodical Letter of the 11th cent. patriarch Nicholas to the bulls of Leo VI, see Kyriakides 25, 26.

The source for c. 50/1–70 is also clearly a bull, the bull issued by Romanus I (50/67) in 922 for the revision of the tribute of Melingoi and Ezeritae (see Kyriakides 20), which again rested in part on 10th cent. oral tradition (50/24–5). It is the better to be relied upon as a historical source in that the incidents at 50/25 ff. took place in C.'s own lifetime.

The question of the chronology, extent and nature of the Slav infiltration into Hellas and Peloponnesus is one which has provoked an enormous literature. It is not relevant to this Commentary to discuss the problem in its wider aspects: see however the capital study of Bon (27–81), and Charanis, *Chr. Mon.*, 164–6.

49/1-3 ʽΟ ζητῶν κτλ.

The chapter heading makes clear that the purpose of the whole narrative was to explain the origin of the dedication of a colony of Slavs to the Church of St Andrew at Patras; hence Kyriakides (19) is right in postulating as the single source the bull of Leo VI, issued between 901 and 907, regulating the status of this colony (49/71–5). For the phraseology, *cf.* 30/6–7.

49/4 Νικηφόρος.

If we assume the historicity of the *Chronicle of Monemvasia* (Kyriakides 47, 48), then the defeat of the Slavs which it records as having taken place in 805 can have no connexion with C.'s narrative. According to the *Chronicle*, when Skleros defeated the Slavs, Patras was still an uninhabited ruin; *cf.* Charanis, *Nicephorus*, 84. If however Patras was re-founded 'while Tarasios was still patriarch' (Kyriakides 49), that is, before February 806, it is just possible to assume a second Slav campaign in 807 (see Introductory Note to this section), which would be the one described by C. But it is certainly hard to suppose that a whole population can have been transported from S. Italy and can have built a whole city, complete with churches, in the short space of one year; and for other im-probabilities, see Kyriakides 56–9.

49/4 οὗτοι. *Cf.* General Introduction p. 8.

49/5 ἀπόστασιν. C.'s account obviously envisages Byzantine authority as established over the *thema*; *cf.* Zakythinos 48, note 4; Ostrogorsky, *Entstehung*, 72.

49/5-6 πρῶτον μὲν . . . ἐξεπόρθουν.

See Zakythinos 49, note 1; Kyriakides 18. The clause certainly implies a mixed popu-lation of Greeks and Slavs living together in the countryside.

49/6 Γραικῶν. *Cf.* Charanis, *ΕΕΒΣ*, 23 (1953), 620; Ferjančić 66, note 248; and Leo, *Taktika*, col. 969 A, γραικώσας.

49/9 ᾿Αφρικοὺς Σαρακηνούς.

This Slav alliance with African Saracens is usually accepted as a fact, and Zakythinos (50) even regards the Saracens as the prime movers in the operation. On the evidence of this passage Hopf (*Geschichte Griechenlands*, 99) dated C.'s narrative from Arab sources to 807; but the date is not by any means certain, and the only safe dating is within the limits of Nicephorus' reign (802–11). The proposal to read ᾿Αθρικοὺς for ᾿Αφρικοὺς is dismissed by Georgakas, *ΒΖ*, 43 (1950), 331–2.

49/13-14 ὁ τηνικαῦτα στρατηγὸς . . . Κορίνθου.

If this passage in fact reflects the true state of affairs in Peloponnesus during the reign of Nicephorus I (which is not certain: *cf.* Introductory Note to this section), then we have to suppose that Peloponnesus became a *thema* either earlier in or else before that reign; *cf.* Bon 45 and note 3; Ostrogorsky, *Entstehung*, 72. This is implied by the *Chronicle of Monemvasia* also (Kyriakides 47; but see K.'s criticism, *ibid.*, 53–4; Setton, *Speculum*, 25 (1950), 522). The words πρὸς τὴν ἄκραν τοῦ θέματος suggest that the whole of Peloponnesus, not just an eastern strip of it, was now comprehended in the *thema*. But we have always to remember that the wording of the passage rests, not on early 9th cent.

written, but on early 10th cent. oral testimony. The *Chronicle of Monemvasia* (Kyriakides 47–8) speaks of a military governor called Skleros who put down the Slavs in 805; but, in view of the fabulous nature of our story and the suspect reliability of the *Chronicle*, it seems idle to ask whether this Skleros was the governor of 49/13. Script. Incert. *de Leone Armenio* (*MPG*, cvⅢ), cols. 1011–12, mentions a Leon Skleros who was made governor of Peloponnesus by Michael I (811–13), and this is the earliest reliable reference to Peloponnesus as a *thema*: cf. *De Them.*, 172. Whether the Skleros of the *Chronicle* and the Leon Skleros of the Scriptor Incertus are one and the same cannot now be determined: see Bon 46.

49/15 Σκλαβήνων.
More properly Σκλαβηνῶν (but see Theoph. Cont. 514/14, etc.). This term (Σθλαβηνός, Σκλαβηνός, Σκλαυινός) for Peloponnesian Slavs of the 8th and early 9th cents. is found also at Theophanes 456/25–9, and in the *Chronicle of Monemvasia* (Kyriakides 45, 47–8); it seems to mean the inhabitant of a Slavonic 'region' (Σκλαβηνία, see on 9/10), such as Peloponnese then was: see Charanis, *Nicephorus*, 82 (but also Kyriakides 13–4). Contrast 50/6: οἱ τοῦ θέματος . . . Σκλάβοι.

49/33 πόρρω τοῦ κάστρου. Yet at 49/38 we find that they προσέφυγον εἰς τὸν πάνσεπτον ναὸν inside the city.

49/54 ἀποδοθῆναι. Cf. Theoph. Cont. 304/12–14.

49/59–60 σιγίλλιον . . . ἀνήγγειλαν.
Nicephorus issued the bull, but by the 10th cent. it was lost and the bull of Leo VI (49/72) was based on oral tradition: see Introductory Note to this section, and Manojlović Ⅱ, 54–5; Kyriakides 19, 26–8.

49/65–71 "Εκτοτε δὲ . . . χρείας.
The situation is explained by Zakythinos 49 and notes 2 and 3. The Slavs were given agricultural holdings on church land, and together they constituted a taxable unit, or ὁμάς (49/71). But, in addition to their ordinary taxes, they had to maintain in the city a ξενοδοχεῖον for the free entertainment of military governors and Byzantine and foreign envoys. Zakythinos, *ibid.*, note 2, cites an apt parallel from the reign of Nicephorus III. In the early 10th cent. this obligation of the Slavs was being abused by Byzantine officials, and this abuse gave rise to the bull of Leo VI, which clearly defined the limits of the obligation, and was prefaced by the historical survey which forms the basis of C.'s narrative.

50/6–7 'Ιστέον, ὅτι . . . ἀποστατήσαντες.
We are here in the realm of historical fact, and this Slav revolt can be dated with accuracy. The 'days of the emperor Theophilus and his son Michael' are the years of their joint rule, 840–2: see G. Ostrogorsky in E. Kornemann, *Doppelprinzipat* (Leipzig and Berlin, 1930), 176. There is good reason to date the expedition of Theoktistos Bryennios (50/10–25) to the year 842, immediately after the death of Theophilus; see Dvornik, *Légendes*, 14, 88. Therefore, the revolt probably broke out in 841. For the revolt, see further Bon 47 and note 5; Zakythinos 51–2. If the archaeological evidence be considered, which suggests that it was Theophilus who first re-established Byzantine power firmly at Corinth after nearly two centuries (see Kent, *Speculum*, 25 (1950), 546, note 2; Lemerle, *Byzantion*, 21 (1951), 344), then the cause of the revolt may well have been discontent at such an unwonted display of Byzantine authority in the province.

50/10–11 Θεόκτιστος . . . ὁ τῶν Βρυεννίων.

Not to be confused with his more celebrated contemporary, the logothete Theoktistos; see F. Hirsch, *Byzantische Studien* (Leipzig, 1876), 220, note 4. Two seals of a Bryennios, possibly Theoktistos, military governor of Dalmatia, date from the middle of the 9th cent.: see Schlumberger, *Sigillographie*, 205–6; Dvornik, *Les Slaves*, 44 and note 1; Ferjančic 70, note 260. Theoktistos Bryennios is very likely mentioned also in the *Life of St Evarestos* (*Anal. Boll.*, 41 (1923), 301/13) as having gone on an embassy to Bulgaria in Theodora's time; *cf.* Theoph. Cont. 162/3–13, and Kyriakides, *Βυζαντιναὶ Μελέται* v (Thessalonike, 1939), 503, note 1.

50/14 λοιποῖς ἀνυποτάκτους. See Zakythinos 51, note 5.

50/15–16 οἱ Ἐζερῖται καὶ οἱ Μηλιγγοί.

For the precise location of these two tribes, see Bon 63 and his map *ibid.*, 40–1. The Melingoi lived to the north, closer to Lacedaemonia, on the western slope of Penta-daktylos (Ταΰγετος), while the Ezeritae lived in the coastal district of Ezero = Helos. For the problems of the origin and nomenclature of these tribes, see Georgakas in *BZ*, 43 (1950): on the Melingoi 302–27 (*cf.* the criticism of Grégoire, *Byzantion*, 21 (1951), 249–50); on the Ezeritae 327–30; on Helos 329–30. Also, Ferjančić 70–1, note 263.

50/23 νομίσματα ξ′ . . . νομίσματα τ′.

The discrepancy between the amounts of tribute paid by the two tribes is explained by Bon (63) as due to the fact that the Ezeritae were the more numerous. But this would not explain why Krinitis did not increase their tribute in the same proportions (50/46–51).

50/24–5 παρὰ τῶν ἐντοπίων . . . φήμη. *Cf.* 49/60–1; and Kyriakides 19–20.

50/25–70 Ἐπὶ δὲ τῆς βασιλείας κτλ.

For the dating of these events, see Jenkins 205–7. It is probable that Protevon (*cf.* 51/201) was succeeded in March 921 by Krinitis Arotras, who was in turn succeeded in November 921 by Platypodis; and that the internal disturbance provoked by Platypodis was followed at once, in early 922, by the 'Sklavesian' or Bulgaro-Slav invasion and occupation of the province. This revolt of Melingoi and Ezeritae therefore began in 920 or early 921, in the troubled period when the Lecapenids were ousting the Macedonians from power, a period marked by innumerable conspiracies at home and revolts in the empire. For a later dating, see Ferjančić, *Zbornik Radova S.A.N.* 44, Viz. Inst. 3 (1955), 37–47; and Ferjančić 72, 73, notes 269, 274.

50/30–2 οὔτε . . . οὔτε . . . οὔτε.

For these three obligations of the Melingoi and Ezeritae, see Vasiliev, *Viz. Vrem.*, 5 (1898), 425–6. For the last, see G. Ostrogorskÿ, *Quelques Problèmes d'Histoire de la Pay-sannerie byzantine* (Bruxelles, 1956), 11–40. The ἄρχων of 50/31 is called δούξ in *Vit. S. Nikonis Metanoeite* (ed. Lambros) 194/7, *i.e.* in the middle 11th cent.

50/34 Κρινίτην τὸν Ἀροτρᾶν.

We must beware of identifying this Krinitis with the Krinitis mentioned in *Vita S. Lucae Junioris* (*MPG*, cxi), cols. 465 D–469 A (*cf. De Cer.*, 668/13). The two may in fact be identical, but the respective incidents must be dated as far apart as twenty-five years (921, 946): see Jenkins 209–11. For the name and family, see also on 43/137; and Ferjančić 72, note 268.

50/53 ἐν τῷ θεοφυλάκτῳ κοιτῶνι.

For κοιτών = 'Staatskasse', see Dölger, *Finanzverwaltung*, 25 and note 3 (*cf. Exodus* 8, 3: τὰ ταμιεῖα τῶν κοιτώνων σου). θεοφύλακτος = the earlier θεῖος: *cf.* Treitinger 51.

50/54-5 Βάρδα τοῦ Πλατυπόδη.

For the name, see also Theoph. Cont. 401/18; Lupus Protospatharius (*MPL*, CLV), cols. 123 B, 128 A. The disturbance with which Platypodis had to contend has been plausibly related by Shanguin (*Viz. Vrem.* n. s. 1 (1947), 247) with that which called for the 'Απολογητικός of Arethas of Caesareia: cf. Jenkins 207-8; also *MPG* CXI, col. 389 B–C. For the invasion of the Sklavesianoi which followed immediately (*i.e.* in 922), and which has been rightly identified by Zakythinos (54-5) with the Bulgarian invasion of Peloponnese mentioned in the *Lives* of SS. Peter of Argos and Luke the Younger, see Jenkins 205-6; and on 50/25-70.

50/58 'Αγέλαστον. *Cf.* Theoph. Cont. 443/21; *AASS*, November III, col. 863 A–B; Jenkins 207. For πρωτοσπαθαρίων καὶ ἀρχόντων, see Guilland, *Byzantion*, 27 (1957), 693.

50/59 Σκλαβησιάνων.

See Amandos, Πρακτικὰ τῆς 'Ακαδημίας τῶν 'Αθηνῶν 7 (1932), 333; Manojlović II, 59-60, note 1; Zakythinos 54-5; Jenkins 205, note 11; Ferjančić, *Zbornik Radova S.A.N.* 44, Viz. Inst. 3 (1955), 46.

50/71-82 οἱ τοῦ κάστρου Μαΐνης κτλ.

For the Maniots, see Bon 71-4 and notes. He observes (72, note 2) that C. has erred in placing Mani εἰς ἄκραν τοῦ Μαλέα: for in fact it is further west. Both F. Hirsch, *Byzantinische Studien* (Leipzig, 1876), 265 and Bury (572-3) have noted that the conversion of the Maniots by Basil I (50/76) is not mentioned in *Vita Basilii*; and indeed, according to Genesios (117/23–118/3), devils were active in the district of Helos (Ezeros) until the time of Leo VI (*cf. AASS*, August III, cols. 494 F–495 A). For the form Ezeros, see Georgakas, *BZ*, 43 (1950), 328; Zakythinos, *EEBΣ*, 18 (1948), 48. For the obligation imposed on the Maniots (50/80-2), see on 50/30-2.

C. 50/83-168

BIBLIOGRAPHY

1. TEXTS

V. Beneševič, 'Die byzantinischen Ranglisten', *Byz.-Neugr. Jhrb.*, 5 (1926-7), 97–167 (Beneševič). *De Velitatione Bellica Domini Nicephori Augusti;* Leo Diaconus, ed. Bonn., 179–258 (*De Vel Bell.*).

2. MODERN WORKS

M. Canard, *Histoire de la dynastie des H'amdanides*, I (Paris, 1953) (Canard). H. Gelzer, 'Ungedruckte . . . Texte der Notitiae Episcopatuum', *Abh. d. bay. Akad. Wiss.* 21 (Munich, 1901), 531–641 (Gelzer). E. Honigmann, *Die Ostgrenze des byzantinischen Reiches* (A. A. Vasiliev, *Byzance et les Arabes*, tom. III, Brussels, 1935) (Honigmann). St. P. Kyriakides, Βυζαντιναὶ Μελέται II–V (Thessalonike, 1939) (Kyriakides, Βυζαντιναὶ Μελέται II–V). G. Ostrogorsky, 'Taktikon Uspenskog i Taktikon Beneshevitcha (Die Entstehungszeit des Taktikon Uspensky und des Taktikon Beneševič)', *Zbornik Radova S. A. N.* 36, Viz. Inst. 2 (1953), 39–59 (Ostrogorsky, *Entstehungszeit*). W. M. Ramsay, *The Historical Geography of Asia Minor* (London, 1890) (Ramsay).

INTRODUCTORY NOTE

This section continues the lesson on provinces, begun at c. 49; but C. now turns from the recovery and taxation of a lost province to the composition and administration of new ones: see General Introduction p. 6. It is very noteworthy that the formation or reorganization of most of these *themata* (Kephallenia, Lagoubardia, Cappadocia, Charsianon, Mesopotamia) was the work of C.'s father Leo VI; *cf.* also 50/133–59 and 43/6–88,

45/43-55. These passages taken together give an illuminating picture of the planned expansion eastwards undertaken by that great emperor during the first decade of the 10th cent. (*cf.* Gelzer 549), which paved the way for the more spectacular campaigns of Kourkouas (see on 45/56) on the 920's and 930's. In the west, though the foundation of the *thema* of Calabria marked the loss of Sicily, that of Lagoubardia equally marked the re-establishment of Byzantine power in S. Italy (see on 50/85, 88).

50/83 Καππαδοκίας στρατηγίς.

See *De Them.*, 64/37-65/1 and 120-1; Honigmann 43-9. C.'s statement is borne out by *Takt. Usp.* (Beneševič 140), no. 111, ὁ τούρμαρχος τῆς Καππαδοκίας, though Beneševič (155, no. 95) thinks this reference an anachronism, since in the Arab list of Al-Garmi, early 9th cent., Cappadocia is already a separate kleisurarchy; whereas *Takt. Usp.* was compiled between 845 and 856 (Ostrogorsky, *Entstehungszeit*, 48, 58). It is worth noting that *Digenis Akritas*, ed. Mavrogordato (Oxford, 1956), 18, vv. 265-6, clearly points to a time when Cappadocia was still a *turma* of the Anatolikoi (late 8th or early 9th cent.), which brings us close to the historical turmarch Diogenes (Theophanes 463/19-20; H. Grégoire, *Digenis Akritas* (New York, 1942), 36-7). The date at which Cappadocia became a *thema* is uncertain; Theoph. Cont. 120/10 mentions a στρατηγός in *c.* 830, and again (181/14) in 863, but Bury (*ERE*, 222, note 5) thinks the former reference anachronistic; *cf.* Honigmann 44. For the term στρατηγίς (= θέμα, see on 50/93), *cf. De Them.*, 73/6; Theoph. Cont. 78/15-16; Anna Comnena, ed. Reifferscheid II, 217/2-7.

50/85 ἡ Κεφαλληνίας στρατηγίς.

De Them., 91/44-5 states that Kephallenia οὐδέποτε . . . εἰς τάξιν ἐχρημάτιζε θέματος, but formed part of the *thema* of Peloponnesus. This is rightly refuted by Beneševič (153), who points to a *Cefaloniae praefectus* as early as 809; see also *Takt. Usp.* (Beneševič 121, no. 22) and, later, Cont. Geo. Mon. 845/7. C.'s statements therefore, both here and at *De Them.*, are inaccurate: it was Lagoubardia which became a separate *thema* only when South Italy was reconquered in the last quarter of the 9th cent. (see Gay 170-2), and the two are mentioned as separate *themata* for the first time at *De Cer.*, 697/14-15 (*c.* 912). See further *De Them.*, 174-6; Ostrogorsky, *Zbornik Radova S.A.N.*, 21, Viz. Inst. I (1952), 73-4 and note 50; Zakythinos, *L'Hellénisme Contemporain*, 2 série, 8 (1954), 303-12; Bury, *Centenario della nascita di M. Amari*, II (Palermo, 1910), 30-1.

50/88 ἡ Καλαβρίας στρατηγίς.

C.'s statement is confirmed by *Takt. Usp.* (Beneševič 121, no. 21, 140, no. 125: ὁ δούξ Καλαβρίας). The στρατηγός of Calabria is first witnessed at Cedrenus II, 355/2-3 (914-17; *cf.* Vasiliev II, 199); and again at *ibid.*, 355/5-6 (920), and at *De Them.*, 96/39 (second quarter of the 10th cent.). Calabria is not listed as a separate *thema* in *De Cer.*, II, cc. 50, 52; but at least its *de facto* existence must date from the expulsion of the Byzantines from Sicily (902); *cf.* Gay 167, 168; Stein, *Byz.-Neugr. Jhrb.*, I (1920), 79. For the use of δουκᾶτον = τούρμα at this period, see Bury, *ERE*, 223, note 3; and *cf.* Kyriakides, Βυζαντιναὶ Μελέται II-V, 278-9.

50/90 ἡ τοῦ Χαρσιανοῦ στρατηγίς.

See *De Them.*, 123-4; Honigmann 49-52. The latter, following H. Gelzer, *Die Genesis der byzantinischen Themenverfassung* (Leipzig, 1899), 96, thinks that Charsianon became a kleisurarchy after the Armeniac mutiny of 793/4 (Theophanes 468-9). It was still a kleisurarchy in 863 (Theoph. Cont. 181/15, 183/9; Genesios' use of the word θέματι at 97/2 seems to be an error), but had become a *thema* by 873 (Genesios 122/22; Theoph. Cont. 272/12, 272/23-273/1). It therefore became so at the beginning of the reign of Basil I. St Eudocimus (*c.* 809-42) was στρατοπεδάρχης of Cappadocia and later of Charsianon (*Izvestiya russk. arkheolog. Inst. v Konst.*, 13 (1908), 196, 207, 214): but, as

Loparëv (*ibid.*, 238, note 111) points out, the term implies no more than a battalion commander. *De Them.*, 65/43–7 is of course inaccurate.

50/92–110 'Ιστέον, ὅτι . . . Καισαρείας.

For these two provincial boundary adjustments, see Ramsay 216–21, 226–7; Honigmann 44; *De Them.*, 121 (Cappadocia); and Ramsay 248–50; Honigmann 51; *De Them.*, 123; Canard 729 (Charsianon); and *cf.* Ramsay 196–7, map of Galatia. For the circumstances which prompted the westward withdrawal of Cappadocia, see Ramsay 316–7. He dates both these adjustments to *c.* 890 (pp. 216, 248), but gives no evidence for this. The settlement of Charsianon was probably disturbed *c.* 916, when part of its new territory was ceded to Lykandos: see on 50/133–66.

50/93 θέματος.

For various attempts to explain the derivation of the word, see Dölger, *Historia*, 4 (1955), 189–98; and for the vexed question of the origin of the thematic system, see bibliography *ibid.*, and Karayannopoulos, *L'Hellénisme contemporain*, 2 sér., 10 (1956), 455 ff.; A. Pertusi, *La formation des thèmes byzantins* (*Berichte zum XI Internationalen Byzantinisten-Kongress* (München, 1958)); J. Karayannopulos, *Die Entstehung der byzantinischen Themenordnung*: Byzantinisches Archiv, Heft 10 (München, 1959).

50/94 βάνδα.

βάνδον is literally a 'standard', φλάμουλον: see Leo, *Taktika*, col. 1100 B; Grosse, *BZ*, 24 (1924), 367, 370. In the military organization, βάνδον = τάγμα, ἀλλάγιον (*cf.* 29/22), that is, a regiment or garrison of 200–400 foot or 50–400 horse, commanded by a κόμης: see Leo, *Taktika*, cols. 709 B–C, 1100 B–C. Territorially, a βάνδον was the sub-division of a τοῦρμα; and it comprised an area whose garrison (τοποτηρησία, ἀλλάγιον) amounted to the said force of up to 400 men. *Cf.* Mayer, *Zeitschrift der Savigny-Stiftung* (Germ. Abt.) 24 (1903), 241–2; Kyriakides, Βυζαντιναὶ Μελέται ιι–ν, 537–8; Bréhier, *Institutions*, 361–2.

50/100 τὰ Κόμματα.

Referred to by Genesios 122/16, who says that the Paulicians reached it in 872; *cf.* Vasiliev ιι, 31. This seems to dispose of the otherwise attractive hypothesis that the name means 'fragments' and is contemporary with Leo's boundary adjustment.

50/105 Σανίανα.

This transfer from the Bukellarioi is reflected at *De Them.*, 71/11–12 (*cf. ibid.*, 135, note 11), where the Bukellarian *thema* ends on the east at the frontier town of Saniana. *Cf.* also Theoph. Cont. 72/1, 19.

50/111–32 'Ιστέον, ὅτι κτλ.

See *De Them.*, 73, 139–40; *De Vel. Bell.*, 250, 251; Honigmann 69–72, 77–8, 90–1; Ramsay 316; Canard 728–9. For the date of the initial foundation of Mesopotamia (Tekis), see Jenkins, *BZ*, 47 (1954), 15: it is most probably 900 (*cf.* on 45/44). The additions of Kamacha and Keltzini (50/127–30) must have been made before 912. The additions of Romanopolis and Chanzit were made between 934 and 938 (Honigmann 70). For the territorial limits, both initial and subsequent, see *id.*, 69, 70.

50/111–12 Χοζάνου . . . 'Ασμοσάτου. For these two short-lived frontier provinces, see Honigmann 77, 78.

50/113–14 Τὸ δὲ Χανζὶτ . . . τῶν Μελιτηνιατῶν.

For the locality, see *De Vel. Bell.*, 250, 251; Honigmann 90, 91. For the status of Melitene before its capture by the Byzantines in 934, see Honigmann 72.

50/116 Κάμαχα . . . Κελτζηνῆς.

For Kamacha, see Honigmann 56, 57; it was the extreme county of Koloneia on the south-east, and it marched with that of Keltzini to the east, across the provincial border with Chaldia. For Keltzini, cf. on 43/92, and Honigmann 69, 70; and for the *thema* of Chaldia, *De Them.*, 138.

50/118–26 Λέων δέ . . . εὐεργεσίας πολλάς.

See Gelzer 565–6. The transaction is rather differently related in the earlier version at *De Them.*, 73, where Manuel is not mentioned, and his sons are given as Pankratoukas, Poukrikas and Tatoukas (*cf.* Manojlović II, 88). Of the five Armenians mentioned in our text, only Pankratoukas is found elsewhere, at Theoph. Cont. 387/14–15. For the origin of the Hicanati, see Ostrogorsky-Stein, *Byzantion*, 7 (1932), 193.

50/119 μετὰ λόγου. *Sc.* ἀπαθείας: see Dölger, *BD*, 87.

50/120 Ἔχει. If this, and not εἶχε, be the correct reading, it implies transcription from a document contemporary with the event described: *cf.* on 43/183, 45/117–8.

50/123–4 εἰς Νικόπολιν στρατηγὸν.

See on 45/146–7. If στρατηγός here means 'provincial governor', then the Nikopolis in question must have been the *thema* of that name in western Greece. But Nikopolis in Koloneia is obviously a more likely place in which to post such a man as Iachnoukas, and perhaps στρατηγός here = κατεπάνω (45/147), and means the commander of the local Armenian garrison in that city: *cf.* on 50/169–70.

50/127 τὸν Ὀρέστην ἐκεῖνον.

See H. Grégoire, *Digenis Akritas* (New York, 1942), 13. Our Orestes was perhaps that δομέστικος τῶν νουμέρων to whose nephew Arethas of Caesareia addressed two unpublished letters (see M. V. Levchenko, *Vizantiyskiy Sbornik* (Moscow, 1945), 229–30).

50/133–66 Ἰστέον, ὅτι ἐπὶ Λέοντος κτλ.

See *De Them.*, 75–6, 143–6; *De Vel. Bell.*, 243/6–16, 250/18; Cedrenus II, 422/21–3; Gelzer 561–3; Honigmann 64–73; Grégoire, *Byzantion*, 8 (1933), 79–88; Ostrogorsky, *ibid.*, 23 (1933), 39–42; Canard 729–30; H. Grégoire, *Digenis Akritas* (New York, 1942), 119–23. The passage deals with the circumstances which led to the creation of the *thema* of Lykandos in or about the year 916 (see on 50/136 ff.). The limits of the *thema* cannot be defined with absolute certainty; but it is clear that it lay south-east of the Halys; that on the north it marched with the *thema* of Sebasteia along a frontier from Larissa to Abara-Amara (50/133, 167); that on the east it was bounded by the semi-independent emirate of Melitene; and that on the south it extended to the Byzantine-Arab frontier, east of the Onopniktes (Karmalas) river. The western limit presents difficulties. To begin with, it is obvious from a comparison with 50/113–17 that the areas mentioned at 50/133–5 (Larissa, Kymbalaios, Symposion) later became (the northern and western) part of the new *thema*. Larissa Honigmann (55) places at Mangulik, and it therefore was the centre of the northern *tourma* of Lykandos. But where were Kymbalaios and Symposion? Grégoire (*Byzantion*, 8 (1933), 85–7) identifies the former with Kamouliana, south of the Halys and a few miles north-*west* of Caesareia; and the latter with Sobeson-Süveš (*cf.* Gelzer 561), south-*west* of Caesareia. If this is right, the two areas correspond closely to the area south of the Halys ceded by Cappadocia to Charsianon in the reign of Leo VI (50/108–10). We must therefore suppose that in 916 the new *thema* derived its western *tourma* from Charsianon, which was from that time confined, as it had been before Leo's reign, to the north of the Halys.

50/136 ff. Καὶ ἐπὶ τῆς βασιλείας Λέοντος κτλ.

The chronology is not quite certain. Grégoire (*Byzantion*, 8 (1933), 84) places the recall of Eustathios Argyros to Charsianon (*cf.* Theoph. Cont. 374/5–6) in about 908, and the escape of Constantine Dux from Baghdad (Theoph. Cont. 373/11–13) a little before. This must be nearly right: Constantine probably returned in 907 (see *Vita Euthymii*, ed. de Boor (Berlin, 1888), 41/6). Eustathios died shortly afterwards (Theoph. Cont. 374/6–8), and was succeeded as governor of Charsianon by Constantine Dux (50/153), that is, *c.* 909. Melias therefore, resident in Euphrateia in 908, occupied Lykandos and built Tzamandos in *c.* 909–10, which accords with the statement of Tabari and other Arab writers (Vasiliev II/2, 22, 60) that the Arabs burnt the fortress of Malih al-Armani (Tzamandos) in 911. Melias' glorious expedition to Germanikeia (Maraš) in A.H. 303 = A.D. 915–16 (Vasiliev II/2, 146) may have been the occasion for the elevation of Lykandos into a *thema*, an event which (despite *De Them.*, 76/46–9) must be placed between 914 and 919 (50/159–62): *cf. De Them.*, 145; Runciman, *Romanus Lecapenus*, 133.

50/136–7 Εὐστάθιος ὁ τοῦ Ἀργυροῦ.

See Theoph. Cont. 368/21–369/5, 374/3–8; and *cf.* Guilland, *BZ*, 43 (1950), 347, 348. Eustathios had been concerned in the revolt of Andronicus Dux (906), for which see Canard, *Bull. d'Et. orient. de Damas*, 13 (1949–51), 55 ff. Cedrenus II, 269/21, seems to identify this Eustathios with the admiral Eustathios of 51/85, 110 (*cf.* Marquart 522, and Jenkins, *Speculum*, 23 (1948), 223, note 42), but this is an error, as Guilland (*loc. cit.*) maintains.

50/138 ὁ δὲ Μελίας.

For this famous Armenian commander, see Grégoire, *Byzantion*, 8 (1933), 79 ff. (bibliography, 79, 83); and Ostrogorsky, *ibid.*, 23 (1953), 39–42 (note). The date, between 916 and his death after 934, at which Melias was made *magister* (50/166) is not known. It is clear from 50/164 that he remained loyal to the emperor in the revolt of Constantine Dux (June, 913), though we may suppose from 50/138 that he had been concerned in that of Andronicus Dux some years previously.

50/139–49 ὁ Βαασάκιος κτλ.

See Honigmann 64–5. These Armenian chiefs are not mentioned elsewhere. They had no doubt been concerned with Melias in the revolt of Andronicus Dux in 906 (see preceding notes). Their recall and establishment at Larissa and Symposion may be dated to *c.* 908 (see on 50/136 ff.); and the destruction of Ismael by the Melitenians to the summer of 909 (*cf.* Tabari's account of the expedition of Mu'nis: Vasiliev II/2, 22). This disaster may have precipitated Melias' retreat westward from Euphrateia to Lykandos in the same year. The second expulsion of Baasakios for treason was probably due to support of Constantine Dux in 913, and was followed by the reversion of Larissa to the *thema* of Sebasteia, in which it remained until ceded to the new *thema* of Lykandos in or about 916 (see on 50/136 ff.).

50/145 εἰς Εὐφράτειαν.

The position of Euphrateia is not quite certain. Honigmann's map (II) places it in an area west of the Euphrates between Tephrike to the north and Abara to the south. If in this initial settlement Euphrateia, the Trypia and Eremia formed one single *turma*, of which Melias was *turmarch*, then the *turma* was presumably attached to the *thema* of Sebasteia. For the Trypia, see Honigmann 65; Canard 243 and note 468.

50/167–8 ἡ Ἄβαρα . . . κλεισούρα. See Honigmann 55–6; *De Them.*, 142; *cf.* Theoph. Cont. 267/15–16; Cedrenus II, 464/15.

50/169–256

At this point C.'s section 4 on internal reforms turns from provincial to naval administration, various aspects of which are discussed until 51/192 (except for 50/222–56). See on 48/22–32 and Introductory Note to c. 51; and for the importance of the navy in the 10th cent., see General Introduction p. 7, and on 51/40–5.

50/169–96 Ἰστέον, ὅτι τύπος κτλ.

The date of this incident can be established with fair accuracy. The reference to Himerios as logothete (cf. Theoph. Cont. 371/20 and De Cer., 651/16) shows that it cannot be dated before 906 (see Vita Euthymii, ed. de Boor (Berlin, 1888), 122). On the other hand, Himerios was deposed and imprisoned in the summer of 912, on his return from the failure of his Cretan expedition (Jenkins, Προσφορὰ εἰς Στ. Π. Κυριακίδην (Thessalonike, 1953), 279). If the start of the Cretan expedition is to be dated, as seems likely, to the summer of 911, and if we must leave time before it for Himerios to quarrel with Eustathios after the dismissal of Staurakios (ὕστερον, 50/192), we can assign the quarrels of Eustathios and Staurakios to c. 909–10. (It is true that at De Cer., 651/19, i.e. in 911, we find a στρατηγὸς τῶν Κιβυρραιωτῶν, where, according to our text, an ἐκ προσώπου would have been more accurate; but the point need not be pressed in the case of a routine military estimate.) An echo of these disturbances is perhaps to be heard in C.'s comment on the Kibyrrhaiotes at De Them., 79/41–3. The details derive from the written report of Eustathios (50/182, ἀνήγαγεν), and from the counter-protest probably submitted by Staurakios: cf. Manojlović II, 83.

50/169–70 κατεπάνω Μαρδαϊτῶν Ἀτταλείας

Cf. De Cer., 657/1–2; 660/7–8. For the office of κατεπάνω at this period, see on 27/69–70, 45/146–7; also Jannaris, BZ, 10 (1901), 204 ff.; Zakythinos, L'Hellénisme Contemporain, 2 série, 2 (1948), 201–6; Glykatzi-Ahrweiler, Bull. Corr. Hell., 84 (1960–1), 64–5. The local commandant of this period must not be confused with the generalissimo of the later 10th cent. (cf. Theoph. Cont. 480/15). For the Mardaïtes, see on 21/4; and Amandos, Ἑλληνικά 5 (1932), 130–6; Bon, Péloponnèse byzantin, 75–6 and 75, note 2.

50/171–2 Σταυράκιος ὁ Πλατύς.

This Staurakios is not certainly known elsewhere: see however Jenkins, Studies presented to D. M. Robinson, II, 1009–10; Vasiliev II, 54; and finally Theoph. Cont. 362/1–10.

50/174 ἐν τῷ τῶν Κιβυρραιωτῶν θέματι ἐκ προσώπου.

For the thema, see De Them., 149–50. For ἐκ προσώπου, see Beneševič 126–7; the office is discussed by Mitard, BZ, 12 (1903), 592–4, Bury, IAS, 46–7, and Glykatzi-Ahrweiler, op. cit. 39–42; cf. especially Leo, Taktika, col. 701 C and De Cer., 788/10. For this dual control in the Kibyrrhaiote thema (50/183), see also De Cer., 657/1–7. This Eustathios seems not to have been a military man (and must therefore not be confused with admiral Eustathios, 51/85, or with Eustathios Argyros, 50/136), but a member of the emperor's chancellery (ἀσηκρῆτις), of which Himerios had until 906 been head (Theoph. Cont. 367/4). He could however be identical with the governor of Calabria, c. 914–17 (Cedrenus II, 355/2).

50/176 Ἡμέριον καὶ λογοθέτην. See on 50/169–96.

50/177 μεσιτευθείς. See Beck, BZ, 48 (1955), 337; Verpeaux, Byzantinoslavica, 16 (1955), 270–1.

50/198–200 ὡς πάντας . . . διεδέξατο.

E.g. St Euthymios (Theoph. Cont. 377/21); Himerios (ibid., 379/22–380/3); Constantine the chamberlain (50/229–31); cf. MPG, cvi col. 803 B–C (= cod. Mosqu. gr. 315, f. 56ᵛ: ἐπαροινοῦντο καὶ ἀπεδοκιμάζοντο οἱ τοῦ ἀδελφοῦ φίλοι).

50/202 Χασέ.

See Theoph. Cont. 388/8–12 ('son of Ioubis'); and *cf. Patrologia Orientalis*, 11 (1916), 269/10. He seems to have been made governor of Hellas by Alexander in 913, and was stoned to death by the Athenians in the Parthenon in the same, or in the following, year: the incident is narrated by the chronicler in the same paragraph as the death of the Saracen admiral Damian, which took place in A. H. 301 (Vasiliev II/2, 145) = A.D. 913 August–914 July, though Dujčev, *BZ*, 41 (1941), 485 dates Chase's death to *c.* 915–16. If Chase had been the slave of Michael III's chamberlain (50/224), he will have been born about 850. For Saracen officials at the imperial court during this period, see Canard, *Bull. d'Et. orient. de Damas*, 13 (1949–51), 61.

50/215 ἐπὶ προελεύσεως . . . Χρυσοτρικλίνου.

See *De Cer.*, 518–28. These morning levées (προελεύσεις) took place daily in the Chrysotriklinos (*ibid.* 5/18), and were the occasion of imperial appointments or promotions of this kind (*cf. ibid.*, 525/17–19, and also 705/15–19).

50/219–20 καθὼς . . . εἴρηται.   See 50/169–70, and General Introduction p. 6.

50/222–56 Ἰστέον, ὅτι κτλ.

These two notices are the only ones in C.'s Section 4 which concern civil administration: see on 48/22–32. They deal (*a*) with the appointment of chamberlains, and (*b*) with the grant of a lay rank to a cleric. For the possible contemporary relevance of both questions, see General Introduction p. 7, where it is suggested that they are connected with the appointments of Basil Nothus (see on 50/233–4) and his nephew Michael Lecapenus, for whom see Laurent, *Ech. d'Or.*, 37 (1938), 132.

50/222 παρακοιμώμενος.

See Bury, *IAS*, 124, 125: the office, mentioned as far back as the reign of Maurice (Theophanes 285/17), no doubt became an independent and important one under Theophilus, with whose reign our list commences. It was normally held by eunuchs (*De Cer.*, 725/14); Basil the Macedonian and, presumably, Barbatos (50/230) were exceptions. Light on the routine duties of the chamberlain is cast by *Vita S. Irenes* (*AASS*, 28th July), col. 628 F.

50/223 ὀστιάριος.

See Bury, *IAS*, 122; and Reiske's note to *De Cer.*, II, 66; Guilland, *Rev. Et. Byz.*, 13 (1955), 79–84.

50/224–5 Δαμιανὸς . . . βασιλεύς.

For Damian, see Theoph. Cont. 234/7–235/5; Cont. Geo. Mon. 827/11–23; *cf.* 50/204. A eunuch and a Slav, he was chamberlain of Michael III in 865, and was deposed in that year owing to the machinations of the Caesar Bardas. Basil was appointed to succeed him, either on the same day (Cont. Geo. Mon. 827/22) or else a short while afterwards (Theoph. Cont. 234/21, 235/4); at all events, in 865. Basil held the post until he was crowned emperor (22:5:866). Pseudo-Symeon (Theoph. Cont. 684/19) says that in 867 Rentakios was chamberlain; but it is more likely that Cont. Geo. Mon. (836/9) is right in calling R. protovestiary, and that Michael III appointed no successor to Basil between May 866 and September 867.

50/228 Σαμωνᾶς ὁ πατρίκιος.

Samonas became chamberlain not before the spring of 907 (*cf. Vita Euthymii*, 48/21, which describes him as πρωτοβεστιάριος in February of that year). Cont. Geo. Mon. (865/14) is therefore inaccurate in dating his appointment *before* the deposition of the patriarch Nicholas. Samonas held the office until his deposition in the following year, *i.e.* June 908 (see Jenkins, *Speculum*, 23 (1948), 234). *Cf.* also 50/239, 250; Janin, *Ech. d'Or.*, 34 (1935), 307 ff.; and Canard, *Bull. d'Et. orient. de Damas*, 13 (1949–51), 54–62.

50/229, 230–2 Κωνσταντῖνος πατρίκιος.
See Theoph. Cont. 375/10–376/22; 386/5; 390/23–392/11; 394/12; 395/4; 713/15–715/6; *cf.* 51/149. A eunuch, previously in the service of Basil Magister, and later of Samonas himself. He succeeded Samonas as chamberlain in 908, was deposed by Alexander in 912, reinstated by Zoë in 914, and finally disappeared in the revolt of his brother-in-law Leo Phocas, in the summer of 919.

50/232 Θεοφάνης πατρίκιος. See Runciman, *Romanus Lecapenus*, 274, *s.v.* Theophanes Protovestiarius; *cf.* Dobschütz, *BZ*, 10 (1901), 170–2.

50/233 Κωνσταντίνου πάλιν τὸ δεύτερον. *Sc.* αὐτοκρατοροῦντος: C. was of course βασιλεύς without intermission: see on 13/161–2.

50/233–4 Βασίλειος πατρίκιος.
See Runciman, *Romanus Lecapenus*, 235, 237; Kyriakides, Βυζαντιναὶ Μελέται, II–V, 270–2; Ostrogorsky² 229; etc. A natural son of Romanus I, emasculated in 945. He played a distinguished part under five sovereigns, until his dismissal by Basil II in 985, after forty years of power and prosperity. He was chamberlain from about or shortly after 945 (Theoph. Cont. 442/18–22) until 959, when he was succeeded by Joseph Bringas (Cedrenus II, 339/3–4; Leo Diac. 46/18–47/2).

50/235–56 Ἰστέον, ὅτι ἐπὶ Λέοντος κτλ.
This incident, by its reference to Samonas as chamberlain (50/239), can be dated to *c.* 907–8 (see on 50/228). As it marks the introduction of an *internal reform*, it can only imply that Leo VI began the practice of conferring on clerics the *substantive* rank of protospatharius (*i.e.* complete with insignia and stipend), whereas they had hitherto received only the *courtesy* title conferred by the laying-on of an ἐπιρριπτάριον βασιλικόν (*De Cer.*, 723/8–11; *cf.* Guilland, *Rev. Et. Byz.*, 4 (1946), 56, 57). The reform may be reflected in *Takt. Ben.* (Beneševič 124, no. 70, 150–1); see also on 50/241–2. For the financial terms of the purchase, see A. M. Andreades, Ἱστορία τῆς ἑλληνικῆς δημοσίας οἰκονομίας (Athens, 1918), 433, note 5, 434, note 3; Ostrogorsky, *BZ*, 32 (1932), 306–8; G. Kolias, *Aemter- u. Würdenkauf im früh- u. mittelbyzantinischen Reich* (Athens, 1939), 103, 106.

50/237 δομέστικος . . . τεχνίτης.
Cf. *Poèmes Prodromiques en grec vulgaire*, ed. Hesseling-Pernot (Amsterdam, 1910), 51, line 60; G. Meyer, *Neugriechische Studien*, III (Vienna, 1895), 21, *s.v.* δεμέστιχος.

50/237 Νέαν Ἐκκλησίαν. See Theoph. Cont. 319/11–20, 325/6–329/3; *De Cer.*, 118–21; Liudprand, *Antapodosis*, I, 10, III, 34.

50/241 ἐπικούτζουλον.
See Du Cange *s. vv.* κάμασος, κούτζουλον ('κουτζούλιον . . . ἐπικούτζουλον, eadem notione'); *cf.* κάμισον, ἐπικάμισον (*Poèmes Prodromiques*, 52, line 89). A long, close-fitting, full-sleeved undergarment. Eunuch protospatharii wore a χιτὼν λευκὸς χρυσοκόλλητος διβητισοειδής (*De Cer.*, 722/6–7), which is presumably the ἐπικούτζουλον here in question. The διβητίσιον was characterized by long sleeves (see Reiske's note at *De Cer.*, II, 425), and it was no doubt this detail which made the chiton διβητισοειδής: *cf.* Du Cange *s.v.* κούτζουλον, and Reiske's note at *De Cer.*, II, 584; τὰ πτερύγια τῶν κουτζούλων. (The English translation is wrong in rendering ἐπικούτζουλον as 'mantle'; 'shirt' would be more accurate.)

50/241–2 προέρχεσθαι εἰς τὸν Λαυσιακὸν κτλ.

That is, to attend the regular Sunday levées in the Lausiacus (*De Cer.*, 523/5–8; 530/5–6). Eunuch protospatharii were the only eunuchs among the so-called ἄρχοντες τοῦ Λαυσιακοῦ (*ibid.*, 787/3–6). For the Lausiacus, see D. Th. Belyaev, *Byzantina*, 1 (St Petersburg, 1891), 46–54; J. Ebersolt, *Le Grand Palais de Constantinople* (Paris, 1910), 93–4. That churchmen were not, until the time of Leo VI, required to attend these levées may be deduced from *Vita Euthymii*, ed. De Boor (Berlin, 1888), 11–12, where St Euthymios violently protests against the senatorial rank attaching to the βασιλικὸν ἀξίωμα of synkellos, and his consequent duty to attend προελεύσεις.

50/242–3 ῥογεύεσθαι . . . τεσσαράκοντα.

For the purchase of ranks, and rates of interest on capital sums invested, see the authorities cited at the end of the note on 50/235–56. Ktenas at first proposes an annuity of 2½% (₁/₄₀); but, owing to the extraordinary nature of his request, he is obliged to accept no more than 1⅔%, or ₁/₆₀. For the *erogatio* of protospatharii, along with other officials, in the week before Palm Sunday, see Liudprand, *Antapodosis*, VI, 10.

50/247 σχολαρίκια.

For the earrings of the empress Irene (12th cent.), see T. Whittemore, *Mosaics of Haghia Sophia at Istanbul* (*Third Preliminary Report* (Oxford, 1942)), 26, 80 and pl. XXIX. For those of the empress Eudocia Ingerina (9th cent.), *cf. Chronicle of Ahimaaz* (tr. Salzman (Columbia University Press, 1924)), 73.

50/248–9 τραπεζίου ἀσήμιν . . . ἀνάγλυφον.

As 50/252 shows, ἀσήμιν is the substantive: the phrase means literally, 'the silver of a table, diversified with gold reliefs representing living creatures'. It is tempting to render ἀσήμιν διάχρυσον as 'silver-gilt', *sc.* deauratum (*cf.* Liudprand, *Antapodosis*, VI, 6), a favourite substance of Byzantine goldsmiths. But the word-order, and the fact that διά- with genitive or in compound adjectives (*cf. De Cer.*, 580/21–2, διὰ μαργαριτῶν; 574/11, διάλιθος) means 'diversified with' or 'picked out in', suggest that the silver table-slab was 'picked out in' gold repoussé. For ἔνζῳδον, *cf.* Cont. Geo. Mon. 896/4. It is possible, though not stated, that the reliefs were a zodiac circle: *cf.* S. J. Gasiorowski, *Malarstwo Minjaturowe Grecko-Rzymskie* (Cracow, 1928), pl. 28.

C. 51

INTRODUCTORY NOTE

This chapter (51/1–191) gives an account of the history of the emperor's private naval flotilla, consisting of pleasure-barges (ἀγράρια, 51/7), a squadron of ten warships (51/13–14), and, since the time of Leo VI, of two large warships converted into yachts (51/25–6, 35). It is important to be clear as to the relation of this flotilla to the imperial navy proper.

The imperial navy (βασιλικοπολώϊμον, or, more colloquially, τὰ ῥούσια χελάνδια, *cf.* Theophanes 446/29, *De Cer.*, 664/9) consisted at this period of a basic force of 12,000 men: see *De Cer.*, 651/18. The standard ship was the χελάνδιον or 'ship-of-war'; *cf.* Cecaumenus 102/5. The standard unit of personnel was the οὐσία, or 'complement', of 108 men; see *De Cer.*, 665/1, 4. The two together formed one οὐσιακὸν χελάνδιον, or 'ship in commission'; see *De Cer.*, 664/8. A larger type of χελάνδιον, the δρόμων or δρομώνιον (51/10, 25), carried, or could on active service carry, two complements; see *De Cer.*, 652/10, 16; 664/14–15; 665/6. A third type of χελάνδιον, swifter and better manned, was the πάμφυλον χελάνδιον or πάμφυλος δρόμων, which was rowed, as the name implies, by complements of foreign mercenaries, each complement being up to 150 strong; see *De Cer.*, 665/3, 8. The οὐσίαι πάμφυλοι were thus the naval counterpart of the ἑταιρεῖαι of the imperial guard. The basic force of the imperial navy was thus composed: 100 standard χελάνδια (*cf. De Cer.*, 664/8) manned by 108 seamen each = 10,800 men; eight πάμφυλοι (*cf. De Cer.*, 664/7-8) manned by 150 seamen each = 1,200 men; total, 12,000 men. The 100 standard complements were organized in four *themata*, or 'divisions' (*cf De Cer.*, 667/14), which corresponded to the four *tagmata*, or 'regiments', of the imperial guards (see on 51/11-12).

The three categories which made up the emperor's private flotilla were all *supernumerary* to the above. They were: first a picked force of ten warships (χελάνδια or δρομώνια) stationed in the Bosphorus; they were reserved for the emperor's private use, but also liable for general active service if directed: see on 51/13-14. It was doubtless one of these vessels that Basil I and his predecessors would employ in such circumstances as those described at 51/7-11, 17-22: see on 51/6. Second, there were the pleasure-barges, painted scarlet or black, used for short trips in the immediate vicinity of the capital. These were based on the private harbour of the Palace, the Bucoleon (see on 51/47); they were in two divisions, one affected to the emperor, the other to the empress, and, until the reign of Romanus I, their respective crews were supervised by two separate officials: see 51/47-51, 63-8, 187-91. Third, Leo VI, combining the two former categories of vessel, constructed his two δρομώνια, large warships converted into pleasure-yachts, and suitable for either long or short progresses. These two yachts were also based on the Bucoleon harbour: see 51/53-4 and *De Cer.*, 601/10-12. Their complements were the emperor's own men in a special sense (*cf.* on 51/40-5), though they still continued to be on the active list of the Navy (see 51/80-2); and inclusion among them might lead to very high promotion: see 51/130-2. For the political importance of the reforms here described, see on 51/40-5.

51/3 καὶ ὅσα. *Cf.* Theoph. Cont. 353/1.

51/6 οὐκ ἦν βασιλικὸν δρομώνιον.

For δρομώνιον, see Introductory Note to this chapter. Emperors before Leo VI are mentioned as possessing χελάνδια or δρομώνια: see Theophanes 471/32 (Constantine VI); Theoph. Cont. 250/11-12 (Michael III); *MPG*, cv, col. 540 B (Basil I). But these vessels were no doubt warships of the sort used by Basil I for longer progresses (see 51/7-11, 17-22). The imperial yacht is frequently mentioned after this time: *cf.* Cedrenus II, 350/18, 552/6.

51/7 ἀγράριον.

Cf. Theophanes 397/22; *De Cer.*, 601/17; Anna Comnena VI, 13, 1-2 (ed. Reifferscheid I, 221/13). The derivation is uncertain: see Reiske's note at *De Cer.*, II, 708; Anna Comnena, ed. Leib, II, 80, note 2. They were obviously not warships, but, in origin, large fishing vessels equipped with oars, and suitable for conversion into state barges. As regards the colouring of the barges, the emperor is here described as embarking in a 'scarlet' barge; but it is clear from 51/49-50 that his fleet of barges included both scarlet and black vessels, as did that of the Augusta. Vogt, *Ech. d'Or.*, 39 (1941-2), 329, says: 'L'impératrice, elle, avait aussi ses *agraria*, mais leur décoration était noire et rouge, d'où la distinction entre les marins "rouges" au service de l'empereur et les marins "noirs" au service de l'impératrice'. There is no evidence in the text for either of these statements; but it certainly seems possible that the barges of the Augusta were red-and-black to distinguish them from those of the emperor; *cf.* Vasiliev II/2, 382, 390. What form the coloured decoration took is as uncertain as it is in the case of the ῥούσια χελάνδια of the imperial navy (see Introductory Note to this chapter). Vogt, *op. cit.*, says that the tackle and sails were coloured; but it is equally probable that the bottoms were also painted in these colours.

51/8 τὰ θέρμα τῆς Προύσης. See on 51/15–19.

51/9 τὸ γεφύριον τοῦ Ῥηγίου.
See Procopius, *De Aed.*, iv, 8, 10–17. The bridge, originally of wood, was rebuilt in stone by Justinian I; it spanned the channel through which the lagoon formed by the mouth of Bathynias river debouched into the sea. For Rhegion, see *De Cer.*, 495/6, 9; K. J. Jireček, *Die Heerstrasse von Belgrad nach Constantinople* (Prague, 1877), 55. Justinian's bridge was apparently destroyed by Krum in 813 (*MPG*, cviii, col. 1020 C), and reconstructed by Basil. See Theoph. Cont. 340/10–16; Millet, *Byzantina-Metabyzantina*, i/2 (1949), 105; but also R. Janin, *Constantinople byzantine* (Paris, 1950), 231–2.

51/11–12 Οἱ δὲ ἐν αὐτῷ . . . πλωΐμων.
Cf. 51/90–2, and *De Cer.*, 698/22–699/1: ἰστέον, ὅτι οὐ δεῖ στρατεύεσθαι ἀπὸ ἄλλου θέματος εἰς τοὺς ἐλάτας τῶν ἀγραρίων εἰ μὴ ἀπὸ τοῦ Στενοῦ, where θέμα means one of the four 'divisions' of the imperial navy (see Introductory Note to this chapter). It was apparently from this *thema* that the rowers of all three categories of vessels in the emperor's private flotilla were recruited. The rowers were seconded by recommendation of the lord admiral: see Theoph. Cont. 391/17.

51/13–14 Τὸ γὰρ παλαιὸν . . . δέκα.
Bréhier, *Institutions*, 411, following A. Vogt, *Basile Ier* (Paris, 1908), 368–9, thinks that the squadron here mentioned was a detachment of the imperial navy reserved for the emperor's personal use. This is not quite certain, but none the less very probable (see Introductory Note to this chapter): *De Cer.*, 664/7–15 gives the strength of the imperial navy in 949 as 108 complements (ρη′ should be read for ρν′ in line 7), whereas the detailed register of duties *ibid.*, adds up to ten more (7 + 3 + 3 + 1 + 24 + 40 + 40 = 118). The extra ten are perhaps the ten here in question, who, as the emperor's private squadron, were not included in the regular strength of the βασιλικοπλώϊμον, but were included in the estimate of the forces available to defend the capital (*ibid.*, 664/12–13).
The Greek is awkward: καὶ τὸ Στενὸν gives little sense, and we should have rather expected καὶ τὸ παλαιόν. But C. clearly means that the emperor's squadron of ten ships was already there in Basil's time, *and still is there*: cf. *De Cer.*, 493/20, 'it used to be, *and still is*, the custom etc.'
For the Stenon, *cf.* J. P. Krug. *Byzantinische Chronologie* (St Petersburg, 1810), 183–201; G. Laskin, *Sochineniya Konstantina Bagryanorodnago* (Moscow, 1899), 187, note 801; Zakythinos, *ΕΕΒΣ*, 22 (1952), 179–81.

51/14 μεταστασίματα.
See Du Cange, *s. vv.* μετάστασις, μεταστάσιμον; he cites Liudprand, *Legatio*, c. 25: habuit Nicephorus metastasin, id est stationem, in loco qui dicitur Εἰς πήγας (*sic*; *cf.* ed. Becker 188/17–19 and note 2): see also Reiske's note at *De Cer.*, ii, 192–3, and Theoph. Cont. 430/2. For specific progresses, see Theoph. Cont. 337/22–338/1 (Hiereia); 465/4–5 (Prousa); 472/19.

51/15–19 εἰς τὰς Πηγὰς . . . τοῦ Ῥηγίου.
For Pegai, see R. Janin, *Constantinople byzantine* (Paris, 1950), 141–2, 423, and pl. I, A6; and for Basil's palace there, see Theoph. Cont. 337/10–19. For Hebdomon, see Janin 137–9, 408–11, and pl. IX; Theoph. Cont. 340/4–5. For Hiereia, see Janin 147–9, 454, and pl. XII; Theoph. Cont. 337/19–20. For Bryas, see Janin 145–6, 447–8, and pls. XIII, XV; *cf.* Bury, *ERE*, 133. These four resorts are suburbs lying east, west and south of the city, close enough to be easily reached by barge. For Prousa (= Pythia, 51/38) ad Olympum, see Mercati, *Riv. degli Stud. Orientali*, 10 (1924), 37, and *cf.* Maas, *BZ*, 25 (1925), 358; W. M. Ramsay, *Historical Geography of Asia Minor* (London, 1890), 180. For Rhegion, lying some twelve miles west of the city, see on 51/9.

51/20 διὰ τό. The reading of P (διότι) is probably correct: cf. 45/155, where, as here, διότι seems to have the force of ὥστε.

51/29–33 εἰ μὴ ὁ δρουγγάριος κτλ.

Cf. De Cer., 551/6–10, 560/13–16, lists which are practically identical with ours if we assume the *mystikos*, *parakoimomenos* and *protovestiarios* to be included in the emperor's οἰκεία θεραπεία (cf. *De Cer.*, 554/12, 556/8), and the military chiefs to be absent on duty (cf. 51/31–2). For the various officials, see Bury, *IAS*, 49 (δομέστικος τῶν σχολῶν: cf. Guilland, *Rev. Et. Byz.*, 8 (1950), 5–63); 60 (δρουγγάριος τῆς βίγλης: cf. Guilland, *BZ*, 43 (1950), 340–51); 77 (ὁ ἐπὶ τῶν δεήσεων: cf. Dölger, *BD*, 63); 91 (λογοθέτης τοῦ δρόμου); 106 (ἑταιρειάρχης: cf. Guilland, *Byzantinoslavica*, 19 (1958), 68); 108 (δρουγγάριος τοῦ πλωΐμου: cf. Guilland, *BZ*, 44 (1951), 212–40); 124 (παρακοιμώμενος: see on 50/222); 125 (πρωτοβεστιάριος). For the *mystikos*, see Reiske's note at *De Cer.*, II, 622; Dölger, *BD*, 64; and cf. Nicephorus, ed. De Boor, 142/21; Cont. Geo. Mon. 860/2; G. Kolias, *Léon Choerosphactès* (Athens, 1939), 127/96.

51/36 δεύτερον . . . ἀκόλουθος.

δεύτερος was a common, and popular, term for a second-in-command or *remplaçant*; see Theoph. Cont. 376/14; Cont. Geo. Mon. 870/4. Ἀκόλουθος was the official name of the vessel. For the word, cf. *De Cer.*, 523/14, 524/9, 18, applied to a palace official who seems to be a Vice-Master of Ceremonies (ἀκόλουθος τοῦ τῆς καταστάσεως). For Ἀκόλουθος as the name of a ship, cf. Niketas Choniata 714/17–19; Anna Comnena x, 8 (ed. Reifferscheid, II, 82/9–10): and Koukoulès, *EEBΣ*, 21 (1951), 10.

51/40–5 Πολλάκις γὰρ κτλ.

The passage is corrupt at 51/44, but it seems likely that a negative must be supplied and that συνεξιοῦσι stands for a main verb (cf. *De Cer.*, 207/12). The meaning is that at this period, despite the fact that Leo VI and C. did not campaign in person (cf. *De Them.*, 60/17–18; *De Cer.*, 503/10–11), their Regiment of the Watch (ἀριθμός: see Bury, *IAS*, 60), which formed one of the four divisions of the Life-Guards, was needed as a fighting unit, and went out on active service with the other regular troops; not under the command of its own chief, the δρουγγάριος τῆς βίγλης, and his officers (see *De Cer.*, 524/22–525/2; cf. *ibid.*, 666/9, 11), but under the command of the δομέστικος τῶν σχολῶν (51/43). This meant that another force was needed for guard duties at the palace, and the complement of an imperial yacht was seconded for this purpose; cf. *De Cer.*, 611/12, 614/18–19; Theoph. Cont. 383/5; Cedrenus II, 404/8–10, 613/13–14. In the absence of the ἀριθμός, the naval detachment (οὐσία) which took over its duties was of course commanded by the δρουγγάριος τῆς βίγλης: cf. *De Cer.*, 10/11, 545/7–9. The night patrol of the ἀριθμός seems to have numbered 100 men (*De Cer.*, 481/7–8), and could thus be replaced by a regular naval complement, which numbered 108 men (see Introductory Note to this chapter). There is probably a political significance attaching to this 'reform' of Leo VI: during the 10th cent. the πλώϊμοι of the βασιλικοπλώϊμον tended to become identified with the imperial, legitimist party and with the populace of the capital, in opposition to the military aristocracy and their armies: cf. Cedrenus II, 370/14–15 (συμβολῆς . . . μέσον πλωΐμων καὶ Ἀρμενίων) = Leo Diac. 64/25 (διαμάχη . . . μεταξὺ Βυζαντίων καὶ Ἀρμενίων); see Jenkins, *Journal of Hellenic Studies*, 73 (1953), 193, col. 2.

Guilland (*Byzantinoslavica*, 19 (1958), 64–71), who shows clearly that the Hippodrome of 51/44 was the Covered Hippodrome (for which see also Bury, *Le Muséon*, 3 sér., I, (1915), 110–15), understands the passage in a rather different sense. He takes ἐναπομένοντες as referring, not to the οὐσία of the second dromon, but to a detachment of the ἀριθμός left behind while the rest of their regiment were on active service under the domestic. This detachment, 'left behind in the Hippodrome', goes off on progress with the emperors, and their place is in turn supplied by the sailors during the emperors' absence. This interpretation has the advantage of dispensing with the ⟨οὐ⟩ supplied before συνεξιοῦσι, but it would also appear to require the insertion of ⟨οἱ⟩ before ἐναπομένοντες. However we take it, the importance of the passage lies in the use of naval guards for the watch.

51/46–7 βασιλικὸν ὀφφίκιον . . . φιάλης.
For this officer, see Guilland, *Byzantion*, 25–7 (1957), 683–6; and for his ὀφφίκιον, *ibid.*, 679. He is not mentioned in contemporary *Ranglisten*: Vogt, *Ech. d'Or.*, 39 (1941–2), 328, suggests that this is because he counted among the judges (*cf.* 51/54–60).

51/47 φιάλης.
The classical meaning is a round drinking-bowl without handles. In later Greek it acquired the technical sense of a 'laver' or 'basin' into which a fountain poured from a jet or jets above: see Reiske's note at *De Cer.*, II, 274; Strzygowski, *Römische Mitteilungen*, 18 (1903), 191–2, 198–9; and *cf.* Theoph. Cont. 451/6–10. This meaning is sometimes extended to include the area in which such a basin stood. The principal φιάλη of the Great Palace was the μυστικὴ τοῦ Τρικόγχου (or τοῦ Σίγματος) φιάλη, constructed by Theophilus (see Theoph. Cont. 141/10–142/3), and often mentioned in connexion with palace ceremonial. A. Vogt, *Basile* Iᵉʳ (Paris, 1908), 369, supposed that this was the φιάλη here in question, though he corrected himself at *Ech. d'Or.*, 39 (1941–2), 330, note 1. But it is clear from 51/56–7, 141–2, *De Cer.*, 601/11–12, *BZ*, 12 (1903), 201/31, and *Vita Euthymii*, ed. De Boor (Berlin, 1888), 46/28–9 that the 'naval' φιάλη was at sea-level, and was a part, not of the Great Palace, but of the palace harbour, the Boucoleon: *cf.* Guilland, *Byzantinoslavica*, 10 (1949), 25. It is possible that a fountain stood on the harbour quay; but it seems more likely that φιάλη here stands for the round 'pool' or 'basin' of the artificial harbour itself: *cf.* Cedrenus II, 375/17–18; Zakythinos, *EEBΣ*, 23 (1953), 661. For similar usages of the word, see Procopius, *De. Aed.*, VI, 1, 3; Pliny, *Nat. Hist.*, VIII, 186; and Josephus, *Bell. Jud.*, III, 511: ἐκ μὲν οὖν τῆς περιφερείας ἐτύμως φιάλη καλεῖται, τροχοειδὴς οὖσα λίμνη. If φιάλη is here the round harbour itself, it seems possible that the name Boucoleon may be a learned embellishment of an original βαυκάλιον (= φιάλη).

51/49–51 τὰ γὰρ . . . τῆς αὐγούστης.   For the ἀγράρια, see on 51/7; for ὁ ⟨ἐπὶ⟩ τῆς τραπέζης see Bury, *IAS*, 126.

51/70, 71, 72 πρωτοσπαθάριος.
That is to say, they became *protospatharii* after, not during, their service as *protokaravoi* and *protospatharii of the basin*; see 51/154–7. Thalasson's subsequent career is unknown. Podaron would become at least a *protospatharius* on his appointment as governor of the Kibyrrhaiote *thema*; see 51/131–2 and *cf. De Cer.*, 730/20–1. Leo Armenius, if he died a τοποτηρητὴς τοῦ πλωΐμου (51/130), should strictly not have risen higher than *spatharo-candidate* (*cf. De Cer.*, 734/11–12); perhaps his promotion was another instance of 'indiscretion' on the part of the patrician Constantine (see 51/149).

51/70–2, 134, 141, 153, 171–2 Ἰωάννης . . . Ποδάρων . . . κτλ.
C. gives a list of seven holders of the office of *protospatharius of the basin* between the years *c.* 902 (see on 51/80–102) and *c.* 921 (see on 51/164–5). Thalasson was succeeded by Podaron in about 902; Podaron and his successor Leo Armenius held the post for not more than ten years between them, since 51/136 implies that Leo's successor, Bimbilides, was appointed before 913. Bimbilides probably held office not after 916, which is all ἐν ἔτεσί τισιν need imply, and his next-but-one successor, Theodotos, was appointed by the chamberlain Constantine, whose power terminated in the summer of 919 (see on

50/229). Old Michael therefore probably served between about 916 and 918, and his son-in-law and successor between 918 and 921, after which he was banished and succeeded by Loricatus.

51/72–3 Ἀρσενίου, καὶ μαγγλαβίτου.

For Arsenios, who, with a colleague in the same corps, conspired against Romanus I in 921, see Theoph. Cont. 398/17–399/7. The μαγγλαβῖται were a body of police closely akin to, if not directly descended from, the *lictores* of Roman times; they preceded the emperor, both on land and by sea (*cf. De Cer.*, 560/22–3), and were armed with rods (Latin *clavae*; *cf. Vita Ignatii, MPG*, cv, col. 529 C, where they are called ῥαβδοῦχοι, and Vasiliev II/2, 429), with which they inflicted summary chastisement (*cf.* Theoph. Cont. 174/23). Command of the corps (*cf.* 46/51, 51/72–3) apparently carried protospatharian rank. See also Vogt, Commentaire I, 32; Canard, *Byzantion*, 21 (1951), 405, note 1.

51/74 πρωτελάται.

There seem to have been one πρωτελάτης and one δευτεροελάτης in each galley (see 51/107, 125); the two πρωτελάται of *De Cer.*, 577/1–2 are one from each of the two imperial δρομώνια. The πρωτελάτης and δευτεροελάτης are probably those described in A. Dain, *Naumachica* (Paris, 1943), 1, 8, as τῶν πρωραίων ἐλατῶν οἱ τελευταῖοι δύο, one of whom managed the gun, the other the anchor. As master-gunner, the πρωτελάτης would have a post hardly inferior in responsibility to that of the starboard steersman (πρῶτος πρωτοκάραβος). It is clear from the passage that the ranks of naval promotion ran from simple ἐλάτης to δευτεροελάτης, πρωτελάτης, δεύτερος πρωτοκάραβος and lastly πρῶτος πρωτοκάραβος (*cf.* Aristophanes, *Equites*, 542–4). Good service in the navy might gain promotion, though in a lower rank, to the emperor's private flotilla (*cf.* 51/76, 110, 125), where the rate of pay was probably higher and was certainly augmented by bonuses: see *De Cer.*, 601/14–19.

51/75 Νάσαρ καὶ δρουγγαρίου.

For the exploits of this famous admiral in the latter part of Basil's reign, see Theoph. Cont. 302/5–305/17; Genesios 35/3, 118–20; *Vita Eliae Jun.* (*AASS*, 17 August) 494×D: Basilius cognomento Nasar. For his victory at Stilo (880), see also Vasiliev II/2, 100, 137, 215–16; Gay 113.

51/80 πρωτοκαράβους.

See Dain, *Naumachica*, 1, 8; *cf.* Vasiliev II/2, 106. The *protokaravoi* managed the star-board and port steering-oars (αὐχένες); the senior of the two, the *protos protokaravos* (see 51/171), presumably took the starboard oar. The *protokaravos* was not, as is often stated, the captain of the ship: as Dain, *Naumachica, loc. cit.* shows, the captain was the *kentarchos*, above whom came the *komes* or commodore (*ibid.*, 1, 25). The *protokaravoi* were what we should now call warrant-officers. As senior warrant-officer of the emperor's first galley, the *protos protokaravos* also became, by custom, *protospatharius of the basin* (see Theoph. Cont. 400/13; 51/171–2), and *ex officio* after 921 (see 51/188–91).

51/80–102 περιστάσεως γενομένης κτλ.

For the word περίστασις, see Theoph. Cont. 57/14; Leo, *Taktika*, col. 961 C; Cecaumenus 61/25. It is not clear whether this engagement is the same as that described lower down at 51/110–25. If in the lacuna in 51/89 we supply Μιχαὴλ (see note *ad loc.*), and suppose that ὁ συνετὸς ἐκεῖνος was Βαρκαλᾶς (*cf.* 51/109), then the two engagements are not identical, since Michael Barkalas is expressly mentioned as serving with the imperial navy in the campaign of 895, and therefore cannot have acted as steersman of the imperial galley simultaneously (51/88–9). The admiral Eustathios is known to have commanded at Taormina in 902 (see Cont. Geo. Mon. 860/22), and also in the Marmora in

904 (see Theoph. Cont. 366/21); the latter occasion was certainly a very urgent περίστασις, but Eustathios appears to have retreated without giving battle, so that the phrase εἰς τὸν πόλεμον (51/95) would be inappropriate. Possibly, therefore, the Sicilian campaign is referred to here; if so, the words τῇ πρὸς τὸν βασιλέα εὐνοίᾳ καὶ ὀρθῇ πίστει (51/98–9; cf. De Cer., 484/7) may be significant, since Eustathios himself was afterwards accused of treachery. For the admiral Eustathios, cf. on 50/136–7; Guilland, BZ, 43 (1950), 347–8.

51/82–4   ἐξόπλισιν πολλὴν κτλ.

This was special heavy armour for the marines, as opposed to the ordinary στρατιῶται (sc. πλώϊμοι) ἤτοι οἱ ἄλλοι ἐλάται: see Dain, Naumachica, 1, 14. σκουτάρια and δόρκαι are two types of shield: σκουτάριον is a generic term (see Leo, Taktika, col. 717 B), but here probably means a metal shield (see ibid., σιδηρᾶ, and cf. Dain, Naumachica, 1, 65); while δόρκα (cf. on 26/31), though also sometimes used generically, means especially a shield of hide (see Reiske's note at De Cer., II, 682: scuta in universum omnia sed praecipue coriacea). σκουτάρια and δόρκαι are perhaps equivalent to the σκουτάρια ῥαπτά and σκουτάρια Λυδιάτικα of De Cer., 669/19, the former meaning a metal plate stitched on to a leather backing, the latter a simple hide or hides. The κλιβάνιον (Attic κρίβανος, 'oven') was a metal corselet, θώραξ (see Leo, Taktika, cols. 724 A, 732 D), made of laminae, πέταλα (see Dain, Naumachica, 1, 14) and worn over the λωρίκιον or ζάβα. The laminae were mostly of steel, but could be made ἐξ ἑτέρας ὕλης (see Leo, Taktika, col. 717 C); for royal personages they were made of gold (cf. De Cer., 500/10; Ch. Diehl, Peinture Byzantine (Paris, 1933), pl. LXXXIII). Cf. the φολιδωτὸς θώραξ of Anna Comnena, x, 8, 7 (ed. Reifferscheid, II, 84/6). The passage proves that though the emperor's flotilla did not form an integral part of the βασιλικοπλώϊμον (cf. 51/76), its personnel were still liable to be seconded for active service: see Introductory Note to this chapter, and on 51/13–14.

51/89   ὁ συνετὸς ἐκεῖνος.

See on 51/80–102. As Moravcsik has seen (cf. Vol. I, Apparatus ad loc.), it seems likely that a second Μιχαὴλ has dropped out here, and that Old Michael and his namesake surnamed Barkalas are the remplaçants in question. The two Michaels are twice referred to lower down as a pair of steersmen (51/105–9, 126), and were probably associated in that employment before their official appointment to the imperial galley in succession to Podaron and Leo Armenius.

51/91–2   Στενῖται . . . Στενοῦ.   For these ten complements of the Stenon, see on 51/11–12, 13–14.

51/100–1   ἀγράμματον . . . κριτής.

A judge had at least to be able to sign his name: see Les Novelles de Léon VI le Sage, ed Noailles-Dain (Paris, 1944), 181/11. For the Hippodrome judges, see Bréhier, Institutions, 227–8; Guilland, Byzantinoslavica, 19 (1958), 51–3.

51/105   τοποτηρητὰς.

For the τοποτηρηταί (locum tenentes, lieutenants) of the βασιλικοπλώϊμον, see De Cer., 734/11–12, where however only one is mentioned. It seems likely that during the following decade (900–10) the βασιλικοπλώϊμον may have been re-modelled in four divisions after the pattern of the Guards regiments (see Introductory Note to this chapter), which would require four τοποτηρηταί: cf. Bury, IAS, 51–3.

51/110–24   Εὐσταθίου . . . ὅτε ἐπέρασεν τοὺς Τούρκους κτλ.

For the Greek sources for this campaign, see 40/7–13, Apparatus 1; cf. on 40/7–12, 45/51. The war lasted from 894 to 896 or 897. The incident here described probably took place in 895.

51/114 λέσας.

Cf. Cedrenus II, 591/18–21; Anon., *De Obsidione Toleranda*, ed. Van den Berg (Leiden 1947), 50, 74; Cecaumenus 30/30; M. A. Triandaphyllides, *Die Lehnwörter der mittelgriechischen Vulgärliteratur* (Strassburg, 1909), 150.

51/121 Τοῦρκοι . . . ὑπερθαυμάσαντες. This was good propaganda for the empire: *cf. BZ*, 17 (1908), 82/4–17.

51/132 ἐν τῷ θέματι τῶν Κιβυρραιωτῶν.

If we were certain that Podaron was appointed to the Kibyrrhaiote *thema* during the reign of Leo VI, it would help us to date more accurately the incidents recorded at 50/169–96, since in that case his appointment must have preceded that of the deputy Eustathios (see on 50/169–96). But his appointment may well have been made between the years 913 and 920.

51/133 Ποδάρωνος. An obvious slip for Λέοντος τοῦ Ἀρμενίου. See 51/71–2.

51/138–9 Μιχαὴλ τὸν γέροντα.

This gallant old seaman, described with a genuine, and very rare, touch of emotion (51/143) which recalls Sophocles, *Electra*, 23–8, cannot have been born much later than 850, since he was already a leading oarsman in the emperor's barge under Basil I (†886); and he would therefore at this time, *c.* 916 (see on 51/70–2 etc.), have been approaching the age of 70.

51/141–92 Καὶ εἰσερχομένου κτλ.

The whole of the rest of this passage on the *protospatharius of the basin* bears abundant traces of editing by C. himself (*cf.* Vol. I, 11, note 44, and General Introduction p. 8): (*a*) 51/141–8 interrupts the catalogue to introduce a personal reminiscence of C. (*cf.* the interpolation at Theoph. Cont. 81/12–15); (*b*) the self-exculpatory parenthesis of 51/148–50, repeated at 51/159–60, is a patent insertion, and a very awkward one, since its proper place is after ἀξίᾳ in 51/140; (*c*) 51/154–62 is tacked on to explain (*b*); and (*d*) in the rancour of 51/162–91 (*cf.* especially 51/162–5, 173–4, 184–6, with which *cf.* 13/146–94) we can certainly again detect C.'s hand, which has so thoroughly recast this last passage that it is hard to say how much, if any, of the original text remains until we pick it up again at 51/188.

51/141–2 ἐν τῇ φιάλῃ ἐν τῷ δρομωνίῳ. See on 51/47.

51/149 τὸ ἀδιάκριτον . . . Κωνσταντίνου.

For Constantine the chamberlain, see on 50/229, 230–2. His second period of office referred to here, dated from early in 914 until 919, while his 'infant' master was between eight years and thirteen years of age. He seems to have been generally unpopular (*cf.* Theoph. Cont. 392/1–2) except with the empress Zoë; and is here charged by C. himself with improperly creating Old Michael a protospatharius in *c.* 916 (51/140, 161–2), and his son-in-law, first spartharocandidate, and then protospatharius in *c.* 918 (51/152–3). This kind of improper promotion was strongly condemned a century later by Cecaumenus, 95/4–97/27.

51/164–5 Θεόδοτον . . . διεδέξατο.

For Theodotos' plot against Romanus I late in 921, see Theoph. Cont. 400/13. It was this plot which gave Romanus the excuse to make himself αὐτοκράτωρ: see *ibid.*, 400/19–401/2; *cf.* Jenkins, *Studies in Honor of A. M. Friend Jr.* (Princeton, 1955), 205.

51/173-4 *'Ιωάννου . . . ῥέκτωρος.*
For the office of rector, see Bury, *IAS*, 115-16; Ostrogorsky, *Sem. Kond.*, 5 (1932), 257; Guilland, *Mémorial L. Petit* (Bucharest, 1948), 185-7. It was created by Basil I, who appointed to it his own nephew Basil, son of his brother Bardas: see Cont. Geo. Mon. 837/11-12; *Σύνοψις Χρονική*, ed. Sathas, *Bibliotheca graeca medii aevi*, 7 (Paris, 1894), 158/7-8. For John the Rector, see Theoph. Cont. 393/12, 399/5, 401/9, 406/3, 419/15, 24; he is probably not to be confused with John Lazanes the rector, *ibid.*, 378/23-379/2, 380/18: see Runciman, *Romanus Lecapenus*, 68, note 1, and Guilland, *op. cit.*, 188. John II was retired from the rectorship by the autumn of 924, but later re-employed on a diplomatic mission to Bulgaria. He is called ὁ πρεσβύτερος *'Ιωάννης* at Theoph. Cont. 393/12, 399/5, perhaps to distinguish him from John the *mystikos*, who succeeded him as παραδυναστεύων: see *ibid.*, 406/2-3.

51/175-91 *'Ο πρωτοσπαθάριος Θεοφύλακτος κτλ.*
This reform, despite C.'s understandable condemnation of it, seems to have been very obvious and sensible. Quite apart from the folly of leaving unstopped a dangerous source of domestic disaffection, in view of the repeated plots laid against Romanus in C.'s interest (*cf.* on 51/72-3, 164-5), it was a clear advantage administratively to have all the seamen of the Boucoleon under one authority, and to make the chief steersman of the galley *ex officio protospatharius of the basin*, which he had hitherto often been by custom: see on 51/80.

51/184-6 *Εὔκολον γὰρ κτλ.* This gnomic utterance is recognizable as another touch from C.'s own hand (see on 51/141-92); *cf.* Theoph. Cont. 286/16-17, 349/16-17.

51/192-204 *'Ιστέον, ὅτι . . . παρέσχον.*
C. here inserts three short items which are connected with provincial rather than naval organization: see on 48/22-33, and General Introduction p. 6. Their proper place would have been at 50/82.

51/192-204 *'Ιστέον, ὅτι ἐπὶ Λέοντος κτλ.*
The reasons for this final 'reform' of Leo VI can only be guessed at, since we cannot date with accuracy its introduction, or identify the military governor Leo Tzikanes (see on 51/193-4). The reform obviously suggests an improvement in the man-power of the empire, and this is in fact demonstrable in the increasing number of Armenians coming into Byzantine service with the eastward expansion of the empire; *cf.* 50/111-66; *De Cer.*, 655/18-656/2. It was therefore good policy to recruit this excellent fighting material and to leave the industrialised western provinces free to equip it; *cf. De Cer.*, 657/12-20; A. Bon, *Péloponnèse byzantin* (Paris, 1951), 119-33. A further reason may have been the flat refusal of Slav elements in the western *themata* to give service, and the unprofitableness of conscribing such unpromising material; *cf.* Ioannes Cameniata, *De Excidio Thessalonicensi*, c. 20 (= Theoph. Cont. 514/11-515/19); 50/25-32. The tax is paid partly in ready money, which would go to the λογοθέσιον τοῦ στρατιωτικοῦ (*cf.* Dölger, *Finanzverwaltung*, 60-1), partly in horses, which would be the province of the λογοθέσιον τῶν ἀγελῶν (see on 52/1). It is suggested in the General Introduction p. 6 and note 2, that the insertion of these notices (51/192-204) was occasioned by similar, contemporary expeditions to S. Italy.

51/193-4 *τῶν τῆς δύσεως θεμάτων . . . Τζικάνη.*
Leo Tzikanes, like his contemporaries Symbatikios and George (see Gay 146-7), was military governor of the western provinces in general (*cf.* Sym. Mag., 665/6), that is to say, of Thrace, Macedonia, Kephallenia, Lombardy, etc., a post which a few years later would have been called κατεπάνω τῆς δύσεως: (*cf.* Theoph. Cont. 480/14-16). The seat

of this command would certainly be Thessalonica; if, therefore, we could suppose Τζικάνης a corruption of Κατζιλάκης (cf. Theoph. Cont. 368/4), we might refer this incident to 904, and compare the passage of Cameniata cited in the previous note. But this is most uncertain and many other alternatives are possible; cf. Gay 143–8. γεγονώς may mean either present or past; for the latter meaning, cf. Theoph. Cont. 441/19 with 443/6.

51/196–8 Ἰστέον, ὅτι καὶ πάλιν κτλ.
The date and circumstances of this incident are, like those of the previous one, quite uncertain. It is possible that the levy was connected with the expedition against Crete in 911: see De Cer., 651–60. At ibid. 657/12–20 four western themata are required to provide war-material, but only one to provide men (ibid., 653/14–16). For John Eladas, see Theoph. Cont. 380/18, 381/11, 386/10–13; Vita Euthymii, ed. De Boor (Berlin, 1888), 70/1–2. Cf. Bees Viz. Vrem., 21 (1914), 95; Bulletin de Correspondence Hellénique, 23 (1899), 123. He was presumably made magister by Alexander.

51/199–204 Ἰστέον, ὅτι καὶ πάλιν κτλ.
The mention of Protevon as military governor of Peloponnese (51/201; cf. 50/26–7) makes it almost certain that this levy should be dated to the first three months of 921; see Jenkins, Studies in Honor of A. M. Friend Jr. (Princeton, 1955), 205; D. Zakythinos, Οἱ Σλάβοι ἐν Ἑλλάδι (Athens, 1945), 53; A. Bon, Péloponnèse byzantin (Paris, 1951), 48, note 1, 188. This commutation differs from the preceding two, in that it concerns one thema in toto; cf. 52/12. The sum paid up is a kentenarion, that is, 7200 gold pieces (nomismata); and in addition 1,000 geldings (cf. De Cer., 461/19–20), with harness, are supplied for the cavalry (cf. ibid., 661/6). See Bon, op. cit., 115, 118; the phrase μετὰ πολλῆς προθυμίας testifies to the economic prosperity of Peloponnese at this time (Bon, op. cit., 119–33).

52/1 ἀπαίτησις τῶν ἱππαρίων.
This chapter consists of two documents (52/4–11, 12–15) on which the statements at 51/202, 203 are based; whether they were intended to form part of the book must remain very doubtful: see General Introduction pp. 1–2. For the requisition of cavalry-horses, cf. Leo, Taktika, col. 1069 B; De Cer., 458/16–461/19. From the latter passage it is clear that such a requisition was the rule on the occasion of a campaign, and it is therefore to be asked, why this requisition from Peloponnese is regarded as exceptional? But a comparison of the figures in the two passages shows that the contributions from Peloponnese are assessed at much higher than the usual rate, perhaps double, in order to compensate for the thema's having contracted out of personal military services; contrast, e.g. De Cer., 460/7–11, 461/9–11 with 52/6–7, 4–6. The assessments were made, and the animals requisitioned, by the λογοθέσιον τῶν ἀγελῶν (see De Cer., 458/16–22, 459/13).

52/4–6 μητρπολίτης . . . ἐπίσκοποι.
For the religious organization of Peloponnese at this time, see A. Bon, Péloponnèse byzantin (Paris, 1951), 106–7; and for requisition of horses from ecclesiastical dignitaries and religious houses, see De Cer., 461/9–11, 17–18.

52/6–7 οἱ πρωτοσπαθάριοι κτλ.
These are the local nobility of the province, the πρωτοσπαθάριοι καὶ ἄρχοντες of 50/57–8 (cf. Guilland, Byzantion, 25–7 (1957), 679), who are expressly distinguished from those who held βασιλικὰ ἀξιώματα (52/10–11), that is to say, διὰ βασιλικοῦ λόγου ἀξιώματα, including the governor and his staff: see De Cer., 707/14–20, 717/1–2.

52/8–10 μοναστήρια.
For the various types of monastery mentioned here, see Herman, Orientalia Christiana Periodica, 6 (1940), 348 ff.; and for their liability to provide horses, cf. De Cer., 461/17–18.

52/10–11　*Οἱ δὲ ἔχοντες . . . οὐ δεδώκασιν.*

For the *βασιλικὰ ἀξιώματα*, see on 52/6–7. The *πλώϊμοι*, or sailors of the thematic fleet (?Mardaïtes, see Theoph. Cont. 304/1) were exempt because still liable to serve in person. The industries of purple- and paper-making were doubtless privileged as being of capital importance for the administration of the imperial bureaucracy. For the *κογχυλευταί*, *cf. Cod. Theodos.*, x, 20: 14, 16, 17; and *Cod. Justin.*, x, 48, 7; and for the significance of their work, see Dölger, *BES*, 15 and note 16. For purple-fishing in general, see Pliny, *Nat. Hist.*, IX, 125–41, and for the 'purples' of Peloponnesus, *ibid.*, 127.

52/12–15　*πᾶς ὁ στρατὸς κτλ.*

For this assessment, see A. Bon. *Péloponnèse Byzantin* (Paris, 1951), 115. As in the case of the horses (see on 52/1), the assessment is a very high one: the campaign allowance for the ordinary thematic soldier/sailor was probably not more than two *nomismata* in 911, and certainly not more than three *nomismata* in 949: see *De Cer.*, 662/15–16. Each soldier therefore has to pay out about double what he would receive if he did his duty in the field. For *χάραγμα*, that is, coined gold pieces, see Dölger, *Finanzverwaltung*, 77.

C. 53

BIBLIOGRAPHY

A. Alföldi, *Archaeologiai Értesítő*, ser. III, 2 (1941), 49–58 (Alföldi). R. Garnett, *English Historical Review*, 12 (1897), 100–5 (Garnett). E. H. Minns, *Scythians and Greeks* (Cambridge, 1913) (Minns). M. Rostovtzeff, *Iranians and Greeks in S. Russia* (Oxford, 1922) (Rostovtzeff). S. P. Shestakov, *Pamyatniki christianskago Chersonesa III. Ocherki po istorii Chersonesa v VI–X vekach* (Moscow, 1908) (Shestakov). A. A. Vasiliev, *The Goths in the Crimea* (Cambridge, Mass., 1936) (Vasiliev, *Goths*).

INTRODUCTORY NOTE

53/1–492 consists of material which cannot have been meant to form part of C.'s *DAI* but which was used as a source and then included by error in the book itself: see General Introduction p. 2, and on 53/512–35. It has no relevance to the present state of the empire; nor can it have been written for inclusion in the original *Περὶ ἐθνῶν*, since the Chersonites were not *ἐθνικοί*. The material gives information about four wars (53/2–123, 53/124–61, 53/162–78, 53/179–233) fought by the men of Cherson during the late 3rd and 4th cents. A.D.; three of them against the neighbour kingdom of Bosporos, said to have been ruled during this period by successive princes called Sauromatos, and the other against revolted 'Scythians' south of the Danube. To this is appended (53/234–492) the legend of the local Chersonite heroine Gykia, which is apparently much older in origin. How much, if any, of the information relating to the Chersonite-Bosporian wars is historical, is disputed: see Th. Mommsen, *Röm. Gesch.*[3] V (Berlin, 1886), 291, note 1; Minns 526, note 5. It seems that whatever kernel of fact may once have existed is so much overlaid with legendary matter that it cannot now be disinterred. But, as Minns (*ibid.*) points out, it is a record at least of what the 10th cent. Chersonites believed about their own past, and, with the story of Gykia, no doubt derives from some Chersonite chronicle (*cf.* Shestakov 5; Manojlović I, 18), a hypothesis supported by the care with which the annual 'primate' in Cherson is named for the year of each event. It is reasonable to suppose that this chronicle was sent to Constantinople by the military governor of Cherson at C.'s request, and formed part of the source-material which C. collected *ἐξ ἁπάσης ἑκασταχοῦ οἰκουμένης* (*MPG*, CXIII, col. 633 C).

The historical background of the Crimean and Maeotic regions in the 4th cent. A.D. shows most of the area in the hands of the Goths, except for Cherson itself; see Rostovtzeff 155, 217; Minns 127, 610; Vasiliev, *Goths*, 21–3. Whether they were actually masters of the city of Bosporos itself in the 4th cent., is not clear; and C.'s account does not make the point any clearer by confounding the terms Sarmatai, Sauromatoi, Sauromatos (see on 53/5), which suggests that the two first were identical and were the people governed by the third. In fact, however, the Sarmatai or Sauromatoi of our text were Goths (see Vasiliev, *Goths*, 22–3); whereas Sauromatos, or, more properly, Sauromates, was a frequent name among the local Bosporian dynasty of the 1st to 3rd cents., and has no Gothic implication whatever. All we can say is, that the first part of c. 53 is a 10th cent. reflection of 3rd and 4th cent. wars of Cherson against the Goths of the Crimea and Maeotis, either controlling or closely allied with the kingdom of Bosporos. If little can be deduced about the value of the Chersonite war-records, even less can be stated about the Gykialegend. Garnett (103) pointed out that it plainly derives from a pre-Christian epoch; and (104, 105) gave reasons for placing the whole incident, which he regarded as historical, in the second half of the 1st cent. B.C. But this, as Minns (530) rightly sees, is to go too far. It is more probable that the story should be linked in origin with other legends characteristic of the Sauromatian region, which tell of the exploits of martial women; cf. Polyaenus (ed. Teubner, 1887), 415–18; Rostovtzeff 33; Harmatta, *Acta Arch. Acad. Sci. Hung.*, 1 (1951) 118–20; and the historical exploits of queen Dynamis, Rostovtzeff, *Journal of Hellenic Studies*, 39 (1919), 93–105. For a possible genesis of the Gykia-legend, see Minns 526, note 6, 530.

At 53/493–535 we come back to the proper text of *DAI*, with two items of extremely important information: the location of oil-wells, and instructions on what to do in the event of a revolt in (contemporary) Cherson: see notes *ad loc.*

53/2 βασιλεύοντος Διοκλητιανοῦ.
Internal evidence would date this campaign on the Halys to between the years 284 and 293, since Diocletian is on the throne, and Constans (*i.e.* Constantius Chlorus, father of Constantine the Great, 53/124–5) is 'tribune' and has not been sent to Gaul: see Minns 526. But this is our only evidence for such a campaign. For the position of Cherson in relation to Rome, see on 53/114, 118.

53/3 πρωτεύοντος. See on 42/45–6, and Minns 526, 541–2.

53/3–4 Σαυρόματος, ὁ ἐκ τῶν Βοσποριανῶν.
The historical ruler of Bosporos during the reign of Diocletian was Thothorses (Minns 608). The nearest Sauromates to this period was Sauromates IV (275–6), son of Rhescuporis, of which name Criscoronos may be a corruption (Minns 526).

53/5 Σαρμάτας . . . οἰκοῦντας.
This people is in C.'s account called indifferently Σαρμάται, Σαυρόματοι (see Vol. 1, 308, *s.v.* Σαρμάται), though the two were originally distinct: see Rostovtzeff 113, 114; Minns 118. Zosimus (85/13–14) speaks of Σαυρομάτας τῇ Μαιώτιδι προσοικοῦντας λίμνῃ in the early 4th cent., and these were Goths: see Vasiliev, *Goths*, 22–3 and Introductory Note to this chapter.

53/10 Κώνστας. See on 53/2. Little is known about the career of Constantius before 293: cf. W. Seston, *Dioclétien et la Tétrarchie* (Paris, 1946), 88–9.

53/25 Χρήστου, τοῦ Παπίου.
The Chersonite names occurring in this chapter, with the exceptions of Supolichos and Gykia, may all be found in *Inscr. orae septent. Pont. Eux.*, and many are common. The -os termination given to Pharnaces and Sauromates is, as Minns (527, note 2) observes, a later corruption.

53/29-30 ἄρματα πολεμικὰ . . . χειροβολίστρας.

For the artillery brigade of Cherson, see on 53/156. The χειροβολίστρα (= χειρο-τοξοβολίστρα, μικρὰ τοξοβολίστρα, De Cer., 669/21–670/1, 671/16, = lat. manubalista) is the English arbalest or cross-bow; see Cecaumenus 30/33; Anna Comnena (ed. Reifferscheid) II, 83/8 ff. The μεγάλη τοξοβολίστρα (De Cer., 670/11; Dain, Naumachica, 3, 3) was a similar but larger and stationary weapon. As the Chersonites are here using 'hand-bows', their ἄρματα πολεμικά are not identical with the ἄμαξαι of Leo, Taktika, col. 720 A, since the τοξοβαλλίστραι mounted on the latter were of the heavy type.

53/69 ποιήσω . . . ἐντεῦθεν. The lost section obviously contained an account of hastily arranged negotiations between Sauromatos and Constans, and of the latter's agreement to buy off the Bosporians.

53/101 ἀθροίλους.

Trypanis, Journal of Hellenic Studies, 72 (1952), 160, proposes ἀθορύβους; Kyriakides, Hellenika, 16 (1958–9), 385 suggests ἀθρόους ὅλους or ἀθρόως ὅλους; cf. Dujčev, BZ 46 (1953), 122.

53/114, 118 ἐλευθερίας . . . ὑπηκόους.

For the position of Cherson as a libera civitas in the empire, see Minns 524; though it seems that the 'freedom' was conferred a century before Diocletian's time.

53/121-3 μετ᾽ ὀλίγον τινὰ χρόνον κτλ. Constantius became Caesar in 293 and emperor in 305. Diocletian abdicated at Nicomedeia in 305, and then retired to Salona.

53/125 ἀντιστάσεως.

For the various dates suggested for this campaign, see Minns 526, note 6. If the phrase ἐπὶ τὸ Βυζάντιον is to be taken literally, the date cannot be before 326. See however the phrase of Zosimus, cited on 53/5, which relates to a campaign across the Danube in 322 (cf. Alföldi 55 and note 130). Năsturel, Dacia 1 (1957), 372, suggests that the Constans and Constantine of this passage are respectively Constans II and Constantine IV, of the 7th cent.

53/142-3 χλαμύδος βασιλικῆς κτλ.

For these imperial insignia, see Lydus, De Magistratibus, ed. Wuensch (Teubner, 1903), 58/13–17; Alföldi, Römische Mitteilungen, 50 (1935), 50–1, 65. Belyaev, Sem. Kond., 3 (1929), 56, shows that the φιβλατούρα here means the clasp only, not a garment with clasp. For the significance of such a gift, cf. Dölger, BES, 19.

53/146, 160 εὐσεβεῖς εἰκόνας . . . θείας φιλοτιμίας.

Cf. Treitinger 42, 50 f., 145; and for the significance of the ikons, ibid., 206, note 204, and 207. For a ring of this type and date, see Ross, American Journal of Archaeology, 61 (1957), 173–4, pl. 67.

53/148 σφραγίζοντες. Cf. Russian Primary Chronicle, ed. Cross and Sherbowitz-Wetzor (Cambridge, Mass., 1953), 74.

53/152 ἀννώνας. See Pauly-Wissowa, RE, I/2, cols. 2317, 2320–1.

53/156 τὸν ἀριθμὸν.

For this artillery regiment at Cherson, see E. Stein, Hist. du Bas-Empire, II (Paris, 1949), 63 and note 2; cf. Shestakov 5 and note 6; Minns 531. For the term ἀριθμός, see Stein, op. cit., 538, note, and cf. on 51/40–5.

53/158–61 *Ἐφοδίοις δὲ κτλ.*
There is no reason to doubt that these privileges were granted by Constantine: *cf.* Th. Mommsen, *Röm. Gesch.*³, v, 291, note 1. But they point to a more precise relationship with the empire, and are to be connected with the formation of the regiment commented on in the previous note.

53/162–79 *Μετὰ δὲ χρόνους τινὰς κτλ.*
These two wars cannot be dated with any accuracy. If the Sauromatos of 53/162 was grandson of the Sauromatos of 53/3–4, his date would be somewhere in the middle of the 4th cent.: see on 53/3–4.

53/170 *Καφᾶ.* See Minns 558; Vasiliev, *Goths*, 171; Manojlović I, 19, who shows that the place-name was older than the Genoese construction.

53/190 *μέγας τὴν ἡλικίαν.* A version of the popular David and Goliath story: see Mommsen *loc. cit.*; Minns 526, note 5.

53/233–4 *Ἔκτοτε . . . κατελύθη.*
See Minns 527. The meaning is not clear. It may refer to the expulsion of the Goths from the eastern Crimea by the Huns in the second half of the 5th cent. (Vasiliev, *Goths*, 39–40); or else to end of the Kingdom of Bosporos: see Minns 609–10.

53/234 ff. *Τούτων δὲ οὕτως γενομένων κτλ.*
For the tale and its possible origins, see Garnett 100–5, and Minns 530. The place-names Limon, Sosae, Symbolon (see on 53/296) bear witness at least to the Chersonite origin; and the name Gykia may possibly by a shortened form of Glycaria (Minns 561).

53/240 *ἐπιγαμβρείαν ποιήσασθαι.*
Cf. Photii *Orat. et. Hom.*, ed. Aristarchis II (Constantinople, 1900), 375: *πόλεις πολλάκις τὰς ἐκ γειτόνων ἄλλας πόλεις εἰς κῆδος συνάπτουσι κτλ.*

53/265 *σεμνοῖς.* = small: *cf.* Vol. I, 328 *s.v.*

53/294–5 *ἐκ διαλειμμάτων . . . νεωτέρους. Cf.* Leo. Diac. 85/13–15.

53/296 *ἐν Συμβόλῳ. Cf.* Theophanes 373/17; it is the modern Balaklava (see Minns 496).

53/418 *ποτήριον πορφυροῦν. Cf. Chronicon Salernitanum (MGH,* Scr. III), 506; *Vita Antonii Minoris (Συλλογὴ Παλ. καὶ Συρ. Ἁγιολογ.,* St Petersburg, 1907), 202.

53/451 *Λαμάχου Σκοπή.* See Minns 530.

53/456 *δύο χαλκοῦς ἀνδριάντας.* See Minns *ibid.*

53/493–511 *Ἰστέον, ὅτι ἔξω τοῦ κάστρου κτλ.*
We here return from myth and fairy-tale to important and contemporary fact: see Introductory Note to this chapter and Manojlović I, 21–2. The passage locates petroleum wells in two areas: (*a*) at Tamatarcha and in Zichia and its hinterland Papagia (53/493–506; *cf.* 42/95–100); this area was known as the naphtha coast to the Arabs also (*cf.* Mas'udi, *Prairies d'Or,* tr. Barbier de Meynard, II (Paris, 1863), 20–1); and (*b*) in two areas of Armenia on the eastern frontier (53/507–11: see on 53/507, 510). The importance of the petroleum lay in its being a vital ingredient of the Greek Fire: see General Introduction p. 7; and on 13/73, 48/22–32.

53/500 Σαπαξί. *Cf.* Manojlović ιν, 7, note 1: Ilovajski suggested a connexion with Russian *sopka*, 'small volcano' or 'hillock'.

53/507, 510 ἐν τῷ θέματι Δερζηνῆς . . . τοῦ Τζιλιάπερτ.

Manojlović doubts if these areas were Byzantine *themata*; but the term would hardly have been used if they had not been so. Derzene (= Τερτζάν, Dergan; *cf.* Gelzer 577) was an Armenian district lying between Keltzini on the west and Theodosioupolis on the east (Honigmann map IV). It may well have been made a frontier *thema* for a few years about the time of the final reduction of Theodosioupolis (949: see on 45/143-4): *cf.* the equally short lived *thema* of Charpezikion (Honigmann 75 ff.; Ostrogorsky, *Zbornik Radova S.A.N.*, 36, Viz. Inst. 3 (1953), 52), whose existence is proved for a single year only (949), since *De Cer.*, 662/17-22 is simply the (misplaced) answer to a query at *ibid.*, 667/1. Of Tziliapert we know nothing but the name, unless it is a corruption of τὸ Παΐπερτε (Theoph. Cont. 404/7; Gelzer 577), in which case it would lie a little north of Derzene (see Honigmann map IV).

53/512-35 Ἰστέον, ὅτι εἰ ἀντάρωσί κτλ.

This passage, which is in the instructive and hortatory tone of cc. 1-8, 10-13, 44/115, 45/156 ff., etc. (see General Introduction pp. 2 ff., 7; Manojlović 1, 22, note 1), is certainly one of the latest in the book (952), and was probably written in conjunction with the diplomatic chapter on the Pechenegs (*cf.* 13/11 and cc. 6, 7); but since Cherson was a *thema*, it properly finds its place in the domestic section (48/22 ff.). It was perhaps for the composition of this short passage that the Chersonite chronicle (53/2-492) was consulted, namely, to verify traditional Chersonite loyalty to successive emperors (*cf.* 53/47-8, 117-19, 135-54). The vigorous reprisals here ordered against Chersonite men and property in the event of a revolt show the vital importance of Cherson's loyalty to the whole imperial policy in Patzinacia. We do not know if the city had revolted recently; but a memorable revolt took place in 896, as a result of the Byzantine defeat at Bulgarophygon (Theoph. Cont. 360/14-16), which was perhaps followed by a reorganization of the *thema*: see *De Them.*, 183.

53/518 θέματος Παφλαγονίας. See 42/31-2; *De Them.*, 136-7.

53/522 ὡς ἂν δέξωνται. *Cf. De Cer.*, 659/2, 6, 7, etc.

53/533 Ἀμινσοῦ. *Cf.* Vasiliev 1, 250-1.

53/534-5 γεννήματα, οὐ δύνανται ζῆσαι. *Cf. MPG*, cv, col. 421 C-D; Wolff, *Speculum*, 23 (1948), 17; Kazhdan, *Sovietskaya Arkheologiya*, 21 (1954), 185.

INDEXES

Subject Index

The Subject Index, and the General Index which follows it, may be supplemented by the Index of Proper Names in Vol. 1, 288 ff.

General Index